The European Tour
Yearbook 2006

OFFICIAL  PUBLICATION

Introduction from The European Tour

Michael Campbell's outstanding US Open Championship triumph and Colin Montgomerie's accomplishment in winning the Order of Merit for a record eighth time are among the many superb achievements by European Tour Members recognised in the 18th edition of The European Tour Yearbook.

Michael holed a six foot putt at Walton Heath to qualify for the 105th US Open and then moved on to Pinehurst No.2 in North Carolina. There he parried the thrust of Tiger Woods, winner of the Masters Tournament and The 134th Open Championship in 2005 in addition to the WGC – NEC Invitational and the WGC – American Express Championship, to become the 30th European Tour Member to win a Major Championship since Severiano Ballesteros captured The Open in 1979. Michael deserves our warmest congratulations in becoming the first New Zealander to win the US Open and he later followed in the footsteps of compatriot Bob Charles by winning the HSBC World Match Play Championship.

Tim Clark (South African Airways Open, The Barclays Scottish Open), Stephen Dodd (Volvo China Open, Nissan Irish Open), Ernie Els (Dubai Desert Classic, Qatar Masters, BMW Asian Open) - whose season was curtailed through injury in July - Niclas Fasth (Holden New Zealand Open, The Deutsche Bank Players' Championship of Europe) and Miguel Angel Jiménez (Omega Hong Kong Open, The Celtic Manor Wales Open) were, like Michael Campbell and Tiger Woods, all multiple winners on The 2005 European Tour International Schedule.

Colin won the dunhill links championship at St Andrews where earlier in the year he finished runner-up to Tiger in The Open. These performances together with 11 other top ten finishes contributed to Colin winning €2,794,222 (£1,888,613) and regaining, through the Number One position on The European Tour Order of Merit, the Harry Vardon Trophy he held for a record seven successive years from 1993 to 1999. Colin has remained a loyal and strong supporter of The European Tour throughout his career, winning 29 titles on our International Schedule and in all 38 worldwide, and he closed 2005 as the leading player in total Career Money Winnings with €23,486,340 (£15,874,404). Colin also captained the Great Britain and Ireland team to victory over the José Maria Olazábal–led Continental Europe in the Seve Trophy.

Success revolves around teamwork. There exists on The European Tour, both on the fairways and in the workshop at Wentworth Headquarters, a team spirit second to none in the world of professional golf which has contributed enormously to our progress. More precisely, it would not be possible to achieve such success without strength-in-depth, commitment and patience and, with

this in mind, we specifically applaud John Bickerton, Emanuele Canonica, Raphaël Jacquelin and Steve Webster. In 2005 all four won for the first time on The European Tour International Schedule and in doing so they had totalled no fewer than 1002 tournament appearances.

Joakim Bäckström, Stephen Dodd, Nick Dougherty, Gonzalo Fernandez-Castano, Peter Hanson, Mark Hensby, Mikael Lundberg, Charl Schwartzel and Thaworn Wiratchant were also first time winners and Joakim (Aa St Omer) and Gonzalo (The KLM Open) did so after graduating from the 2004 European Tour Qualifying School. Gonzalo also followed in the footsteps of fellow Spaniards José Maria Olazábal (1986) and Sergio Garcia (1999) by being named the Sir Henry Cotton Rookie of the Year.

On a personal note my first full year as the Executive Director of The European Tour began in January with the announcement that BMW was to become our newest and highly distinguished partners in the PGA Championship – the Tour's flagship event – and the success of the BMW Championship, won superbly by Angel Cabrera at Wentworth Club, was a wonderful highlight in what we regard as a new era for The European Tour.

The many other highlights included Paul McGinley's excellent triumph in the season-ending Volvo Masters and Retief Goosen's victory in the Linde German Masters which contributed to them finishing third and fourth respectively in the Order of Merit ahead of Angel Cabrera, Sergio Garcia (winner of the Omega European Masters), David Howell (BMW International Open), Henrik Stenson, Thomas Björn (The Daily Telegraph Dunlop Masters) and José Maria Olazábal (Mallorca Classic).

Our byword for the future both on and off the fairways is: PRIDE. We must have Pride in our Performance, Pride in our Reputation, Pride in our Image, Pride in our Dedication and Determination and Pride in the Excellence of all we strive to deliver. This relates to our desire to achieve substantial growth coupled with maximum exposure to enhance the popularity of the game at all levels as we administer three Tours which, in 2005, resulted in 100 tournaments played in 37 countries with total prize money in excess of €121,000,000 (£82,000,000).

Carl Mason and Sam Torrance took the European Seniors Tour to a new level with their wonderful duel for Order of Merit honours and The John Jacobs Trophy, with Sam eventually denying Carl by €20,307 (£13,718), and we also congratulate Des Smyth for winning the season-ending Arcapita Seniors Tour Championship in Bahrain and twice on American soil on the US Champions Tour on which Mark James and Mark McNulty also triumphed, while Sergio Garcia, Retief Goosen, Padraig Harrington, Adam Scott and Vijay Singh enjoyed success on the US PGA Tour.

The European Challenge Tour has now produced 73 players who between them have accounted for 141 victories on The European Tour. In 2005, Scotland's Marc Warren led the graduates ahead of Spain's Carl Suneson, Sweden's Fredrik Widmark, England's Andrew Butterfield and South

Africa's Michael Kirk and he was part of history as for the first time one nation – Scotland – provided the Number One player on all three European Tours.

It is not a coincidence that four of our blue chip partners – BMW, HSBC, Johnnie Walker and Volvo – host tournaments in both China and on European soil on our International Schedule and we are equally proud of the partners who head the family of sponsors supporting The Ryder Cup which, in 2006, will be played at The K Club in Ireland. With the co-operation of the two Captains, Ian Woosnam and Tom Lehman, we look forward in this, the 18th edition of The European Tour Yearbook, to the biennial match between Europe and the United States and we hope you will enjoy their hole-by-hole view of the Palmer Course in addition to recalling the many exciting and enthralling events from 2005.

George O'Grady
George O'Grady
Executive Director
The European Tour

Acknowledgments

Executive Editor
Mitchell Platts

Production Editor
Vanessa O'Brien

Editorial Consultants
Scott Crockett
Chris Plumridge

Picture Editors
Andrew Redington
Richard Martin-Roberts
Rob Harborne

Art Direction
Tim Leney
Andrew Wright
TC Communications Plc

Print Managed by
London Print & Design Plc

The European Tour Yearbook 2006 is published by The PGA European Tour, Wentworth Drive, Virginia Water, Surrey GU25 4LX. Distributed through Aurum Press Ltd. 25 Bedford Avenue London WC1B 3AT.

© PGA European Tour.

ISBN 1 84513 150 9

THERE IS A MEASUREMENT FOR
UNRELENTING FOCUS:
THE EUROPEAN TOUR.

TREVOR IMMELMAN

Golf is an extremely demanding sport. The practice, the shot-making, the mental toughness – all are part of the self-imposed pressure to constantly improve. Compound that dedication with fierce competition, high-stake prize money, constant media visibility, and a non-stop travel schedule, and you have the PGA European Tour.

OYSTER PERPETUAL DATEJUST · WWW.ROLEX.COM

ROLEX

Contents

Breathtaking Return of A Colossus

The abiding image is of a natural golfer, a player sublimely unconcerned with the demanding technique of this gloriously perverse game, but who is also the very picture of a hunter searching down his prey with the cunning of a lion.

There are some who say that Colin Stuart Montgomerie OBE is so perfectly balanced because he always wears a heart on both sleeves. It is a theory hard to displace because it has ever been thus since the artist - soon to be known universally by the sobriquet Monty - turned professional in 1987. He enjoyed a plus three handicap at the time and had won, amongst other amateur titles, the Scottish Amateur Championship. Right from the start he laid down the template for his new professional life. "My aim," he said in that intensely authoritative style of his: "Is to make a decent living and to improve each year if I can."

Well, he did, and he did. Despite his disappointment, an occurrence more revolving on bad luck in not winning – thus far – a Major Championship, he did bestride the 1990s like a colossus. More than this, his personality and his readiness to voice an opinion in a coherent and often entertaining fashion, set him apart from the herd. Monty never just invited you to look at his medals, his seven consecutive European Tour Order of Merit titles, he talked you through them richly and along the way always offered an opinion on those people who failed to offer an opinion.

Too often in this squared and modern world, professional sportsmen feel uncomfortable talking about anything other than themselves. Theirs can be a tiny world, a small and rather monosyllabic planet. A dull place.

Well Monty's World has never been dull. His life is a perpetual drama waiting to happen. Now, just when some believed the truly great days were over, his game retreating before the inevitable onslaught of age, he

has reinvented himself. Or rather rebuilt himself. For it was not the new Monty we witnessed emerging from a turbulent few years in 2005, it was, in fact, the old one.

At the beginning of the season it was depressingly easy to view him as something of a lost soul, a man understandably impaled on the sharp emotions of a very public divorce and a golfer traumatised by his inability to reach out and to consistently touch the old competitive sharpness he had caressed since his teenage years.

He was ranked 83rd in the world and he was not happy. He told us he was determined to return to the top 50 on the Official World Golf Ranking, two score and ten players who, by virtue of their standing, enjoy the sweetest ride through the most coveted tournaments. He told us he could do this

The European Tour Order of Merit Winner

Colin Montgomerie OBE

His form continued through the early months with top ten finishes in Dubai, China (twice) and Indonesia. He was clearly in improving fettle but the old, cocky spring was not yet in his stride. He was still searching for The X Factor, that indefinable something which turns the accomplished player into a winner. His mood, though, was increasingly confident. The fact was Monty was testing himself and, for the most part, being reassured with what he found.

Forced, frustratingly, to sit out the Masters Tournament in April, he continued to work on mind and body and his first missed cut of the year did not come until June when he slid out of The Celtic Manor Wales Open. The sceptics immediately began to emerge once more. The old flame, they said, was extinguished forever.

They were, of course, spectacularly wrong but then with Montgomerie, it had never been a mere flame. In his case it had been a roaring bush fire, a volcanic ignition that takes some serious extinguishing. Slowly, despite this setback, he was rekindling some serious heat, a process helped hugely by his qualification for the US Open Championship at Pinehurst No.2 in North Carolina where he finished in a creditable tie for 42nd place.

His second runners-up spot of the year came at the Smurfit European Open in Ireland but it was to be his third second place that finally shifted all his component parts into the correct competitive order. This arrived in the epicentre of his heartland, St Andrews, the Old Course and Scotland.

He had to concede victory in The Open Championship to an irresistible Tiger Woods that weekend in July but his joust with the best golfer in the world caught the public's imagination and the support extended to him by Scottish fans on that final Sunday offered up the vital last piece of reassurance he had been seeking. To understand this you must first know that while Monty has

and, what is more, he would. But those of us who have ridden with him through so much of his life and his career, the majority clinging on desperately as momentum and mood swung this way and that, felt that more than a place back in the top 50, Monty was searching for an inner peace.

As the curtain came down on 2005, it appeared he had found both. Contentment for Colin Montgomerie has always come ultimately from a job well done and as he contemplated his eighth European Number One title he felt good both inside and out.

It is quite simply a phenomenal achievement. The European scene is alive to the bravado calls of a posse of talented golfers these days, most of them significantly younger than the Scot, and for him to hold them off and then to move forward himself is breathtaking. We should not, of course, be surprised.

As early as January he hoisted his flag of intent via a second place in the Caltex Masters, presented by Carlsberg, Singapore 2005 before, a week later, he finished tied for 11th in the Heineken Classic staged at the classically impressive Royal Melbourne Golf Club. Monty was off but not quite running.

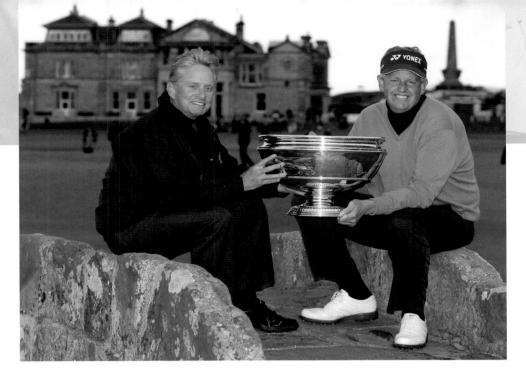

always been an overtly confident person, he has retained an attractive vulnerability to the slings and arrows of outrageous fortune. It is this most human of faces that continues to endear him to a public who remain fascinated by his progress through the game.

Sometimes, it must be added, his inability to restrain his emotions and his susceptibility to a rash word or action has caused dismay but, for the most part, he has been man enough to own up to these ill-chosen sentences or deeds and his repentance has been transparently sincere.

Having started his total rehabilitation on the Old Course in July, he completed the process at the same venue 11 weeks later when he won the dunhill links championship. His amateur partner for the week was Hollywood superstar Michael Douglas and the actor was so charmed by his professional that he stayed on long after the prizegiving, just another spectator caught up in the narrative of Monty's life.

It was after the pair had been photographed together on the Swilcan Bridge (pictured above) that Monty finally allowed us briefly inside the farthest reaches of his head and heart. He admitted he had wondered if his last victory – in Singapore some 19 months earlier - had indeed been just that, his last. "Who was to know?" he said. "You get down, of course you get down, and self-doubt creeps in. Now everything has changed again. This is the most important victory of my life."

So it has proved. The following week he overcame tiredness and jet-lag to finish tied for third place in the WGC - American Express Championship in San Francisco, a supreme example of will triumphing even if the actual victory went to Woods again. Those two weeks took him above Michael Campbell at the top of The European Tour Order of Merit. Just a couple of months earlier this had seemed the most unlikely of situations, and there he stayed with another superb performance in the season-ending Volvo Masters.

We should, of course, have taken into account not just an outstanding talent but his lifelong ability to bounce back from adversity. After the dunhill links championship, the old Monty was before us once more, the rhythm silkily restored and the familiar pose, whereby he stands with his club sheathed like a hussar about to meet the Queen, was on view again.

His delight at recovering the Harry Vardon Trophy after an absence of six years was obvious for all to see, and second only to his pleasure at now being all but a certainty for The 2006 European Ryder Cup Team and a match he always illuminates. He has never really been away but it is still good to welcome him back to where he so deservedly belongs. Let the fun begin once more.

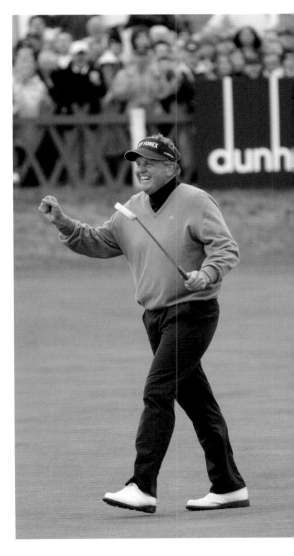

Bill Elliott
The Observer / Golf Monthly

EUROPEAN TOUR

Michael Campbell on his celebratory Welcome Home Parade in the streets of Wellington following his historic achievement in becoming the first New Zealander to win the US Open Championship. He was accompanied by his wife, Julie, their children, Thomas and Jordan, and Michael's parents, Maria and Tom

Keeping the Romance Alive

While glittering names such as Michael Campbell, Ernie Els, Colin Montgomerie and Tiger Woods continued to embroider The European Tour story in 2005, another fourball comprising John Bickerton, Emanuele Canonica, Raphaël Jacquelin and Steve Webster captured the romance that golf can offer possibly better than any other sport.

This latter quartet were among the 13 first-time victors on The 2005 European Tour International Schedule. For each of them the wait for such a moment had been long. Forbiddingly long. Between them they had teed-up in a total of 1002 events on The European Tour before, at last, the dark bird of doubt took wing and flew forever from their shoulders. Quite a feat but, then again, it only goes to emphasise the strength of talent on the Tour. And, of course, the virtue of patience where golf is concerned.

Bickerton is top of this class simply because he had played more tournaments than the other three without winning. What is more, when he headed for the Abama Open de Canarias at the Abama Golf Club, Tenerife, Spain, he did so not only to contest his 287th European Tour event but also in the knowledge that he was on the cusp of losing the playing privileges he had earned by graduating from the European Challenge Tour in 1998.

On top of the alarm this understandably caused to Bickerton, he had to endure the frustration that comes when you have finished runner-up on no fewer than five occasions, beaten by the likes of Thomas Björn, Darren Clarke and Paul Lawrie, a catalogue of close-calls that can sometimes turn a nearly man into a crazy man. To his eternal credit he preserved his sanity and remained cheerfully optimistic before finally, and gloriously, his day arrived.

To be specific it arrived on Sunday October 9 when he clinched the Abama Open de Canarias and secured a one year exemption to The 2006 European Tour International Schedule, representing the

sharp pinnacle of a career centred on the word *almost*. Since that moment he has never stopped grinning.

Webster, too, had endured the frustration of finishing runner-up five times, including being beaten in a play-off by Retief Goosen in the 2001 Telefonica Open de Madrid, so when he arrived to play in his 247th European Tour event in the Telecom Italia Open at Castello di Tolcinasco Golf & Country Club in Milan you could understand if he felt a sense of injustice weighing down on his 30 year old shoulders. Four rounds in the 60s, however, under a hot sun provided a good thirst and a delicious reason to celebrate.

Webster's win might have also fired the emotions of one of the Italians in the field because after finishing fifth in Milan, Canonica later teed up for his 231st European Tour event in the Johnnie Walker

John Bickerton

Steve Webster

Emanuele Canonica

Championship at Gleneagles and duly ended a 14 year wait for success. The 34 year old from Turin, runner-up to Lee Westwood in the Deutsche Bank – SAP Open TPC of Europe in the year 2000, closed with a 71 for a two shot win.

For Jacquelin, runner-up twice in 2004, there was more reason for him to mark his 238th European Tour appearance with a win because he arrived at the Open de Madrid at Club de Campo in October with his wife, Fanny, expecting their second child. There was also more than a hint of romance in the air since this event marked the return of Seve Ballesteros to competitive action. If Jacquelin had chosen to reflect on the eve of the event that Ballesteros had won 50 European Tour events alone, that the Spaniard's last success had come in 1995 at Club de Campo and that he had won all of his five Major Championships by the age of 31, which happened to be Jacquelin's age, then the Frenchman might have dwelled on what might have been since he turned professional in 1995. Instead he decided that this would

be his time to wrestle a tournament in his direction, as Ballesteros did so many times, and no-one could accuse him of not doing so in real style as he pulled seven shots clear after three rounds on the way to victory. He was, as is traditional at these times, surrounded by his delighted countrymen on the 18th green and drenched in bubbly.

While there are those who are forced to wait there are others who sprint into pole position almost before they are properly warmed up. Australian Mark Hensby won the Scandinavian Masters by Carlsberg at the Kungsängen Golf Club on only his eighth European Tour outing while Spain's Gonzalo Fernandez-Castano (The KLM Open), the Sir Henry Cotton Rookie of the Year winner for 2005, and Sweden's Joakim Bäckström (Aa St Omer Open), both graduates of the 2004 European Challenge Tour, won on their 16th and 17th appearances respectively.

To the untutored Western ear, the wonderfully named Thaworn Wiratchant may sound like an anagram of a particularly challenging grocery list but in his native Thailand his name now means only one thing: Winner. His victory in the Enjoy Jakarta Standard Chartered Indonesia Open at Cengkareng Golf Club, Jakarta, Indonesia, in late March brought great joy to the game's rapidly increasing number of followers in the Far East. Enjoy indeed.

It was a win that has changed Wiratchant's life for he took up full Tour membership shortly after his stunning victory, confident in the knowledge that he is now exempt until 2007 and thus able to mould his career into a more coherent and certainly more lucrative shape.

Similar joy, of course, was felt by the other rookie victors in 2005. Stephen Dodd won not just his first Tour title but the season's first event, the Volvo China Open at the Shanghai Silport Golf Club, China. As openers go, it is not bad given that the Welshman became

Raphaël Jacquelin

champion of the country that can boast not only the world's largest population but also the planet's oldest continuing civilisation. Six months later Dodd followed up by winning the Nissan Irish Open held at Carton House Golf Club, Maynooth, Co. Kildare, Ireland.

Elsewhere, South Africa's Charl Schwartzel invigorated his fellow countrymen when he lifted the trophy at the dunhill championship staged at Leopard Creek, Mpumalanga, South Africa; Nick Dougherty lived up to his reputation by winning the Caltex Masters, presented by Carlsberg, Singapore 2005 at the Laguna National Golf & Country Club, Singapore; Peter Hanson won the Jazztel Open de España en Andalucia at San Roque Club, Cadiz, Spain; and Mikael Lundberg raised a deserved toast to himself after landing The Cadillac Russian Open at Le Meridien Moscow Country Club, Moscow, Russia.

So the first, and largest, obstacle to abiding success had been breached by these players. The romance of their victories will lie well with them for some time but each now also knows – Dodd apart - that the clock is ticking on how long it takes for them to win again. Professional sport is like that. No matter what the game may be, the sweet taste of success lasts for only a short time before the pressure builds on a man to construct his next victory. Some, of course, never do. There are a variety of reasons for that – loss of form and then, inevitably, confidence, brutally poor luck or, perhaps, other, even more debilitating problems in life.

For the chosen few, however, victories come and then come again, their games riding high, their self-esteem pumped up, their expectations always keen. No-one, of course, expects more than Tiger Woods who has now won at least one title on The European Tour for the last nine years.

In 2005 he maintained his record with some brilliance when he emerged victorious in the

Ernie Els

Masters Tournament at Augusta National, Georgia, USA; The 134th Open Championship at the Old Course, St Andrews, Scotland; the WGC-NEC Invitational at Firestone Country Club, Akron, Ohio, USA; and the WGC-American Express Championship at Harding Park Golf Club, San Francisco, California, USA, where he defeated a crestfallen John Daly in a play-off that ended with the big man three-putting from 15 feet.

Another big man was unlucky in 2005, too. Ernie Els began his year in impressive fashion with back-to-back victories in the Dubai Desert Classic at the Emirates Golf Club, Dubai, and in the Qatar Masters at Doha Golf Club, Qatar, before also taking the BMW Asian Open at the Tomson Shanghai Pudong Golf Club in Shanghai, China. Everyone was expecting a stellar year from the South African but it never quite happened. The European Tour Number One in both 2003 and 2004 injured a knee whilst on holiday and retired early from 2005 to undergo surgery. He will, of course, be back.

Back already is Colin Montgomerie, whose victory on the Old Course at St Andrews in

Gonzalo Fernandez-Castano - The 2005 Sir Henry Cotton Rookie of the Year

Michael Campbell

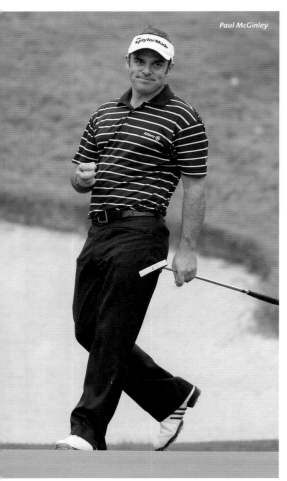

Paul McGinley

he had to withstand several challengers, Thomas Björn being amongst the most dogged that week. The Dane, of course, had already tasted success earlier in the year when he saw off Brian Davis and David Howell to win the The Daily Telegraph Dunlop Masters at the Marriott Forest of Arden, Warwickshire, England.

But pride of place in the Major arena from a European Tour perspective, went to Michael Campbell, whose US Open Championship victory on the delectable Pinehurst No.2 course in North Carolina, USA, was the outstanding performance of the year. The affable New Zealander has shown many times that, when injury free, his is a world class talent, but this win in the American heartland endorsed his curriculum vitae magnificently. As did his late summer triumph in the glittering HSBC World Match Play Championship at Wentworth Club, Surrey, England, where he beat the gallant Paul McGinley 2 and 1 in the final. The West Course is no place for the faint hearted while match play is the game of choice for those possessing real character. Campbell is such a player.

the dunhill links championship was the catalyst for an exhilarating eighth Order of Merit win, and the Scot also skippered his Great Britain & Ireland side to victory over the José Maria Olazábal-led Continental Europe in the Seve Trophy at The Wynyard Golf Club, Billingham, Tees Valley, England.

Meanwhile, with or without Els in their ranks, the South Africans continued to impress. Tim Clark won the South African Airways Open at the Durban Country Club, Durban, South Africa, and followed that up impressively by taking The Barclays Scottish Open title at Loch Lomond, Glasgow, Scotland, while Retief Goosen finally interrupted an unusually subdued campaign by winning the Linde German Masters at Gut Lärchenhof, Cologne, Germany.

The year's four Major Championships were memorable for several reasons. First, Woods re-established himself as the dominant global force with his two wins while Phil Mickelson added his second Major title with the US PGA Championship at Baltusrol Golf Club, Springfield, New Jersey, USA, where

As is the big-hitting Angel Cabrera. The Argentine was seven shots adrift of the lead at the halfway stage of the BMW Championship at Wentworth Club but seemed to borrow some oomph from the sponsors' engines to make it up and more to win the most significant title of his career in real style. There was style, also, from Miguel Angel Jiménez whose pony-tail bobbed in approval at his victories in the Omega Hong Kong Open, Hong Kong Golf Club, Fanling, Hong Kong, and in The Celtic Manor Wales Open at The Celtic Manor Resort, Newport, South Wales, where his opening 63 tied as one of the three lowest opening rounds by a winner in 2005. The others were Adam Scott in the Johnnie Walker Classic at Pine Valley Golf Resort & Country Club, Beijing, China, and the aforementioned Thaworn Wiratchant in Indonesia. Scott, by the way,

also achieved the highest winning finish of the season in the same event when he carded a 75. Nice symmetry there.

The highest start by a winner was Englishman Kenneth Ferrie's 75 during the Smurfit European Open at The K Club, Straffan, County Kildare, Ireland. The lowest finish by a winner to par was Niclas Fasth's nine under par 63 to take the Holden New Zealand Open at the Gulf Harbour Country Club, Auckland, New Zealand, while the Swede also won The Deutsche Bank Players' Championship of Europe at Gut Kaden, Hamburg, Germany.

Elsewhere England's Paul Broadhurst recorded his first victory on Tour for ten years when he won the Estoril Open de Portugal Caixa Geral de Depositos at Oitavos Golfe, Quinta da Marinha, Portugal; Craig Parry triumphed at home in the Heineken Classic at Royal Melbourne Golf Club, Victoria, Australia; Thongchai Jaidee won the Carlsberg Malaysian Open at Saujana Golf & Country Club, Kuala Lumpur, Malaysia; David Toms won the WGC - Accenture Match Play, at La Costa Resort & Spa in Carlsbad, California, USA; Robert-Jan Derksen triumphed in the Madeira Island Open Caixa Geral de Depositos at Santo da Serra, Madeira, Portugal; Paul Casey returned to form by winning the TCL Classic at Yalong Bay Golf Club, Sanya, Hainan Island, China; French hearts fluttered when Jean-Francois Remesy successfully defended the Open de France at Le Golf National, Paris, France; David Howell returned from injury to win the BMW International Open at Golfclub München Nord-Eichenried, Munich, Germany; Sergio Garcia flew high to win the Omega European Masters at Crans-sur-Sierre, Crans Montana, Switzerland; while fellow Spaniard José Maria Olazábal ended over three winless years with victory in the Mallorca Classic at Pula Golf Club, Mallorca, Spain.

Club de Golf Valderrama again hosted the final event of the season, the Volvo Masters,

in which Paul McGinley was another to rekindle the art of winning. Three runners-up finishes - in the TCL Classic, BMW Championship and HSBC World Match Play Championship - had made it a year of near misses for the Irishman, but all that changed with a final round 67 that saw him come from behind to clinch a famous win and a personal best third place behind Montgomerie and Campbell in The European Tour Order of Merit.

And finally, as mentioned earlier, Seve Ballesteros made that long anticipated comeback to The European Tour when he contested the Open de Madrid some 18 months after he suggested he might never play again. The great man, understandably after such a long lay-off, missed the cut but said he would play more in 2006. And better too. Of course he will. You simply cannot keep a great romantic down.

Bill Elliott
The Observer / Golf Monthly

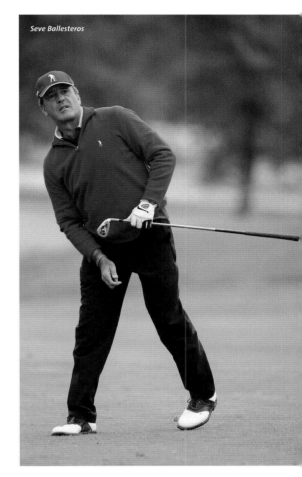

Seve Ballesteros

From left to right: Bertie Ahern, T.D. (the Taoiseach), Ian Woosnam (The 2006 European Ryder Cup Captain), John O'Donoghue, T.D. (Minister for Arts, Sport and Tourism) and George O'Grady (Executive Director of The European Tour) with The Ryder Cup during 'The Year To Go' Ryder Cup Gala Dinner at Citywest Hotel and Golf Resort in September, 2005

Volvo China Open

China
November 25-28 • 2004

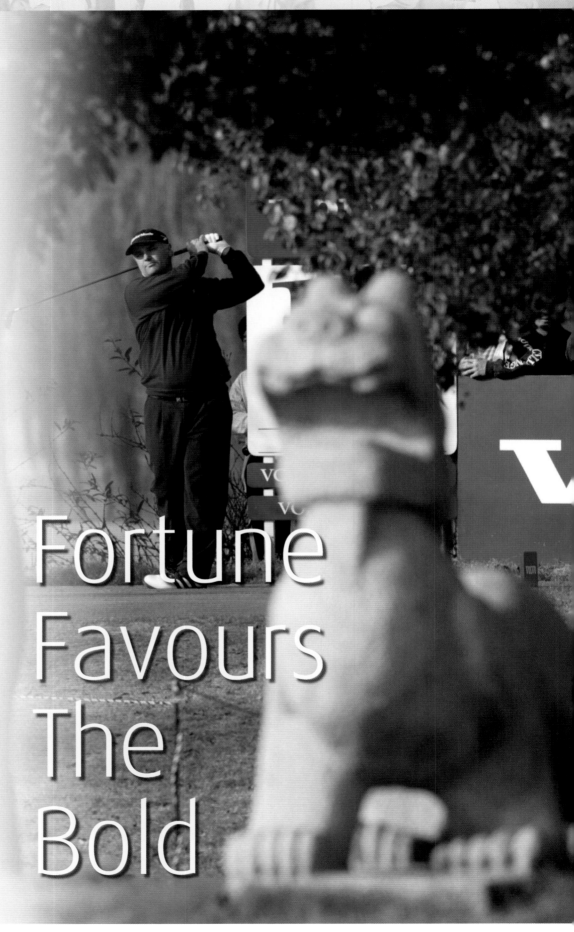

Shanghai Silport Golf Club

Par	Yards	Metres
72	7073	6467

Pos	Name	Score	To Par	
1	**Stephen DODD**	276	-12	
2	Thomas BJÖRN	279	-9	
3	Jason DAWES	282	-6	
	Chawalit PLAPHOL	282	-6	
	Thaworn WIRATCHANT	282	-6	
6	Amandeep JOHL	283	-5	
	Steve WEBSTER	283	-5	
8	Søren HANSEN	284	-4	
	Barry LANE	284	-4	
	Jonathan LOMAS	284	-4	

Round One   Round Two   Round Three   Round Four

EUROPEAN TOUR ORDER OF MERIT
(After one tournament)

Pos		€	
1	**Stephen DODD**	127,621.20	
2	Thomas BJÖRN	85,083.38	
3	Jason DAWES	39,564.16	
4	Amandeep JOHL	24,887.14	
	Steve WEBSTER	24,887.14	
6	Søren HANSEN	17,204.03	
	Barry LANE	17,204.03	
	Jonathan LOMAS	17,204.03	
9	Mark FOSTER	12,826.45	
	Gregory HAVRET	12,826.45	

Fortune Favours The Bold

When Stephen Dodd turned up at Shanghai Silport Golf Club for the Volvo China Open, there were some who were mildly surprised. The city, formerly known as the Paris of the Orient, is halfway round the world from Barry where the former Amateur Champion has his home, and the Welshman has always made it clear he dislikes flying - a major problem for someone trying to make a name for himself on The European Tour International Schedule.

Back in the old days when another well-known Welshman, the late Dai Rees, was playing, 'overseas' meant a quick trip to France, Italy or Spain. Now it is very different as The European Tour spreads its message around the world. Dodd, who had come through the Qualifying School on three occasions before establishing himself as the Tour moved into the new millennium, had packed his bags for China, however, with a strengthened belief in his ability and a singular goal for 2005 – victory.

Although his best performance in his previous 165 events had been a second place finish in the 2001 North West of Ireland Open, Dodd's ambition was no pipe dream. At the end of the 2004 season, he had finished in a creditable tie for 15th in the Volvo Masters at the Club de Golf Valderrama, one of the most testing courses in Europe.

In addition to that, the work Dodd was doing with psychologist Alan Fine was beginning to pay off. The Welshman had a new attitude.

Søren Hansen

Barry Lane

Volvo China Open

China
November 25-28 • 2004

Bradley Dredge

He practised more and was giving himself a better chance of winning, but he had no idea that his much desired breakthrough would come as quickly as it did at entrepreneur Beta Soong's stylish golf course, an hour's drive from downtown Shanghai.

Soong had liberally sprinkled the course with old Chinese statues which, it was alleged, brought good luck to those who touched them. Whether or not the phlegmatic Dodd went near the impressive stone animals, far less rubbed them, is not on record but nevertheless, good fortune was with him.

He led by three shots at the halfway stage, maintained that advantage after the penultimate round and, despite the strong attentions of Denmark's Thomas Björn on the final afternoon, went on to win by three on 12 under par 276 after respective closing 68s from the tournament's leading pair. The success finally proved to the 38 year old that he was just as capable of handling the

pressure on The European Tour as he had been when winning the Amateur title or as a member of the history-making Great Britain and Ireland Walker Cup side which became the first to win on American soil, at Peachtree, Atlanta, in 1989.

Dodd had joined the ever growing list of winners on The European Tour and achieved his 2005 goal, ironically, even before the year had started. For this was November 2004 and the Volvo China Open , a co-sanctioned event between The European and Asian Tours, was the first of three on the 2005 schedule in place before Christmas 2004.

Dodd did not care what year it was, just that he had won, from Björn, and a trio in third place; talented Australian Jason Dawes, who had an ace at the eighth hole in his closing 66, and two of Thailand's top golfers, Chawalit Plaphol and Thaworn Wiratchant. Now, however, he knew he would have to reassess his situation.

With his 58th place finish in 2004 having been his highest on The European Tour Order of Merit, he knew more consistency would help him earn a better placing at the end of the 2005 season, as well as, of course, trying to win again now he had proved to himself he could do it once.

Yet, keeping his feet firmly planted on the ground, Dodd tried to remain cool and not become overwhelmed at what he had achieved. In the post tournament interview he explained the victory really meant he had done what he always believed deep down he could do. "If I had thought I was not good enough to win out here I would have given up long before now," he said. Ironically, Dodd ended up a champion on two Tours because after ten years of running the event as a purely Asian Tour tournament, Volvo Event Management CEO and President Mel Pyatt, himself a former professional, had made his own breakthrough in helping secure co-sanctioned status with The European Tour.

" A good all round golf course with a little bit of water and some very interesting holes, some very strong par fours in particular. It was pretty flat but they made it very interesting on some holes, for example, where you had to hit irons off tees. It was a long journey to get there from the city but it was worth the trip " – Barry Lane

Gregory Havret

To celebrate the achievement, there was a new trophy to be presented.

Few have done more to foster professional golf in China than Pyatt, who had worked hard to persuade his board that a golfing expansion into the country made sound commercial sense when it came to selling cars, vans and heavy equipment. After all, a similar strategy in Europe had proved amazingly successful. "It wasn't easy but I knew how the game was expanding in the country," he said. "In 1995 there were just ten courses. Today there are over 200 and golf is growing in popularity."

He was a happy man indeed, but the week belonged to Dodd and when he looks back on what he hopes will be the first of many wins, he can remember with pride many parts of the week, including the second round 70 he shot in icily cold conditions. It was by far the toughest scoring day of the week when the wind whistled down from the north, lowering temperatures and making everyone shiver.

Appropriate really as, come Sunday, it was the Ice Man who triumphed.

Renton Laidlaw
The Golf Channel

Marc Cayeux

Final Results

Pos	Name		Rd1	Rd2	Rd3	Rd4	Total		€	£
1	Stephen DODD	Wal	68	70	70	68	276	-12	127,621.20	89,602.12
2	Thomas BJÖRN	Den	71	72	68	68	279	-9	85,083.38	59,736.56
3	Thaworn WIRATCHANT	Thai	71	74	69	68	282	-6	39,564.16	27,777.77
	Jason DAWES	Aus	68	74	74	66	282	-6	39,564.16	27,777.77
	Chawalit PLAPHOL	Thai	75	69	72	66	282	-6	39,564.16	27,777.77
6	Steve WEBSTER	Eng	70	75	70	68	283	-5	24,887.14	17,473.12
	Amandeep JOHL	Ind	68	76	70	69	283	-5	24,887.14	17,473.12
8	Søren HANSEN	Den	70	71	70	73	284	-4	17,204.03	12,078.85
	Jonathan LOMAS	Eng	72	71	72	69	284	-4	17,204.03	12,078.85
	Barry LANE	Eng	68	75	70	71	284	-4	17,204.03	12,078.85
11	Mark FOSTER	Eng	70	72	71	72	285	-3	12,826.45	9,005.38
	Simon YATES	Scot	70	73	70	72	285	-3	12,826.45	9,005.38
	Joon CHUNG	Kor	69	72	72	72	285	-3	12,826.45	9,005.38
	Gregory HAVRET	Fr	71	75	67	72	285	-3	12,826.45	9,005.38
15	Bradley DREDGE	Wal	67	75	70	74	286	-2	10,797.19	7,580.65
	Wen-Chong LIANG	PRC	72	74	73	67	286	-2	10,797.19	7,580.65
	Anthony WALL	Eng	73	72	71	70	286	-2	10,797.19	7,580.65
18	Damien MCGRANE	Ire	71	74	73	69	287	-1	9,361.39	6,572.58
	Peter LAWRIE	Ire	72	78	70	67	287	-1	9,361.39	6,572.58
	Mads VIBE-HASTRUP	Den	69	77	68	73	287	-1	9,361.39	6,572.58
	David PARK	Wal	73	77	70	67	287	-1	9,361.39	6,572.58
22	Chris WILLIAMS	Eng	72	72	73	71	288	0	8,538.20	5,994.62
	Paul BROADHURST	Eng	73	73	71	71	288	0	8,538.20	5,994.62
24	Andrew PITTS	USA	69	77	74	69	289	1	8,078.75	5,672.04
	James KINGSTON	SA	69	78	70	72	289	1	8,078.75	5,672.04
26	Edward MICHAELS	USA	72	74	72	72	290	2	7,619.29	5,349.46
	Philip GOLDING	Eng	71	75	70	74	290	2	7,619.29	5,349.46
28	Lian-Wei ZHANG	PRC	69	76	74	72	291	3	6,585.52	4,623.66
	Rick GIBSON	Can	70	79	68	74	291	3	6,585.52	4,623.66
	Maarten LAFEBER	NL	74	75	70	72	291	3	6,585.52	4,623.66
	Ter-Chang WANG	Tpe	72	74	73	72	291	3	6,585.52	4,623.66
	Prayad MARKSAENG	Thai	70	76	73	72	291	3	6,585.52	4,623.66
	Mikko ILONEN	Fin	72	78	73	68	291	3	6,585.52	4,623.66
	Matthew KING	Eng	68	73	77	73	291	3	6,585.52	4,623.66
35	Terry PILKADARIS	Aus	75	72	72	73	292	4	5,666.61	3,978.49
	Anthony KANG	Kor	72	76	73	71	292	4	5,666.61	3,978.49
37	Pablo DEL OLMO	Mex	72	76	73	72	293	5	5,360.31	3,763.44
	Graeme STORM	Eng	72	78	76	67	293	5	5,360.31	3,763.44
39	Simon DYSON	Eng	72	78	72	72	294	6	4,517.97	3,172.04
	Gary RUSNAK	USA	73	75	69	77	294	6	4,517.97	3,172.04
	Unho PARK	Aus	67	80	70	77	294	6	4,517.97	3,172.04
	Louis OOSTHUIZEN	SA	72	75	74	73	294	6	4,517.97	3,172.04
	Marc CAYEUX	Zim	68	75	77	74	294	6	4,517.97	3,172.04
	Hendrik BUHRMANN	SA	71	79	73	71	294	6	4,517.97	3,172.04
	Stephen SCAHILL	NZ	72	75	74	73	294	6	4,517.97	3,172.04
	Fredrik ANDERSSON HED	Swe	71	75	74	74	294	6	4,517.97	3,172.04
	Kwang-Soo CHOI	Kor	75	72	70	77	294	6	4,517.97	3,172.04
48	Scott BARR	Aus	73	78	74	70	295	7	3,369.34	2,365.59
	Paul LAWRIE	Scot	71	78	73	73	295	7	3,369.34	2,365.59
	Miguel Angel MARTIN	Sp	75	74	74	72	295	7	3,369.34	2,365.59
	Jyoti RANDHAWA	Ind	71	76	72	76	295	7	3,369.34	2,365.59
	Robert KARLSSON	Swe	74	75	73	73	295	7	3,369.34	2,365.59
	Nick DOUGHERTY	Eng	72	79	69	75	295	7	3,369.34	2,365.59
54	Gregory HANRAHAN	USA	73	71	77	75	296	8	2,680.15	1,881.72
	Andrew MARSHALL	Eng	73	75	72	76	296	8	2,680.15	1,881.72
	Pat GILES	Aus	75	74	74	73	296	8	2,680.15	1,881.72
57	Mardan MAMAT	Sing	71	80	74	72	297	9	2,220.70	1,559.14
	Robert-Jan DERKSEN	NL	72	78	78	69	297	9	2,220.70	1,559.14
	Des TERBLANCHE	SA	72	77	77	71	297	9	2,220.70	1,559.14
	Raymond RUSSELL	Scot	70	80	71	76	297	9	2,220.70	1,559.14
	Robert COLES	Eng	71	76	73	77	297	9	2,220.70	1,559.14
62	Thammanoon SRIROT	Thai	72	77	77	72	298	10	1,990.97	1,397.85
	Henry LIAW (AM)	USA	73	77	74	74	298	10		
64	Lei SHANG	PRC	71	79	74	76	300	12	1,837.82	1,290.32
	Emanuele CANONICA	It	76	70	74	80	300	12	1,837.82	1,290.32
	Arjun SINGH	Ind	73	77	78	72	300	12	1,837.82	1,290.32
67	Jamie DONALDSON	Wal	73	78	75	75	301	13	1,646.38	1,155.91
	Johan AXGREN	Swe	76	75	73	77	301	13	1,646.38	1,155.91
69	Harmeet KAHLON	Ind	74	77	76	75	302	14	1,493.23	1,048.39
	Danny CHIA	Mal	72	79	75	76	302	14	1,493.23	1,048.39
71	Ming Jie HUANG	PRC	73	77	76	77	303	15	1,275.17	895.29
	Nobuhito SATO	Jpn	75	76	78	74	303	15	1,275.17	895.29

Total Prize Fund
€766,910   £538,441

Hong Kong Golf Club

Par	Yards	Metres
70	6749	6170

Pos	Name	Score	Par	
1	**Miguel Angel JIMÉNEZ**	266	-14	
2	Padraig HARRINGTON	267	-13	
	James KINGSTON	267	-13	
4	Thomas BJÖRN	270	-10	
	Thammanoon SRIROT	270	-10	
6	Nick FALDO	272	-8	
	David HOWELL	272	-8	
8	José Maria OLAZÁBAL	273	-7	
	Charl SCHWARTZEL	273	-7	
	Alessandro TADINI	273	-7	
	Lian-Wei ZHANG	273	-7	

Round One	Round Two	Round Three	Round Four

Infectious Enthusiasm

EUROPEAN TOUR ORDER OF MERIT
(After two tournaments)

Pos	Name	€	
1	**Stephen DODD**	129,126.32	
2	Thomas BJÖRN	112,898.00	
3	Miguel Angel JIMÉNEZ	100,338.80	
4	James KINGSTON	60,366.62	
5	Padraig HARRINGTON	52,287.87	
6	Jason DAWES	40,465.66	
7	Steve WEBSTER	31,907.02	
8	Amandeep JOHL	30,967.83	
9	Søren HANSEN	24,223.91	
10	Barry LANE	22,291.34	

A quick glance at the record books shows what Miguel Angel Jiménez means when he says he would be happy if more events on The European Tour International Schedule were played in the Far East. For the smiling señor had just won the second event on the 2005 calendar – the Omega Hong Kong Open – for his fifth success in ten months and three of them had a distinct Eastern flavour.

Victories in the Algarve Open de Portugal Caixa Geral de Depositos and the BMW International Open aside, the 2004 season had also included successes in the Johnnie Walker Classic at the Alpine Golf & Sports Club in Bangkok and the BMW Asian Open at the Tomson Shanghai Pudong Golf Club in China.

Now Jiménez was celebrating glory in the East again. Whatever it is that makes him so ruthlessly efficient when he tees it up in co-sanctioned events with the Asian Tour, Jiménez was certain of one thing: Life had begun at 40. He had reached that milestone birthday in January, 2004, and since that time he had been reaching for the stars, which seemed rather appropriate, as this latest success was achieved in the Fanling district of Hong Kong where the skyscrapers seem to disappear at times into the clouds.

Over the years, several composite courses have been used at the Hong Kong Golf Club with the quality of the winners, whatever the layout, equally impressive. It all started with Mr Lu back in 1959 and he won again in 1974. Peter Thomson took the title three times between 1960 and 1967 and, as well as including many of the top Asian golfers, the Roll of Honour also features notable names such as Bernhard Langer, Greg Norman, Tom Watson and Ian Woosnam.

Jiménez's compatriot José Maria Olazábal is also there, his triumph coming in the first co-sanctioned tournament in 2002, and he was subsequently followed onto the winners' rostrum by Fredrik Jacobson and Padraig Harrington.

Harrington was back to defend the title and remained on the leaderboard from day one before finally losing out by a shot and finishing tied second with South African James Kingston. It was such a tense battle for first place that just two shots separated the top nine players going into the last round, one of them in the mix being Nick Faldo who had won the Johnnie Walker Classic at the course in 1990, setting a new record at the time.

It would be one of the last times that Faldo and his long time caddie Fanny Sunesson would work together. With Sunesson wishing to curtail her programme and widen her other interests, victory would have been one of the most fitting ways to bring the curtain down on one of golf's most successful partnerships. But it was

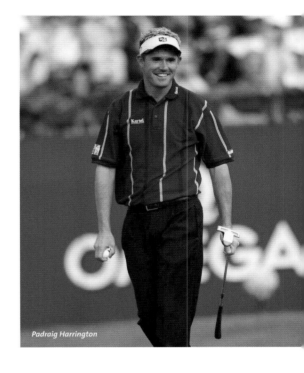

Padraig Harrington

Nick Faldo

José María Olazábal

> *A great course and I thought the layout was fantastic. Even though it was an old course, it still played up to the standards required. The wind made it very tricky due to the variety of heights on the course too. It was my first time in Hong Kong. I had heard good stories about the course and I would definitely go back* – Robert-Jan Derksen

not to be. Despite a stirring third round 65, a closing 71 saw Faldo share sixth place with David Howell, six shots adrift of Jiménez.

Set high in the hills above Hong Kong not far from the border with China, Fanling can be reached these days in 30 minutes by fast train. Five minutes by taxi from the station and you are at the gate of the Hong Kong Golf Club where Ian Roberts, successor to long time professional Joe Hardwick, has his well stocked shop.

Of course, getting there in previous years was not always this easy. Early settlers must have been desperately keen because the trip involved travelling by rickshaw, horse and boat and when none of those were available, Shank's Pony. Yet the dedication of the early golfers created, over the years, a golf club and course of which they can be justifiably proud. Not just one course but three, all named after courses

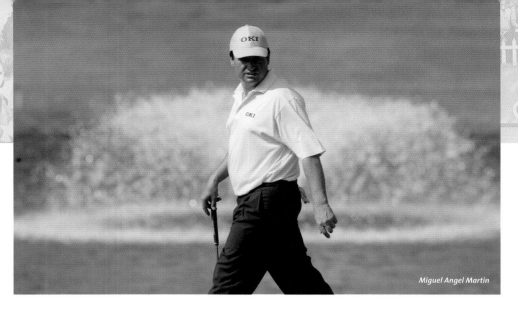

Miguel Angel Martin

at St Andrews – the Old, the New and the Eden - on ground once inhospitably barren, but now lush and beautiful with flowers cared for as dedicatedly as the fairways and greens.

Similar care for his game was taken by Jiménez who held his nerve over the closing holes to disappoint Harrington, seeking to successfully defend a title for the first time but who was beaten by the better man on the day.

Near the end it looked as if the Irishman might do it. One behind Jiménez and Kingston, Harrington hit a superb approach to four feet at the difficult 17th, with the Spaniard and the South African 25 and 35 feet away respectively. Cruelly for Harrington, however, they both holed for birdie to take a one shot advantage to the 18th where Kingston drove poorly to drop a shot, Harrington left his putt to tie just short, and Jiménez closed with a par four for a 66 and a 14 under par 266 total to claim the Red Jacket.

Once again the Omega Hong Kong Open had produced a class winner, someone who had remained loyal to his commitment to play after turning down a late invitation to replace Darren Clarke in the lucrative Nedbank Challenge in South Africa the same week.

Moreover, Jiménez's enjoyment of the game is so truly infectious that the people in the East warm to him as much as he warms to the task of competing in golf's New Territories.

Renton Laidlaw
The Golf Channel

Pos	Name		Rd1	Rd2	Rd3	Rd4	Total		€	£
1	Miguel Angel JIMÉNEZ	Sp	65	64	71	66	266	-14	100,338.80	70,303.17
2	Padraig HARRINGTON	Ire	65	68	67	67	267	-13	52,287.87	36,635.91
	James KINGSTON	SA	71	67	62	67	267	-13	52,287.87	36,635.91
4	Thammanoon SRIROT	Thai	67	68	66	69	270	-10	27,814.62	19,488.53
	Thomas BJÖRN	Den	69	67	65	69	270	-10	27,814.62	19,488.53
6	David HOWELL	Eng	65	66	70	71	272	-8	19,566.56	13,709.47
	Nick FALDO	Eng	69	67	65	71	272	-8	19,566.56	13,709.47
8	Lian-Wei ZHANG	PRC	70	64	73	66	273	-7	12,913.93	9,048.25
	José Maria OLAZÁBAL	Sp	67	68	71	67	273	-7	12,913.93	9,048.25
	Alessandro TADINI	It	66	67	72	68	273	-7	12,913.93	9,048.25
	Charl SCHWARTZEL	SA	65	70	70	68	273	-7	12,913.93	9,048.25
12	Louis OOSTHUIZEN	SA	69	64	71	70	274	-6	9,121.03	6,390.72
	Adam GROOM	Aus	64	70	68	72	274	-6	9,121.03	6,390.72
	Miguel Angel MARTIN	Sp	68	69	69	68	274	-6	9,121.03	6,390.72
	Robert-Jan DERKSEN	NL	68	70	69	67	274	-6	9,121.03	6,390.72
	Gregory HAVRET	Fr	66	68	68	72	274	-6	9,121.03	6,390.72
	Bryan SALTUS	USA	66	68	71	69	274	-6	9,121.03	6,390.72
18	Andrew PITTS	USA	72	66	69	68	275	-5	7,766.42	5,441.60
19	Steve WEBSTER	Eng	69	68	71	68	276	-4	7,019.88	4,918.53
	Maarten LAFEBER	NL	72	67	70	67	276	-4	7,019.88	4,918.53
	Søren HANSEN	Den	68	71	69	68	276	-4	7,019.88	4,918.53
	Wen-Chong LIANG	PRC	67	68	71	70	276	-4	7,019.88	4,918.53
	Jamie DONALDSON	Wal	71	65	71	69	276	-4	7,019.88	4,918.53
24	Amandeep JOHL	Ind	71	69	68	69	277	-3	6,080.69	4,260.48
	Markus BRIER	Aut	70	72	66	69	277	-3	6,080.69	4,260.48
	Christopher HANELL	Swe	72	68	69	68	277	-3	6,080.69	4,260.48
	Ted OH	Kor	68	69	71	69	277	-3	6,080.69	4,260.48
	Philippe LIMA	Port	67	70	70	70	277	-3	6,080.69	4,260.48
29	Terry PILKADARIS	Aus	68	73	67	70	278	-2	5,087.31	3,564.46
	Thaworn WIRATCHANT	Thai	69	70	70	69	278	-2	5,087.31	3,564.46
	Boonchu RUANGKIT	Thai	71	71	67	69	278	-2	5,087.31	3,564.46
	Clay DEVERS	USA	67	72	73	66	278	-2	5,087.31	3,564.46
	Barry LANE	Eng	68	71	69	70	278	-2	5,087.31	3,564.46
	Damien MCGRANE	Ire	72	67	71	68	278	-2	5,087.31	3,564.46
35	Mardan MAMAT	Sing	68	72	67	72	279	-1	4,334.75	3,037.17
	Richard BLAND	Eng	71	66	72	70	279	-1	4,334.75	3,037.17
	Harmeet KAHLON	Ind	66	71	70	72	279	-1	4,334.75	3,037.17
	Nick DOUGHERTY	Eng	69	67	72	71	279	-1	4,334.75	3,037.17
39	Thongchai JAIDEE	Thai	67	68	72	73	280	0	3,792.90	2,657.53
	Simon WAKEFIELD	Eng	71	71	72	66	280	0	3,792.90	2,657.53
	Gwang-Soo CHOI	Kor	69	67	70	74	280	0	3,792.90	2,657.53
	Robert JACOBSON	USA	70	70	73	67	280	0	3,792.90	2,657.53
	Paul LAWRIE	Scot	69	71	68	72	280	0	3,792.90	2,657.53
44	Simon YATES	Scot	70	72	68	71	281	1	3,371.47	2,362.25
	Leif WESTERBERG	Swe	70	70	70	71	281	1	3,371.47	2,362.25
46	Ter-Chang WANG	Tpe	71	71	70	70	282	2	2,950.04	2,066.97
	Jason KNUTZON	USA	69	69	70	74	282	2	2,950.04	2,066.97
	Jonathan LOMAS	Eng	72	68	76	66	282	2	2,950.04	2,066.97
	Gaurav GHEI	Ind	68	70	72	72	282	2	2,950.04	2,066.97
	Nico Van RENSBURG	SA	70	69	74	69	282	2	2,950.04	2,066.97
51	Rick GIBSON	Can	70	66	72	75	283	3	2,287.78	1,602.95
	Adam FRASER	Aus	68	72	73	70	283	3	2,287.78	1,602.95
	Raymond RUSSELL	Scot	68	74	71	70	283	3	2,287.78	1,602.95
	Prayad MARKSAENG	Thai	69	68	74	72	283	3	2,287.78	1,602.95
	Gerry NORQUIST	USA	70	70	71	72	283	3	2,287.78	1,602.95
	David GLEESON	Aus	69	72	71	71	283	3	2,287.78	1,602.95
57	Stephen SCAHILL	NZ	70	71	71	72	284	4	1,806.14	1,265.49
	Jonathan CHEETHAM	Eng	68	73	71	72	284	4	1,806.14	1,265.49
	Des TERBLANCHE	SA	71	69	73	71	284	4	1,806.14	1,265.49
60	Stephen DODD	Wal	68	72	75	70	285	5	1,505.12	1,054.57
	Paul BROADHURST	Eng	69	71	74	71	285	5	1,505.12	1,054.57
	Philip GOLDING	Eng	73	69	73	70	285	5	1,505.12	1,054.57
	Derek FUNG	HK	66	75	72	72	285	5	1,505.12	1,054.57
	Pablo DEL OLMO	Mex	67	72	71	75	285	5	1,505.12	1,054.57
	Chih-Bing LAM	Sing	68	69	75	73	285	5	1,505.12	1,054.57
	Chao LI	PRC	69	69	69	78	285	5	1,505.12	1,054.57
67	Scott BARR	Aus	66	72	75	73	286	6	1,204.10	843.66
	Gary RUSNAK	USA	69	71	71	75	286	6	1,204.10	843.66
	Jeev Milkha SINGH	Ind	69	73	72	72	286	6	1,204.10	843.66
70	Sung-Man LEE	Kor	69	72	74	72	287	7	1,106.26	775.11
71	David PARK	Wal	70	70	76	72	288	8	901.50	631.64
	Jason DAWES	Aus	71	67	76	74	288	8	901.50	631.64
73	Lee SLATTERY	Eng	68	73	74	74	289	9	895.50	627.44
	Nobuhito SATO	Jpn	70	72	68	79	289	9	895.50	627.44
75	Gary EMERSON	Eng	71	71	74	74	290	10	888.00	622.18
	Andrew MARSHALL	Eng	70	72	78	70	290	10	888.00	622.18
	Eiji MIZUGUCHI	Jpn	71	71	73	75	290	10	888.00	622.18
78	Danny CHIA	Mal	69	71	72	79	291	11	882.00	617.98
79	Edward LOAR	USA	70	70	74	78	292	12	879.00	615.88
80	Anthony SUMMERS	Aus	71	71	72	79	293	13	876.00	613.78
81	Mike CUNNING	USA	74	67	75	81	297	17	873.00	611.67

Thomas Björn

Total Prize Fund
€611,820   £428,673

dunhill championship

Mpumalanga, South Africa
December 9-12 • 2004

3 PAR 4 410m

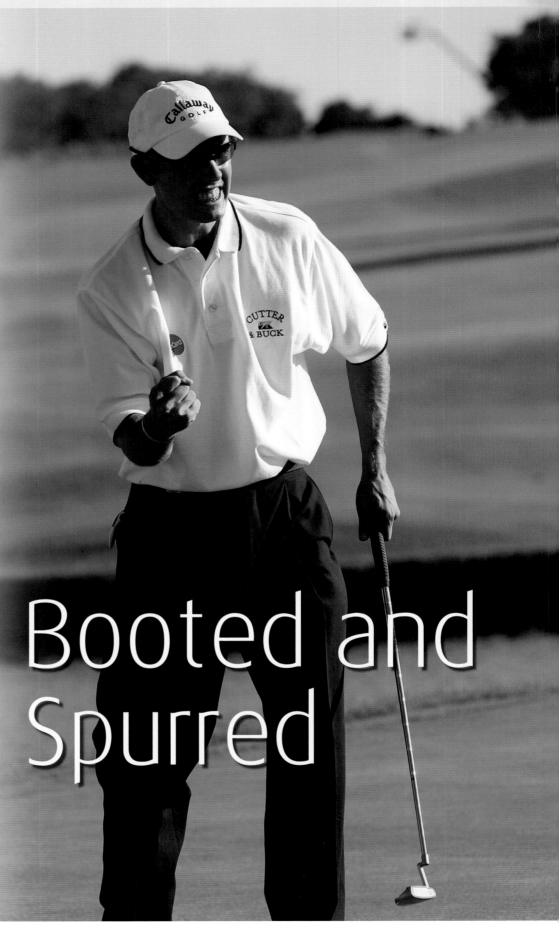

Booted and Spurred

Leopard Creek Golf Club

Par	Yards	Metres
72	7316	6692

Pos	Name	Score	To Par	
1	**Charl SCHWARTZEL**	281	-7	
2	Neil CHEETHAM	281	-7	
3	Warren ABERY	282	-6	
	Ernie ELS	282	-6	
	Oliver WHITELEY	282	-6	
6	David FROST	283	-5	
	Marcel SIEM	283	-5	
8	Euan LITTLE	284	-4	
	Damien McGRANE	284	-4	
	Graeme STORM	284	-4	

Round One	Round Two	Round Three	Round Four

EUROPEAN TOUR ORDER OF MERIT
(After three tournaments)

Pos		€	
1	**Stephen DODD**	129,126.32	
2	Charl SCHWARTZEL	127,225.35	
3	Thomas BJÖRN	112,898.00	
4	Miguel Angel JIMÉNEZ	100,338.80	
5	Neil CHEETHAM	83,201.35	
6	James KINGSTON	60,366.62	
7	Padraig HARRINGTON	52,287.87	
8	Jason DAWES	40,465.66	
9	Ernie ELS	38,562.02	
	Oliver WHITELEY	38,562.02	

His youthfulness might be emphasised by the braces on his teeth but he produced a mature performance which belied his tender years. At 20, Charl Schwartzel did not simply win the dunhill championship at the Leopard Creek - he let rip another mighty roar for the young lions of South African golf.

In October, 2004, 23 year old Richard Sterne won the Open de Madrid at Club de Campo to retain his card in spectacular fashion, and now here was his young compatriot guaranteeing his playing privileges on The European Tour International Schedule until the end of the 2007 season.

Over the years many lions have roared. Hugh Baiocchi, John Bland, Sid Brews, Bobby Cole, David Frost, Dale Hayes, Bobby Locke, Gary Player, Wayne Westner and, more recently, Ernie Els, Retief Goosen and Trevor Immelman. Now it is in the guise of players such as Darren Fichardt and Louis Oosthuizen, Andrew McLardy and Hennie Otto, Schwartzel and Sterne, that the conveyor belt of South African golfing talent shows no sign of expiring.

In the end it took the first hole of a sudden-death play-off with brave English challenger Neil Cheetham before Schwartzel engraved his name on the trophy. They had tied on seven under par 281 and, on their return to the par five 18th moments later, a pitch and putt birdie four was sufficient for the South African as his rival was unable to repeat the birdie he carded on the 72nd hole to force the play-off.

Understandably, Schwartzel's victory was popular in South Africa. Even so, romantics in the northern hemisphere might have preferred victory to have gone to Cheetham, ranked 561st at the time on the Official World Golf Ranking, and who for years had struggled to make a living in the margins of the game.

Ernie Els

Andrew McLardy

George O'Grady (second from left) began his role as Executive Director of The European Tour by visiting the dunhill championship where he was joined by Johann Rupert (Chairman of The Sunshine Tour) (left), Johan Immelman (Commissioner of The Sunshine Tour) (second right) and Ernie Els (right)

Though Cheetham has the remarkable record of having won 50 Pro-Ams, he had attempted the Qualifying School route on ten occasions but graduated only twice, the second time at the San Roque Club in Spain in 2004. However, for four days in the searing heat and humidity of Leopard Creek he produced a performance of which his good friend and fellow Worksop resident, Lee Westwood, would have been proud.

Leopard Creek is 250 miles east of Johannesburg, and arguably the most unusual and distinctive golf course on The European Tour International Schedule. Courses in Hong Kong, Shanghai and Madrid have skyscrapers peering over them while play on the West Course at Wentworth Club takes place in front of a series of sprawling houses with manicured lawns and tall pines. Leopard Creek resembles these courses only in so far as it has 18 tees, fairways and greens and a clubhouse.

To the east of Leopard Creek is Mozambique.

Swaziland is just over the hill and a few holes on the inward nine border the sprawling Kruger National Park. There is not a view in golf like the one from the 13th green, 50 feet above the bed of the Crocodile River, where, at dusk or early in the morning, the animals come to feed and drink. From here it is possible to see every one of those that make up Africa's Big Five - elephant, buffalo, rhinoceros, lion and giraffe. Elsewhere, there is a hippopotamus known as 'Harry' in a lagoon by the 15th and 16th holes, while two crocodiles lurk in the water between the ninth and 18th greens.

In such an environment you would have been forgiven for putting money on Ernie Els winning over a course he knows well and where he has built a house. He was the highest ranked player in the world among the competitors, and he flew down the day after celebrating the centenary of a golf club in the Transvaal where he had played nine holes with Nico van Rensburg, one of his childhood friends.

"Leopard Creek is unique, a truly fantastic golf course, and what Mr Rupert has done here is very special. Having grown up in the Bushveld, I felt very at home with the Kruger National Park by my side on the back nine on Sunday. There is no golf course in the world like this and it was a dream come true for me to win both my first tournament in South Africa and my first event on The European Tour here" – Charl Schwartzel

Marcel Siem

Final Results

Pos	Name		Rd1	Rd2	Rd3	Rd4	Total		€	£
1	Charl SCHWARTZEL	SA	71	69	70	71	281	-7	120,576.80	83,330.00
2	Neil CHEETHAM	Eng	68	71	69	73	281	-7	80,379.74	55,550.00
3	Ernie ELS	SA	67	75	70	70	282	-6	37,380.32	25,833.33
	Warren ABERY	SA	69	70	73	70	282	-6	37,380.32	25,833.33
	Oliver WHITELEY	Eng	72	67	72	71	282	-6	37,380.32	25,833.33
6	Marcel SIEM	Ger	76	69	71	67	283	-5	23,513.43	16,250.00
	David FROST	SA	70	70	69	74	283	-5	23,513.43	16,250.00
8	Damien MCGRANE	Ire	74	68	72	70	284	-4	16,254.41	11,233.33
	Euan LITTLE	Scot	71	69	72	72	284	-4	16,254.41	11,233.33
	Graeme STORM	Eng	73	68	75	68	284	-4	16,254.41	11,233.33
11	Tim CLARK	SA	77	68	73	67	285	-3	12,878.12	8,900.00
	Michael KIRK	SA	71	72	69	73	285	-3	12,878.12	8,900.00
13	Richard FINCH	Eng	72	69	72	73	286	-2	11,648.19	8,050.00
14	Martin MARITZ	SA	75	72	68	72	287	-1	10,635.30	7,350.00
	Des TERBLANCHE	SA	69	70	76	72	287	-1	10,635.30	7,350.00
	Johan EDFORS	Swe	70	74	71	72	287	-1	10,635.30	7,350.00
17	Ian GARBUTT	Eng	71	72	76	69	288	0	8,886.87	6,141.67
	Iain STEEL	Mal	70	73	75	70	288	0	8,886.87	6,141.67
	Mark MURLESS	SA	76	69	73	70	288	0	8,886.87	6,141.67
	Darren FICHARDT	SA	70	71	78	69	288	0	8,886.87	6,141.67
	Garry HOUSTON	Wal	80	68	69	71	288	0	8,886.87	6,141.67
	Leif WESTERBERG	Swe	70	70	76	72	288	0	8,886.87	6,141.67
23	Lee SLATTERY	Eng	73	69	77	70	289	1	7,632.82	5,275.00
	Matthew MORRIS	Eng	72	72	73	72	289	1	7,632.82	5,275.00
	Manuel QUIROS	Sp	69	72	78	70	289	1	7,632.82	5,275.00
	Anton HAIG	SA	77	69	74	69	289	1	7,632.82	5,275.00
27	Bruce MCDONALD	Zim	66	76	73	75	290	2	6,656.11	4,600.00
	Gregory BOURDY	Fr	74	73	70	73	290	2	6,656.11	4,600.00
	Mark DAVIS	Eng	70	72	72	76	290	2	6,656.11	4,600.00
	Ulrich VAN DEN BERG	SA	72	75	72	71	290	2	6,656.11	4,600.00
	André BOSSERT	Swi	74	72	72	72	290	2	6,656.11	4,600.00
32	Joakim BÄCKSTRÖM	Swe	71	77	71	72	291	3	5,457.18	3,771.43
	Peter LAWRIE	Ire	75	67	75	74	291	3	5,457.18	3,771.43
	Grant MULLER	SA	76	71	72	72	291	3	5,457.18	3,771.43
	Phillip ARCHER	Eng	73	71	75	72	291	3	5,457.18	3,771.43
	Michael LAMB	Zim	72	70	78	71	291	3	5,457.18	3,771.43
	Peter GUSTAFSSON	Swe	69	68	79	75	291	3	5,457.18	3,771.43
	Roope KAKKO	Fin	73	74	75	69	291	3	5,457.18	3,771.43
39	Matthew KING	Eng	75	73	72	72	292	4	4,268.59	2,950.00
	Alan MICHELL	SA	72	76	70	74	292	4	4,268.59	2,950.00
	Stephen BROWNE	Ire	76	71	76	69	292	4	4,268.59	2,950.00
	Louis OOSTHUIZEN	SA	72	69	78	73	292	4	4,268.59	2,950.00
	Alessandro TADINI	It	71	70	73	78	292	4	4,268.59	2,950.00
	Titch MOORE	SA	72	76	73	71	292	4	4,268.59	2,950.00
	Hennie OTTO	SA	73	71	75	73	292	4	4,268.59	2,950.00
	Sam LITTLE	Eng	72	71	80	69	292	4	4,268.59	2,950.00
	Keith HORNE	SA	71	72	72	77	292	4	4,268.59	2,950.00
48	Mathias GRÖNBERG	Swe	70	71	77	75	293	5	3,111.01	2,150.00
	Francesco MOLINARI	It	73	71	76	73	293	5	3,111.01	2,150.00
	Andrew MCLARDY	SA	72	72	72	77	293	5	3,111.01	2,150.00
	Lindani NDWANDWE	SA	70	71	73	79	293	5	3,111.01	2,150.00
	Johan SKOLD	Swe	74	74	73	72	293	5	3,111.01	2,150.00
	Matthew BLACKEY	Eng	77	71	74	71	293	5	3,111.01	2,150.00
	Paul BRADSHAW	Eng	73	71	76	73	293	5	3,111.01	2,150.00
55	Bertrand CORNUT	Fr	74	71	75	74	294	6	2,286.23	1,580.00
	Chris DAVISON	SA	72	73	76	73	294	6	2,286.23	1,580.00
	Liam BOND	Eng	78	70	74	72	294	6	2,286.23	1,580.00
	Raphael EYRAUD	Fr	68	78	75	73	294	6	2,286.23	1,580.00
	Sammy DANIELS	SA	76	71	72	75	294	6	2,286.23	1,580.00
60	Bobby LINCOLN	SA	71	74	77	73	295	7	1,953.42	1,350.00
	André CRUSE	SA	70	72	76	77	295	7	1,953.42	1,350.00
	Omar SANDYS	SA	79	68	73	75	295	7	1,953.42	1,350.00
63	Benoit TEILLERIA	Fr	68	78	77	73	296	8	1,664.03	1,150.00
	Sarel SON-HOUI	Fr	69	73	78	76	296	8	1,664.03	1,150.00
	Jan-Are LARSEN	Nor	74	74	73	75	296	8	1,664.03	1,150.00
	Johan AXGREN	Swe	73	72	74	77	296	8	1,664.03	1,150.00
	Nico LE GRANGE	SA	71	74	76	75	296	8	1,664.03	1,150.00
68	Oliver WILSON	Eng	69	73	76	79	297	9	1,410.81	975.00
	David PATRICK	Scot	75	72	75	75	297	9	1,410.81	975.00
70	Stuart MANLEY	Wal	74	72	75	77	298	10	1,331.22	920.00
71	Ryan TIPPING	SA	72	74	75	78	299	11	1,080.50	746.73
	Martin ERLANDSSON	Swe	72	75	78	74	299	11	1,080.50	746.73
	Callie SWART	SA	71	76	77	75	299	11	1,080.50	746.73
	Julien CLÉMENT	Swi	73	73	80	73	299	11	1,080.50	746.73
75	Steve BASSON	SA	74	72	76	78	300	12	1,073.00	741.54
76	Brett LIDDLE	SA	74	74	77	76	301	13	1,068.50	738.43
	Ryan REID	SA	75	69	82	75	301	13	1,068.50	738.43
78	James KAMTE	SA	68	76	84	84	312	24	1,064.00	735.32
79	Thomas AIKEN	SA	72	75	71	W/D	218	2		

At the end of a long year Els was at peace with himself. His wife Liezl would be at Leopard Creek for the weekend and as Els and van Rensburg played, seven year old Cjristoff van Rensburg, Els's godson, frolicked between the two of them. It was a tranquil scene.

Less tranquil was what happened to the pre-tournament favourite in the second round after he had opened with a 67. A hooked drive and a yanked second shot, both ending in water, saw Els run up a seven on the par five 13th. Another wild drive on the 15th and Els had taken 41 for the inward nine in a round of 75.

Nevertheless, Els almost caught Cheetham and Schwartzel. Birdies on the 71st and 72nd holes got him to within one stroke of the play-off. Cheetham, the overnight leader, had gone round in 73 to tie Schwartzel, who carded a 71. One hole later though, it was all over.

It was Schwarzel's maiden victory on The European Tour but it will not be his last. The son of a professional, he has been booted and spurred for success, but was nevertheless delighted when it eventually arrived. "This is a dream," he said. "It is indescribable, something I have worked really hard for. You don't want to finish second."

Maybe not, but for Cheetham, coming second was a performance to be proud of and earned him far and away the biggest cheque of his career to date.

John Hopkins
The Times

Ian Garbutt

Total Prize Fund
€732,090 £506,673

South African Airways Open

Durban, South Africa
January 20-23 • 2005

Local Hero

Durban Country Club

Par	Yards	Metres
72	6747	6167

1	**Tim CLARK**	273	-15	
2	Gregory HAVRET	279	-9	
	Charl SCHWARTZEL	279	-9	
4	Darren CLARKE	280	-8	
	Nick DOUGHERTY	280	-8	
	James KINGSTON	280	-8	
	Graeme STORM	280	-8	
8	Gregory BOURDY	281	-7	
	David HOWELL	281	-7	
	Titch MOORE	281	-7	
	Tjaart VAN DER WALT	281	-7	

Round One   Round Two   Round Three   Round Four

EUROPEAN TOUR ORDER OF MERIT
(After four tournaments)

Pos		€	
1	**Charl SCHWARTZEL**	192,949.04	
2	Stephen DODD	129,126.32	
3	Thomas BJÖRN	112,898.00	
4	Miguel Angel JIMÉNEZ	100,338.80	
5	Neil CHEETHAM	91,522.31	
6	James KINGSTON	88,093.24	
7	Gregory HAVRET	87,671.17	
8	Padraig HARRINGTON	52,287.87	
9	Graeme STORM	48,955.47	
10	Jason DAWES	40,465.66	

It is a venue to delight the traditionalists, a course that, at 6,747 yards, is short by modern standards but so cunningly and beautifully designed that length simply does not matter. Precision and finesse are the bywords for success around Durban Country Club, qualities possessed in abundance by the eventual champion Tim Clark, who won his second South African Airways Open title at the venue in four years.

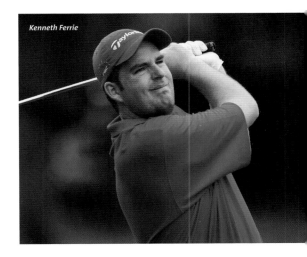
Kenneth Ferrie

Those who try to overpower the course tend not to succeed and never was that better illustrated than over four glorious, sun-drenched January days in which 156 competitors from The European Tour and The Sunshine Tour came together to contest one of the oldest tournaments in the world of professional golf.

Among the big hitters were Northern Ireland's Darren Clarke, playing for the first time in two months, and Titch Moore of South Africa, who is consistently one of the longest drivers on Tour and comfortable on home soil. Yet despite the fact that five of the par fours measured less than 400 yards and all four of the par threes were shorter than 200 yards, this was one tournament that was not about to turn into a pitch-and-putt contest.

As the highest world ranked player in the field, much was expected of Clarke, although he had warned beforehand that, in the past, he had struggled to get the measure of what he described as a "fantastic" course.

Darren Clarke

Graeme Storm

When the wind blows off the Indian Ocean and out of the north-east, the first five holes offer as tough a test as any opening stretch in the game. Yet that is but a part of what lies in wait. With its twists and turns, bumps, deep hollows and penal rough, anything that strays from the straight and narrow nearly always proves costly.

As it turned out, Clarke's pessimism had seemed well founded by the time he arrived at the 18th hole of the second round needing an eagle two to make the cut. Yet if any hole was going to offer up such a chance, this was it. At 274 yards, it is one of the shortest par fours in tournament golf, so when Clarke reached the green with his tee shot and proceeded to roll in a 30 foot putt for a two, he had guaranteed himself some weekend work. In point of fact, he had learned his lesson well. On Saturday and Sunday he was a revelation, finishing with two rounds of 67 for a share of fourth place.

By way of contrast, Moore had got off to a good start, opening with a seven under par 65 and sharing, or holding, the lead for each of the first three days. But his play never again touched the heights of the first round and he started to suffer for a few errant shots that eventually cost him the chance to challenge seriously for the title. He had begun the final round on nine under par and in a tie for the lead with three of his compatriots - Hendrik Buhrmann, Tjaart van der Walt and Clark - but ended it eight shots adrift of the eventual winner, who cruised to victory virtually unchallenged.

Durban born and bred, Clark used his local knowledge to devastating effect. With rounds of 68-71-68, he had manoeuvred himself nicely into position by the end of the third round and was convinced that he had the game and the know-how to seal victory on the final day. That he did in style with a round of 66, for a total of 273, 15 under par,

People say how technology has changed the game but this is a course which doesn't need any more length to be great. You have to plot your way around and I am finding that I am hitting from the same spots I was hitting from ten years ago. It is not worth taking driver and risking it because there is such a lot of trouble out there - that is why it is such a great course and a great test of golf – Tim Clark

and victory by six shots over Gregory Havret and Charl Schwartzel.

It was little wonder that nobody could live with him. As a 14 year old, Clark played the course for the first time and took to the layout so well that he went on to win three successive Natal Junior Championships and also equalled the amateur course record with a round of 66. Then, competing there in 2002, he became the only qualifier in the history of the South African Airways Open to win, blowing away the rest of the field with an aggregate total of 19 under par 269.

Clark is not the biggest hitter in the professional game, but his play was an illustration of course management at its best. He would not use a driver when an iron would do and he was able to draw on past experience to help him through. That he did not drop a shot in his final 45 holes says it all.

"I stand up there and don't see the trouble," he said. "A lot of guys see the bushes, but I am always looking to where I want to hit the ball."

And there, perhaps, lies a lesson to designers the world over. A course does not have to be ridiculously long to protect itself from modern technology. An imaginatively designed course demands imaginative golf and the ability to shape the ball through the air. At the Durban Country Club, brute force had been reduced to a side issue. A delight to witness, golf needs more of the same.

Peter Dixon
The Times

David Howell

Final Results

Pos	Name		Rd1	Rd2	Rd3	Rd4	Total		€	£
1	Tim CLARK	SA	68	71	68	66	273	-15	112,689.50	79,000.00
2	Charl SCHWARTZEL	SA	68	72	71	68	279	-9	65,723.69	46,075.00
	Gregory HAVRET	Fr	69	69	72	69	279	-9	65,723.69	46,075.00
4	Graeme STORM	Eng	71	68	69	72	280	-8	27,726.62	19,437.50
	Nick DOUGHERTY	Eng	73	73	68	66	280	-8	27,726.62	19,437.50
	Darren CLARKE	N.Ire	72	74	67	67	280	-8	27,726.62	19,437.50
	James KINGSTON	SA	71	70	72	67	280	-8	27,726.62	19,437.50
8	Titch MOORE	SA	65	70	72	74	281	-7	14,924.23	10,462.50
	Tjaart VAN DER WALT	SA	66	71	70	74	281	-7	14,924.23	10,462.50
	David HOWELL	Eng	73	70	67	71	281	-7	14,924.23	10,462.50
	Gregory BOURDY	Fr	75	70	68	68	281	-7	14,924.23	10,462.50
12	Hendrik BUHRMANN	SA	70	67	70	75	282	-6	10,930.17	7,662.50
	Paul EALES	Eng	74	69	70	69	282	-6	10,930.17	7,662.50
	Des TERBLANCHE	SA	68	72	73	69	282	-6	10,930.17	7,662.50
	Louis OOSTHUIZEN	SA	69	69	73	71	282	-6	10,930.17	7,662.50
16	Mårten OLANDER	Swe	72	73	71	67	283	-5	9,592.88	6,725.00
	Werner GEYER	SA	71	72	71	69	283	-5	9,592.88	6,725.00
18	Bruce VAUGHAN	USA	65	73	73	73	284	-4	8,320.96	5,833.33
	Hennie OTTO	SA	71	72	71	70	284	-4	8,320.96	5,833.33
	Jaco VAN ZYL	SA	70	70	72	72	284	-4	8,320.96	5,833.33
	Lee SLATTERY	Eng	73	68	71	72	284	-4	8,320.96	5,833.33
	Bobby LINCOLN	SA	71	70	69	74	284	-4	8,320.96	5,833.33
	Neil CHEETHAM	Eng	70	70	70	74	284	-4	8,320.96	5,833.33
24	Jonathan LOMAS	Eng	72	73	70	70	285	-3	6,656.77	4,666.67
	Ian GARBUTT	Eng	71	70	71	73	285	-3	6,656.77	4,666.67
	Simon HURD	Eng	75	66	73	71	285	-3	6,656.77	4,666.67
	Fulton ALLEM	SA	74	69	72	70	285	-3	6,656.77	4,666.67
	Johan EDFORS	Swe	74	69	73	69	285	-3	6,656.77	4,666.67
	Lars BROVOLD	Nor	68	72	73	72	285	-3	6,656.77	4,666.67
	Phillip ARCHER	Eng	72	70	71	72	285	-3	6,656.77	4,666.67
	Garry HOUSTON	Wal	74	69	75	73	285	-3	6,656.77	4,666.67
	Kenneth FERRIE	Eng	72	72	69	72	285	-3	6,656.77	4,666.67
33	Darren FICHARDT	SA	70	73	72	71	286	-2	5,349.19	3,750.00
	Marcel SIEM	Ger	69	77	72	68	286	-2	5,349.19	3,750.00
	Fredrik HENGE	Swe	71	69	76	70	286	-2	5,349.19	3,750.00
	Andrew MCLARDY	SA	69	69	75	73	286	-2	5,349.19	3,750.00
	Leif WESTERBERG	Swe	74	71	73	68	286	-2	5,349.19	3,750.00
	Richard STERNE	SA	74	71	73	68	286	-2	5,349.19	3,750.00
	Stuart MANLEY	Wal	76	67	72	71	286	-2	5,349.19	3,750.00
40	Scott DUNLAP	USA	71	75	71	70	287	-1	4,635.96	3,250.00
	Trevor IMMELMAN	SA	70	73	69	75	287	-1	4,635.96	3,250.00
	Gavan LEVENSON	SA	74	70	71	72	287	-1	4,635.96	3,250.00
43	Jean HUGO	SA	74	67	73	74	288	0	4,136.71	2,900.00
	Francesco MOLINARI	It	72	71	71	74	288	0	4,136.71	2,900.00
	John MASHEGO	SA	71	72	73	72	288	0	4,136.71	2,900.00
	Ross WELLINGTON	SA	69	70	77	72	288	0	4,136.71	2,900.00
47	David GRIFFITHS	Eng	74	72	73	70	289	1	3,494.80	2,450.00
	Andrew BUTTERFIELD	Eng	75	71	70	73	289	1	3,494.80	2,450.00
	Ashley ROESTOFF	SA	74	70	75	70	289	1	3,494.80	2,450.00
	Nicolas COLSAERTS	Bel	71	74	70	74	289	1	3,494.80	2,450.00
	Warren ABERY	SA	73	70	75	71	289	1	3,494.80	2,450.00
52	Marc CAYEUX	Zim	72	69	80	69	290	2	2,710.26	1,900.00
	Malcolm MACKENZIE	Eng	68	76	77	69	290	2	2,710.26	1,900.00
	Søren KJELDSEN	Den	72	74	72	72	290	2	2,710.26	1,900.00
	Matthew BLACKEY	Eng	72	72	71	75	290	2	2,710.26	1,900.00
	Ben MASON	Eng	75	70	70	75	290	2	2,710.26	1,900.00
	Lindani NDWANDWE	SA	69	72	73	76	290	2	2,710.26	1,900.00
58	Martin MARITZ	SA	75	68	76	72	291	3	2,139.68	1,500.00
	Michiel BOTHMA	SA	70	73	75	73	291	3	2,139.68	1,500.00
	Martin ERLANDSSON	Swe	75	71	70	75	291	3	2,139.68	1,500.00
	Niki ZITNY	Aut	75	69	74	73	291	3	2,139.68	1,500.00
	Jason KELLY	Eng	73	70	76	72	291	3	2,139.68	1,500.00
63	Thomas AIKEN	SA	72	73	76	71	292	4	1,783.06	1,250.00
	Andrea MAESTRONI	It	74	69	75	74	292	4	1,783.06	1,250.00
	Philip GOLDING	Eng	69	76	70	77	292	4	1,783.06	1,250.00
	Stephen BROWNE	Ire	78	67	74	73	292	4	1,783.06	1,250.00
	Michael KIRK	SA	72	70	75	75	292	4	1,783.06	1,250.00
68	Oliver WILSON	Eng	72	73	76	72	293	5	1,569.10	1,100.00
69	Chris WILLIAMS	Eng	68	78	73	76	295	7	1,331.35	933.33
	Gary MURPHY	Ire	76	70	81	68	295	7	1,331.35	933.33
	David FROST	SA	72	72	77	74	295	7	1,331.35	933.33
72	Chris DAVISON	SA	72	73	77	74	296	8	1,066.84	747.90
73	Joakim BÄCKSTRÖM	Swe	73	70	78	76	297	9	1,063.84	745.80
74	Alain NORRIS	SA	73	72	83	71	299	11	1,060.84	743.69
75	Jakobus ROOS (AM)	SA	73	72	79	77	301	13		
76	Tony JOHNSTONE	Zim	77	68	83	75	303	15	1,057.84	741.59
77	Cody FREEMAN	USA	71	75	77	81	304	16	1,054.84	739.49

Total Prize Fund
€719,600   £504,468

Caltex Masters, presented by Carlsberg, Singapore 2005

Singapore
January 27-30 • 2005

Laguna National Golf & Country Club

Par	Yards	Metres
72	7207	6589

1	**Nick DOUGHERTY**	270	-18	
2	Maarten LAFEBER	275	-13	
	Colin MONTGOMERIE	275	-13	
4	Thomas BJÖRN	277	-11	
5	Robert COLES	280	-8	
	Marcus FRASER	280	-8	
	Gregory HAVRET	280	-8	
	Peter LAWRIE	280	-8	
	Wen-Chong LIANG	280	-8	
	Lee WESTWOOD	280	-8	

Round One   Round Two   Round Three   Round Four

EUROPEAN TOUR ORDER OF MERIT
(After five tournaments)

Pos		€	
1	**Charl SCHWARTZEL**	192,949.04	
2	Nick DOUGHERTY	163,148.80	
3	Thomas BJÖRN	151,214.97	
4	Stephen DODD	129,126.32	
5	Gregory HAVRET	109,997.19	
6	Miguel Angel JIMÉNEZ	100,338.80	
7	James KINGSTON	99,128.53	
8	Neil CHEETHAM	91,522.31	
9	Maarten LAFEBER	80,165.81	
10	Colin MONTGOMERIE	66,560.41	

Turning Point

32

Had Nick Dougherty pulled a brace of rabbits from his golf bag, he could not have done more to startle his audience as he played the 445 yard 16th at Laguna National Golf & Country Club in the final round of the Caltex Masters, presented by Carlsberg, Singapore 2005. Having pulled his drive into a cavernous bunker, the 22 year old climbed out of the depths with ball in hand. Then, under the auspices of European Tour Chief Referee John Paramor, he was given a free drop at the top.

The Singaporeans, of course, knew their local rule. If, like Dougherty, you finish on the grass fringe between the sand and the wooden sleepers in the face of the bunker rather than in the sand itself, you are entitled to a drop. It is all down to the dangers of ball and club cannoning into the supports.

Paramor had taken note of the rule when he arrived at the start of the week and had seen no reason to change it. Dougherty appreciated that his luck was in but, having seen players such as Ernie Els and Tiger Woods seize upon their good fortune so often in the past, he was not about to let embarrassment intrude, even if he was playing with two greats of the game in Thomas Björn and Colin Montgomerie. Rather he compounded his good fortune by hitting the boldest of seconds to within three feet of the pin, a shot later voted RBS Shot of the Month for January.

Maarten Lafeber

Colin Montgomerie

Lee Westwood

As proven a competitor as Montgomerie is, he was nevertheless floored by this double whammy. Two shots behind Dougherty overnight, the Scot had cut the deficit to one and was seemingly set to draw level when he bisected the 16th fairway before Dougherty disappeared into the pit.

"The ruling was a turning point," admitted Montgomerie, afterwards. "I was one behind and in the middle of the fairway and Nick is in the bunker on the left and up against the face. Next minute you know he's a couple of feet away from the hole in two…"

Montgomerie followed up with a second hit short and right of the pin, and any chance he had of making a successful defence of his title faded when he took three putts.

Not unnaturally, Montgomerie arrived at the conclusion that this was not his moment. "When you have a day, you have a day and this was Nick's," he said. "He played well. He

Robert Coles

"I think it is a really great golf course. If you are not on your game you can be punished as there is so much water and the rough is tricky. You need to be hitting it really well. If you take advantage of the par fives and play the par threes in par you are on to a winner. A lot of thought has gone into the design" – **Nick Dougherty**

Jamie Donaldson

Final Results

attacked the pins when he had to and for someone to play as well as he did in winning his first tournament was terrific."

Aside from the free drop, the last round was mostly a battle of irons as well as wills. Time after time, Montgomerie, whose latest clubs seem to have given him back the uncanny judgement of distance he enjoyed during his seven successive European Tour Order of Merit victories, put the pressure on his young rival by hitting his irons down the stick.

It might have been too much for most 22 year olds but Dougherty refused to capitulate. With a smile no less grooved than his swing, the youngster gave as good as he got. His final round 67 gave him a four round aggregate as many as 18 under par, and he finished five clear of the fast-finishing Maarten Lafeber and Montgomerie. If the Scot's second place was a disappointment, Lafeber's was a minor triumph after a 2004 season in which elbow trouble had played a significant part. The heat in Singapore, though too oppressive for some, was precisely what was required for Lafeber and others with injury concerns.

When all was said and done, Dougherty admitted that he felt a little like the character from Rocky IV as the crowd, which early on had eyes only for Björn and Montgomerie, ended up rooting for him. They did not find it difficult to relate to a young Englishman, however, who, instead of disappearing into his own little world, fed off their encouragement and acknowledged it.

The former Walker Cup player was no less disarming when he came to speak to the

Press. "We've talked before about the things I've done wrong," he began. "But here at last is something I've done right!"

The old mistakes to which Dougherty referred embraced those wild times which followed the 2002 season when he won the Sir Henry Cotton Rookie of the Year on The European Tour and bagged in excess of half a million euro in prize money. It was, he admitted, like winning the lottery and, like a few lottery winners, he had blown the lot.

"It's not a mistake I am going to make twice," he said, as he left Singapore with the €127,718 (£88,932) winner's cheque in hand.

Lewine Mair
The Daily Telegraph

Anders Hansen

Pos	Name		Rd1	Rd2	Rd3	Rd4	Total		€	£
1	Nick DOUGHERTY	Eng	68	67	68	67	270	-18	127,718.10	88,932.75
2	Colin MONTGOMERIE	Scot	65	71	69	70	275	-13	66,560.41	46,347.39
	Maarten LAFEBER	NL	69	70	67	69	275	-13	66,560.41	46,347.39
4	Thomas BJÖRN	Den	72	66	67	72	277	-11	38,316.97	26,680.90
5	Robert COLES	Eng	72	69	71	68	280	-8	22,326.02	15,546.07
	Lee WESTWOOD	Eng	70	73	70	67	280	-8	22,326.02	15,546.07
	Gregory HAVRET	Fr	70	70	69	71	280	-8	22,326.02	15,546.07
	Peter LAWRIE	Ire	74	72	68	66	280	-8	22,326.02	15,546.07
	Wen-Chong LIANG	PRC	70	68	71	71	280	-8	22,326.02	15,546.07
	Marcus FRASER	Aus	71	70	70	69	280	-8	22,326.02	15,546.07
11	Peter HEDBLOM	Swe	71	69	66	75	281	-7	14,100.65	9,818.57
12	Joong Kyung MO	Kor	72	72	68	70	282	-6	12,759.55	8,884.74
	Peter SENIOR	Aus	72	71	70	69	282	-6	12,759.55	8,884.74
14	Jamie DONALDSON	Wal	70	68	72	73	283	-5	11,035.29	7,684.10
	Paul MARANTZ	Aus	73	68	71	71	283	-5	11,035.29	7,684.10
	Kim FELTON	Aus	70	73	69	71	283	-5	11,035.29	7,684.10
	James KINGSTON	SA	73	73	68	69	283	-5	11,035.29	7,684.10
18	Søren HANSEN	Den	69	70	69	76	284	-4	9,528.15	6,634.65
	Graeme MCDOWELL	N.Ire	74	69	69	72	284	-4	9,528.15	6,634.65
	Angleo QUE	Phil	70	70	70	74	284	-4	9,528.15	6,634.65
21	Jason KNUTZON	USA	69	71	70	75	285	-3	8,314.78	5,789.75
	Philippe LIMA	Port	76	68	70	71	285	-3	8,314.78	5,789.75
	Jean-François LUCQUIN	Fr	69	74	69	73	285	-3	8,314.78	5,789.75
	Anders HANSEN	Den	72	73	70	70	285	-3	8,314.78	5,789.75
	Lian-Wei ZHANG	PRC	72	72	70	71	285	-3	8,314.78	5,789.75
	Barry LANE	Eng	73	73	71	68	285	-3	8,314.78	5,789.75
27	Mardan MAMAT	Sing	74	72	71	69	286	-2	6,935.37	4,829.24
	Philip GOLDING	Eng	75	70	71	70	286	-2	6,935.37	4,829.24
	Boonchu RUANGKIT	Thai	73	72	73	68	286	-2	6,935.37	4,829.24
	Fredrik ANDERSSON HED	Swe	75	69	75	67	286	-2	6,935.37	4,829.24
	Yuan-Chi CHEN	Tpe	72	72	71	71	286	-2	6,935.37	4,829.24
	Mads VIBE-HASTRUP	Den	73	71	72	70	286	-2	6,935.37	4,829.24
33	Graeme STORM	Eng	75	69	73	70	287	-1	4,678.70	3,257.88
	Adam GROOM	Aus	69	72	75	71	287	-1	4,678.70	3,257.88
	Brad KENNEDY	Aus	72	71	68	76	287	-1	4,678.70	3,257.88
	Terry PILKADARIS	Aus	73	71	67	76	287	-1	4,678.70	3,257.88
	Klas ERIKSSON	Swe	74	71	70	72	287	-1	4,678.70	3,257.88
	Greg CHALMERS	Aus	71	70	75	71	287	-1	4,678.70	3,257.88
	Marcus BOTH	Aus	75	69	69	74	287	-1	4,678.70	3,257.88
	Raymond RUSSELL	Scot	73	67	72	75	287	-1	4,678.70	3,257.88
	Paul LAWRIE	Scot	72	73	71	71	287	-1	4,678.70	3,257.88
	Thaworn WIRATCHANT	Thai	74	72	69	72	287	-1	4,678.70	3,257.88
	Danny CHIA	Mal	68	70	75	74	287	-1	4,678.70	3,257.88
	Jyoti RANDHAWA	Ind	73	68	74	72	287	-1	4,678.70	3,257.88
	Simon YATES	Scot	71	74	75	67	287	-1	4,678.70	3,257.88
	Trevor IMMELMAN	SA	76	70	71	70	287	-1	4,678.70	3,257.88
	Scott DRUMMOND	Scot	72	74	70	71	287	-1	4,678.70	3,257.88
	David BRANSDON	Aus	72	74	69	72	287	-1	4,678.70	3,257.88
	Søren KJELDSEN	Den	69	73	73	72	287	-1	4,678.70	3,257.88
	José Manuel LARA	Sp	73	70	73	71	287	-1	4,678.70	3,257.88
	Mike CUNNING	USA	72	74	71	70	287	-1	4,678.70	3,257.88
52	Steve WEBSTER	Eng	74	70	72	72	288	0	2,988.72	2,081.11
	Keng-Chi LIN	Taiw	74	72	73	69	288	0	2,988.72	2,081.11
	Amandeep JOHL	Ind	74	72	70	72	288	0	2,988.72	2,081.11
55	Simon DYSON	Eng	72	70	73	74	289	1	2,375.65	1,654.22
	Corey HARRIS	USA	75	69	69	76	289	1	2,375.65	1,654.22
	David HOWELL	Eng	73	72	70	74	289	1	2,375.65	1,654.22
	Edward LOAR	USA	74	71	75	69	289	1	2,375.65	1,654.22
	Gwang-Soo CHOI	Kor	72	74	69	74	289	1	2,375.65	1,654.22
	Simon KHAN	Eng	72	72	72	73	289	1	2,375.65	1,654.22
61	Prayad MARKSAENG	Thai	72	71	72	75	290	2	1,915.85	1,334.05
	Peter O'MALLEY	Aus	74	71	72	73	290	2	1,915.85	1,334.05
	Peter HANSON	Swe	76	68	72	74	290	2	1,915.85	1,334.05
	Edward MICHAELS	USA	71	75	75	69	290	2	1,915.85	1,334.05
	Rick GIBSON	Can	72	70	71	77	290	2	1,915.85	1,334.05
66	Mark FOSTER	Eng	68	76	71	76	291	3	1,571.00	1,093.92
	Costantino ROCCA	It	72	73	67	79	291	3	1,571.00	1,093.92
	Joon CHUNG	Kor	73	72	70	76	291	3	1,571.00	1,093.92
	Joakim HAEGGMAN	Swe	73	71	74	73	291	3	1,571.00	1,093.92
70	Gerry NORQUIST	USA	74	72	71	75	292	4	1,179.63	821.40
	Richard BLAND	Eng	72	72	74	74	292	4	1,179.63	821.40
	Hendrik BUHRMANN	SA	70	76	73	73	292	4	1,179.63	821.40
	Eiji MIZUGOCHI	Jpn	75	71	72	74	292	4	1,179.63	821.40
	Roger CHAPMAN	Eng	72	71	74	75	292	4	1,179.63	821.40
	Harmeet KAHLON	Ind	71	75	75	71	292	4	1,179.63	821.40
	Brett RUMFORD	Aus	69	72	77	74	292	4	1,179.63	821.40
77	Unho PARK	Aus	72	74	75	72	293	5	1,127.50	785.10
	Ted OH	Kor	73	71	74	75	293	5	1,127.50	785.10
	Rahil GANGJEE	Ind	77	69	74	73	293	5	1,127.50	785.10
	Markus BRIER	Aut	74	71	72	76	293	5	1,127.50	785.10
81	Gaurav GHEI	Ind	74	72	74	74	294	6	1,115.50	776.75
	Jamie SPENCE	Eng	71	75	74	74	294	6	1,115.50	776.75
	Pablo DEL OLMO	Mex	74	70	74	76	294	6	1,115.50	776.75
	Eng-Wah POH	Sing	74	70	76	74	294	6	1,115.50	776.75
85	Carlos RODILES	Sp	73	73	74	75	295	7	1,108.00	771.52
86	Jarmo SANDELIN	Swe	72	72	80	72	296	8	1,103.50	768.39
	Chawalit PLAPHOL	Thai	74	69	84	69	296	8	1,103.50	768.39
88	Bill FUNG	Sing	75	68	76	78	297	9	1,097.50	764.21
	Ross BAIN	Scot	75	70	77	75	297	9	1,097.50	764.21
90	Sushi ISHIGAKI	Jpn	73	68	76	81	298	10	1,093.00	761.08

Total Prize Fund
€788,770 £549,235

Heineken Classic

Victoria, Australia
February 3-6 • 2005

Royal Melbourne Golf Club

Par	Yards	Metres
71	6954	6370

#	Player	Score	To Par	
1	**Craig PARRY**	270	-14	
2	Nick O'HERN	270	-14	
3	Simon DYSON	271	-13	
	Jarrod LYLE	271	-13	
5	Ernie ELS	272	-12	
6	Trevor IMMELMAN	273	-11	
	Henrik STENSON	273	-11	
8	Simon KHAN	274	-10	
	Peter LONARD	274	-10	
10	Camilo VILLEGAS	275	-9	

Round One · Round Two · Round Three · Round Four

EUROPEAN TOUR ORDER OF MERIT
(After six tournaments)

Pos	Player	€	
1	**Charl SCHWARTZEL**	192,949.04	
2	Nick DOUGHERTY	165,164.59	
3	Thomas BJÖRN	151,214.97	
4	Gregory HAVRET	133,285.18	
5	Stephen DODD	129,126.32	
6	Nick O'HERN	127,708.40	
7	Miguel Angel JIMÉNEZ	100,338.80	
8	James KINGSTON	99,128.53	
9	Neil CHEETHAM	91,522.31	
10	Maarten LAFEBER	91,434.19	

Parry
And Thrust

The tone for what was announced as the last Heineken Classic, won in dramatic fashion by Craig Parry following a play-off with Nick O'Hern, was set early in the week, on Tuesday night to be precise. It was, as it turned out, the farewell party for one of golf's great sponsors, and a glittering occasion it was too.

Heineken provided an A-list of celebrities with the night themed on the imminent 50th birthday of Australia's most charismatic sportsman, Greg Norman. The Great White Shark's parents had been secretly spirited down from Queensland to enjoy, alongside their son, a wonderful evening whose centrepiece was a compilation film celebrating Norman's remarkable life and career.

It reached its height when two former US Presidents appeared on film in the same room, the Republican George Bush Snr and the Democrat Bill Clinton, sitting in adjoining chairs and, for once, not making petty political points. Instead they were in total agreement on one thing; that Greg Norman was a great guy. Even Norman, he of the ocean-going yacht, the helicopter, the seven or so Ferraris, and a man not easily impressed, was almost overcome by that one.

Many of the week's field attended, including Nick Dougherty, whose win in Singapore

the previous week was his first on The European Tour International Schedule and one which led to him being named The European Tour Golfer of the Month for January. He was to start well but the last two rounds caught up with him, as they often do with those who have had to dig the deepest the previous week.

His closest challenger at Laguna National Golf & Country Club, Colin Montgomerie, was also at the party and delighted the sponsors when he was interviewed about his weight loss. "I've stopped eating," he said, "I'm just drinking Heineken!"

If Tuesday night was glittering, the weather for all of Wednesday was ghastly. A storm dropped more rain on Melbourne than had been recorded in one day for over 100 years; roads were flooded, and strong winds blew down huge eucalyptus trees across roads leading into the golf course. The Pro-Am was washed out and it was a fantastic

Simon Khan

Paul Kimmage took time out from his sports writing duties with the Sunday Times to work alongside Nick Faldo

Simon Dyson

Costantino Rocca

tribute to the greenkeeping staff that play on Thursday was only delayed by two and a half hours.

On Tuesday night it had seemed that the tournament itself might struggle to match the party, but by Sunday night it had managed it comfortably. In fact, the result of the event was splashed all over the front pages of Melbourne's newspapers. But more of that later.

Over the first two days, most of the publicity was grabbed by Montgomerie, whose rounds of 68-65 over a layout made receptive by the storm, gave him a chance to improve on Singapore. But like Dougherty, the inspiration vanished over the weekend and he had to settle for a share of 11th place after closing rounds of 72-71.

Instead it was left to a South African and a trio of Australians to headline a final day which provided a finish as fine as any Heineken

Classic has witnessed. At the outset Ernie Els, Jarrod Lyle, Nick O'Hern and Craig Parry had the tournament between them, and with Els having won the previous three stagings of the event at Royal Melbourne, it was hard to look past the defending champion.

But The Big Easy had been nowhere near his best for three days and only his innate class and utter determination had given him a chance. It was not enough on the final day, however, and when he needed to birdie the final hole, he bogeyed it.

However, the reason the tournament featured on the front pages of the newspapers as well as the back was 23 year old Lyle, who for much of Sunday had a chance to win the event in his rookie professional year. Lyle was everyone's sentimental favourite, given that he had fought a huge battle against leukaemia in his late teens, spending much of one year bedridden, and had recovered to become a star in the amateur ranks.

"It's one of the best courses we play all year and the condition is fantastic. It has everything - long par threes, short par threes, par fives you can get up in two, good par fours and the bunkering is good as well. The greens were fantastic to putt on for all four days, too, so it was just a real pleasure to play there" – Simon Dyson

Ignacio Garrido

Final Results

Now he was trying to prove himself against some of the world's best professionals and, but for four errant drives, each of which cost him a bogey, he might have done so. The last of them came at the 72nd, and although it cost him a place in the play-off he was cheered off the course, with scarcely a dry eye in the stands.

That left O'Hern and Parry to fight it out, with the latter the last man the former wanted to see opposite him on the tee as he searched for his maiden title. Parry is a tenacious opponent, although if golf were

boxing, the fight might have been stopped in O'Hern's favour. The left-hander hit better shots off the tee at all four of the extra holes, and better seconds into the green, but had to watch Parry hole long putt after long putt, including from 15 feet for a winning birdie three.

"I thought I'd lost on every extra hole," Parry admitted afterwards, but his doggedness, and O'Hern's fallibility with the long putter, saw the lovingly nicknamed Popeye home.

David Davies

Pos	Name		Rd1	Rd2	Rd3	Rd4	Total		€	£
1	Craig PARRY	Aus	69	66	65	70	270	-14	225,367.70	155,820.39
2	Nick O'HERN	Aus	69	67	63	71	270	-14	127,708.40	88,298.24
3	Simon DYSON	Eng	68	70	65	68	271	-13	72,305.47	49,992.37
	Jarrod LYLE	Aus	68	66	66	71	271	-13	72,305.47	49,992.37
5	Ernie ELS	SA	72	64	66	70	272	-12	50,081.71	34,626.75
6	Trevor IMMELMAN	SA	65	69	70	69	273	-11	42,569.45	29,432.74
	Henrik STENSON	Swe	69	66	68	70	273	-11	42,569.45	29,432.74
8	Peter LONARD	Aus	65	68	70	71	274	-10	35,057.20	24,238.73
	Simon KHAN	Eng	69	71	68	66	274	-10	35,057.20	24,238.73
10	Camilo VILLEGAS	Col	66	71	68	70	275	-9	31,301.07	21,641.72
11	Christopher HANELL	Swe	69	71	67	69	276	-8	23,287.99	16,101.44
	Brett RUMFORD	Aus	70	66	66	74	276	-8	23,287.99	16,101.44
	Colin MONTGOMERIE	Scot	68	65	72	71	276	-8	23,287.99	16,101.44
	Gregory HAVRET	Fr	72	66	71	67	276	-8	23,287.99	16,101.44
	Richard BLAND	Eng	70	67	71	68	276	-8	23,287.99	16,101.44
16	Nobuhito SATO	Jpn	72	70	69	66	277	-7	17,152.98	11,859.66
	Steve WEBSTER	Eng	65	72	66	74	277	-7	17,152.98	11,859.66
18	David SMAIL	NZ	69	67	75	67	278	-6	14,210.68	9,825.34
	Mark FOSTER	Eng	68	73	68	69	278	-6	14,210.68	9,825.34
	Stuart APPLEBY	Aus	72	67	71	68	278	-6	14,210.68	9,825.34
21	David MCKENZIE	Aus	71	70	70	68	279	-5	11,268.38	7,791.02
	Robert KARLSSON	Swe	72	65	71	71	279	-5	11,268.38	7,791.02
	Brad LAMB	Aus	66	72	70	71	279	-5	11,268.38	7,791.02
	Graeme MCDOWELL	N.Ire	70	70	67	72	279	-5	11,268.38	7,791.02
	Martin DOYLE	Aus	73	67	70	69	279	-5	11,268.38	7,791.02
	Brad KENNEDY	Aus	70	68	70	71	279	-5	11,268.38	7,791.02
	Barry LANE	Eng	73	67	66	73	279	-5	11,268.38	7,791.02
	Maarten LAFEBER	NL	70	70	67	72	279	-5	11,268.38	7,791.02
29	Richard GREEN	Aus	70	69	70	71	280	-4	8,013.07	5,540.28
	Chris CAMPBELL	Aus	71	69	69	71	280	-4	8,013.07	5,540.28
	James NITTIES	Aus	68	67	71	74	280	-4	8,013.07	5,540.28
	Jamie DONALDSON	Wal	69	68	71	72	280	-4	8,013.07	5,540.28
	Raymond RUSSELL	Scot	72	67	71	70	280	-4	8,013.07	5,540.28
	Matthew ECOB	Aus	72	67	71	70	280	-4	8,013.07	5,540.28
35	Peter O'MALLEY	Aus	70	66	72	73	281	-3	6,635.83	4,588.04
	Gary SIMPSON	Aus	70	71	65	75	281	-3	6,635.83	4,588.04
	Paul SHEEHAN	Aus	70	70	71	70	281	-3	6,635.83	4,588.04
	Søren KJELDSEN	Den	69	68	72	72	281	-3	6,635.83	4,588.04
39	Peter FOWLER	Aus	73	67	73	69	282	-2	5,383.78	3,722.38
	Lee SLATTERY	Eng	69	71	71	71	282	-2	5,383.78	3,722.38
	Niclas FASTH	Swe	71	70	72	69	282	-2	5,383.78	3,722.38
	Stephen SCAHILL	NZ	74	67	69	72	282	-2	5,383.78	3,722.38
	Fredrik HENGE	Swe	70	69	70	73	282	-2	5,383.78	3,722.38
	Garry HOUSTON	Wal	72	69	73	68	282	-2	5,383.78	3,722.38
45	Paul LAWRIE	Scot	71	70	72	70	283	-1	3,881.33	2,683.57
	Markus BRIER	Aut	71	71	70	71	283	-1	3,881.33	2,683.57
	Gavin COLES	Aus	73	67	68	75	283	-1	3,881.33	2,683.57
	Alastair FORSYTH	Scot	70	69	74	70	283	-1	3,881.33	2,683.57
	Adam SCOTT	Aus	72	68	75	68	283	-1	3,881.33	2,683.57
	Klas ERIKSSON	Swe	71	67	73	72	283	-1	3,881.33	2,683.57
51	Greg CHALMERS	Aus	73	68	67	76	284	0	2,472.78	1,709.70
	Adam CRAWFORD	Aus	68	72	69	75	284	0	2,472.78	1,709.70
	Stephen GALLACHER	Scot	69	73	71	71	284	0	2,472.78	1,709.70
	Simon WAKEFIELD	Eng	68	72	72	72	284	0	2,472.78	1,709.70
	John BICKERTON	Eng	66	72	72	74	284	0	2,472.78	1,709.70
	Mathew GOGGIN	Aus	73	69	72	70	284	0	2,472.78	1,709.70
57	Nick DOUGHERTY	Eng	68	69	71	77	285	1	2,015.79	1,393.73
	Andrew BUCKLE	Aus	71	69	68	77	285	1	2,015.79	1,393.73
	Mat HENDRIX	USA	68	74	72	71	285	1	2,015.79	1,393.73
	Danny VERA	Aus	69	70	71	75	285	1	2,015.79	1,393.73
	David BRANSDON	Aus	70	71	69	75	285	1	2,015.79	1,393.73
62	Sven STRÜVER	Ger	71	71	71	73	286	2	1,903.11	1,315.82
	José Manuel LARA	Sp	70	72	73	71	286	2	1,903.11	1,315.82
	Terry PRICE	Aus	70	67	71	78	286	2	1,903.11	1,315.82
	Miles TUNNICLIFF	Eng	69	72	73	72	286	2	1,903.11	1,315.82
66	Emanuele CANONICA	It	73	67	67	80	287	3	1,807.12	1,249.45
	Steven O'HARA	Scot	73	69	73	72	287	3	1,807.12	1,249.45
	Steve CONRAN	Aus	73	66	73	75	287	3	1,807.12	1,249.45
69	Phillip ARCHER	Eng	70	71	72	75	288	4	1,610.54	1,113.54
	Peter SENIOR	Aus	73	69	76	70	288	4	1,610.54	1,113.54
	Martin MARITZ	SA	70	71	72	75	288	4	1,610.54	1,113.54
	Steven BOWDITCH	Aus	72	68	71	77	288	4	1,610.54	1,113.54
	Dean ALABAN	Aus	72	70	68	78	288	4	1,610.54	1,113.54
	Tony CHRISTIE	NZ	70	68	73	77	288	4	1,610.54	1,113.54
75	Mads VIBE-HASTRUP	Den	69	72	73	75	289	5	1,498.70	1,036.21
76	Graeme STORM	Eng	69	68	75	78	290	6	1,415.44	978.64
	Philippe LIMA	Port	74	68	79	69	290	6	1,415.44	978.64
	Philip GOLDING	Eng	71	70	75	74	290	6	1,415.44	978.64
	Scott DRUMMOND	Scot	73	68	73	76	290	6	1,415.44	978.64
	Ignacio GARRIDO	Sp	70	72	72	76	290	6	1,415.44	978.64
	Costantino ROCCA	It	73	69	76	72	290	6	1,415.44	978.64
82	Chris DOWNES	Aus	71	71	78	71	291	7	1,332.17	921.07

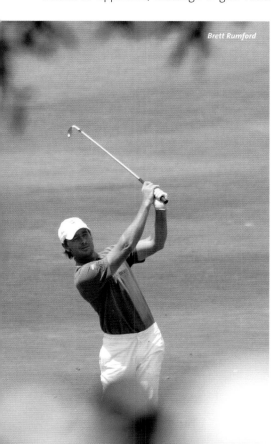

Brett Rumford

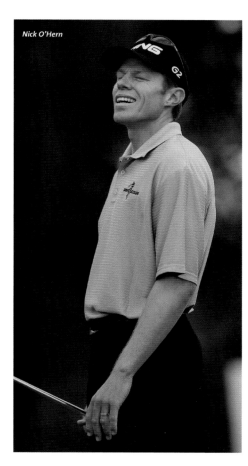

Nick O'Hern

Total Prize Fund
€1,207,000 £834,523

Holden New Zealand Open

Auckland, New Zealand
February 10-13 • 2005

Gulf Harbour Country Club

Par	Yards	Metres
72	6978	6381

1	Niclas FASTH	266	-22	
2	Miles TUNNICLIFF	266	-22	
3	Richard GREEN	270	-18	
	Simon NASH	270	-18	
5	Robert KARLSSON	271	-17	
	Peter O'MALLEY	271	-17	
7	Steve ALKER	273	-15	
	José Manuel LARA	273	-15	
	Damien McGRANE	273	-15	
	Jarrod MOSELEY	273	-15	
	Rolf MUNTZ	273	-15	
	Oliver WILSON	273	-15	

Round One   Round Two   Round Three   Round Four

EUROPEAN TOUR ORDER OF MERIT
(After seven tournaments)

Pos		€	
1	Charl SCHWARTZEL	192,949.04	
2	Nick DOUGHERTY	171,953.68	
3	Niclas FASTH	162,054.98	
4	Thomas BJÖRN	151,214.97	
5	Gregory HAVRET	133,285.18	
6	Stephen DODD	129,126.32	
7	Nick O'HERN	127,708.40	
8	Miguel Angel JIMÉNEZ	100,338.80	
9	James KINGSTON	99,128.53	
10	Neil CHEETHAM	91,522.31	

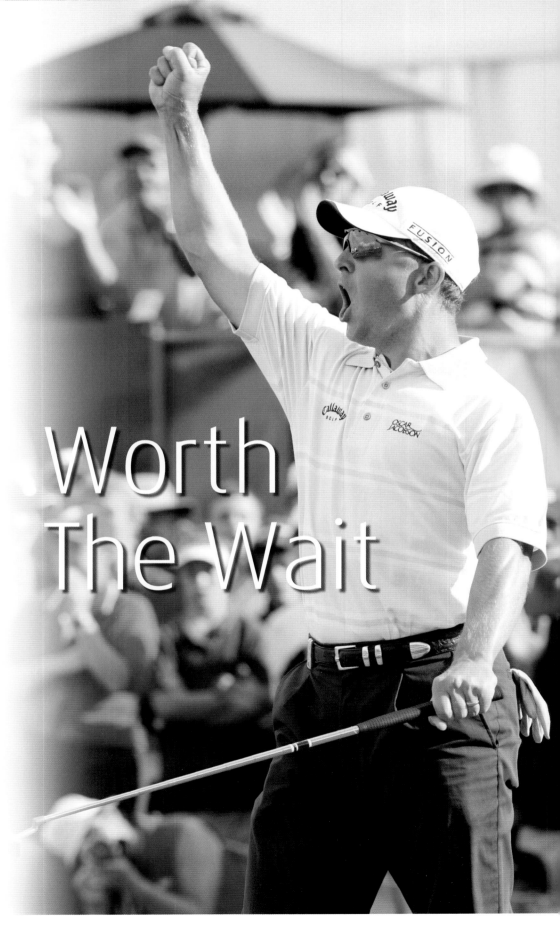

Worth The Wait

It was a long time coming, but there was perhaps a good reason for the five year wait for Niclas Fasth's second victory on The European Tour International Schedule. It seems the Swedish golfer was simply waiting for a course which provided spectacular views and breathtaking scenery, and one which could match those offered by the site of his first triumph in the 2000 Madeira Island Open.

Perched some 2,300ft above sea level, the Santo da Serra course in Madeira affords breathtaking views and it was a similar story at the Gulf Harbour Country Club, site of the Holden New Zealand Open, and The European Tour's historic first visit to New Zealand for a co-sanctioned event with the Australasian Tour.

The reward for conquering the steeply undulating back nine was found on the 16th and 17th holes in particular, and proved well worth the effort. Reminiscent of Pebble Beach's daunting stretch of holes around the turn, the long par four and fearsome par five run perilously along the cliff's edge, stunning vistas of the Whangaparaoa Peninsula and harbour below, distracting players from the daunting task ahead.

"It is a spectacular and beautiful place and it also reminds me of home a little bit," admitted Fasth after his thrilling play-off victory over Englishman Miles Tunnicliff. "We are very lucky to come to a lot of nice places and this is one of them."

Presumably, a job with the Auckland Tourist Board beckons if Fasth should decide to hang up his clubs, but that seems a remote possibility after a win which put him back at the forefront of European golf, a position he last occupied at the end of the 2003 season.

A year on from a successful Ryder Cup debut which saw him denied the glory of holing the winning putt only by Paul Azinger's holed bunker shot on the 18th at

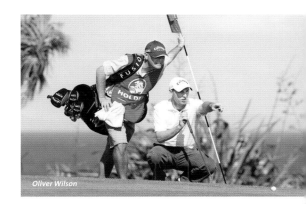

Oliver Wilson

Joakim Haeggman

Marcus Fraser

Richard Green

The Belfry, the Swede finished 22nd on The European Tour Order of Merit.

That followed a 17th place finish in 2002 and a tenth in 2001, the year he confirmed his potential with a superb second place finish behind American David Duval in The Open Championship at Royal Lytham & St Annes.

However, his subsequent decision to have a crack at the US PGA Tour in 2004 was one which Fasth admitted backfired badly. During his year in America, he dropped over 100 places on the Official World Golf Ranking and was 155th by the time he arrived in Auckland. However, again epitomising the strength of The European Tour, his win in New Zealand saw him move in the right direction, up almost 50 places to 106th.

With precious little wind to protect the course's large greens and generous fairways, 116 of the 156-strong field broke par on the first day, and the feast of low scoring continued throughout the week.

Australia's Richard Green, Fasth and Tunnicliff all equalled the course record 63 on the second day, the Swede posting three eagles on his card for the first time in his career, on his way to a two shot weekend lead.

His advantage, however, was blown away by Saturday's strong winds, a third round 75 leaving him four shots adrift of English rookie professional Oliver Wilson, the Challenge Tour graduate storming into the lead with a 68 in only his fifth outing on The European Tour.

"We played a great course that was in fantastic condition. We are quite demanding and this was great. We try to enjoy what we do and it is important to me that the course is beautiful" – Niclas Fasth

Miles Tunnicliff

Final Results

Pos	Name		Rd1	Rd2	Rd3	Rd4	Total		€	£
1	Niclas FASTH	Swe	65	63	75	63	266	-22	156,671.20	107,442.24
2	Miles TUNNICLIFF	Eng	67	63	70	66	266	-22	88,780.35	60,883.94
3	Simon NASH	Aus	65	67	71	67	270	-18	50,265.35	34,471.06
	Richard GREEN	Aus	70	63	69	68	270	-18	50,265.35	34,471.06
5	Robert KARLSSON	Swe	68	65	72	66	271	-17	33,075.03	22,682.25
	Peter O'MALLEY	Aus	68	70	66	67	271	-17	33,075.03	22,682.25
7	Rolf MUNTZ	NL	67	66	72	68	273	-15	22,485.22	15,419.95
	Jarrod MOSELEY	Aus	66	66	73	68	273	-15	22,485.22	15,419.95
	Oliver WILSON	Eng	66	65	68	74	273	-15	22,485.22	15,419.95
	Steve ALKER	NZ	69	65	72	67	273	-15	22,485.22	15,419.95
	José Manuel LARA	Sp	66	67	72	68	273	-15	22,485.22	15,419.95
	Damien MCGRANE	Ire	67	66	72	68	273	-15	22,485.22	15,419.95
13	Lee SLATTERY	Eng	68	70	66	70	274	-14	14,230.97	9,759.34
	Marcus FRASER	Aus	68	67	68	71	274	-14	14,230.97	9,759.34
	Ricky SCHMIDT	Aus	68	69	73	64	274	-14	14,230.97	9,759.34
	Peter LAWRIE	Ire	68	68	70	68	274	-14	14,230.97	9,759.34
17	Stephen SCAHILL	NZ	69	71	70	65	275	-13	10,238.03	7,021.05
	Alastair FORSYTH	Scot	65	71	71	68	275	-13	10,238.03	7,021.05
	Andrew BUCKLE	Aus	67	69	74	65	275	-13	10,238.03	7,021.05
	Greg CHALMERS	Aus	71	66	74	64	275	-13	10,238.03	7,021.05
21	Anders HANSEN	Den	69	69	72	66	276	-12	8,529.88	5,849.63
	Barry CHEESEMAN	USA	69	69	69	69	276	-12	8,529.88	5,849.63
	Simon KHAN	Eng	66	70	69	71	276	-12	8,529.88	5,849.63
	Peter SENIOR	Aus	68	71	71	66	276	-12	8,529.88	5,849.63
25	Peter HEDBLOM	Swe	73	67	71	66	277	-11	6,789.09	4,655.83
	James NITTIES	Aus	69	71	72	65	277	-11	6,789.09	4,655.83
	Paul SHEEHAN	Aus	67	67	75	68	277	-11	6,789.09	4,655.83
	Nick DOUGHERTY	Eng	70	69	71	67	277	-11	6,789.09	4,655.83
	Brett RUMFORD	Aus	67	69	69	72	277	-11	6,789.09	4,655.83
	Andrew TSCHUDIN	Aus	68	72	66	71	277	-11	6,789.09	4,655.83
31	Joakim HAEGGMAN	Swe	65	70	73	70	278	-10	5,135.33	3,521.72
	Craig PARRY	Aus	68	68	69	73	278	-10	5,135.33	3,521.72
	Fredrik HENGE	Swe	71	68	70	69	278	-10	5,135.33	3,521.72
	Mathew GOGGIN	Aus	69	69	70	70	278	-10	5,135.33	3,521.72
	David BRANSDON	Aus	68	70	71	69	278	-10	5,135.33	3,521.72
	Garry HOUSTON	Wal	66	67	72	73	278	-10	5,135.33	3,521.72
37	Philippe LIMA	Port	68	66	75	70	279	-9	4,439.02	3,044.20
	Steven JEFFRESS	Aus	68	71	73	67	279	-9	4,439.02	3,044.20
39	Costantino ROCCA	It	71	68	73	68	280	-8	4,090.86	2,805.44
	Peter FOWLER	Aus	69	71	71	69	280	-8	4,090.86	2,805.44
41	Steve WEBSTER	Eng	70	69	80	62	281	-7	2,872.31	1,969.77
	Marcus CAIN	Aus	68	67	76	70	281	-7	2,872.31	1,969.77
	Kenneth FERRIE	Eng	72	65	74	70	281	-7	2,872.31	1,969.77
	Matthew ECOB	Aus	69	69	72	70	281	-7	2,872.31	1,969.77
	Andrew MARSHALL	Eng	69	70	71	71	281	-7	2,872.31	1,969.77
	Christopher HANELL	Swe	65	70	76	70	281	-7	2,872.31	1,969.77
	Adam GROOM	Aus	66	72	69	74	281	-7	2,872.31	1,969.77
	Martin MARITZ	SA	66	70	75	70	281	-7	2,872.31	1,969.77
	Steven BOWDITCH	Aus	64	69	79	69	281	-7	2,872.31	1,969.77
	Wayne PERSKE	Aus	69	68	71	73	281	-7	2,872.31	1,969.77
	Brad LAMB	Aus	68	72	72	69	281	-7	2,872.31	1,969.77
	Gary SIMPSON	Aus	70	69	74	68	281	-7	2,872.31	1,969.77
53	Nathan GREEN	Aus	70	67	73	72	282	-6	1,493.82	1,024.43
	Martin DOYLE	Aus	70	68	74	70	282	-6	1,493.82	1,024.43
	Dean ALABAN	Aus	70	68	74	70	282	-6	1,493.82	1,024.43
	Terry PRICE	Aus	69	69	74	70	282	-6	1,493.82	1,024.43
	Kim FELTON	Aus	67	72	74	69	282	-6	1,493.82	1,024.43
	Paul LAWRIE	Scot	71	69	71	71	282	-6	1,493.82	1,024.43
	Emanuele CANONICA	It	69	68	72	73	282	-6	1,493.82	1,024.43
	Peter HANSON	Swe	69	68	77	68	282	-6	1,493.82	1,024.43
61	Christian CÉVAËR	Fr	69	70	74	70	283	-5	1,323.00	907.29
	Graeme STORM	Eng	71	69	72	71	283	-5	1,323.00	907.29
	John BICKERTON	Eng	69	71	72	71	283	-5	1,323.00	907.29
	Craig CARMICHAEL	Aus	70	69	73	71	283	-5	1,323.00	907.29
	Scott GARDINER	Aus	69	70	71	73	283	-5	1,323.00	907.29
	Mattias ELIASSON	Swe	70	69	74	70	283	-5	1,323.00	907.29
67	Barry LANE	Eng	69	69	76	70	284	-4	1,178.95	808.50
	Mårten OLANDER	Swe	70	68	73	73	284	-4	1,178.95	808.50
	Mark FOSTER	Eng	69	71	73	71	284	-4	1,178.95	808.50
	Phillip ARCHER	Eng	69	67	78	70	284	-4	1,178.95	808.50
	Gareth PADDISON	NZ	70	70	75	69	284	-4	1,178.95	808.50
	Nobuhito SATO	Jpn	67	71	73	73	284	-4	1,178.95	808.50
73	Craig JONES	Aus	70	70	75	70	285	-3	1,074.94	737.17
74	Mikko ILONEN	Fin	69	71	74	72	286	-2	1,050.13	720.16
	Jamie DONALDSON	Wal	71	68	74	73	286	-2	1,050.13	720.16
76	Jason DAWES	Aus	67	73	75	72	287	-1	1,025.33	703.15
77	Ben BURGE	Aus	69	71	74	74	288	0	1,008.79	691.81
78	Alistair PRESNELL	Aus	66	73	77	74	290	2	992.25	680.47
79	Adam CRAWFORD	Aus	66	71	77	79	293	5	975.71	669.12

Total Prize Fund
€836,250   £573,486

But as Sunday dawned with barely a breath of wind, Fasth reasserted his credentials. Two early birdies and yet another eagle helped him to another brilliant 63, good enough to book his spot in the play-off, but not good enough for another share of the record, a new mark of 62 having been set by England's Steve Webster in the final round.

Tunnicliff, the winner at another beautiful destination on The European Tour in 2004 – The Gleneagles Hotel – showed bravery to hole from 12 feet on the 72nd hole to join Fasth, after having missed from four feet at the 17th.

On the first extra hole, the Malaga-based 36 year old was distressed to see his approach strike a young female spectator in the crowd, but after ensuring she was uninjured, he scrambled for par to keep the play-off alive.

But on the return to the 18th again - the sixth time of asking in the tournament as a whole - Fasth produced a birdie putt from 12 feet to seal a memorable victory.

Phil Casey
Press Association

Carlsberg Malaysian Open

Kuala Lumpur, Malaysia
February 17-20 • 2005

Saujana Golf & Country Club

Par	Yards	Metres
72	6971	6373

1	**Thongchai JAIDEE**	267	-21	
2	Jyoti RANDHAWA	270	-18	
3	Henrik STENSON	271	-17	
4	Niclas FASTH	276	-12	
	Paul McGINLEY	276	-12	
6	Miguel Angel JIMÉNEZ	277	-11	
	Prom MEESAWAT	277	-11	
8	Padraig HARRINGTON	278	-10	
	Wen-Chong LIANG	278	-10	
	Gary ORR	278	-10	

Round One	Round Two	Round Three	Round Four

EUROPEAN TOUR ORDER OF MERIT
(After eight tournaments)

Pos		€	
1	**Niclas FASTH**	205,511.14	
2	Charl SCHWARTZEL	192,949.04	
3	Nick DOUGHERTY	171,953.68	
4	Thomas BJÖRN	160,715.13	
5	Thongchai JAIDEE	160,556.00	
6	Gregory HAVRET	133,285.18	
7	Miguel Angel JIMÉNEZ	130,908.61	
8	Stephen DODD	129,126.32	
9	Nick O'HERN	127,708.40	
10	Jyoti RANDHAWA	112,556.74	

Bucking The Trend

Former British Prime Minister Benjamin Disraeli is remembered for a variety of reasons but perhaps mainly for his much-used quotation which stated: "There are lies, damn lies and statistics." After the Carlsberg Malaysian Open, 149 of the 150 competitors no doubt agreed with him.

When Thongchai Jaidee launched the defence of his title with a superb eight under par 64 on Thursday morning at the Saujana Golf & Country Club in Kuala Lumpur, few believed the celebrated Thai golfer would go on to win.

It was not intended at all as a slight on Jaidee's ability, but instead, as Thomas Björn pointed out, statistically, the first day leader is usually reined in. "It is very rare for the guy who leads on Thursday to win the tournament," he stated. He was quite right.

Until the Carlsberg Malaysian Open, no-one had won a tournament on The 2005 European Tour International Schedule having led at the end of the first day and, indeed, only three players claimed wire-to-wire victories the previous season.

Even fewer players successfully defend their titles, only 39 have managed it since 1972. The odds of your first two victories on The European Tour coming in the same event are even greater, as only six players in history have got off the mark with a brace of wins in the same tournament.

But every once in a while statistics are turned on their heads and the unexpected happens. The chances of Jaidee winning were stacked against him, but by Sunday night the former Thai paratrooper had bucked the trend.

Jaidee was a late starter in golf, his first love being football, and he only took up the sport after becoming injured in a freak accident when a wooden skewer became embedded in his foot. While recuperating, he and his friends sneaked onto the Army Golf Club behind his home, tied the discarded head of a five iron to a bamboo stick and started playing.

Jyoti Randhawa

It was some time before he joined the paid ranks at the age of 31, having served in the Royal Thai Army, but those humble beginnings served him well. His swing is still grooved on the flat plane caused by years of striking the ball with the open face of his bamboo-shafted five iron.

With skill and audacity, Jaidee snaked his way around 'The Cobra', as the Palm Course at Saujana Golf & Country Club is colloquially known, sharing an affinity in particular with the back nine.

When he won the title in 2004, he covered the final nine holes in a staggering 30 strokes which included a hole in one on

Henrik Stenson

Carlsberg Malaysian Open

Kuala Lumpur, Malaysia
February 17-20 • 2005

the 16th, a stroke later voted Royal Bank of Scotland Shot of the Month for February. In the first two rounds in 2005, he required only 31 strokes to play the back nine in each round which made him 16 under par for that 27 hole stretch.

Jaidee's opening 64 gave him a three stroke lead but that was cut to two after a second round 66. The third day is often the one in which the chasing pack make their move but in Kuala Lumpur it was in the wrong direction as Jaidee pulled six strokes clear with a third round 67.

Six shot advantages have been squandered in the past going into the final round through a combination of a member of the chasing pack's brilliance added to the leader faltering, but this was not one of those occasions.

Padraig Harrington

"This is a tough golf course. You will get a few knocks but that is the beauty of it, for it tests your mentality as well as your physical ability to hit the ball. It is very easy for the golf course to get the upper hand so you have to stay patient" – *Padraig Harrington*

Gary Murphy

India's Jyoti Randhawa, playing in the final group alongside Ireland's Padraig Harrington and Jaidee, battled well and on another day the golfing gods may have been a little kinder as chips lipped out and putts slipped by. He clawed back three shots but Jaidee was always just out of reach. A closing 67 for an 18 under par total of 270 was good enough, however, for second place, his highest finish on The European Tour.

Henrik Stenson made a bold challenge by making up five shots in the first 11 holes on the leader to move to within two, but the 13th proved unlucky for the Swede as he chased a third title on The European Tour. He was rightly pushing to put pressure on Jaidee but his aggressive ploy ultimately proved his undoing. Going for an eagle three he pulled his seven iron second and

the ball trickled off the edge of the green onto the rocks above the water. He tried to nick a pitch off the stone but the clubhead bounced and he was left with another tricky shot. Although he got the ball within eight feet of the hole, the putt stayed out and he was left to rue a bogey six.

Jaidee, in the group behind, seized the opportunity to pull clear, birdieing the same hole to re-establish his four stroke cushion. Three holes later he applied the coup de grace with a birdie on the 16th and it was game over - a closing 70 giving him a 21 under par total of 267.

But, as always, such mere statistics only tell half the story.

Rod Williams

Pos	Name		Rd1	Rd2	Rd3	Rd4	Total		€	£
1	Thongchai JAIDEE	Thai	64	66	67	70	267	-21	156,763.10	108,070.75
2	Jyoti RANDHAWA	Ind	70	68	65	67	270	-18	104,508.70	72,047.14
3	Henrik STENSON	Swe	69	64	71	67	271	-17	58,882.16	40,592.71
4	Paul MCGINLEY	Ire	68	70	70	68	276	-12	43,456.16	29,958.20
	Niclas FASTH	Swe	67	70	71	68	276	-12	43,456.16	29,958.20
6	Prom MEESAWAT	Thai	68	65	71	73	277	-11	30,569.81	21,074.49
	Miguel Angel JIMÉNEZ	Sp	68	67	73	69	277	-11	30,569.81	21,074.49
8	Gary ORR	Scot	71	69	70	68	278	-10	21,132.36	14,568.41
	Padraig HARRINGTON	Ire	71	66	67	74	278	-10	21,132.36	14,568.41
	Wen-Chong LIANG	PRC	70	70	69	69	278	-10	21,132.36	14,568.41
11	Thaworn WIRATCHANT	Thai	69	70	71	69	279	-9	16,209.84	11,174.88
	Scott BARR	Aus	73	71	67	68	279	-9	16,209.84	11,174.88
	Simon YATES	Scot	69	69	69	72	279	-9	16,209.84	11,174.88
14	Anders HANSEN	Den	69	68	72	71	280	-8	13,262.60	9,143.09
	Pelle EDBERG	Swe	67	69	71	73	280	-8	13,262.60	9,143.09
	Adam BLYTH	SA	69	71	70	70	280	-8	13,262.60	9,143.09
	Graeme STORM	Eng	71	72	69	68	280	-8	13,262.60	9,143.09
	Simon DYSON	Eng	68	68	73	71	280	-8	13,262.60	9,143.09
19	Peter GUSTAFSSON	Swe	70	65	72	74	281	-7	10,817.01	7,457.13
	Gregory HANRAHAN	USA	71	73	69	68	281	-7	10,817.01	7,457.13
	Francois DELAMONTAGNE	Fr	69	70	71	71	281	-7	10,817.01	7,457.13
	Terry PILKADARIS	Aus	67	76	67	71	281	-7	10,817.01	7,457.13
	Mattias ELIASSON	Swe	71	70	73	67	281	-7	10,817.01	7,457.13
	Robert-Jan DERKSEN	NL	71	69	67	74	281	-7	10,817.01	7,457.13
25	Maarten LAFEBER	NL	69	68	72	73	282	-6	9,500.16	6,549.30
	Marcus FRASER	Aus	73	71	70	68	282	-6	9,500.16	6,549.30
	Thomas BJÖRN	Den	68	64	73	77	282	-6	9,500.16	6,549.30
28	Simon WAKEFIELD	Eng	70	74	70	69	283	-5	8,089.24	5,576.63
	Stuart MANLEY	Wal	70	71	66	76	283	-5	8,089.24	5,576.63
	Peter LAWRIE	Ire	71	70	70	72	283	-5	8,089.24	5,576.63
	Chawalit PLAPHOL	Thai	73	70	74	66	283	-5	8,089.24	5,576.63
	Rick GIBSON	Can	73	68	70	72	283	-5	8,089.24	5,576.63
	James KINGSTON	SA	75	69	70	69	283	-5	8,089.24	5,576.63
	Danny CHIA	Mal	73	70	70	70	283	-5	8,089.24	5,576.63
35	Francesco MOLINARI	It	69	73	71	71	284	-4	6,396.15	4,409.43
	Ian GARBUTT	Eng	73	70	70	71	284	-4	6,396.15	4,409.43
	David BRANSDON	Aus	68	71	68	77	284	-4	6,396.15	4,409.43
	Thammanoon SRIROT	Thai	72	66	78	68	284	-4	6,396.15	4,409.43
	Brad KENNEDY	Aus	74	68	69	73	284	-4	6,396.15	4,409.43
	Richard MOIR	Aus	69	73	71	71	284	-4	6,396.15	4,409.43
	Ter-Chang WANG	Tpe	71	70	74	69	284	-4	6,396.15	4,409.43
	Prayad MARKSAENG	Thai	70	71	76	67	284	-4	6,396.15	4,409.43
43	Henrik NYSTROM	Swe	75	67	72	71	285	-3	4,797.11	3,307.07
	Johan SKOLD	Swe	70	71	70	74	285	-3	4,797.11	3,307.07
	Angelo QUE	Phil	73	70	71	71	285	-3	4,797.11	3,307.07
	Richard FINCH	Eng	72	70	70	73	285	-3	4,797.11	3,307.07
	Adam GROOM	Aus	68	72	72	73	285	-3	4,797.11	3,307.07
	Mardan MAMAT	Sing	70	71	73	71	285	-3	4,797.11	3,307.07
	Emanuele CANONICA	It	67	70	74	74	285	-3	4,797.11	3,307.07
	Jarrod MOSELEY	Aus	67	73	76	69	285	-3	4,797.11	3,307.07
	Olle NORDBERG	Swe	71	71	71	72	285	-3	4,797.11	3,307.07
52	Hendrik BUHRMANN	SA	70	71	72	73	286	-2	3,668.38	2,528.94
	Gary MURPHY	Ire	71	66	71	78	286	-2	3,668.38	2,528.94
	Gwang-Soo CHOI	Kor	74	70	67	75	286	-2	3,668.38	2,528.94
55	Keng-Chi LIN	Taiw	70	70	73	74	287	-1	3,033.47	2,091.24
	Leif WESTERBERG	Swe	73	68	72	74	287	-1	3,033.47	2,091.24
	Mikko ILONEN	Fin	71	71	72	73	287	-1	3,033.47	2,091.24
	Jeev Milkha SINGH	Ind	71	70	73	73	287	-1	3,033.47	2,091.24
59	Costantino ROCCA	It	74	70	73	71	288	0	2,539.65	1,750.80
	Ross BAIN	Scot	72	69	73	74	288	0	2,539.65	1,750.80
	Amandeep JOHL	Ind	69	73	76	70	288	0	2,539.65	1,750.80
	Jason KNUTZON	USA	72	72	71	73	288	0	2,539.65	1,750.80
	Muda SHAIFUBARI	Mal	69	75	74	70	288	0	2,539.65	1,750.80
64	Unho PARK	Aus	72	70	71	76	289	1	2,163.40	1,491.43
	Sushi ISHIGAKI	Jpn	70	73	73	73	289	1	2,163.40	1,491.43
	Jean-François LUCQUIN	Fr	71	71	75	72	289	1	2,163.40	1,491.43
67	Jan-Are LARSEN	Nor	73	71	72	74	290	2	1,928.25	1,329.31
	Anthony KANG	USA	71	68	71	80	290	2	1,928.25	1,329.31
69	S MOORRTHY	Mal	72	72	77	70	291	3	1,754.90	1,209.81
	Corey HARRIS	USA	69	74	70	78	291	3	1,754.90	1,209.81
71	Terry PRICE	Aus	70	74	76	72	292	4	1,406.50	969.63
	David DRYSDALE	Scot	69	72	74	77	292	4	1,406.50	969.63
	Søren HANSEN	Den	70	74	76	72	292	4	1,406.50	969.63
	Raphaël JACQUELIN	Fr	74	70	74	74	292	4	1,406.50	969.63
75	Tze-Chung CHEN	PRC	70	74	78	78	300	12	1,399.00	964.46

PETRONAS MALAYSIAN GRAND PRIX
KUALA LUMPUR
18-19-20 MARCH 2005

Formula 1

Thomas Björn

Total Prize Fund
€947,630 £653,287

WGC – Accenture Match Play

Carlsbad, California, USA
February 23-27 • 2005

La Costa Resort & Spa

Par	Yards	Metres
72	7247	6628

Champion - David TOMS

Runner-Up - Chris DiMARCO

Third - Retief GOOSEN

Fourth - Ian POULTER

Day One	Day Two	Day Three	Day Four	Day Five

EUROPEAN TOUR ORDER OF MERIT
(After nine tournaments)

Pos		€	
1	**Retief GOOSEN**	**428,297.00**	
2	Ian POULTER	344,167.30	
3	Nick O'HERN	311,264.30	
4	Niclas FASTH	205,511.14	
5	Miguel Angel JIMÉNEZ	195,917.98	
6	Charl SCHWARTZEL	192,949.04	
7	Thomas BJÖRN	187,483.69	
8	Adam SCOTT	187,437.23	
9	Nick DOUGHERTY	171,953.68	
10	Thongchai JAIDEE	160,556.00	

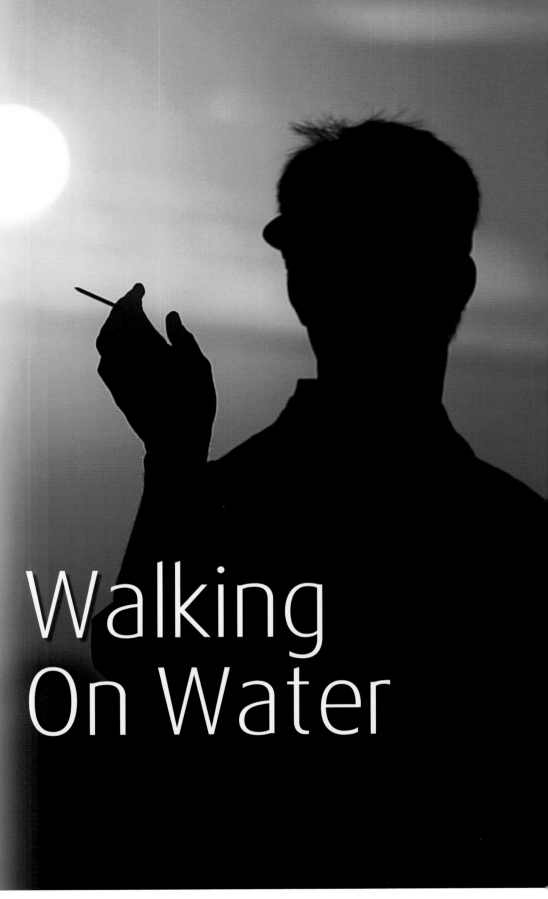

Walking On Water

Mudslides, rockfalls, flash floods and cliff-top houses trembling on their precarious perches provided the rain-soaked backdrop to the WGC - Accenture Match Play Championship at La Costa Resort & Spa in California. The tournament was won by American David Toms, but the week was illuminated by Ian Poulter.

With the opening day abandoned because of the weather that left standing water across fairways and greens, it naturally took time for Poulter to step into his stride although he was smart enough to use the indoor facilities at the nearby TaylorMade factory to warm up. Even then, he was often walking between shots with his trousers hitched up above the mud.

But once Poulter got started, he was scintillating, accounting for 2003 US Open Champion Jim Furyk then Stuart Appleby, Rory Sabbatini and Nick O'Hern on his way to the semi-finals.

He did not win his semi-final, that honour going to Toms who subsequently swept to a 6 and 5 win over his fellow American, Chris DiMarco in the 36 hole final, but there was acclaim all round for the Englishman who brightened a week where grey skies replaced the normal Californian blue.

Using indoor practice facilities, of course, is something Poulter will rapidly become accustomed to for he revealed during the week that his new purpose-built house near Woburn in the south of England would have an indoor studio in addition to a 200 yard driving range.

It was Poulter's enthusiasm, aggression and individual fashion sense that endeared him to the American galleries. He spoke with a smile, and insisted: "Bad greens? What bad greens? There's nothing wrong with them. They're perfect. Everybody's going to miss the odd putt. There is no time for whingeing; it's time to get out there and play some golf."

The Americans had fun trying to interpret

the word 'whingeing' while Poulter got on with it. His play that took him to the quarter-final against O'Hern involved 48 holes, a stretch he covered in 16 under par with 17 birdies, one eagle and only three bogeys. He spoke freely of his love for the match play format and it reminded people of his 3 and 2 win over Chris Riley in The 35th Ryder Cup at Oakland Hills Country Club in September 2004.

There was passion and power to his play that week and echoes of that also appeared in his third round victory over Sabbatini. Poulter was two down with five to play against the South African, who appeared to be marching to a victory of his own. It made Poulter's eventual fight back to win on the final green all the more remarkable.

While he appeared to be relishing the challenge thrown up by conditions, there

Darren Clarke

Tiger Woods and Nick O'Hern

Angel Cabrera

was no such joy for the top three seeds who all fell at some stage during Friday's play. Number One Vijay Singh went out to the veteran American Jay Haas in the second round, Number Two Tiger Woods fell to O'Hern at the same stage and Number Three Phil Mickelson succumbed to Toms in round three.

By the end of play on Friday, eight players were still standing, including four European Tour Members – Retief Goosen, Adam Scott, O'Hern and Poulter - an excellent return from another fine week in which 23 teed up in the first round.

Goosen and Poulter progressed to Saturday afternoon's semi-finals and the drama intensified. For a while there was a genuine belief that they would contest the final, as both held the upper hand in the early stages of their respective contests. Alas, it was not to be, as both DiMarco and Toms rallied to win.

Poulter had been in imperious form but now it was Toms who produced some of the most inspired golf of the entire week in an enthralling contest. His ball-striking from the ninth through to the 16th, where he eventually ended the match 3 and 2, was a joy to behold. The killer blow, Poulter agreed, was the nine iron the American holed from 123 yards on the tenth to go two up. Not far behind in its majesty, however, was the five wood from 234 yards on the 11th that stopped two feet from the cup for his second consecutive eagle to go three up and, despite Poulter's steely determination, it was game over.

Meanwhile, it seemed that Goosen was set for a semi-final success when he moved three up early in his match with DiMarco. His rhythm was upset on the eighth hole, however, when his tee shot strayed into a tree to the right of the fairway and stayed in the tightly-woven branches. Goosen's caddie,

Retief Goosen

"Considering the amount of rain they had in the run up to the tournament and at the beginning of the week, we did well to get any golf at all and I think the course played fantastic. The fairways, especially, were really good by the end of the week" – Ian Poulter

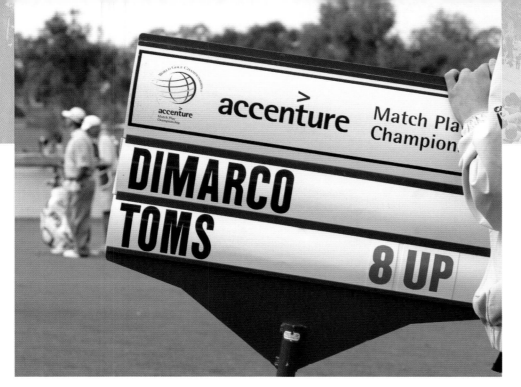

Final Results

Total Prize Fund
€5,736,120   £3,957,992

Colin Byrne, climbed the tree and spent the allotted five minutes shaking branches and poking a club into them. He finally dislodged a ball but, amazingly, it did not belong to the South African! At that point, Goosen conceded the hole rather than play another ball and never looked confident afterwards. DiMarco clawed his way back into the match and eventually closed out proceedings on the 17th green by 2 and 1.

In many respects it was unfortunate the 18 hole third and fourth place play-off was not the final itself for the standard of golf produced by Goosen and Poulter was, at times, breathtaking. On the inward half six out of seven holes from the tenth were halved in birdies and in the end it was appropriate that a sublime shot won such a contest. It came on the 20th green with Goosen pitching in from the fringe of the putting surface to triumph.

The final did not reach such heights largely because of Toms's dominance which saw him six ahead by lunch and nine up at one stage in the afternoon before DiMarco mounted a mini revival to ensure his final deficit of defeat was 'only' 6 and 5. It was a richly deserved win as Toms, taken to the last green in each of the first two rounds, had included Mickelson, Scott and, of course, the inspirational Poulter along the way.

James Mossop
Sunday Telegraph

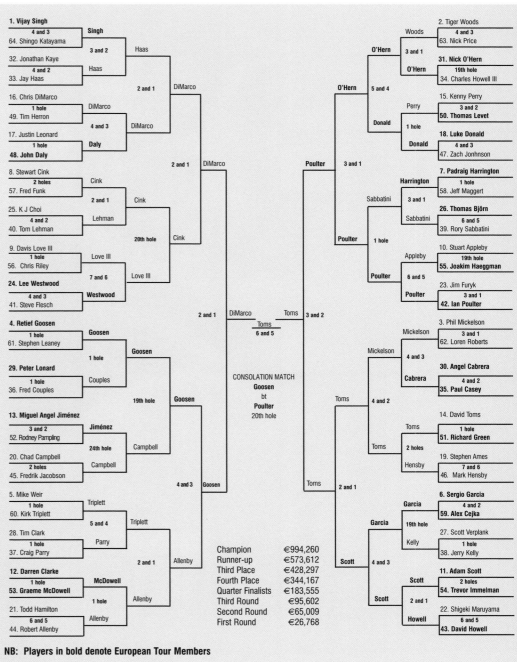

1. Vijay Singh	Singh		
64. Shingo Katayama	4 and 3	Haas	
32. Jonathan Kaye	Haas	3 and 2	
33. Jay Haas	4 and 2		DiMarco 2 and 1
16. Chris DiMarco	DiMarco		
49. Tim Herron	1 hole	DiMarco	
17. Justin Leonard	Daly	4 and 3	
48. John Daly	1 hole		
			DiMarco 2 and 1
8. Stewart Cink	Cink		
57. Fred Funk	2 holes	Cink	
25. K J Choi	Lehman	2 and 1	
40. Tom Lehman	4 and 2		Cink 20th hole
9. Davis Love III	Love III		
56. Chris Riley	1 hole	Love III	
24. Lee Westwood	Westwood	7 and 6	
41. Steve Flesch	4 and 3		
			DiMarco 2 and 1
4. Retief Goosen	Goosen		
61. Stephen Leaney	1 hole	Goosen	
29. Peter Lonard	Couples	1 hole	
36. Fred Couples	1 hole		Goosen 19th hole
13. Miguel Angel Jiménez	Jiménez		
52. Rodney Pampling	3 and 2	Campbell	
20. Chad Campbell	Campbell	24th hole	
45. Fredrik Jacobson	2 holes		Goosen 4 and 3
5. Mike Weir	Triplett		
60. Kirk Triplett	1 hole	Triplett	
28. Tim Clark	Parry	5 and 4	
37. Craig Parry	1 hole		Allenby 2 and 1
12. Darren Clarke	McDowell		
53. Graeme McDowell	1 hole	Allenby	
21. Todd Hamilton	Allenby	1 hole	
44. Robert Allenby	6 and 5		

2. Tiger Woods	Woods		
63. Nick Price	4 and 3	O'Hern	
31. Nick O'Hern	O'Hern	3 and 1	
34. Charles Howell III	19th hole		O'Hern 5 and 4
15. Kenny Perry	Perry		
50. Thomas Levet	3 and 2	Donald	
18. Luke Donald	Donald	1 hole	
47. Zach Jonhnson	4 and 3		Poulter 3 and 1
7. Padraig Harrington	Harrington		
58. Jeff Maggert	1 hole	Sabbatini	
26. Thomas Björn	Sabbatini	3 and 1	
39. Rory Sabbatini	6 and 5		Poulter 1 hole
10. Stuart Appleby	Appleby		
55. Joakim Haeggman	19th hole	Poulter	
23. Jim Furyk	Poulter	6 and 5	
42. Ian Poulter	3 and 1		
			Toms 3 and 2
3. Phil Mickelson	Mickelson		
62. Loren Roberts	3 and 1	Mickelson	
30. Angel Cabrera	Cabrera	4 and 3	
35. Paul Casey	4 and 2		Toms 4 and 2
14. David Toms	Toms		
51. Richard Green	1 hole	Toms	
19. Stephen Ames	Hensby	2 holes	
46. Mark Hensby	7 and 6		Toms 2 and 1
6. Sergio Garcia	Garcia		
59. Alex Cejka	4 and 2	Garcia	
27. Scott Verplank	Kelly	19th hole	
38. Jerry Kelly	1 hole		Scott 4 and 3
11. Adam Scott	Scott		
54. Trevor Immelman	2 holes	Scott	
22. Shigeki Maruyama	Howell	2 and 1	
43. David Howell	6 and 5		

Final: DiMarco — Toms 6 and 5

CONSOLATION MATCH
Goosen bt Poulter 20th hole

Champion	€994,260
Runner-up	€573,612
Third Place	€428,297
Fourth Place	€344,167
Quarter Finalists	€183,555
Third Round	€95,602
Second Round	€65,009
First Round	€26,768

NB: Players in bold denote European Tour Members

51

Dubai Desert Classic

Dubai
March 3-6 • 2005

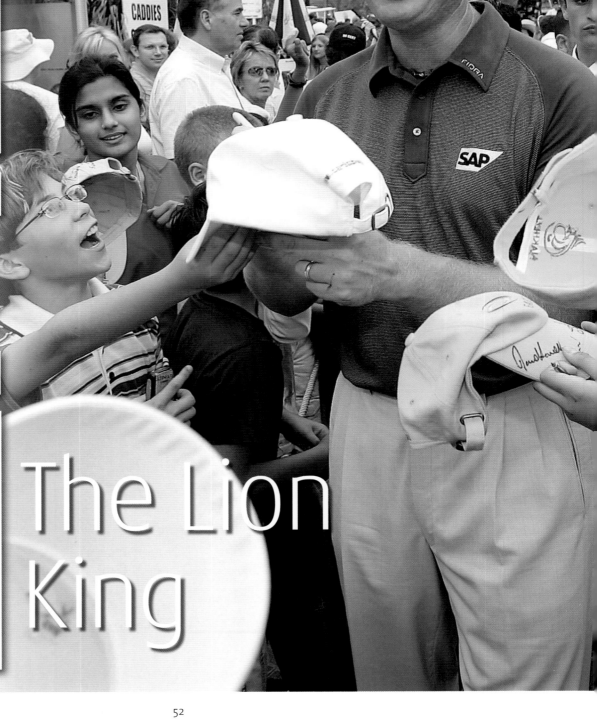

Emirates Golf Club

Par	Yards	Metres
72	7264	6643

1	**Ernie ELS**	**269**	**-19**	
2	Stephen DODD	270	-18	
	Miguel Angel JIMÉNEZ	270	-18	
4	Colin MONTGOMERIE	272	-16	
5	Gregory HAVRET	275	-13	
6	Nick DOUGHERTY	276	-12	
	Robert KARLSSON	276	-12	
	Lee WESTWOOD	276	-12	
9	David HOWELL	277	-11	
	Søren KJELDSEN	277	-11	

 Round One   Round Two   Round Three Round Four

EUROPEAN TOUR ORDER OF MERIT
(After ten tournaments)

Pos		€	
1	**Retief GOOSEN**	**428,297.00**	
2	Ernie ELS	366,521.43	
3	Ian POULTER	344,167.30	
4	Miguel Angel JIMÉNEZ	340,730.28	
5	Nick O'HERN	311,264.30	
6	Stephen DODD	273,938.62	
7	Niclas FASTH	222,851.02	
8	Nick DOUGHERTY	221,972.58	
9	Thomas BJÖRN	204,823.57	
10	Gregory HAVRET	203,978.56	

The Lion King

Afrian or Indian? The talk was of elephants. Camels might have been a more appropriate conversational topic given that the discussion took place in the desert, or perhaps even a magnificent eagle, for it was such a beautiful bird that won Ernie Els the Dubai Desert Classic in sensational fashion. But no, most definitely, elephants were the hot topic of the day.

Francesco Molinari

To be more precise, the concern centred around just how digestible this giant animal might be? Indeed what it might taste like, cooked or raw, and what is one supposed to do with the tusks? However, what does this have to do with golf?

Well, post round press conferences can sometimes be odd affairs for player and reporter alike. Often the standard of questioning goes along the lines of: To Mike Weir – "Say Mike, why do they call you Weirsy?" Or to Phil Mickelson – "Phil, are you hitting your drives longer to make your second shots shorter?"

Both these questions have actually been asked and, amazingly, have been rewarded with thorough, earnest answers. Rarely, though, does the level of conversation plumb such depths when Colin Montgomerie is fielding the questions, especially if he has just beaten par by some distance.

The Scot was the man who put elephants on the agenda after his third round 66 had given him a decent chance of landing his second Dubai Desert Classic title, his first success having come back in 1996.

He was two shots adrift of Els and three

Miguel Angel Jiménez

Dubai
March 3-6 • 2005

Stephen Dodd

behind leader Miguel Angel Jiménez and, having discussed his tournament position, was in the process of explaining how tough a task it was trying to climb back up the Official World Golf Ranking in an attempt to qualify for the Masters Tournament at Augusta National.

"It's like eating an elephant, for God's sake," he said, before musing: "You can eat an elephant, can't you? I suppose you can, but it would have to be one chunk at a time!"

The arguments over the digestibility of the great beast raged on but what was not in doubt was the fact that Montgomerie, winner of The European Tour Order of Merit on seven successive occasions in the 1990s, a feat never likely to be equalled, had struck a rich vein of form in his attempt to regain a seat at golf's top table.

"When the golf course is firm and fast, you've got to always be careful. The Majlis course is very well designed and as a result you've got to shape it both ways. If you're on your game though, you can score well round here" – Ernie Els

Final Results

Pos	Name		Rd1	Rd2	Rd3	Rd4	Total		€	£
1	Ernie ELS	SA	66	68	67	68	269	-19	277,877.70	191,477.37
2	Stephen DODD	Wal	70	65	69	66	270	-18	144,812.30	99,785.91
	Miguel Angel JIMÉNEZ	Sp	67	65	68	70	270	-18	144,812.30	99,785.91
4	Colin MONTGOMERIE	Scot	70	67	66	69	272	-16	83,364.83	57,444.26
5	Gregory HAVRET	Fr	70	68	69	68	275	-13	70,693.38	48,712.73
6	Robert KARLSSON	Swe	69	70	68	69	276	-12	50,018.90	34,466.56
	Lee WESTWOOD	Eng	70	68	67	71	276	-12	50,018.90	34,466.56
	Nick DOUGHERTY	Eng	69	70	69	68	276	-12	50,018.90	34,466.56
9	David HOWELL	Eng	67	71	69	70	277	-11	35,346.69	24,356.37
	Søren KJELDSEN	Den	70	70	68	69	277	-11	35,346.69	24,356.37
11	Steve WEBSTER	Eng	72	69	72	65	278	-10	27,243.63	18,772.79
	Jyoti RANDHAWA	Ind	72	68	71	67	278	-10	27,243.63	18,772.79
	Jamie DONALDSON	Wal	70	68	69	71	278	-10	27,243.63	18,772.79
	Ian GARBUTT	Eng	72	67	72	67	278	-10	27,243.63	18,772.79
	Paul MCGINLEY	Ire	70	71	69	68	278	-10	27,243.63	18,772.79
16	James KINGSTON	SA	69	68	69	73	279	-9	21,258.03	14,648.28
	Stephen SCAHILL	NZ	70	71	66	72	279	-9	21,258.03	14,648.28
	Bradley DREDGE	Wal	70	68	68	73	279	-9	21,258.03	14,648.28
	Peter HEDBLOM	Swe	69	72	69	69	279	-9	21,258.03	14,648.28
	David MCKENZIE	Aus	70	72	70	67	279	-9	21,258.03	14,648.28
	Mårten OLANDER	Swe	70	70	70	69	279	-9	21,258.03	14,648.28
22	Richard GREEN	Aus	71	70	72	67	280	-8	17,339.88	11,948.40
	Raphaël JACQUELIN	Fr	71	72	69	68	280	-8	17,339.88	11,948.40
	Anthony WALL	Eng	71	70	69	70	280	-8	17,339.88	11,948.40
	Henrik STENSON	Swe	69	73	71	67	280	-8	17,339.88	11,948.40
	Thomas BJÖRN	Den	69	68	73	70	280	-8	17,339.88	11,948.40
	Niclas FASTH	Swe	72	66	69	73	280	-8	17,339.88	11,948.40
	Jarrod LYLE	Aus	68	70	68	74	280	-8	17,339.88	11,948.40
29	Steven O'HARA	Scot	70	72	68	71	281	-7	13,065.54	9,003.08
	Sam OSBORNE	Eng	68	71	72	70	281	-7	13,065.54	9,003.08
	Gary EMERSON	Eng	72	69	70	70	281	-7	13,065.54	9,003.08
	Anders HANSEN	Den	70	71	70	70	281	-7	13,065.54	9,003.08
	Darren FICHARDT	SA	70	70	72	69	281	-7	13,065.54	9,003.08
	Joakim HAEGGMAN	Swe	70	70	70	71	281	-7	13,065.54	9,003.08
	Toru TANIGUCHI	Jpn	70	68	71	72	281	-7	13,065.54	9,003.08
	Maarten LAFEBER	NL	70	70	69	72	281	-7	13,065.54	9,003.08
	Mattias ELIASSON	Swe	72	71	70	68	281	-7	13,065.54	9,003.08
	José Manuel LARA	Sp	74	70	67	70	281	-7	13,065.54	9,003.08
	Peter FOWLER	Aus	69	70	69	74	281	-7	13,065.54	9,003.08
40	Ian WOOSNAM	Wal	74	69	70	69	282	-6	9,837.05	6,778.42
	Barry LANE	Eng	73	71	66	72	282	-6	9,837.05	6,778.42
	Lian-Wei ZHANG	PRC	74	67	70	71	282	-6	9,837.05	6,778.42
	Phillip ARCHER	Eng	72	66	71	73	282	-6	9,837.05	6,778.42
	Søren HANSEN	Den	71	69	70	72	282	-6	9,837.05	6,778.42
	Gary EVANS	Eng	74	68	71	69	282	-6	9,837.05	6,778.42
	Paul SHEEHAN	Aus	70	68	70	74	282	-6	9,837.05	6,778.42
47	Wade ORMSBY	Aus	73	71	69	70	283	-5	8,003.02	5,514.65
	Graeme STORM	Eng	72	70	69	72	283	-5	8,003.02	5,514.65
	Charl SCHWARTZEL	SA	69	70	72	72	283	-5	8,003.02	5,514.65
	Francesco MOLINARI	It	71	70	73	69	283	-5	8,003.02	5,514.65
51	Andrew MARSHALL	Eng	69	71	75	69	284	-4	6,023.11	4,150.35
	Louis OOSTHUIZEN	SA	73	69	72	70	284	-4	6,023.11	4,150.35
	Marcus FRASER	Aus	74	69	69	72	284	-4	6,023.11	4,150.35
	Simon DYSON	Eng	71	70	71	72	284	-4	6,023.11	4,150.35
	Alastair FORSYTH	Scot	70	71	72	71	284	-4	6,023.11	4,150.35
	Stephen GALLACHER	Scot	72	71	71	70	284	-4	6,023.11	4,150.35
	Marc CAYEUX	Zim	72	70	68	74	284	-4	6,023.11	4,150.35
	Ben CURTIS	USA	70	71	70	73	284	-4	6,023.11	4,150.35
59	Matthew KENT	SA	74	69	72	70	285	-3	4,585.07	3,159.43
	David CARTER	Eng	72	70	71	72	285	-3	4,585.07	3,159.43
	Sandy LYLE	Scot	71	70	71	73	285	-3	4,585.07	3,159.43
	Santiago LUNA	Sp	74	70	72	69	285	-3	4,585.07	3,159.43
63	Robert-Jan DERKSEN	NL	74	70	71	71	286	-2	3,834.78	2,642.44
	Peter HANSON	Swe	70	74	71	71	286	-2	3,834.78	2,642.44
	Peter GUSTAFSSON	Swe	72	70	74	70	286	-2	3,834.78	2,642.44
	Richard STERNE	SA	72	70	72	72	286	-2	3,834.78	2,642.44
	Pierre FULKE	Swe	69	73	71	73	286	-2	3,834.78	2,642.44
68	Lee SLATTERY	Eng	73	71	69	74	287	-1	3,012.52	2,075.84
	Martin MARITZ	SA	71	73	67	76	287	-1	3,012.52	2,075.84
	Mikko ILONEN	Fin	71	73	70	73	287	-1	3,012.52	2,075.84
	Gordon BRAND JNR	Scot	74	70	70	73	287	-1	3,012.52	2,075.84
72	Damien MCGRANE	Ire	71	69	73	75	288	0	2,490.50	1,716.13
	Paul BROADHURST	Eng	73	71	66	78	288	0	2,490.50	1,716.13
	Fredrik HENGE	Swe	72	72	70	74	288	0	2,490.50	1,716.13
	Thongchai JAIDEE	Thai	72	71	76	69	288	0	2,490.50	1,716.13
	David PARK	Wal	71	72	73	72	288	0	2,490.50	1,716.13
	Raymond RUSSELL	Scot	72	70	74	72	288	0	2,490.50	1,716.13
78	Patrik SJÖLAND	Swe	70	72	73	74	289	1	2,480.00	1,708.90
79	Jonathan LOMAS	Eng	73	70	69	78	290	2	2,475.50	1,705.79
	Francois DELAMONTAGNE	Fr	75	69	73	73	290	2	2,475.50	1,705.79

Total Prize Fund
€1,692,170 £1,166,025

He was playing as good a game as he was talking, but would it be good enough to win the tournament? Ultimately, the answer was no. The elephant gave way to the lion, for that is surely the beast we should associate with Els. The South African is a golfer whose elegant, seemingly effortless power and timing bear all the hallmarks of the languid king of the jungle.

Montgomerie could not summon up the accuracy to sustain his challenge on the final day and for a long while it seemed Els would suffer similar frustration. But he swooped on his prey in dramatic fashion at the very last moment.

With Jiménez alongside him on the 18th tee a shot to the good, as was Welshman Stephen Dodd who had birdied the final hole up ahead, Els knew exactly what was required and, to the delight of the huge and adoring gallery, he produced it.

A monstrous drive down the 547 yard hole left him needing only a six iron to find the putting surface. That he did before rolling in the 22 foot eagle putt to leapfrog the Welshman and the Spaniard, who could do no better than a par five.

It was a first class finish to a week which had begun for Els in unfamiliar surroundings. The winner of The European Tour Order of Merit in 2003 and 2004 had been late to the check-in desk at Johannesburg Airport and his usual seat at the sharp end of the aircraft had been allocated elsewhere.

Rather than pout or strop, Els did what most of us have to do on occasion with air travel, and simply got on with it. As well as endearing himself to the flight crew, he also made several new friends in his economy row by insisting that, if he was given the first-class food service for the duration of the flight, then so should they.

"You know what they say, start in the toilet but finish in the penthouse," he said afterwards. Clutching the distinctive Arabian coffee pot trophy for the third time, he admitted the view from there was pretty good.

Iain Carter
BBC Radio Five Live

The 2006 European Ryder Cup Team Captain - Ian Woosnam

Qatar Masters

Qatar
March 10-13 • 2005

Doha Golf Club

Par	Yards	Metres
72	7311	6685

Pos	Player	Score	To Par	
1	**Ernie ELS**	276	-12	
2	Henrik STENSON	277	-11	
3	Pierre FULKE	279	-9	
	Richard GREEN	279	-9	
5	Robert KARLSSON	280	-8	
	James KINGSTON	280	-8	
	Barry LANE	280	-8	
8	Gregory HAVRET	281	-7	
	Raphaël JACQUELIN	281	-7	
	Louis OOSTHUIZEN	281	-7	

Round One	Round Two	Round Three	Round Four

EUROPEAN TOUR ORDER OF MERIT
(After 11 tournaments)

Pos	Player	€	
1	**Ernie ELS**	555,286.23	
2	Retief GOOSEN	428,297.00	
3	Ian POULTER	344,167.30	
4	Miguel Angel JIMÉNEZ	340,730.28	
5	Nick O'HERN	311,264.30	
6	Stephen DODD	282,481.57	
7	Henrik STENSON	244,629.59	
8	Niclas FASTH	237,829.50	
9	Nick DOUGHERTY	234,447.23	
10	Gregory HAVRET	229,424.05	

Twin Peaks

The problem with doing something spectacular - not that many of us ever get the opportunity to find out apart from in our dreams - is that it creates an almost impossible act to follow. Ernie Els realised this as he took the hour-long flight from Dubai to Doha for his first appearance in the Qatar Masters, flushed with the euphoria of his tournament-winning eagle three on the final green at the Emirates Golf Club.

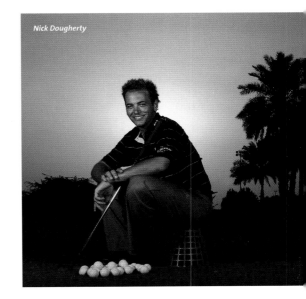

Nick Dougherty

Even if he had not captured the Dubai Desert Classic, Els would have been a strong favourite for the second leg of The European Tour's double-header in the Gulf, such is his standing in the game. As it was, he was an overwhelming favourite and that, in itself, added pressure.

Unbeknown to him, it had been four years since anyone had lifted back-to-back titles on The European Tour International Schedule, a fact which tells its own story. As tall orders go, this one is skyscraper high. In golf, even the best lose more often than they win and, therefore, winning twice in a

row is a mighty achievement to which few even come close.

The last to accomplish the feat was Vijay Singh in the Carlsberg Malaysian Open and Caltex Singapore Masters in 2001, but there was a feeling that if anyone was capable of scaling these particular twin peaks it was the winner of the last two European Tour Orders of Merit, a player at the height of his powers and with a burning desire to stamp his authority wherever he goes.

It had not gone unnoticed to Els that in America, Phil Mickelson had done exactly

Gregory Havret

Robert-Jan Derksen

what he was now trying to do, namely capture two successive tournaments – the FBR Open and the AT&T Pebble Beach National Pro-Am. Or, that on the same day he triumphed in Dubai, Tiger Woods had pipped Mickelson for the Ford Championship at Doral and with it had reclaimed the Number One spot from Singh on the Official World Golf Ranking.

The game's leading lights were well and truly switched on as the first of the season's Major Championships approached and Els, denied by Mickelson at the Masters Tournament the previous April, was determined not to be left in the shade.

After the adrenalin rush of the previous Sunday, it was not totally surprising to see the South African a little flat on the opening day. He is human after all, not a

" This is a great golf course. It has a lot of length and is a tough test of golf all round. The greens are really good and it is a different type of grass – Bermuda – to last week in Dubai and they are running beautifully. The course overall is in great shape " – Ernie Els

Barry Lane

Final Results

robot, and the result was a one over par 73 which left him in a share of 81st place. Now a different question had to be asked. While still wondering if he could triumph from such a position, the first hurdle to be negotiated was the halfway cut.

Not since the 2000 Johnnie Walker Classic, 58 European Tour events earlier, had the 35 year old failed to make it to the weekend, a run second only to Bernhard Langer's 69 tournaments from the 1991 Volvo PGA Championship to the same event five years later.

That particular record remained in his sights, as his second round 69 saw him safely through with three shots to spare and lifted him to joint 24th. Not that he was any closer to the lead though, Australian left-hander Richard Green having taken over at the top from Sweden's Pierre Fulke.

Pierre Fulke

Els still had a seven stroke deficit to make up and even when he was one of just six players to break 70 in Saturday's difficult conditions, his 69 narrowed the gap by only two shots, thanks to Henrik Stenson's superb 66 which moved him to ten under par.

The wind, always a factor in Doha, switched direction for the final round and did so at the same time as Els moved up the gears. He did well to save par at the short third and from then on, this enormously gifted athlete launched a hugely impressive charge.

Birdies at the next three holes, then two more at the tenth and 12th, brought him onto the heels of Green and Stenson. Crucially then, he picked up another stroke on the driveable 16th, at the same time as the leaders both bogeyed the 13th.

With Stenson proceeding to double-bogey the 14th after driving into thick rough, Els, for the first time in the week, was in the lead and he hammered home the advantage by two-putting the 18th for his eighth birdie of the day in a blistering 65, the low round of the week.

Green, a man looking for his own desert double after capturing the Dubai title in 1997, could have caught him with a closing eagle, but a wayward drive ended his hopes of that eventuality. Stenson, after birdies at the 15th and 16th, was left needing an eagle as well, but his chip shot from the back of the green failed to drop.

It left Els the winner - again.

Mark Garrod
Press Association

Pos	Name		Rd1	Rd2	Rd3	Rd4	Total		€	£
1	Ernie ELS	SA	73	69	69	65	276	-12	188,764.80	129,917.41
2	Henrik STENSON	Swe	67	73	66	71	277	-11	125,838.10	86,608.10
3	Pierre FULKE	Swe	66	70	73	70	279	-9	63,764.73	43,886.09
	Richard GREEN	Aus	67	68	73	71	279	-9	63,764.73	43,886.09
5	Barry LANE	Eng	71	69	69	71	280	-8	40,546.67	27,906.25
	Robert KARLSSON	Swe	69	67	74	70	280	-8	40,546.67	27,906.25
	James KINGSTON	SA	70	72	69	69	280	-8	40,546.67	27,906.25
8	Louis OOSTHUIZEN	SA	72	71	70	68	281	-7	25,445.49	17,512.86
	Gregory HAVRET	Fr	71	67	72	71	281	-7	25,445.49	17,512.86
	Raphaël JACQUELIN	Fr	70	68	73	70	281	-7	25,445.49	17,512.86
11	Steve WEBSTER	Eng	73	69	69	71	282	-6	20,839.63	14,342.88
12	Jyoti RANDHAWA	Ind	73	70	71	69	283	-5	17,923.21	12,335.65
	Marcus FRASER	Aus	69	71	70	73	283	-5	17,923.21	12,335.65
	David PARK	Wal	68	70	74	71	283	-5	17,923.21	12,335.65
	Graeme STORM	Eng	71	71	72	69	283	-5	17,923.21	12,335.65
16	Niclas FASTH	Swe	68	71	69	76	284	-4	14,978.48	10,308.94
	Charl SCHWARTZEL	SA	70	75	70	69	284	-4	14,978.48	10,308.94
	Ricardo GONZALEZ	Arg	69	70	74	71	284	-4	14,978.48	10,308.94
	Thaworn WIRATCHANT	Thai	69	68	75	72	284	-4	14,978.48	10,308.94
20	Simon YATES	Scot	71	73	71	70	285	-3	12,474.65	8,585.68
	Arjun ATWAL	Ind	70	69	71	75	285	-3	12,474.65	8,585.68
	Miguel Angel MARTIN	Sp	70	71	74	70	285	-3	12,474.65	8,585.68
	Nick DOUGHERTY	Eng	73	68	71	73	285	-3	12,474.65	8,585.68
	Steven O'HARA	Scot	70	74	71	70	285	-3	12,474.65	8,585.68
	David LYNN	Eng	72	71	72	70	285	-3	12,474.65	8,585.68
	Bradley DREDGE	Wal	70	74	70	71	285	-3	12,474.65	8,585.68
27	David DRYSDALE	Scot	70	73	71	72	286	-2	10,419.81	7,171.44
	Richard STERNE	SA	72	71	73	70	286	-2	10,419.81	7,171.44
	Jeev Milkha SINGH	Ind	71	73	73	69	286	-2	10,419.81	7,171.44
	Clay DEVERS	USA	70	71	72	73	286	-2	10,419.81	7,171.44
	Anders HANSEN	Den	71	71	71	73	286	-2	10,419.81	7,171.44
32	Andrew PITTS	USA	69	74	73	71	287	-1	8,542.95	5,879.69
	Darren FICHARDT	SA	69	75	70	73	287	-1	8,542.95	5,879.69
	Søren HANSEN	Den	70	72	74	71	287	-1	8,542.95	5,879.69
	Peter HEDBLOM	Swe	70	73	74	70	287	-1	8,542.95	5,879.69
	Terry PILKADARIS	Aus	72	72	72	71	287	-1	8,542.95	5,879.69
	Stephen DODD	Wal	71	74	70	72	287	-1	8,542.95	5,879.69
	Christopher HANELL	Swe	71	70	75	71	287	-1	8,542.95	5,879.69
39	Mads VIBE-HASTRUP	Den	72	73	74	69	288	0	6,569.01	4,521.12
	Prayad MARKSAENG	Thai	71	72	73	72	288	0	6,569.01	4,521.12
	Robert COLES	Eng	71	70	74	73	288	0	6,569.01	4,521.12
	Thongchai JAIDEE	Thai	71	71	73	73	288	0	6,569.01	4,521.12
	Nobuhito SATO	Jpn	69	72	73	74	288	0	6,569.01	4,521.12
	Miles TUNNICLIFF	Eng	73	68	71	76	288	0	6,569.01	4,521.12
	Garry HOUSTON	Wal	67	76	76	69	288	0	6,569.01	4,521.12
	Scott DRUMMOND	Scot	74	71	71	72	288	0	6,569.01	4,521.12
	José Manuel LARA	Sp	70	73	71	74	288	0	6,569.01	4,521.12
	Søren KJELDSEN	Den	69	75	72	72	288	0	6,569.01	4,521.12
49	Robert-Jan DERKSEN	NL	74	71	70	74	289	1	4,756.87	3,273.92
	Gary EMERSON	Eng	72	72	74	71	289	1	4,756.87	3,273.92
	Paul BROADHURST	Eng	73	68	74	74	289	1	4,756.87	3,273.92
	Anthony KANG	USA	68	72	77	72	289	1	4,756.87	3,273.92
	Sung-Man LEE	Kor	73	70	75	71	289	1	4,756.87	3,273.92
	Christian CÉVAËR	Fr	73	70	74	72	289	1	4,756.87	3,273.92
55	Matthew KENT	SA	74	71	72	73	290	2	3,578.98	2,463.23
	Martin MARITZ	SA	75	70	74	71	290	2	3,578.98	2,463.23
	Mark ROE	Eng	74	70	73	73	290	2	3,578.98	2,463.23
	Mårten OLANDER	Swe	71	72	71	76	290	2	3,578.98	2,463.23
	Anthony WALL	Eng	70	73	74	73	290	2	3,578.98	2,463.23
60	Philip GOLDING	Eng	74	70	76	71	291	3	2,888.10	1,987.74
	Carlos RODILES	Sp	70	75	74	72	291	3	2,888.10	1,987.74
	Peter HANSON	Swe	70	74	71	76	291	3	2,888.10	1,987.74
	Jose-Filipe LIMA	Port	75	68	76	72	291	3	2,888.10	1,987.74
	Adam GROOM	Aus	69	75	73	74	291	3	2,888.10	1,987.74
	Rolf MUNTZ	NL	71	73	74	73	291	3	2,888.10	1,987.74
66	Adam FRASER	Aus	71	74	71	76	292	4	2,378.44	1,636.96
	Johan AXGREN	Swe	74	69	74	75	292	4	2,378.44	1,636.96
	Maarten LAFEBER	NL	69	71	77	75	292	4	2,378.44	1,636.96
69	Kenneth FERRIE	Eng	74	70	76	73	293	5	2,110.39	1,452.48
	Paul LAWRIE	Scot	70	74	78	71	293	5	2,110.39	1,452.48
71	Paul MCGINLEY	Ire	71	71	76	76	294	6	1,696.00	1,167.27
	Gary RUSNAK	USA	70	74	78	72	294	6	1,696.00	1,167.27
	Lian-Wei ZHANG	PRC	71	74	74	75	294	6	1,696.00	1,167.27
74	Ian WOOSNAM	Wal	72	72	76	76	296	8	1,690.00	1,163.14
75	Fredrik ANDERSSON HED	Swe	69	75	88	72	304	16	1,687.00	1,161.08

Total Prize Fund
€1,141,050 £1,511,211

Yalong Bay Golf Club

Par	Yards	Metres
72	7097	6490

1	**Paul CASEY**	266	-22	
2	Paul McGINLEY	266	-22	
3	Thomas BJÖRN	267	-21	
	Wook-Soon KANG	267	-21	
	Chawalit PLAPHOL	267	-21	
6	Colin MONTGOMERIE	268	-20	
7	Ivo GINER	269	-19	
	Wen-Tang LIN	269	-19	
	Edward LOAR	269	-19	
10	Wen Teh LU	271	-17	
	Alex QUIROZ	271	-17	

Round One	Round Two	Round Three	Round Four

EUROPEAN TOUR ORDER OF MERIT
(After 12 tournaments)

Pos		€	
1	**Ernie ELS**	555,286.23	
2	Retief GOOSEN	428,297.00	
3	Ian POULTER	344,167.30	
4	Miguel Angel JIMÉNEZ	340,730.28	
5	Nick O'HERN	311,264.30	
6	Stephen DODD	282,481.57	
7	Henrik STENSON	244,629.59	
8	Thomas BJÖRN	243,194.67	
9	Niclas FASTH	237,829.50	
10	Nick DOUGHERTY	234,447.23	

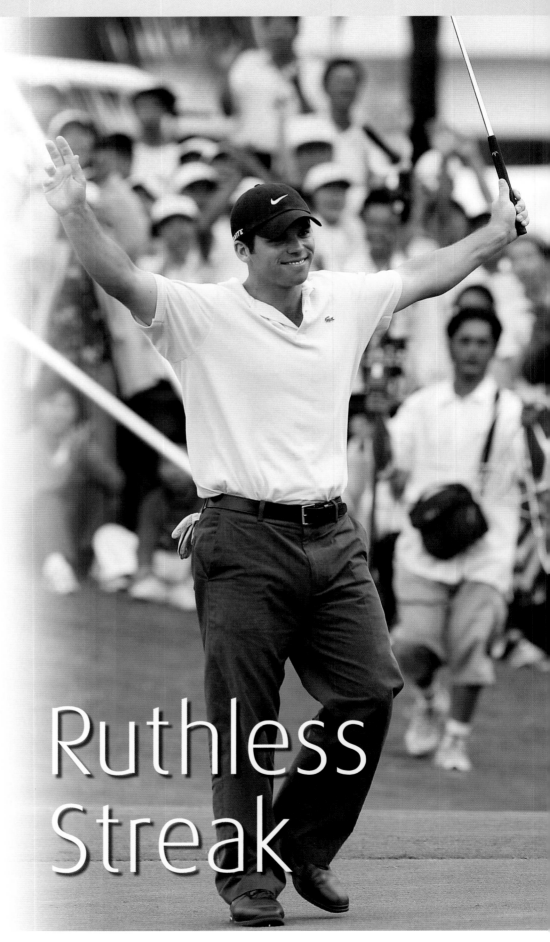

Ruthless Streak

It is one of Paul Casey's favourite photographs. Taken in the summer of 2003 to later feature on the front page of The Radio Times television magazine, it showed the Englishman, resplendent in a dinner jacket with a seven iron resting menacingly on his shoulder, recreating a pose straight from the film Reservoir Dogs.

In many ways it was appropriate that the 27 year old should be linked to writer and director Quentin Tarantino, for they view their respective work on celluloid and grass with a similarly no nonsense approach to success. Another fabled Tarantino screenplay was Natural Born Killers and in the play-off for the TCL Classic, Casey certainly exhibited such a ruthless streak.

Facing up to his Ryder Cup team-mate Paul McGinley, Casey was favourite as the duo returned to the 18th hole at the Yalong Bay Golf Club, Sanya, Hainan Island, for the second time. McGinley found two bunkers

and was 15 feet from the pin in three with Casey safely on the back of the green in two. Many in his position would have opted for caution but Casey went for the kill, and slammed the 25 foot birdie putt into the back of the hole for his fourth victory on The European Tour International Schedule.

Once again the Englishman, with a gait and stature likened by many to a young Tony Jacklin, was centre stage but this time, thankfully, for events on the golf course. Because, ever since he knocked a full tumbler of water all over the top table during the press conference following his

Gary Evans

Colin Montgomerie

61

James Kingston

maiden Tour victory in the 2001 Gleneagles Scottish PGA Championship, Paul Casey has been known to make a splash or two.

At the start of 2005 it centred around his relationship with the United States, a bond which is strong due to his successful college career at Arizona State University, his second home in Scottsdale and his American girlfriend Jocelyn, but one which had been stretched due to the mischievous nature of certain sections of the British tabloid press, who highlighted and expanded comments made within the context of a reasoned and expansive broadsheet interview.

Perhaps not surprisingly, given what latterly appeared, his reception in America at the beginning of the year was cool. But having spoken personally to many players and having appeared on television through the auspices of The Golf Channel, Casey embraced the situation and sorted matters out.

Facing up to things is a facet of life that the former English Amateur champion never shirks from and one which emerged again during the final round in China, when an adrenalin-fuelled drive on the 317 yard 14th hole caught a favourable bounce and rolled across the right edge of a green still occupied by Colin Montgomerie and Terry Pilkadaris.

Although neither the Scot nor the Australian were actually putting at the time, Casey immediately realised his mistake and, before even looking at the line of his resulting eagle putt, walked straight to the 15th tee to apologise to his fellow title challengers.

It also says a lot for Casey's strength of mind that he was able to refocus on his own task in hand immediately afterwards, two putting for birdie on the 14th, saving par from sand at the 15th, two putting for birdie on the par five 16th, and pitching and putting to save par on the 17th. Such an inspired run brought him level with

"I'm sure a lot of people are not aware there is such a great facility as this out here. The golf course is fantastic and the people are so friendly that I have really enjoyed my time here. In fact, the course reminds me of a few back in England which helped me feel really at home" – Paul Casey

Michael Campbell

Final Results

McGinley who, an hour earlier, had thrilled the large gallery with a course record equalling 63.

With both men on 22 under par 266, it meant a play-off and one underpinned by a strange coincidence. While Casey had only contested one play-off in his European Tour career to McGinley's three, incredibly, both their last experiences of the genre had come some 5000 miles west of Hainan Island, in The Celtic Manor Wales Open.

Ironically, given what was about to unfold, McGinley had pleasant memories of the shoot-out in 2001 when he emerged victorious over Paul Lawrie and Daren Lee, while Casey's recollections, although fresher, were less fragrant, considering he had lost to Simon Khan only nine months earlier in the midst of the 2004 season.

This time though, there was no sadness for Casey as he put the events of what had happened against Khan to good effect to help him pocket the title and the €123,772 (£86,527) first prize.

Golf, as in life itself, is all about learning from past experiences and, as he milked the applause around the 18th green, he would have certainly appreciated another of Tarantino's memorable quotes which states: "Failure can bring great rewards – I don't think there is anything to be afraid of."

He might have failed in Wales but got his rewards in China and proved, when he is on form, it is the rest of the golfing world who need to be fearful.

Steven O'Hara

Scott Crockett

Total Prize Fund
€744,890 £520,738

Enjoy Jakarta Standard Chartered Indonesia Open

Jakarta, Indonesia
March 24-27 • 2005

Cengkareng Golf Club

Par	Yards	Metres
70	6851	6262

1	Thaworn WIRATCHANT	255	-25	
2	Raphaël JACQUELIN	260	-20	
3	Adam FRASER	261	-19	
4	Frankie MINOZA	262	-18	
	Colin MONTGOMERIE	262	-18	
6	Eiji MIZOGUCHI	263	-17	
7	Marcus BOTH	265	-15	
	Ariel CANETE	265	-15	
	Gary SIMPSON	265	-15	
	Chris WILLIAMS	265	-15	

Round One	Round Two	Round Three	Round Four

EUROPEAN TOUR ORDER OF MERIT
(After 13 tournaments)

Pos		€	
1	Ernie ELS	555,286.23	
2	Retief GOOSEN	428,297.00	
3	Ian POULTER	344,167.30	
4	Miguel Angel JIMÉNEZ	340,730.28	
5	Nick O'HERN	311,264.30	
6	Stephen DODD	282,481.57	
7	Henrik STENSON	244,629.59	
8	Thomas BJÖRN	243,194.67	
9	Niclas FASTH	237,829.50	
10	Nick DOUGHERTY	234,447.23	

United
In Glory

Adam Fraser

What chance is there of a player shooting three 63s, winning a European Tour event by five shots, and not once carding the outright lowest score in any round?

You could answer about as much chance as the Enjoy Jakarta Standard Chartered Indonesia Open grabbing the lead headlines on the same weekend as The Players Championship – regarded by many observers as the fifth Major Championship – unfolded in the shadow of the US PGA Tour headquarters at Ponte Vedra, Florida.

Yet all that happened, and so much more, over four fabulous days at the Cengkareng Golf Club in Jakarta on the island of Java. Thaworn Wiratchant became the second Thai golfer to win a tournament on The European Tour International Schedule – following in the footsteps of Thongchai Jaidee – when he posted scores of 63-63-66-63 for a 25 under par winning total of 255 which, along with just about everything else, would have found a place in the record books except that the players were allowed

to lift, clean and place the ball in the final two rounds.

In the first round, India's Arjun Atwal and Northern Ireland's Michael Hoey shot 62 – one shot lower than Wiratchant – then in round two Belgium's Nicolas Colsaerts and Canada's Darren Griff both carded 62s to Wiratchant's second successive 63. Frankie Minoza of the Philippines went low on day three with another 62 then in the last round came the pièce de résistance when Colin Montgomerie came within inches of breaking the magical 60 barrier.

Even so, when the last putt in the first Enjoy Jakarta Standard Chartered Indonesia Open to be co-sanctioned by The European and Asian Tours disappeared into the cup, Wiratchant had good reason to celebrate. His achievement in compiling a third 63

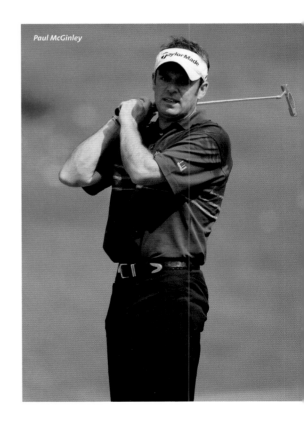

Paul McGinley

Enjoy Jakarta Standard Chartered Indonesia Open

Jakarta, Indonesia
March 24-27 • 2005

Terry Price

during a week in which he played golf of the highest calibre enabled him to coast to a famous win. He finished five ahead of Raphaël Jacquelin of France, six in front of Adam Fraser of Australia and seven clear of Minoza and Montgomerie.

Wiratchant said: "Winning a co-sanctioned event has been on my mind. I've been trying for a while and my dream has now become reality. I concentrated on every shot, every day, and if I missed one then I didn't let it bother me. I had a good feeling starting the week."

A week disrupted by rain - The Players Championship actually went to a Monday finish with 48 year old Fred Funk denying Luke Donald – almost brought glory for another member of the over 40 brigade as, with his 60, Montgomerie shot the lowest score of his career. It was not quite enough to secure a victory which would have given him a place in the top 50 of the Official World Golf Ranking, and automatic exemption to the Masters Tournament, but it was the

" *The course was in very good condition. It was a good test of golf, especially on the greens, which had some tricky undulation. You need to drive the ball well to set up opportunities. There are some hazards on the course which can take you by surprise but overall, I enjoyed playing on it* " – *Thaworn Wiratchant*

Final Results

David Garland, The European Tour's Director of Tour Operations, visits the Banda Aceh region of Indonesia which suffered enormous devastation when the Tsunami hit the coastline on December 26, 2004

eighth tournament in a row where he had not finished outside the top 11.

He said: "It's the best golf I have ever played, even back in the mid-1990s. I had a golden opportunity to make a 59 but my ten foot putt on the last didn't really roll the way the other putts had – the grain grabbed the ball."

Even so Montgomerie achieved another lifetime best on The European Tour with nine successive birdies, although with preferred lies in operation it will not feature in the record books. He had played the course back to front, starting at the tenth, and embarked on his great run at the 15th.

This was also a week when The European Tour and The Asian Tour united before a shot was struck, and remembered the Tsunami disaster. David Garland, The European Tour's Director of Tour Operations, and representatives of the Indonesian Central Bank and Standard Chartered Bank visited the Banda Aceh region of Indonesia which suffered enormous devastation when the Tsunami hit the coastline on December 26, 2004. More than 126,000 people lost their lives; tens of thousands were missing and 400,000 had been made homeless. Paul McGinley and Montgomerie presented a cheque for $100,000 from The European Tour International Relief Golf Fund to the Bank of Indonesia and more than $40,000 was raised from a charity auction at a Pro-Am dinner which included Ryder Cup memorabilia.

When the tournament began Wiratchant, a lover of fast cars, raced into contention with his opening 63 then moved ahead at the

halfway stage when he repeated the feat. Thereafter the 38 year old from Bangkok, who enjoyed an impressive amateur career in the 1980s, remained in control. His self-taught swing has been described as highly unorthodox, with his hands directly above his head at the top of the backswing and a long, extended follow through, but as he said: "It worked well for me during my amateur days, and it works now."

Wiratchant, who grew up next to the Army golf course in Bangkok where he became hooked on the game after becoming a caddie to earn a few extra Baht as pocket money, took home a cheque for €125,205 (£86,838) and earned a two year exemption to The European Tour. "My dream just became a reality," he declared.

Mitchell Platts

Raphaël Jacquelin

Pos	Name		Rd1	Rd2	Rd3	Rd4	Total		€	£
1	Thaworn WIRATCHANT	Thai	63	63	66	63	255	-25	125,205.20	86,838.30
2	Raphaël JACQUELIN	Fr	64	67	64	65	260	-20	83,472.61	57,893.92
3	Adam FRASER	Aus	66	65	68	62	261	-19	47,028.94	32,617.76
4	Colin MONTGOMERIE	Scot	67	69	66	60	262	-18	34,708.26	24,072.53
	Frankie MINOZA	Phil	67	67	62	66	262	-18	34,708.26	24,072.53
6	Eiji MIZOGUCHI	Jpn	64	69	64	66	263	-17	26,294.13	18,236.76
7	Chris WILLIAMS	Eng	63	68	66	68	265	-15	18,293.21	12,687.58
	Ariel CANETE	Arg	69	68	63	65	265	-15	18,293.21	12,687.58
	Gary SIMPSON	Aus	67	67	64	67	265	-15	18,293.21	12,687.58
	Marcus BOTH	Aus	67	69	66	63	265	-15	18,293.21	12,687.58
11	Richard MOIR	Aus	66	70	65	65	266	-14	11,995.13	8,319.44
	Thongchai JAIDEE	Thai	66	69	65	66	266	-14	11,995.13	8,319.44
	Hennie OTTO	SA	67	66	67	66	266	-14	11,995.13	8,319.44
	Clay DEVERS	USA	67	67	68	64	266	-14	11,995.13	8,319.44
	Mardan MAMAT	Sing	65	65	66	70	266	-14	11,995.13	8,319.44
	Paul MCGINLEY	Ire	69	68	64	65	266	-14	11,995.13	8,319.44
17	Terry PILKADARIS	Aus	67	64	67	69	267	-13	9,916.65	6,877.87
	Mahal PEARCE	NZ	66	66	68	67	267	-13	9,916.65	6,877.87
19	Shiv KAPUR	Ind	65	66	71	66	268	-12	8,521.45	5,910.20
	Boonchu RUANGKIT	Thai	65	70	66	67	268	-12	8,521.45	5,910.20
	Simon HURD	Eng	70	67	63	68	268	-12	8,521.45	5,910.20
	Terry PRICE	Aus	66	66	68	68	268	-12	8,521.45	5,910.20
	Thammanoon SRIROT	Thai	68	66	68	66	268	-12	8,521.45	5,910.20
	Arjun ATWAL	Ind	62	69	71	66	268	-12	8,521.45	5,910.20
	Gaurav GHEI	Ind	64	70	68	66	268	-12	8,521.45	5,910.20
26	Jochen LUPPRIAN	Ger	67	69	65	68	269	-11	7,136.98	4,949.98
	Lian-Wei ZHANG	PRC	67	67	69	66	269	-11	7,136.98	4,949.98
	Miguel Angel MARTIN	Sp	68	67	71	63	269	-11	7,136.98	4,949.98
	Andrew BUCKLE	Aus	64	69	67	69	269	-11	7,136.98	4,949.98
	Ron WON	USA	64	71	68	66	269	-11	7,136.98	4,949.98
31	Satoshi TOMIYAMA	Jpn	69	63	68	70	270	-10	5,684.54	3,942.62
	Daniel VANCSIK	Arg	66	66	68	70	270	-10	5,684.54	3,942.62
	Peter GUSTAFSSON	Swe	68	66	67	69	270	-10	5,684.54	3,942.62
	Harmeet KAHLON	Ind	70	67	65	68	270	-10	5,684.54	3,942.62
	Brad KENNEDY	Aus	66	69	66	69	270	-10	5,684.54	3,942.62
	Unho PARK	Aus	66	68	66	68	270	-10	5,684.54	3,942.62
	Gonzalo FERNANDEZ-CASTANO	Sp	69	67	68	66	270	-10	5,684.54	3,942.62
	Ivo GINER	Sp	71	66	65	68	270	-10	5,684.54	3,942.62
	Michael HOEY	N.Ire	62	68	69	71	270	-10	5,684.54	3,942.62
40	Francesco MOLINARI	It	67	70	67	67	271	-9	4,357.31	3,022.09
	Anthony KANG	USA	66	67	67	71	271	-9	4,357.31	3,022.09
	Simon YATES	Scot	69	68	67	67	271	-9	4,357.31	3,022.09
	Matthew BLACKEY	Eng	70	66	65	70	271	-9	4,357.31	3,022.09
	Peter FOWLER	Aus	66	68	69	68	271	-9	4,357.31	3,022.09
	Mike CUNNING	USA	65	71	67	68	271	-9	4,357.31	3,022.09
	Jarrod LYLE	Aus	68	68	68	67	271	-9	4,357.31	3,022.09
	Wade ORMSBY	Aus	68	69	67	67	271	-9	4,357.31	3,022.09
48	Scott BARR	Aus	64	69	69	70	272	-8	3,305.55	2,292.62
	David GRIFFITHS	Eng	67	66	70	69	272	-8	3,305.55	2,292.62
	Ted OH	Kor	67	68	67	70	272	-8	3,305.55	2,292.62
	Paul MARANTZ	Aus	66	69	68	69	272	-8	3,305.55	2,292.62
	Matthew CORT	Eng	63	73	70	66	272	-8	3,305.55	2,292.62
	Alessandro TADINI	It	66	70	68	68	272	-8	3,305.55	2,292.62
54	Cesar MONASTERIO	Arg	69	67	69	68	273	-7	2,347.69	1,628.28
	Johan SKOLD	Swe	65	70	69	69	273	-7	2,347.69	1,628.28
	Ter-Chang WANG	Tpe	67	70	67	69	273	-7	2,347.69	1,628.28
	Nicolas COLSAERTS	Bel	65	62	71	75	273	-7	2,347.69	1,628.28
	Mike CAPONE	USA	68	68	66	71	273	-7	2,347.69	1,628.28
	Scott STRANGE	Aus	69	67	67	70	273	-7	2,347.69	1,628.28
	Darren GRIFF	Can	70	62	73	68	273	-7	2,347.69	1,628.28
	Jeppe HULDAHL	Den	69	67	70	67	273	-7	2,347.69	1,628.28
62	Stephen BROWNE	Ire	67	66	70	71	274	-6	1,953.28	1,354.73
63	Amandeep JOHL	Ind	68	69	67	71	275	-5	1,727.90	1,198.42
	David ORR	Scot	65	71	68	71	275	-5	1,727.90	1,198.42
	Keith HORNE	SA	68	69	67	71	275	-5	1,727.90	1,198.42
	Gerry NORQUIST	USA	70	66	68	71	275	-5	1,727.90	1,198.42
	Benoit TEILLERIA	Fr	65	71	64	75	275	-5	1,727.90	1,198.42
68	Wen Teh LU	Tpe	70	66	70	70	276	-4	1,434.91	995.21
	Sam WALKER	Eng	65	71	72	68	276	-4	1,434.91	995.21
	Pablo DEL OLMO	Mex	67	69	69	71	276	-4	1,434.91	995.21
71	Edward MICHAELS	USA	68	69	69	71	277	-3	1,125.50	780.61
	Prayad MARKSAENG	Thai	69	68	70	70	277	-3	1,125.50	780.61
73	Søren KJELDSEN	Den	67	70	71	70	278	-2	1,119.50	776.45
	Mao-Chang SUNG	Tpe	71	66	68	73	278	-2	1,119.50	776.45
75	Bo Song KAO	Tpe	70	65	74	70	279	-1	1,113.50	772.29
	Sung-Man LEE	Kor	68	69	67	75	279	-1	1,113.50	772.29
77	Kariem BARAKA	Ger	67	70	75	68	280	0	1,107.50	768.13
	Philip WALTON	Ire	67	69	71	73	280	0	1,107.50	768.13
79	Corey HARRIS	USA	69	68	73	74	284	4	1,103.00	765.01

Total Prize Fund
€761,290   £528,010

Estoril Open de Portugal Caixa Geral de Depositos

Quinta da Marinha, Portugal
March 31-April 3 • 2005

Caixa Geral de Depositos

Oitavos Golfe

Par	Yards	Metres
71	6893	6303

1	Paul BROADHURST	271	-13	
2	Paul LAWRIE	272	-12	
3	Jose-Filipe LIMA	273	-11	
4	Richard STERNE	274	-10	
5	Barry LANE	275	-9	
6	Stephen DODD	276	-8	
7	Gary EMERSON	277	-7	
8	Jamie DONALDSON	279	-5	
	Niclas FASTH	279	-5	
	Ian GARBUTT	279	-5	
	Ignacio GARRIDO	279	-5	
	Stephen SCAHILL	279	-5	
	Charl SCHWARTZEL	279	-5	

Round One   Round Two   Round Three   Round Four

EUROPEAN TOUR ORDER OF MERIT
(After 14 tournaments)

Pos		€	
1	Ernie ELS	555,286.23	
2	Retief GOOSEN	428,297.00	
3	Ian POULTER	344,167.30	
4	Miguel Angel JIMÉNEZ	340,730.28	
5	Stephen DODD	326,231.57	
6	Nick O'HERN	311,264.30	
7	Niclas FASTH	262,642.00	
8	Nick DOUGHERTY	245,384.73	
9	Henrik STENSON	244,629.59	
10	Thomas BJÖRN	243,194.67	

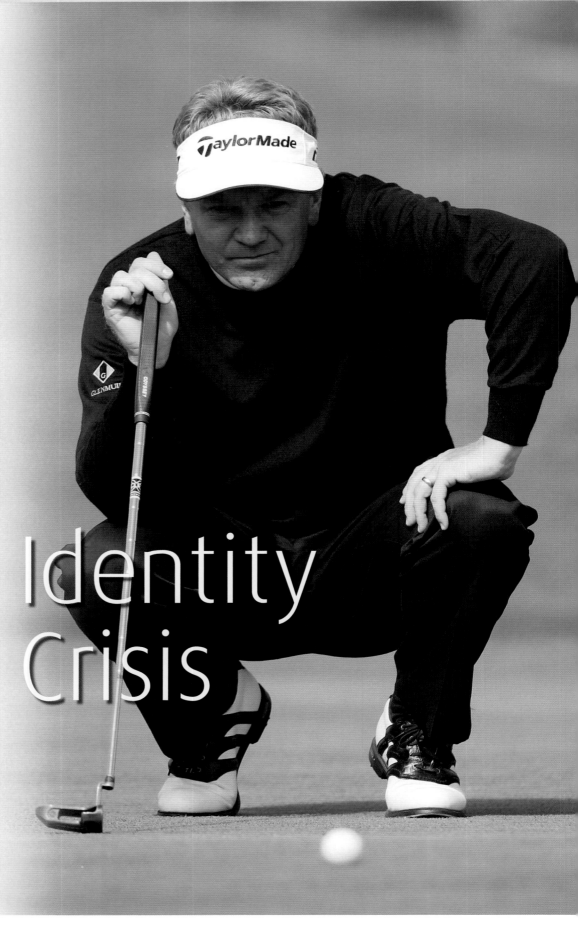

Identity Crisis

WHile the Oitavos Golfe crowd favourite Jose-Filipe Lima knew he was Portuguese, having changed his first name and his nationality from French at the end of the 2004 season, Englishman Paul Broadhurst was facing another form of identity crisis at the start of the week. Quite simply, the eventual champion's dilemma was that he did not know whether it would be Dr Jekyll or Mr Hyde who turned up.

One minute he was hitting the ball "purely," the next he was not. And that was not the only thing. While worried about hitting the ball way right in practice when he desired the majority of his shots to go left, he was also missing his little lad Aaron, who had only recently turned six months old. In fact he was missing all his family, including one of the other little fellows, Alex, the one that once announced in a West Midlands supermarket: "My dad used to be famous, you know. He used to be a top golfer!"

'Broady', as he has been familiarly known on The European Tour since first joining the circuit in 1989, has known success. Indeed, prior to Portugal, he had won four times on The European Tour International Schedule, but the last victory came a decade ago in 1995, hence the reason behind Alex's unintentional howler in the freezer aisle. Therefore, standing on the practice range at Oitavos Golfe, he was not only homesick, but a little golf sick too and not far off packing up and going home, so he could see Aaron's disarming smile in person instead of having to snatch a quick peak at him on his mobile phone wallpaper.

But this was Broadhurst's job and he knew that a little fortitude was called for alongside a little psychology, not too much of either, just enough of both. So the decision was simple: get to the course early to try to straighten out the swing, and bring in the mental coach.

Broadhurst did not have a clue what he did to put things right on the range, but perhaps his sports psychologist John Pates had hit the nail on the head. It wasn't earth-shattering advice, just a bit of the simple

Barry Lane

Estoril Open de Portugal Caixa Geral de Depositos

Quinta da Marinha, Portugal
March 31-April 3 • 2005

Markus Brier

stuff: "Relax, and stop being so uptight." That might stop him carving the ball right.

Whether that was the key or not, the man who was part of Europe's Ryder Cup Team at Kiawah Island in 1991 found a way of getting around the tricky Oitavos Golfe layout and even worked out a way to navigate the testing 18th. The umbrella-pine-protected finishing hole took many a scalp in the first round. Barry Lane, for instance, sent his ball out of bounds to deny himself the chance of sharing the lead. It was to get much worse for Barry there, though.

By Thursday night, Broadhurst had warmed to his task, and he was lying there or thereabouts. By Friday night, though, he was hot, while alongside him at the business end of the golf tournament it was well and truly Bravo Lima. Versailles-born Lima, who had adopted the land of his mother and father, was looking at a unique Tour double, having won the 2004 Aa St Omer Open in France as Frenchman Philippe and now trying to

Jose-Filipe Lima

Paul Lawrie

Final Results

Pos	Name		Rd1	Rd2	Rd3	Rd4	Total		€	£
1	Paul BROADHURST	Eng	68	66	70	67	271	-13	208,330.00	144,439.90
2	Paul LAWRIE	Scot	69	67	66	70	272	-12	138,880.00	96,288.64
3	Jose-Filipe LIMA	Port	69	65	69	70	273	-11	78,250.00	54,252.49
4	Richard STERNE	SA	71	67	70	66	274	-10	62,500.00	43,332.66
5	Barry LANE	Eng	68	67	68	72	275	-9	53,000.00	36,746.10
6	Stephen DODD	Wal	68	69	70	69	276	-8	43,750.00	30,332.86
7	Gary EMERSON	Eng	73	71	66	67	277	-7	37,500.00	25,999.60
8	Ian GARBUTT	Eng	70	66	73	70	279	-5	24,812.50	17,203.07
	Ignacio GARRIDO	Sp	71	66	71	71	279	-5	24,812.50	17,203.07
	Stephen SCAHILL	NZ	67	70	72	70	279	-5	24,812.50	17,203.07
	Niclas FASTH	Swe	70	71	68	70	279	-5	24,812.50	17,203.07
	Jamie DONALDSON	Wal	75	68	72	64	279	-5	24,812.50	17,203.07
	Charl SCHWARTZEL	SA	72	65	74	68	279	-5	24,812.50	17,203.07
14	Gonzalo FERNANDEZ-CASTANO	Sp	71	68	72	69	280	-4	19,125.00	13,259.79
15	Simon HURD	Eng	71	69	71	70	281	-3	17,250.00	11,959.82
	Peter BAKER	Eng	70	71	71	69	281	-3	17,250.00	11,959.82
	Neil CHEETHAM	Eng	67	71	71	72	281	-3	17,250.00	11,959.82
	Jonathan LOMAS	Eng	68	71	69	73	281	-3	17,250.00	11,959.82
19	Marcel SIEM	Ger	72	67	72	71	282	-2	14,575.00	10,105.18
	Stuart LITTLE	Eng	69	67	75	71	282	-2	14,575.00	10,105.18
	Steve WEBSTER	Eng	71	71	75	65	282	-2	14,575.00	10,105.18
	David PARK	Wal	73	66	75	68	282	-2	14,575.00	10,105.18
	Alastair FORSYTH	Scot	69	69	69	75	282	-2	14,575.00	10,105.18
24	Leif WESTERBERG	Swe	69	70	71	73	283	-1	12,812.50	8,883.20
	Fredrik ANDERSSON HED	Swe	69	72	70	72	283	-1	12,812.50	8,883.20
	Jean-Francois REMESY	Fr	70	70	73	70	283	-1	12,812.50	8,883.20
	Roger CHAPMAN	Eng	71	67	73	72	283	-1	12,812.50	8,883.20
28	Cesar MONASTERIO	Arg	69	67	74	74	284	0	10,937.50	7,583.22
	Titch MOORE	SA	67	70	76	71	284	0	10,937.50	7,583.22
	Carlos RODILES	Sp	71	69	73	71	284	0	10,937.50	7,583.22
	Patrik SJÖLAND	Swe	70	71	73	70	284	0	10,937.50	7,583.22
	Nick DOUGHERTY	Eng	72	67	74	71	284	0	10,937.50	7,583.22
	Stuart MANLEY	Wal	72	71	68	73	284	0	10,937.50	7,583.22
34	Simon DYSON	Eng	71	64	78	72	285	1	8,875.00	6,153.24
	Henrik NYSTROM	Swe	70	68	73	74	285	1	8,875.00	6,153.24
	Jean-François LUCQUIN	Fr	72	71	76	66	285	1	8,875.00	6,153.24
	Kenneth FERRIE	Eng	71	71	74	69	285	1	8,875.00	6,153.24
	David GILFORD	Eng	71	67	74	73	285	1	8,875.00	6,153.24
	Klas ERIKSSON	Swe	70	71	71	73	285	1	8,875.00	6,153.24
	Gary MURPHY	Ire	69	68	73	75	285	1	8,875.00	6,153.24
41	Mark FOSTER	Eng	73	70	76	67	286	2	7,500.00	5,199.92
	Damien MCGRANE	Ire	70	70	78	68	286	2	7,500.00	5,199.92
	Jan-Are LARSEN	Nor	74	69	76	67	286	2	7,500.00	5,199.92
	Raymond RUSSELL	Scot	70	70	76	70	286	2	7,500.00	5,199.92
45	David GRIFFITHS	Eng	74	69	76	68	287	3	6,250.00	4,333.27
	Mads VIBE-HASTRUP	Den	67	70	76	74	287	3	6,250.00	4,333.27
	Sam LITTLE	Eng	72	68	74	73	287	3	6,250.00	4,333.27
	Peter HANSON	Swe	74	70	76	67	287	3	6,250.00	4,333.27
	Phillip ARCHER	Eng	73	71	70	73	287	3	6,250.00	4,333.27
	Hernan REY	Arg	77	66	75	69	287	3	6,250.00	4,333.27
51	Johan AXGREN	Swe	72	70	73	73	288	4	4,625.00	3,206.62
	Søren KJELDSEN	Den	73	68	76	71	288	4	4,625.00	3,206.62
	Garry HOUSTON	Wal	72	72	75	69	288	4	4,625.00	3,206.62
	José Manuel LARA	Sp	74	70	72	72	288	4	4,625.00	3,206.62
	Philip GOLDING	Eng	73	69	73	73	288	4	4,625.00	3,206.62
	John BICKERTON	Eng	71	72	73	72	288	4	4,625.00	3,206.62
	Van PHILLIPS	Eng	73	69	74	72	288	4	4,625.00	3,206.62
58	Simon WAKEFIELD	Eng	72	69	76	72	289	5	3,562.50	2,469.96
	Martin MARITZ	SA	76	66	74	73	289	5	3,562.50	2,469.96
	Richard BLAND	Eng	72	71	77	69	289	5	3,562.50	2,469.96
	Peter LAWRIE	Ire	72	70	77	70	289	5	3,562.50	2,469.96
62	Bradley DREDGE	Wal	73	69	76	72	290	6	3,250.00	2,253.30
63	David CARTER	Eng	72	71	75	73	291	7	2,875.00	1,993.30
	Matthew BLACKEY	Eng	73	71	76	71	291	7	2,875.00	1,993.30
	Ben MASON	Eng	69	74	77	71	291	7	2,875.00	1,993.30
	Sam TORRANCE	Scot	73	71	74	73	291	7	2,875.00	1,993.30
	Gabriel CANIZARES	Sp	75	68	74	74	291	7	2,875.00	1,993.30
68	Sven STRÜVER	Ger	72	72	77	71	292	8	2,260.00	1,566.91
	Niki ZITNY	Aut	74	70	77	71	292	8	2,260.00	1,566.91
	Stephen GALLACHER	Scot	70	68	80	74	292	8	2,260.00	1,566.91
	Johan SKOLD	Swe	75	68	79	70	292	8	2,260.00	1,566.91
72	Markus BRIER	Aut	65	79	77	72	293	9	1,870.50	1,296.86
	Fredrik HENGE	Swe	72	72	76	73	293	9	1,870.50	1,296.86
74	André CRUSE	SA	73	71	77	75	296	12	1,866.00	1,293.74
75	Sergio RIBEIRO	Port	74	70	81	75	300	16	1,863.00	1,291.66

Total Prize Fund
€1,259,350 £873,132

win the 2005 Estoril Open de Portugal Caixa Geral de Depositos as Portuguese Jose-Filipe. He shared the lead with Broadhurst.

As if sympathising with the adjacent tournament on the US PGA Tour, the BellSouth Classic, that had been bedevilled by bad weather, Saturday was the day the rains came, too, to Quinta da Marinha. Broadhurst did not quite finish his third round but when he did the next morning, he found himself trailing the leader, the 1999 Open Champion Paul Lawrie, by two strokes.

The Scot, anxious to continue his rehabilitation after a thin time over the past couple of seasons, had taken a chance and finished off in the dark the night before. Lima was no creature of the night, though, and he and Lane left it to the next morning to finish just one behind.

The final round began looking like a foregone conclusion but ended a two-gone one. In an often calamitous finale and one for which no script could surely have been penned, Lawrie let it slip at the 17th to forfeit his chance of his first victory since The 2002 Celtic Manor Wales Open. Next Lane lost his way along the 18th and went from winning to losing in a heartbeat.

It had taken Broadhurst ten years to get back to the top, just as it had Lane the previous year in The Daily Telegraph Damovo British Masters at the Marriott Forest of Arden. The closing holes in Portugal were hit or miss and Broadhurst was definitely the hit. Wasn't he now glad he'd stayed around and given it his best shot?

Norman Dabell

Sam Little

Madeira Island Open Caixa Geral de Depositos

Madeira, Portugal
April 7-10 • 2005

Santo da Serra

Par	Yards	Metres
72	6826	6241

1	**Robert-Jan DERKSEN**	**275**	**-13**
2	Andrew MCLARDY	277	-11
	Gary ORR	277	-11
4	David HIGGINS	278	-10
5	Tom WHITEHOUSE	280	-8
6	John BICKERTON	281	-7
7	Andrew COLTART	282	-6
	Mikko ILONEN	282	-6
	Kyron SULLIVAN	282	-6
	Simon WAKEFIELD	282	-6

Round One   Round Two   Round Three   Round Four

EUROPEAN TOUR ORDER OF MERIT
(After 15 tournaments)

Pos		€
1	**Ernie ELS**	**555,286.23**
2	Retief GOOSEN	428,297.00
3	Ian POULTER	344,167.30
4	Miguel Angel JIMÉNEZ	340,730.28
5	Stephen DODD	326,231.57
6	Nick O'HERN	311,264.30
7	Niclas FASTH	262,642.00
8	Nick DOUGHERTY	245,384.73
9	Henrik STENSON	244,629.59
10	Thomas BJÖRN	243,194.67

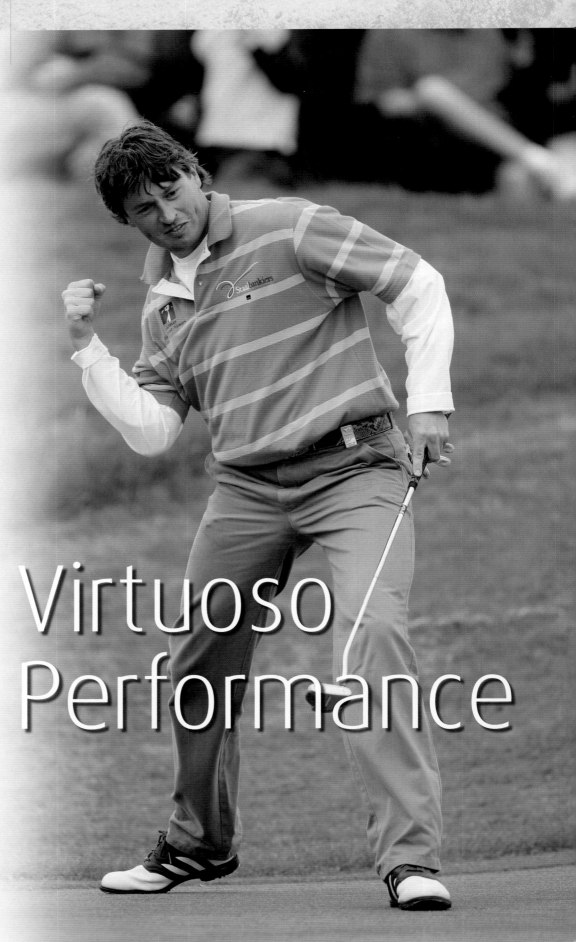

Virtuoso Performance

Antonio Vivaldi's most famous concerto, The Four Seasons, would have made the perfect musical accompaniment to the 2005 Madeira Island Open Caixa Geral de Depositos. Vivaldi, the famous Italian Baroque composer, could easily have drawn the inspiration for his masterpiece by spending four days atop any of the stunning vantage points around Santo da Serra, which is beautifully positioned more than 2000 feet above sea level amongst the mountain ranges of the Portuguese island of Madeira.

Not only would Vivaldi have experienced the spring, summer, autumn and winter seasons he so vividly portrays in his classic violin works, he would also have witnessed some of the most breathtaking views in Europe. Those four seasons all played a part in the tournament where, ultimately, Robert-Jan Derksen of The Netherlands secured his second victory on The European Tour.

The tournament began and ended in warm sunshine, with Thursday's opening round blossoming into the perfect summer's day. The light shone particularly brightly for Scotland's Andrew Coltart, who got proceedings underway in astounding fashion when he holed a magnificent six iron from 226 yards for a stunning albatross two at his second hole of the day, the par five 11th.

As summer drew to a close on Thursday evening, and the sound of Vivaldi's autumn strings were heard in the distance, New Zealand's Stephen Scahill and Welshman Kyron Sullivan shared the lead on eight under par after posting a pair of impressive 64s.

By Friday morning, autumn had truly arrived, and as the day progressed you could feel the temperature drop and the chill of winter appear in the air as clouds began to cover the mountain tops, forcing a suspension of play during round two.

The harsh winter had set in by Saturday and, as the players fought against the sternest of the elements in the form of cold driving wind and icy rain, you could almost hear Vivaldi's

Gary Orr

Andrew Coltart

David Higgins

Madeira Island Open Caixa Geral de Depositos

Madeira, Portugal
April 7-10 • 2005

Andrew McLardy

violins and strings battling for supremacy in the darkest of his Four Seasons.

Thankfully winter drew to a close as Sunday morning, and the final round, dawned in crisp sunshine, turning thoughts to the spring allegro. Sullivan was still in a share of the lead – this time alongside South African Andrew McLardy – with Derksen just one shot behind in a tie for third place with Scotland's Gary Orr.

As the day progressed and the temperatures rose, Derksen and Orr established a two way tussle for the title. Both players were looking to restore former European Tour glories, Derksen having won the 2003 Dubai Desert Classic and Orr the 2000 Victor Chandler British Masters and the Algarve Portuguese Open.

They provided an intriguing battle and by the time Derksen reached the 18th tee in

"I have been to Santo da Serra seven times and I would go so far as to say that of all the improvements on all the golf courses that the Tour make, we have seen the biggest and best improvements here. The fairways are magnificent – probably some of the best we play on all year" – Andrew Coltart

Graeme Storm

Final Results

Pos	Name		Rd1	Rd2	Rd3	Rd4	Total		€	£
1	Robert-Jan DERKSEN	NL	67	70	71	67	275	-13	100,000.00	68,636.06
2	Andrew MCLARDY	SA	67	71	69	70	277	-11	52,110.00	35,766.25
	Gary ORR	Scot	69	70	69	69	277	-11	52,110.00	35,766.25
4	David HIGGINS	Ire	69	66	74	69	278	-10	30,000.00	20,590.82
5	Tom WHITEHOUSE	Eng	71	69	71	69	280	-8	25,440.00	17,461.01
6	John BICKERTON	Eng	66	69	74	72	281	-7	21,000.00	14,413.57
7	Andrew COLTART	Scot	68	71	72	71	282	-6	14,610.00	10,027.73
	Simon WAKEFIELD	Eng	68	71	73	70	282	-6	14,610.00	10,027.73
	Mikko ILONEN	Fin	67	74	69	72	282	-6	14,610.00	10,027.73
	Kyron SULLIVAN	Wal	64	70	73	75	282	-6	14,610.00	10,027.73
11	David DRYSDALE	Scot	70	73	70	70	283	-5	10,680.00	7,330.33
	Knud STORGAARD	Den	69	74	71	69	283	-5	10,680.00	7,330.33
13	Jarmo SANDELIN	Swe	71	72	74	67	284	-4	8,844.00	6,070.17
	Rolf MUNTZ	NL	70	67	73	74	284	-4	8,844.00	6,070.17
	Michael KIRK	SA	68	76	71	69	284	-4	8,844.00	6,070.17
	Richard MCEVOY	Eng	65	74	73	72	284	-4	8,844.00	6,070.17
	Stuart MANLEY	Wal	70	70	72	72	284	-4	8,844.00	6,070.17
18	Matthew MORRIS	Eng	65	74	76	70	285	-3	7,335.00	5,034.46
	Graeme STORM	Eng	74	69	74	68	285	-3	7,335.00	5,034.46
	Van PHILLIPS	Eng	70	69	70	76	285	-3	7,335.00	5,034.46
	Stephen SCAHILL	NZ	64	73	72	76	285	-3	7,335.00	5,034.46
22	Henrik NYSTROM	Swe	72	72	71	71	286	-2	5,970.00	4,097.57
	Erol SIMSEK	Ger	70	74	69	73	286	-2	5,970.00	4,097.57
	Richard FINCH	Eng	72	70	72	72	286	-2	5,970.00	4,097.57
	Kariem BARAKA	Ger	68	72	73	73	286	-2	5,970.00	4,097.57
	Roger CHAPMAN	Eng	69	75	73	69	286	-2	5,970.00	4,097.57
	Mark FOSTER	Eng	70	69	76	71	286	-2	5,970.00	4,097.57
	Sven STRÜVER	Ger	70	72	72	72	286	-2	5,970.00	4,097.57
	Jean VAN DE VELDE	Fr	68	72	72	74	286	-2	5,970.00	4,097.57
	Francesco MOLINARI	It	69	71	74	72	286	-2	5,970.00	4,097.57
	Nicolas COLSAERTS	Bel	67	74	73	72	286	-2	5,970.00	4,097.57
32	Robert KARLSSON	Swe	70	69	79	69	287	-1	4,525.71	3,106.27
	Ian GARBUTT	Eng	73	71	71	72	287	-1	4,525.71	3,106.27
	Magnus P. ATLEVI	Swe	69	68	79	71	287	-1	4,525.71	3,106.27
	Fredrik HENGE	Swe	70	72	74	71	287	-1	4,525.71	3,106.27
	Gregory BOURDY	Fr	66	77	75	69	287	-1	4,525.71	3,106.27
	Mads VIBE-HASTRUP	Den	69	71	75	72	287	-1	4,525.71	3,106.27
	Markus BRIER	Aut	66	76	68	77	287	-1	4,525.71	3,106.27
39	Benn BARHAM	Eng	67	74	76	71	288	0	3,780.00	2,594.44
	Simon HURD	Eng	71	73	70	74	288	0	3,780.00	2,594.44
	Gordon BRAND JNR	Scot	72	72	70	74	288	0	3,780.00	2,594.44
	Gary EMERSON	Eng	66	77	70	75	288	0	3,780.00	2,594.44
	Peter BAKER	Eng	70	74	75	69	288	0	3,780.00	2,594.44
44	Joakim BÄCKSTRÖM	Swe	72	69	73	75	289	1	3,000.00	2,059.08
	Marc CAYEUX	Zim	69	72	73	75	289	1	3,000.00	2,059.08
	Gary MURPHY	Ire	68	71	78	72	289	1	3,000.00	2,059.08
	Santiago LUNA	Sp	69	71	72	77	289	1	3,000.00	2,059.08
	Shaun P WEBSTER	Eng	68	72	75	74	289	1	3,000.00	2,059.08
	Martin ERLANDSSON	Swe	72	72	74	71	289	1	3,000.00	2,059.08
	Lee S JAMES	Eng	68	70	75	76	289	1	3,000.00	2,059.08
	Roope KAKKO	Fin	70	72	75	72	289	1	3,000.00	2,059.08
52	Gary CLARK	Eng	73	68	78	71	290	2	2,400.00	1,647.22
	Paul DWYER	Eng	71	71	77	71	290	2	2,400.00	1,647.22
54	Marco RUIZ	Par	67	75	71	78	291	3	2,100.00	1,441.36
	Miguel Angel MARTIN	Sp	67	72	71	81	291	3	2,100.00	1,441.36
	Jesus Maria ARRUTI	Sp	72	70	71	78	291	3	2,100.00	1,441.36
57	Peter LAWRIE	Ire	69	75	76	72	292	4	1,800.00	1,235.45
	Garry HOUSTON	Wal	67	73	79	73	292	4	1,800.00	1,235.45
	Matthew BLACKEY	Eng	72	72	74	74	292	4	1,800.00	1,235.45
60	Gareth PADDISON	NZ	68	75	76	74	293	5	1,530.00	1,050.13
	Sam WALKER	Eng	75	69	77	72	293	5	1,530.00	1,050.13
	Johan AXGREN	Swe	70	71	79	73	293	5	1,530.00	1,050.13
	Massimo FLORIOLI	It	69	71	75	78	293	5	1,530.00	1,050.13
	Andrew MARSHALL	Eng	74	70	75	74	293	5	1,530.00	1,050.13
	Sam LITTLE	Eng	70	71	74	78	293	5	1,530.00	1,050.13
66	Nuno CAMPINO	Port	74	69	75	76	294	6	1,290.00	885.41
	André CRUSE	SA	69	73	75	77	294	6	1,290.00	885.41
68	Robert COLES	Eng	70	73	76	76	295	7	1,085.00	744.70
	Titch MOORE	SA	72	70	77	76	295	7	1,085.00	744.70
	Kalle BRINK	Swe	75	69	77	74	295	7	1,085.00	744.70
	Stuart LITTLE	Eng	68	71	76	80	295	7	1,085.00	744.70
72	Raul BALLESTEROS	Sp	71	73	73	79	296	8	897.00	615.67
73	Fernando ROCA	Sp	72	71	78	76	297	9	894.00	613.61
74	António SOBRINHO	Port	72	71	78	77	298	10	891.00	611.55
75	Andrea MAESTRONI	It	68	71	79	81	299	11	888.00	609.49
76	Alvaro SALTO	Sp	72	69	79	80	300	12	885.00	607.43
77	Raymond RUSSELL	Scot	70	73	81	77	301	13	880.50	604.34
	Robert ROCK	Eng	75	69	73	84	301	13	880.50	604.34
79	Julien CLÉMENT	Swi	71	68	77	86	302	14	876.00	601.25
80	Duarte FREITAS	Port	73	71	81	82	307	19	873.00	599.19

Total Prize Fund
€608,870 £417,900

---

a tie for the lead with Orr on 12 under par, he knew that a birdie at the last hole of the tournament would apply the pressure on the Scotsman, who was in the final group behind with McLardy and Sullivan.

Derksen proceeded to do just that, sinking a testing 15 foot putt to set the seal on a fine final round of five under par 67. His four round aggregate of 13 under par 275 to win in the end by two shots from McLardy and Orr, ensured he became the first player from The Netherlands to record multiple wins on The European Tour International Schedule, as well as registering the 133rd European Tour win by a former Challenge Tour player.

"Obviously I am delighted to have won," smiled Derksen after collecting the winner's cheque for €100,000 (£68,636). "My birdie on the 18th was excellent and won the tournament for me. I have been coming to Madeira the past eight years and I really like the place. I felt confident and comfortable coming here but the win also means a lot because I am now exempt on Tour until the end of the 2006 season."

With that, Derksen drew the curtain on a virtuoso performance for which Vivaldi himself would have been proud.

Michael Gibbons

75

Masters Tournament

Augusta, Georgia, USA
April 7-10 • 2005

Augusta National

Par	Yards	Metres
72	7290	6665

1	**Tiger WOODS**	276	-12	
2	Chris DiMARCO	276	-12	
3	Luke DONALD	283	-5	
	Retief GOOSEN	283	-5	
5	Mark HENSBY	284	-4	
	Trevor IMMELMAN	284	-4	
	Rodney PAMPLING	284	-4	
	Vijay SINGH	284	-4	
	Mike WEIR	284	-4	
10	Phil MICKELSON	285	-3	

Round One Round Two Round Three Round Four

EUROPEAN TOUR ORDER OF MERIT
(After 16 tournaments)

Pos		€	
1	**Retief GOOSEN**	743,122.60	
2	Ernie ELS	573,198.72	
3	Luke DONALD	410,427.61	
4	Miguel Angel JIMÉNEZ	376,826.66	
5	Ian POULTER	374,889.93	
6	Nick O'HERN	330,805.20	
7	Stephen DODD	326,231.57	
8	Thomas BJÖRN	290,961.31	
9	David HOWELL	267,495.10	
10	Trevor IMMELMAN	262,662.78	

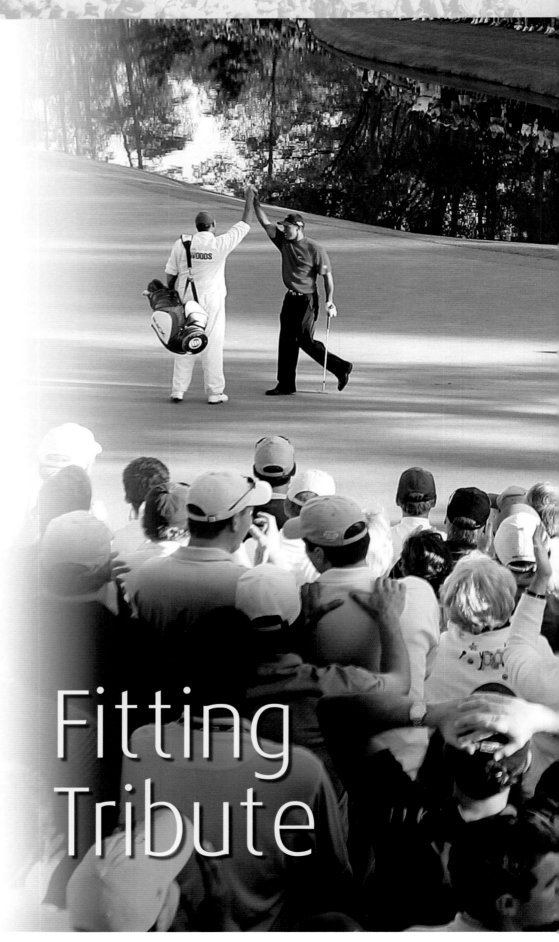

Fitting
Tribute

Masters Tournament

Augusta, Georgia, USA
April 7-10 • 2005

When the time comes to assess the career of Tiger Woods, golfing historians will surely conclude that his ninth Major Championship victory, at the 69th Masters Tournament, was neither first in terms of performance or significance. After all, we are talking here about a talent so unique that he has won Majors by margins as great as 12 and 15 strokes; as well as being the only professional to win all four of golf's great championships in a row.

Darren Clarke

But it will be remembered for the drama of a finish that produced a stroke people will talk about as long as the tournament is played; as the hour of redemption following heavy criticism of changes to Woods's swing; but most of all, as a fitting tribute to a sick father, who instilled in his son the qualities of fortitude and indomitability that ultimately prevailed in claiming his fourth Green Jacket before his 30th birthday.

Chris DiMarco, too, will remember with pride his full contribution to the stirring last afternoon, while two European Tour newcomers to the Masters Tournament arena, Luke Donald and David Howell, are probably still smiling now.

Three players, Gene Sarazen, Horton Smith and Fuzzy Zoeller, have all won at Augusta National in their first attempt. That is the context in which Donald's share of third place alongside Retief Goosen should be placed, achieved with a wondrous finish of two eagles and two birdies in his last eight holes. As for fellow Englishman Howell, he finished a creditable tied 11th to earn a return trip in 2006.

This edition of the Masters Tournament took place against a heavy backdrop as far as Woods was concerned. Swing changes had coincided with a run of ten Majors without a win, and in a society that demands immediate results, that meant criticism at every turn.

"*The whole aura of Augusta National is totally amazing. You stand up at the top of the hill and look out and it is just wonderful. The crowds there are very knowledgeable and you get an echoey sound through the valley when there are cheers, which gives a great atmosphere. It is a special place because I watched it so much growing up as a youngster and I am pleased to say it is everything I thought it would be*" – Luke Donald

Trevor Immelman

Luke Donald

When it was over, when the gallant DiMarco had finally been subdued with a typically pitiless birdie at the first extra hole, it was hardly surprising that Woods regarded the victory as validation of his decision to change.

What was more shocking, however, were the tears at the closing ceremony. Woods regards Major wins as his rightful reward for talent and hard work, so when they arrive the pleasure is never so unexpected as to precipitate tears of joy.

But in dedicating the win to his seriously ill father, the 29 year old American displayed a human frailty his fellow players rarely see in competition. "I didn't expect to cry, I didn't know what was happening, but it just shows the place my father holds in my life," he admitted later.

Indeed, if ever a victory could be said to be down to Earl Woods, this was it, for it was his

father who instilled in his son the "quitter never wins, and a winner never quits" mentality on his 13th birthday, when Tiger was pouting and whining in a tournament.

Earl took his son into a back room that day, and told him that he was a disgrace to himself, his family, and that pouting and whining was just another form of quitting. Legend has it that they did not speak for three days. Then son came to father and said: "Pop, I heard every word. It will never happen again."

It never has, of course, as he demonstrated on day one, stoically accepting a series of bizarre events, from putting into Rae's Creek at the 13th to watching a precision iron shot hit the flag at the first hole and rebound into a bunker, two occurrences which led to an opening 74.

A series of storms interrupted the flow of

Thomas Levet and son Gregoire

Over the course of 18 holes, you can see how far you've come, and how far the game can still take you.

United is proud to support the European Tour.

It's time to fly.® UNITED

www.unitedairlines.co.uk

A STAR ALLIANCE MEMBER ✷ ™

Vijay Singh

Final Results

Chris DiMarco

Jack Nicklaus

the tournament, but not Woods. He shot 66 in the second round and then a marvellous 65 that contained seven birdies in a row. Three strokes clear with a round to play, no-one expected anything other than him to make it nine wins out of nine when leading going into the final 18 holes of a Major. No-one, that is, apart from a gritty 37 year old New Yorker with a love of Augusta National.

DiMarco was ultimately undone by events beyond his control, a chip shot from Woods at the par three 16th that had skill, timing, and fate all rolled into one. Hopelessly out of position with his tee shot, Woods aimed his chip 20 feet left of the flag, using the contours of the green to bring the ball back towards the hole. For two full seconds it quivered on the lip. When it fell, the roars echoed down the halls of history.

Meanwhile, somewhere in Florida, a Golden Bear must have allowed himself a wry smile. After missing the halfway cut, Jack Nicklaus had tearfully announced this was his last Masters Tournament. Now, the man intent on staring down his record total of 18 Majors had marked the occasion by reaching the turn.

Like the best courses, the back nine will be harder for Woods but, armed with a new method, renewed belief, and the words of a wise father that will never be forgotten, we can be sure he will stride boldly on.

Derek Lawrenson
Daily Mail

Pos	Name		Rd1	Rd2	Rd3	Rd4	Total		€	£
1	Tiger WOODS	USA	74	66	65	71	276	-12	977,044.80	670,605.10
2	Chris DiMARCO	USA	67	67	74	68	276	-12	586,226.90	402,363.07
3	Retief GOOSEN	SA	71	75	70	67	283	-5	314,825.60	216,083.90
	Luke DONALD	Eng	68	77	69	69	283	-5	314,825.60	216,083.90
5	Trevor IMMELMAN	SA	73	73	65	73	284	-4	184,010.10	126,297.29
	Mike WEIR	Can	74	71	68	71	284	-4	184,010.10	126,297.29
	Vijay SINGH	Fiji	68	73	71	72	284	-4	184,010.10	126,297.29
	Rodney PAMPLING	Aus	73	71	70	70	284	-4	184,010.10	126,297.29
	Mark HENSBY	Aus	69	73	70	72	284	-4	184,010.10	126,297.29
10	Phil MICKELSON	USA	70	72	69	74	285	-3	146,556.70	100,590.75
11	Tim HERRON	USA	76	68	70	72	286	-2	130,272.60	89,413.99
	David HOWELL	Eng	72	69	76	69	286	-2	130,272.60	89,413.99
13	Thomas LEVET	Fr	71	75	68	73	287	-1	104,941.60	72,027.78
	Justin LEONARD	USA	75	71	70	71	287	-1	104,941.60	72,027.78
	Tom LEHMAN	USA	74	74	70	69	287	-1	104,941.60	72,027.78
	Ryan MOORE (Am)	USA	71	71	75	70	287	-1		
17	Chad CAMPBELL	USA	73	73	67	75	288	0	86,848.43	59,609.34
	Kirk TRIPLETT	USA	75	68	72	73	288	0	86,848.43	59,609.34
	Darren CLARKE	N.Ire	72	76	69	71	288	0	86,848.43	59,609.34
20	Scott VERPLANK	USA	72	75	69	73	289	1	65,787.69	45,154.08
	Jeff MAGGERT	USA	74	74	72	69	289	1	65,787.69	45,154.08
	Stewart CINK	USA	72	72	74	71	289	1	65,787.69	45,154.08
	Jerry KELLY	USA	75	70	73	71	289	1	65,787.69	45,154.08
	Bernhard LANGER	Ger	74	74	70	71	289	1	65,787.69	45,154.08
25	Craig PARRY	Aus	72	75	69	74	290	2	47,766.64	32,785.14
	Thomas BJÖRN	Den	71	67	71	81	290	2	47,766.64	32,785.14
	Joe OGILVIE	USA	74	73	73	70	290	2	47,766.64	32,785.14
28	Jim FURYK	USA	76	67	74	74	291	3	41,795.80	28,686.99
29	Steve FLESCH	USA	76	70	70	76	292	4	39,353.20	27,010.49
	Kenny PERRY	USA	76	68	71	77	292	4	39,353.20	27,010.49
31	Miguel Angel JIMÉNEZ	Sp	74	74	73	72	293	5	36,096.38	24,775.13
	Mark O'MEARA	USA	74	74	72	75	293	5	36,096.38	24,775.13
33	Kyoung-Ju CHOI	Kor	73	72	76	73	294	6	30,722.63	21,086.80
	Ian POULTER	Eng	72	74	72	76	294	6	30,722.63	21,086.80
	Luke LIST (Am)	USA	77	69	78	70	294	6		
	Shingo KATAYAMA	Jpn	72	74	73	75	294	6	30,722.63	21,086.80
	Adam SCOTT	Aus	71	76	72	75	294	6	30,722.63	21,086.80
	Casey WITTENBERG	USA	72	72	74	76	294	6	30,722.63	21,086.80
39	Ryan PALMER	USA	70	74	74	77	295	7	24,968.92	17,137.68
	Tim CLARK	SA	74	74	72	75	295	7	24,968.92	17,137.68
	Todd HAMILTON	USA	77	70	71	77	295	7	24,968.92	17,137.68
	Fred COUPLES	USA	75	71	77	72	295	7	24,968.92	17,137.68
43	Stuart APPLEBY	Aus	69	76	72	79	296	8	21,712.11	14,902.34
	Jonathan KAYE	USA	72	74	76	74	296	8	21,712.11	14,902.34
45	Stephen AMES	T&T	73	74	75	75	297	9	19,540.90	13,412.10
	Nick O'HERN	Aus	72	72	76	77	297	9	19,540.90	13,412.10
47	Ernie ELS	SA	75	73	78	72	298	10	17,912.49	12,294.43
48	Jay HAAS	USA	76	71	76	78	301	13	16,826.88	11,549.31
49	Chris RILEY	USA	71	77	78	78	304	16	15,741.28	10,804.20
50	Craig STADLER	USA	75	73	79	79	306	18	14,872.79	10,208.10

Total Prize Fund
€5,320,690 £3,651,912

Jazztel Open de España en Andalucia

Cadiz, Spain
April 14-17 • 2005

San Roque Club

Par	Yards	Metres
72	7103	6494

1	**Peter HANSON**	**280**	**-8**
2	Peter GUSTAFSSON	280	-8
3	Peter LAWRIE	283	-5
	Hennie OTTO	283	-5
5	Stephen DODD	285	-3
	Robert KARLSSON	285	-3
7	Miguel Angel MARTIN	286	-2
8	Raphaël JACQUELIN	287	-1
	Simon KHAN	287	-1
	Paul McGINLEY	287	-1
	Steven O'HARA	287	-1

Round One · Round Two · Round Three · Round Four

EUROPEAN TOUR ORDER OF MERIT
(After 17 tournaments)

Pos		€	
1	**Retief GOOSEN**	**743,122.60**	
2	Ernie ELS	573,198.72	
3	Luke DONALD	410,427.61	
4	Stephen DODD	390,086.57	
5	Miguel Angel JIMÉNEZ	376,826.66	
6	Ian POULTER	374,889.93	
7	Nick O'HERN	330,805.20	
8	Peter HANSON	291,382.55	
9	Thomas BJÖRN	290,961.31	
10	David HOWELL	267,495.10	

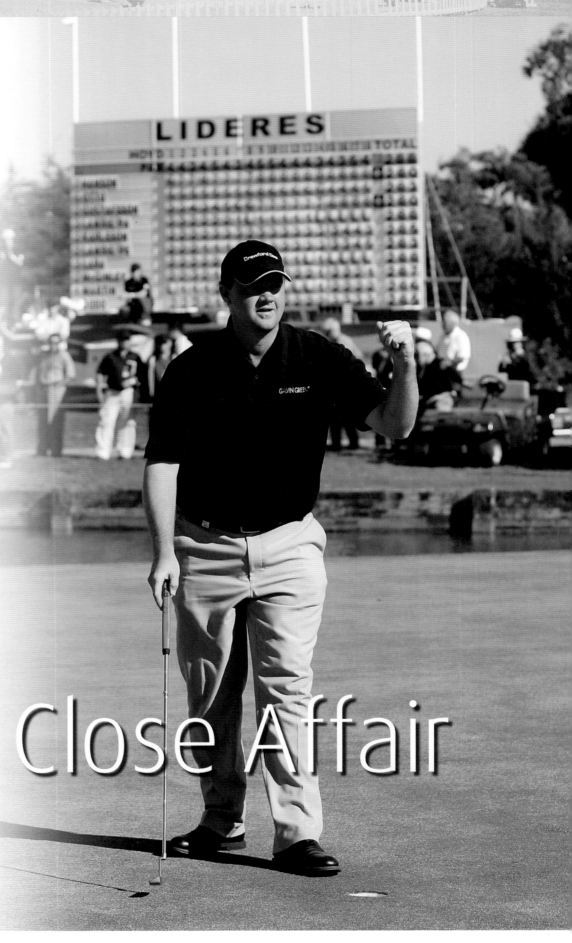

Close Affair

S o, what can we say about Freidrich Nietzsche's existentialist musings on Ecce Homo: How What One Becomes What One Is? Well, not a lot, actually, so let's talk about a golf tournament instead.

The event under discussion is the Jazztel Open de España en Andalucia and involves at centre stage a man with a collection of funny hats and another with a more conventional taste in headgear. The one with the eccentric line in cranial protection came second. The other one won. Which all goes to prove that charming, if very silly examples of the milliner's craft, are not reasons, in and of themselves, to ensure victory in one of Europe's oldest and most distinguished National Open Championships.

Ask Peter Gustafsson. He was the one with the hats and he lost on the first hole of a sudden-death play-off to Peter Hanson, his Swedish compatriot. It was not placed on record in the aftermath of his defeat what Gustafsson proposed to do about the hats. The best informed guess was he would stick

with them. He does love those dinky little fabric flower pots he sports.

One of the most interesting, and recurring, curiosities throughout the tournament was that Gustafsson's skull remained in full and constant contact with what he was wearing above his eyes and ears. It would have been entirely more in line with what was happening out there had it been whipped off and got itself blown off towards Gibraltar.

What it would have done to Gustafsson's psyche had the unthinkable occurred does not bear lengthy consideration. But no matter. It didn't happen. It might well have done, though. Because, my, did it ever blow.

Citizens used to a British climate usually associate wind with dark clouds scudding

José Manuel Lara

Peter Gustafsson

Jazztel Open de España en Andalucia

Cadiz, Spain
April 14-17 • 2005

Jean Van de Velde

"I love this course. It's a beautiful place and it's really tough even without the wind. The greens were unbelievably good when we got here and have improved through the week. But the whole course has been in fantastic condition. Everybody associated with it should be proud of what they have created for us" – Peter Hanson

across an angry sky. Dirty weather is a gale's best friend. But on this April week on the Costa del Sol, the skies were clear blue and guileless, the sun beating down in the friendliest of manners, the very picture of meteorological probity. So why somebody up there decided that they would get frisky and cause such inconveniences is anybody's guess.

Whatever, it blew many a score to smithereens and temporarily broke a few hearts on the immaculately prepared San Roque course. For instance, on the first day, the exalted threesome of Paul Broadhurst, Paul Lawrie and Paul McGinley, Ryder Cup players all, were a combined eight over par after only three holes.

However, that is to dwell, in the greater scheme of things, on irrelevancies, although McGinley, bless his indefatigable Dublin heart, did recover to finish in a share of eighth place. We must return to more significant and much weightier matters, such as the man with the hat and his pal.

Mark Foster

If local knowledge is a factor, which by all that is right and proper it ought to be, Gustafsson should have strolled it. He lives in Malaga, 85 miles from the tournament venue, and has an intimate knowledge of the course - he had won The European Tour Qualifying School Finals there the previous November - and had played it, by his own estimation, not less than 70 and probably closer to 100 times before the tournament.

He demonstrated that fact, too, by producing a round of 66, jointly the best of the last day, in the final round while Hanson, who had led him by five strokes overnight, put in a solid, if slightly staid, 71 to leave them locked on eight under par 280.

By no more than an inch was the affair decided. The combatants made errors of various degrees of magnitude on the play-off hole, the 18th, Hanson putting his second shot on the bank of a bunker left of the green while Gustafsson hooked his second 60 feet wide, also to the left.

Gustafsson did as well as any human could to put the ball 12 feet past the flag from a horrid lie, but Hanson did even better, his cute chip leaving his ball no more than two feet from the hole. Gustafsson's brave, bold putt lipped out and Hanson made no mistake.

It was the winner's maiden victory on The European Tour and no matter how many more he might win in his career, none will seem any sweeter.

Hanson said afterwards that he would be buying dinner that night, for which Gustafsson, hat intact, was duly grateful. Talk about Ecce Homo. For these precious few moments, the pleasant young chap from Trelleborg knew that he had become what he was, all right.

Mel Webb
The Times

Peter Lawrie

Final Results

Pos	Name		Rd1	Rd2	Rd3	Rd4	Total		€	£
1	Peter HANSON	Swe	70	68	71	71	280	-8	275,000.00	190,614.82
2	Peter GUSTAFSSON	Swe	70	69	75	66	280	-8	183,330.00	127,074.24
3	Peter LAWRIE	Ire	71	70	73	69	283	-5	92,895.00	64,389.69
	Hennie OTTO	SA	71	71	69	72	283	-5	92,895.00	64,389.69
5	Robert KARLSSON	Swe	72	71	71	71	285	-3	63,855.00	44,260.76
	Stephen DODD	Wal	74	73	72	66	285	-3	63,855.00	44,260.76
7	Miguel Angel MARTIN	Sp	71	72	72	71	286	-2	49,500.00	34,310.67
8	Raphaël JACQUELIN	Fr	73	71	74	69	287	-1	35,392.50	24,532.13
	Paul MCGINLEY	Ire	76	70	72	69	287	-1	35,392.50	24,532.13
	Simon KHAN	Eng	73	73	72	69	287	-1	35,392.50	24,532.13
	Steven O'HARA	Scot	70	75	74	68	287	-1	35,392.50	24,532.13
12	Ian GARBUTT	Eng	72	74	73	69	288	0	25,542.00	17,704.30
	Paul LAWRIE	Scot	72	72	69	75	288	0	25,542.00	17,704.30
	José Manuel LARA	Sp	73	72	68	75	288	0	25,542.00	17,704.30
	David GILFORD	Eng	75	71	70	72	288	0	25,542.00	17,704.30
	Sam LITTLE	Eng	74	70	74	70	288	0	25,542.00	17,704.30
17	Stuart LITTLE	Eng	72	74	74	69	289	1	20,955.00	14,524.85
	Damien MCGRANE	Ire	73	74	69	73	289	1	20,955.00	14,524.85
	Sebastian FERNANDEZ	Arg	73	72	70	74	289	1	20,955.00	14,524.85
	Francois DELAMONTAGNE	Fr	73	72	75	69	289	1	20,955.00	14,524.85
21	Stephen GALLACHER	Scot	73	75	75	67	290	2	16,912.50	11,722.81
	Jamie DONALDSON	Wal	74	68	74	74	290	2	16,912.50	11,722.81
	Martin MARITZ	SA	72	73	74	71	290	2	16,912.50	11,722.81
	David GRIFFITHS	Eng	77	68	73	72	290	2	16,912.50	11,722.81
	David PARK	Wal	72	72	73	73	290	2	16,912.50	11,722.81
	Jarmo SANDELIN	Swe	72	72	78	68	290	2	16,912.50	11,722.81
	Søren KJELDSEN	Den	72	76	68	74	290	2	16,912.50	11,722.81
	Jean-Francois REMESY	Fr	75	73	71	71	290	2	16,912.50	11,722.81
	Andrew MARSHALL	Eng	72	71	75	72	290	2	16,912.50	11,722.81
	Nicolas COLSAERTS	Bel	77	69	73	71	290	2	16,912.50	11,722.81
31	Mark FOSTER	Eng	72	72	74	73	291	3	13,035.00	9,035.14
	Johan AXGREN	Swe	72	74	73	72	291	3	13,035.00	9,035.14
	Adam MEDNICK	Swe	72	74	71	74	291	3	13,035.00	9,035.14
	Jonathan LOMAS	Eng	73	74	71	73	291	3	13,035.00	9,035.14
	Carlos DEL CORRAL	Sp	74	73	72	72	291	3	13,035.00	9,035.14
	Oliver WILSON	Eng	75	72	74	70	291	3	13,035.00	9,035.14
37	Diego BORREGO	Sp	70	73	77	72	292	4	11,220.00	7,777.08
	David LYNN	Eng	74	71	76	71	292	4	11,220.00	7,777.08
	Jose-Filipe LIMA	Port	73	71	73	75	292	4	11,220.00	7,777.08
	Carl SUNESON	Sp	76	72	74	70	292	4	11,220.00	7,777.08
41	Andrea MAESTRONI	It	72	76	73	72	293	5	9,570.00	6,633.40
	José Manuel CARRILES	Sp	72	75	74	72	293	5	9,570.00	6,633.40
	Steve WEBSTER	Eng	79	69	75	70	293	5	9,570.00	6,633.40
	Graeme STORM	Eng	73	70	77	73	293	5	9,570.00	6,633.40
	David DRYSDALE	Scot	74	73	74	72	293	5	9,570.00	6,633.40
	Alfredo GARCIA	Sp	75	72	71	75	293	5	9,570.00	6,633.40
47	Fernando ROCA	Sp	72	75	75	72	294	6	7,920.00	5,489.71
	Ben MASON	Eng	72	75	75	72	294	6	7,920.00	5,489.71
	Titch MOORE	SA	75	73	71	75	294	6	7,920.00	5,489.71
	Marcel SIEM	Ger	73	75	70	76	294	6	7,920.00	5,489.71
51	Jean VAN DE VELDE	Fr	73	71	77	74	295	7	6,435.00	4,460.39
	Darren FICHARDT	SA	75	72	71	77	295	7	6,435.00	4,460.39
	Robert ROCK	Eng	73	75	77	70	295	7	6,435.00	4,460.39
	Mikko ILONEN	Fin	73	70	75	77	295	7	6,435.00	4,460.39
	Gregory BOURDY	Fr	73	68	74	80	295	7	6,435.00	4,460.39
56	Leif WESTERBERG	Swe	73	73	79	71	296	8	4,983.00	3,453.94
	Emanuele CANONICA	It	70	77	78	71	296	8	4,983.00	3,453.94
	Johan SKOLD	Swe	75	73	71	77	296	8	4,983.00	3,453.94
	Gary MURPHY	Ire	73	74	77	72	296	8	4,983.00	3,453.94
	Roger CHAPMAN	Eng	75	72	75	74	296	8	4,983.00	3,453.94
61	José RIVERO	Sp	70	72	76	79	297	9	4,290.00	2,973.59
	Andrew COLTART	Scot	73	75	74	75	297	9	4,290.00	2,973.59
	John BICKERTON	Eng	73	75	76	73	297	9	4,290.00	2,973.59
64	Oskar BERGMAN	Swe	71	74	76	77	298	10	3,877.50	2,687.67
	Malcolm MACKENZIE	Eng	72	74	78	74	298	10	3,877.50	2,687.67
66	David CARTER	Eng	74	74	74	78	300	12	3,630.00	2,516.12
67	Ricardo GONZALEZ	Arg	74	74	79	74	301	13	3,382.50	2,344.56
	Niclas FASTH	Swe	74	71	78	78	301	13	3,382.50	2,344.56
69	Fredrik HENGE	Swe	75	71	79	77	302	14	3,135.00	2,173.01
70	Raul BALLESTEROS	Sp	75	72	82	78	307	19	3,010.00	2,086.37
71	Santiago LUNA	Sp	70	77	82	79	308	20	2,475.00	1,715.53

Total Prize Fund
€1,652,480 £1,145,404

The San Roque Club

Johnnie Walker Classic

Beijing, China
April 21-24 • 2005

Pine Valley Golf Resort & Country Club

Par	Yards	Metres
72	7224	6604

1	Adam SCOTT	270	-18	
2	Retief GOOSEN	273	-15	
3	Michael CAMPBELL	275	-13	
	Henrik STENSON	275	-13	
	Richard STERNE	275	-13	
6	Ernie ELS	276	-12	
	Colin MONTGOMERIE	276	-12	
	Brett RUMFORD	276	-12	
9	Luke DONALD	277	-11	
10	Scott DRUMMOND	278	-10	
	Sergio GARCIA	278	-10	
	Santiago LUNA	278	-10	
	Steven O'HARA	278	-10	

Round One   Round Two   Round Three   Round Four

EUROPEAN TOUR ORDER OF MERIT
(After 18 tournaments)

Pos		€	
1	Retief GOOSEN	946,479.00	
2	Ernie ELS	628,108.47	
3	Adam SCOTT	523,209.16	
4	Luke DONALD	451,426.89	
5	Stephen DODD	390,086.57	
6	Miguel Angel JIMÉNEZ	379,721.45	
7	Ian POULTER	374,889.93	
8	Henrik STENSON	339,196.38	
9	Nick O'HERN	330,805.20	
10	Peter HANSON	305,887.88	

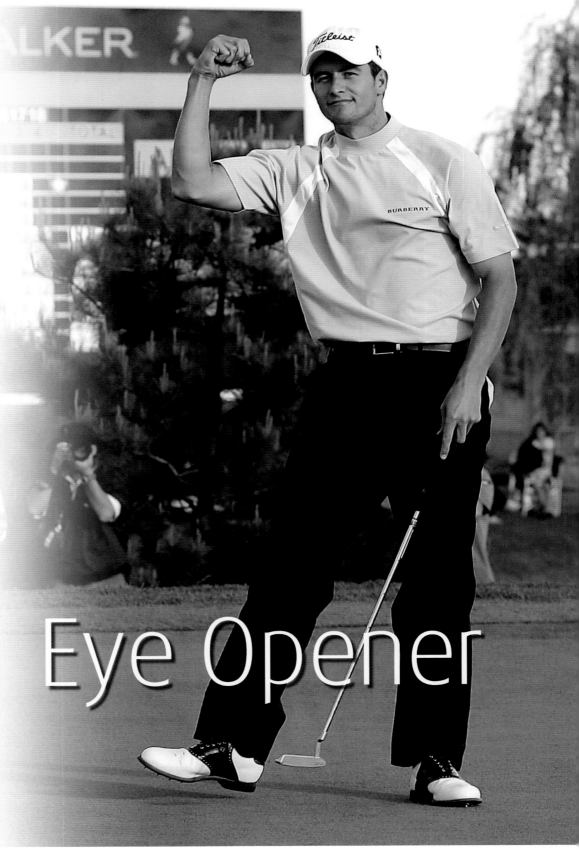

Eye Opener

Adam Scott is prone to blushing and it did not take too long to establish this fact if you were in his company in China. On only his second day in Beijing it was apparent the Australian was a hit. Questions from female reporters dominated his pre-tournament press conference and invariably they made reference to the 24 year old being "a very good looking young man". He tried hard, but he could not prevent his cheeks from flushing, although this was about as uncomfortable as it got for Scott in a week in which he led from start to finish to win the Johnnie Walker Classic.

It gave him a victory that may prove more valuable than most. He arrived at the Pine Valley Golf Resort & Country Club for the event, co-sanctioned between The European and Asian Tours, as the pin-up of the Chinese fans and did nothing to harm that reputation while, at the same time, enhancing his golfing credentials in the most exciting marketplace the game has at this time.

Big business is looking to invest in the country's vast potential at every opportunity and not surprisingly regards golf as the ideal tool to further its interests. This was the main reason for staging the Johnnie Walker Classic - Asia's most prestigious tournament - on the Chinese mainland for the first time.

Only around 300,000 people in the country are able to play golf at the moment, but no fewer than 15 million have expressed an interest in taking up the game. The vast majority of them fall into the marketing world's dream category – men under the age of 34.

These figures cannot be ignored by anyone involved in the sport; the administrators, sponsors or the players. It was why four of the World's Top Ten – Ernie Els, Sergio Garcia, Retief Goosen and Scott - were competing for the Johnnie Walker Classic and why so many leading players have China firmly placed in their course design portfolios.

On the lighter side there was also a rare opportunity for the players to be tourists as well as competitors during The European Tour's visit to the Chinese capital. At the official welcome dinner, Nick Faldo, wrapped up warmly against the bitterly cold wind, could be seen scrambling up onto The Great Wall, camera in hand, looking every inch the awestruck sightseer.

Scott was the same. "I couldn't believe it," he said. "I didn't expect the arid landscape as we were driving along, it was just like being in the country back home in Australia. Then we reached The Wall and drove for about an hour and it was there all along, snaking its way over the mountains. It was incredible."

Then there were the players who took themselves into central Beijing to see first hand the Forbidden City, Tiananmen Square and check out the abundant bargains available at the Silk Market.

Henrik Stenson

Richard Sterne

Luke Donald

Many of these trips were hastily arranged because the playing schedule was re-written as the weather restricted play to around three hours on the first day. But even that, like the week in general, was different. Rarely can play have been rendered impossible in such agreeable conditions. There was not a cloud in the skies over the course but golf was made impossible by the warm, dry, and gusting winds which swept across exposed greens.

Play was suspended with Scott halfway towards an extraordinary course record 63 which was completed the following morning in calmer conditions. Then, as the rest of the field tried to play catch-up, he headed off to walk The Great Wall. Maybe the trip was an inspiration or perhaps a mere metaphor.

The Wall had been erected to repel invaders from the north and it seemed Scott found the means to erect an impregnable barrier of his own around him on the leaderboard

"Pine Valley is a fantastic golf course and it is worthy of having a tournament like the Johnnie Walker Classic on it. It played very tough in the wind and with a little more rough, it would be a very difficult golf course all round. I'm sure we'll be back here somewhere down the line " – Adam Scott

Steven O'Hara

Final Results

Pos	Name		Rd1	Rd2	Rd3	Rd4	Total		€	£
1	Adam SCOTT	Aus	63	66	69	72	270	-18	305,049.30	208,330.00
2	Retief GOOSEN	SA	68	67	68	70	273	-15	203,356.40	138,880.00
3	Michael CAMPBELL	NZ	70	65	68	72	275	-13	94,566.79	64,583.33
	Richard STERNE	SA	68	66	70	71	275	-13	94,566.79	64,583.33
	Henrik STENSON	Swe	70	67	66	72	275	-13	94,566.79	64,583.33
6	Colin MONTGOMERIE	Scot	68	70	69	69	276	-12	54,909.75	37,500.00
	Ernie ELS	SA	71	67	69	69	276	-12	54,909.75	37,500.00
	Brett RUMFORD	Aus	71	71	65	69	276	-12	54,909.75	37,500.00
9	Luke DONALD	Eng	73	67	65	72	277	-11	40,999.28	28,000.00
10	Steven O'HARA	Scot	72	65	69	72	278	-10	32,808.57	22,406.25
	Santiago LUNA	Sp	70	70	66	72	278	-10	32,808.57	22,406.25
	Sergio GARCIA	Sp	67	71	67	73	278	-10	32,808.57	22,406.25
	Scott DRUMMOND	Scot	69	71	65	73	278	-10	32,808.57	22,406.25
14	Gary RUSNAK	USA	68	65	71	75	279	-9	27,454.88	18,750.00
	David PARK	Wal	70	68	67	74	279	-9	27,454.88	18,750.00
16	Terry PRICE	Aus	73	66	70	71	280	-8	24,206.05	16,531.25
	Thongchai JAIDEE	Thai	70	72	64	74	280	-8	24,206.05	16,531.25
	Simon DYSON	Eng	72	71	66	71	280	-8	24,206.05	16,531.25
	Gregory HAVRET	Fr	71	70	67	72	280	-8	24,206.05	16,531.25
20	Trevor IMMELMAN	SA	71	70	66	74	281	-7	21,292.78	14,541.67
	Unho PARK	Aus	70	71	69	71	281	-7	21,292.78	14,541.67
	Wade ORMSBY	Aus	71	67	68	75	281	-7	21,292.78	14,541.67
23	Gareth PADDISON	NZ	71	68	72	71	282	-6	18,486.28	12,625.00
	Terry PILKADARIS	Aus	70	73	67	72	282	-6	18,486.28	12,625.00
	Prayad MARKSAENG	Thai	68	71	66	77	282	-6	18,486.28	12,625.00
	Emanuele CANONICA	It	72	66	68	76	282	-6	18,486.28	12,625.00
	K J CHOI	Kor	72	65	70	75	282	-6	18,486.28	12,625.00
	Kenneth FERRIE	Eng	74	67	68	73	282	-6	18,486.28	12,625.00
	Anthony WALL	Eng	73	66	69	74	282	-6	18,486.28	12,625.00
30	David BRANSDON	Aus	69	70	71	73	283	-5	14,505.33	9,906.25
	Steve COLLINS	Aus	74	68	71	70	283	-5	14,505.33	9,906.25
	Maarten LAFEBER	NL	73	68	70	72	283	-5	14,505.33	9,906.25
	Peter HANSON	Swe	70	65	73	75	283	-5	14,505.33	9,906.25
	Thomas BJÖRN	Den	72	70	68	73	283	-5	14,505.33	9,906.25
	Søren HANSEN	Den	70	69	71	73	283	-5	14,505.33	9,906.25
	Martin DOYLE	Aus	74	68	69	72	283	-5	14,505.33	9,906.25
	Paul CASEY	Eng	72	68	70	73	283	-5	14,505.33	9,906.25
38	Simon WAKEFIELD	Eng	70	70	69	75	284	-4	10,981.95	7,500.00
	Ter-Chang WANG	Tpe	68	72	75	69	284	-4	10,981.95	7,500.00
	Christian CÉVAËR	Fr	74	69	72	69	284	-4	10,981.95	7,500.00
	Kim FELTON	Aus	71	70	69	74	284	-4	10,981.95	7,500.00
	Scott GARDINER	Aus	72	67	71	74	284	-4	10,981.95	7,500.00
	Miles TUNNICLIFF	Eng	68	71	70	75	284	-4	10,981.95	7,500.00
	Peter LAWRIE	Ire	69	71	69	75	284	-4	10,981.95	7,500.00
	Anders HANSEN	Den	72	70	71	71	284	-4	10,981.95	7,500.00
	Peter SENIOR	Aus	72	71	73	68	284	-4	10,981.95	7,500.00
	Richard MOIR	Aus	73	65	70	76	284	-4	10,981.95	7,500.00
48	James NITTIES	Aus	72	69	70	74	285	-3	8,236.46	5,625.00
	José Manuel LARA	Sp	72	69	69	75	285	-3	8,236.46	5,625.00
	Barry LANE	Eng	69	72	69	75	285	-3	8,236.46	5,625.00
	Ricky SCHMIDT	Aus	72	70	70	73	285	-3	8,236.46	5,625.00
	Wen-Ko LIN	Tpe	71	70	66	78	285	-3	8,236.46	5,625.00
53	Adam GROOM	Aus	70	71	74	71	286	-2	6,589.17	4,500.00
	Wen-Chong LIANG	PRC	71	72	70	73	286	-2	6,589.17	4,500.00
	Simon YATES	Scot	70	71	71	74	286	-2	6,589.17	4,500.00
	Paul LAWRIE	Scot	70	69	72	75	286	-2	6,589.17	4,500.00
57	Peter O'MALLEY	Aus	68	74	71	74	287	-1	5,399.46	3,687.50
	Patrik SJÖLAND	Swe	74	69	72	72	287	-1	5,399.46	3,687.50
	Marcus FRASER	Aus	71	70	71	75	287	-1	5,399.46	3,687.50
	Yuan-Chi CHEN	Tpe	67	71	74	75	287	-1	5,399.46	3,687.50
61	Chawalit PLAPHOL	Thai	66	71	72	79	288	0	4,850.36	3,312.50
	Peter FOWLER	Aus	71	71	73	73	288	0	4,850.36	3,312.50
63	Lian-Wei ZHANG	PRC	73	68	71	77	289	1	4,026.72	2,750.00
	Anthony KANG	USA	71	72	71	75	289	1	4,026.72	2,750.00
	Jean-François LUCQUIN	Fr	71	71	70	77	289	1	4,026.72	2,750.00
	Edward LOAR	USA	70	72	71	76	289	1	4,026.72	2,750.00
	Marcus BOTH	Aus	73	69	71	76	289	1	4,026.72	2,750.00
	Christopher D GRAY	Aus	70	72	74	73	289	1	4,026.72	2,750.00
	Wayne PERSKE	Aus	74	68	72	75	289	1	4,026.72	2,750.00
70	Richard LEE	NZ	71	70	70	79	290	2	2,894.79	1,976.96
	Miguel Angel JIMÉNEZ	Sp	71	71	71	77	290	2	2,894.79	1,976.96
	Peter HEDBLOM	Swe	73	69	72	76	290	2	2,894.79	1,976.96
	Kurt BARNES	Aus	73	70	71	76	290	2	2,894.79	1,976.96
74	Carlos RODILES	Sp	72	71	73	76	292	4	2,736.00	1,868.52
75	Marcus CAIN	Aus	74	68	72	79	293	5	2,733.00	1,866.47
76	Gary SIMPSON	Aus	72	70	74	78	294	6	2,730.00	1,864.42

as none of his fellow competitors proved able to overhaul him in the course of the tournament.

Immediately after seeing off the reigning US Open Champion, Retief Goosen, by three shots with an 18 under par total of 270, Scott's first thoughts were of achieving a tournament victory that followed in the footsteps of his great hero Greg Norman. But even as he looked into the future, he could see the wider implications.

"I really enjoyed my experience this week," he said. "There are so many things I had no idea about and they've really opened my eyes being here. The way things are going there will be a lot more golf to be played here in China and I think that's a fantastic thing. I'm thrilled that in the first week I've played here I've won and I'm sure that'll bring me back."

That will be music to the ears of his growing Chinese fan base – especially those as interested in his looks as his golf.

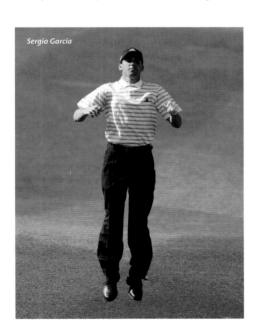

Sergio Garcia

Iain Carter
BBC Radio Five Live

Total Prize Fund
€1,846,750   £1,261,217

BMW Asian Open

Shanghai, China
April 28-May 1 • 2005

Tomson Shanghai Pudong Golf Club

Par	Yards	Metres
72	7300	6674

1	Ernie ELS	262	-26	
2	Simon WAKEFIELD	275	-13	
3	Thomas BJÖRN	276	-12	
4	Eddie LEE	278	-10	
	Jean-François LUCQUIN	278	-10	
6	Luke DONALD	279	-9	
	Stuart LITTLE	279	-9	
8	Søren HANSEN	280	-8	
	James KINGSTON	280	-8	
10	Peter HEDBLOM	281	-7	
	Edward MICHAELS	281	-7	
	David PARK	281	-7	
	Jeev Milkha SINGH	281	-7	

Round One	Round Two	Round Three	Round Four	Round Four

EUROPEAN TOUR ORDER OF MERIT
(After 19 tournaments)

Pos		€	
1	Retief GOOSEN	946,479.00	
2	Ernie ELS	819,415.77	
3	Adam SCOTT	523,209.16	
4	Luke DONALD	488,731.80	
5	Miguel Angel JIMÉNEZ	390,281.61	
6	Stephen DODD	390,086.57	
7	Thomas BJÖRN	377,321.64	
8	Ian POULTER	374,889.93	
9	Henrik STENSON	339,196.38	
10	Nick O'HERN	330,805.20	

Class is
Permanent

Out of sorts and out of luck at the Masters Tournament a few weeks earlier, Ernie Els nevertheless arrived in Shanghai for the BMW Asian Open in a better frame of mind and with his swing beginning to resemble the beautifully oiled creature we have come to expect from one of the game's true greats.

Colin Montgomerie

In the days leading up to the co-sanctioned event between The European and Asian Tours, the South African could be found at the Tomson Shanghai Pudong Golf Club working assiduously on his game and putting into practice a drill that had been given to him by David Leadbetter, his coach, who had noticed that Els had become too stooped over the ball and was cramped in the backswing.

As a result, he was unable to move the ball through the air as he would have liked and his confidence had started to suffer. However, as if to prove that form is temporary but class is permanent, it did not take Els long to turn his game around. Once it had been pointed out to him what

changes needed to be made to his set-up, it was just a matter of time before his golf returned to its previously sublime level.

The signs were good when he finished in a share of sixth place in the Johnnie Walker Classic in Beijing a week earlier and by the time the weather affected BMW Asian Open finally concluded on Monday morning, the evidence was conclusive. Els had claimed his 21st title on The European Tour International Schedule but even more impressively, he had won by a country mile.

After opening with a round of 67 over the 7,300 yard course, Els shared the lead on five under par with six other players, among them Simon Wakefield, who had lost his

Anthony Wall

Simon Wakefield

European Tour card the previous year, but had won it back at the Qualifying School. For the 31 year old Englishman however, it would prove to be a week he would never forget.

Ominously for his rivals, Els suggested after the first round that he was close to rediscovering his 'A' game and awarded himself seven out of ten. He is not a man given to idle boasting so it was not surprising that by the next day everyone else was giving him full marks after an outstanding, virtually blemish-free 62, a ten under par effort only denied course record status by the existence of preferred lies.

The round comprised eight birdies, nine pars and "one of the nicest things in golf - a tap-in eagle." That came at his final hole of the day, the 570 yard ninth, where he fired a sublime four iron second to within eight

inches of the hole, a shot later voted RBS Shot of the Month for April. It was enough for Els to open up a gap of four shots over the unheralded Eddie Lee of New Zealand - who came into the event on the back of ten successive missed cuts – and five over Frenchman Raphaël Jacquelin.

A straw poll amongst the players at this stage had already conceded the title to the World Number Three and they were not to be proved wrong. A third round of 68 was followed by one of 65 - with the last 11 holes completed on Monday morning because of a weather delay the previous day - to give Els victory by a staggering 13 shots over Wakefield and 14 over Denmark's Thomas Björn.

He had led from the opening day, had finished with a tournament record total

" This is a pretty decent golf course. There are some good par fives, some really tough par threes and some tricky dog-legs on the par fours that keep you on your toes. The greens are really good, the surfaces are good and it is a course which tests everyone's game from the driver to the putter " – Ernie Els

Final Results

Pos	Name		Rd1	Rd2	Rd3	Rd4	Total		€	£
1	Ernie ELS	SA	67	62	68	65	262	-26	191,307.30	130,541.53
2	Simon WAKEFIELD	Eng	67	69	66	73	275	-13	127,533.10	87,024.20
3	Thomas BJÖRN	Den	71	65	68	72	276	-12	71,855.00	49,031.38
4	Jean-François LUCQUIN	Fr	70	66	69	73	278	-10	53,030.37	36,186.10
	Eddie LEE	NZ	67	66	73	72	278	-10	53,030.37	36,186.10
6	Luke DONALD	Eng	70	69	68	72	279	-9	37,304.91	25,455.59
	Stuart LITTLE	Eng	71	70	72	66	279	-9	37,304.91	25,455.59
8	Søren HANSEN	Den	69	70	68	73	280	-8	27,203.89	18,563.00
	James KINGSTON	SA	70	71	69	70	280	-8	27,203.89	18,563.00
10	David PARK	Wal	70	69	71	71	281	-7	20,575.09	14,039.73
	Peter HEDBLOM	Swe	72	69	70	70	281	-7	20,575.09	14,039.73
	Jeev Milkha SINGH	Ind	69	68	70	74	281	-7	20,575.09	14,039.73
	Edward MICHAELS	USA	74	69	67	71	281	-7	20,575.09	14,039.73
14	Simon DYSON	Eng	70	74	66	72	282	-6	17,217.65	11,748.73
	Lian-Wei ZHANG	PRC	70	69	68	75	282	-6	17,217.65	11,748.73
16	Raphaël JACQUELIN	Fr	67	67	75	74	283	-5	15,180.23	10,358.47
	Joong Kyung MO	Kor	73	68	70	72	283	-5	15,180.23	10,358.47
	Patrik SJÖLAND	Swe	70	68	72	73	283	-5	15,180.23	10,358.47
	Jyoti RANDHAWA	Ind	70	74	67	72	283	-5	15,180.23	10,358.47
20	Christian CÉVAËR	Fr	70	69	73	72	284	-4	12,468.45	8,508.04
	Anthony WALL	Eng	71	69	72	72	284	-4	12,468.45	8,508.04
	Kenneth FERRIE	Eng	72	68	74	70	284	-4	12,468.45	8,508.04
	Niki ZITNY	Aut	75	69	71	69	284	-4	12,468.45	8,508.04
	Mark FOSTER	Eng	72	72	70	72	284	-4	12,468.45	8,508.04
	Jason KNUTZON	USA	71	72	71	70	284	-4	12,468.45	8,508.04
	Adam GROOM	Aus	72	71	69	72	284	-4	12,468.45	8,508.04
	Wade ORMSBY	Aus	72	67	71	74	284	-4	12,468.45	8,508.04
28	Francois DELAMONTAGNE	Fr	72	70	71	72	285	-3	10,560.16	7,205.89
	Miguel Angel JIMÉNEZ	Sp	70	73	69	73	285	-3	10,560.16	7,205.89
	Jean VAN DE VELDE	Fr	67	69	72	77	285	-3	10,560.16	7,205.89
31	Colin MONTGOMERIE	Scot	73	70	73	70	286	-2	8,562.91	5,843.04
	Miles TUNNICLIFF	Eng	72	70	73	71	286	-2	8,562.91	5,843.04
	José Manuel LARA	Sp	73	71	69	73	286	-2	8,562.91	5,843.04
	Peter HANSON	Swe	73	69	70	74	286	-2	8,562.91	5,843.04
	Peter LAWRIE	Ire	70	71	71	78	286	-2	8,562.91	5,843.04
	Gregory HANRAHAN	USA	72	72	67	75	286	-2	8,562.91	5,843.04
	Christopher HANELL	Swe	70	73	74	69	286	-2	8,562.91	5,843.04
	Terry PRICE	Aus	74	70	69	73	286	-2	8,562.91	5,843.04
	Richard STERNE	SA	69	69	71	77	286	-2	8,562.91	5,843.04
	Larry AUSTIN	Aus	67	72	73	74	286	-2	8,562.91	5,843.04
41	Jarrod LYLE	Aus	72	70	71	74	287	-1	6,772.28	4,621.17
	Marcus BOTH	Aus	70	72	70	75	287	-1	6,772.28	4,621.17
	David BRANSDON	Aus	71	70	70	76	287	-1	6,772.28	4,621.17
	Peter FOWLER	Aus	71	70	71	75	287	-1	6,772.28	4,621.17
	Philip GOLDING	Eng	74	70	71	72	287	-1	6,772.28	4,621.17
46	Anders HANSEN	Den	70	72	70	76	288	0	5,509.65	3,759.59
	Adam BLYTH	SA	74	69	72	73	288	0	5,509.65	3,759.59
	Oliver WILSON	Eng	71	70	75	72	288	0	5,509.65	3,759.59
	Wen-Tang LIN	Tpe	72	72	71	73	288	0	5,509.65	3,759.59
	Michael CAMPBELL	NZ	73	71	70	74	288	0	5,509.65	3,759.59
	Alastair FORSYTH	Scot	72	70	75	71	288	0	5,509.65	3,759.59
52	Wen-Chong LIANG	PRC	70	71	72	76	289	1	4,247.02	2,898.02
	Brad KENNEDY	Aus	71	71	75	72	289	1	4,247.02	2,898.02
	Thammanoon SRIROT	Thai	72	70	74	73	289	1	4,247.02	2,898.02
	Mardan MAMAT	Sing	73	71	71	74	289	1	4,247.02	2,898.02
	Ross BAIN	Scot	72	68	74	75	289	1	4,247.02	2,898.02
57	Carlos RODILES	Sp	69	71	74	76	290	2	3,156.57	2,153.93
	Peter O'MALLEY	Aus	70	74	73	73	290	2	3,156.57	2,153.93
	Thaworn WIRATCHANT	Thai	74	69	68	79	290	2	3,156.57	2,153.93
	Charl SCHWARTZEL	SA	71	71	70	78	290	2	3,156.57	2,153.93
	Edward LOAR	USA	72	68	74	76	290	2	3,156.57	2,153.93
	Ted OH	Kor	71	73	71	75	290	2	3,156.57	2,153.93
	Kim FELTON	Aus	70	72	74	74	290	2	3,156.57	2,153.93
	Nick DOUGHERTY	Eng	71	72	70	77	290	2	3,156.57	2,153.93
65	Prom MEESAWAT	Thai	71	72	70	78	291	3	2,525.26	1,723.15
	Rahil GANGJEE	Ind	75	69	73	74	291	3	2,525.26	1,723.15
	Costantino ROCCA	It	74	68	71	78	291	3	2,525.26	1,723.15
68	Jason DAWES	Aus	73	71	74	74	292	4	2,295.69	1,566.50
69	James HEATH	Eng	73	70	73	77	293	5	1,929.66	1,316.73
	Ben MASON	Eng	76	67	72	78	293	5	1,929.66	1,316.73
	Nick FALDO	Eng	72	70	73	78	293	5	1,929.66	1,316.73
	Anthony KANG	USA	72	68	75	78	293	5	1,929.66	1,316.73
73	Bryan SALTUS	USA	73	71	72	80	296	8	1,716.00	1,170.94
74	Paul CASEY	Eng	73	71	78	76	298	10	1,713.00	1,168.89
75	Sung-Man LEE	Kor	70	74	75	82	301	13	1,710.00	1,166.85

Total Prize Fund
€1,156,420 £789,102

of 26 under par 262 and had recorded the second largest margin of victory on The European Tour International Schedule, two behind Tiger Woods who won the US Open Championship in 2000 by 15 shots. It was his third victory of the year on The European Tour – following his back-to-back wins in Dubai and Qatar – and he picked up the winner's cheque for €191,307 (£130,541).

"I knew the parts of my game that I was working on but I am a little surprised it came so fast," he admitted. "The 62 was the key to victory, but in the last two rounds I had to play really steady and not make mistakes. The changes I have made gave me a clear vision of what I wanted to do. They made me really focus and, in a sense, made it a little bit easier to win."

The key for Els at this stage of the season

Jean-François Lucquin

was to keep his game in good shape for the challenges that lay ahead. He had come close in all four of the Major Championships in 2004, but he will not be satisfied until he has at least another one under his belt.

For Wakefield, who partnered Els in the final grouping of the last day, the year had already reached a high point. He had been forced back to the Qualifying School Finals five times in eight years, but on the back of his performance in Shanghai, he effectively secured his card for 2006. With scores of 67-69-66-73 for a 13 under par total of 275, Wakefield earned himself a career-best cheque of €127,533 (£87,024) and the chance to reflect on his day in the sun.

"Just being in Ernie's presence and seeing how he goes about his business was an education," said Wakefield. "Walking down the tenth, I was thinking to myself that I wasn't enjoying it after having made a couple of bogeys. Then I gave myself a kick up the backside by reminding myself, 'You're playing golf with Ernie Els for goodness sake, and you are not enjoying it. What's going on?'"

It was a pep talk that worked wonders as Wakefield kept his game together to keep Björn at bay and claim the runners-up spot for himself. Given such exalted company, that is a pretty good effort in anybody's book.

Peter Dixon
The Times

Telecom Italia Open

Milan, Italy
May 5-8 • 2005

Castello di Tolcinasco Golf & Country Club

Par	Yards	Metres
72	7224	6610

1	**Steve WEBSTER**	270	-18	
2	Bradley DREDGE	273	-15	
	Richard FINCH	273	-15	
	Anders HANSEN	273	-15	
5	Emanuele CANONICA	274	-14	
6	Gonzalo FERNANDEZ-CASTANO	278	-10	
	Simon KHAN	278	-10	
	Andrew McLARDY	278	-10	
	Jamie SPENCE	278	-10	
10	Adam GROOM	279	-9	
	Stuart LITTLE	279	-9	
	Gary ORR	279	-9	
	Marcel SIEM	279	-9	

Round One	Round Two	Round Three	Round Four

EUROPEAN TOUR ORDER OF MERIT
(After 20 tournaments)

Pos		€	
1	**Retief GOOSEN**	946,479.00	
2	Ernie ELS	819,415.77	
3	Adam SCOTT	523,209.16	
4	Luke DONALD	488,731.80	
5	Miguel Angel JIMÉNEZ	390,281.61	
6	Stephen DODD	390,086.57	
7	Thomas BJÖRN	377,321.64	
8	Ian POULTER	374,889.93	
9	Steve WEBSTER	343,809.29	
10	Henrik STENSON	339,196.38	

Positively Mental

Increasingly, tournament professionals are pinpointing the power of positive thinking as the key to glory, with sports psychologists becoming as vital a part of a top golfer's armoury as the latest drivers and irons.

To prove that point, Steve Webster insisted the input of 'mind magician' Jamil Qureshi was the vital element in his breakthrough victory on The European Tour in the Telecom Italia Open at Castello di Tolcinasco Golf & Country Club on the outskirts of Milan.

The 30 year old Englishman joked that after a decade of near-misses – including five second places – he seriously wondered if he should look for another job. Six more top 20s in his previous nine starts underlined the frustration of a golfer whose powerful hitting belies his modest physical proportions.

Indeed no less an authority on the game than five time Major Champion Severiano

Ballesteros spoke to him during the Jazztel Open de España en Andalucia at the San Roque Club, and warned: "Time is running out."

Webster admitted: "Seve was my hero when I was growing up and he still is – it was great of him to come over and ask how I was doing. What he said clicked. It was the push I needed to get into the winner's circle. Also, when Ernie Els and I shot 69s playing together in Qatar, he said he was surprised I hadn't won yet and said once I did, I'd win a few."

The Ballesteros-Els effect manifested itself in Webster intensifying his work with the 36 year old stage performer Qureshi, dubbed 'a new-wave mentalist' on his website. Linking up with Qureshi came on the

Bradley Dredge

Marcel Siem

Telecom Italia Open

Milan, Italy
May 5-8 • 2005

Francois Delamontagne

> *It's a wonderful layout. In Europe we don't play a course in better condition or with purer greens. The rough is thick and you must hit the fairways to score. It's a classically designed course which gets away from the modern ethos of slopey greens with relatively few pin positions* — Mark Roe

recommendation of good friend and Golf Management International stablemate Gary Evans. Webster explained: "I've definitely been an under-achiever. When I look at players who have done well, no names mentioned, I know I'm better than them. It's just a case of getting the mind right.

"Jamil has got me thinking much more positively. He did the same for Nick Dougherty, who had been really struggling but won for the first time in Singapore earlier in the year. Jamil had changed him completely. He's amazing. He's a guy who can almost put you under like a hypnotist. But his main achievement has been getting me focused on my pre-shot routine and impressing on me how strong the mind is.

"He told me stories before the final round about how other sportsmen, like Mohammed Ali and Aussie cricketer Steve Waugh, think and what they do to help themselves concentrate. I've felt a big change in myself

Anders Hansen

Final Results

Pos	Name		Rd1	Rd2	Rd3	Rd4	Total		€	£
1	Steve WEBSTER	Eng	68	68	66	68	270	-18	216,660.00	146,377.06
2	Anders HANSEN	Den	72	68	67	66	273	-15	96,940.00	65,493.36
	Bradley DREDGE	Wal	67	66	71	69	273	-15	96,940.00	65,493.36
	Richard FINCH	Eng	69	63	71	70	273	-15	96,940.00	65,493.36
5	Emanuele CANONICA	It	68	68	71	67	274	-14	55,120.00	37,239.47
6	Andrew MCLARDY	SA	72	69	68	69	278	-10	36,530.00	24,679.93
	Jamie SPENCE	Eng	69	71	65	73	278	-10	36,530.00	24,679.93
	Gonzalo FERNANDEZ-CASTANO	Sp	66	73	69	70	278	-10	36,530.00	24,679.93
	Simon KHAN	Eng	67	69	68	74	278	-10	36,530.00	24,679.93
10	Gary ORR	Scot	70	71	67	71	279	-9	23,302.50	15,743.34
	Stuart LITTLE	Eng	72	64	69	74	279	-9	23,302.50	15,743.34
	Marcel SIEM	Ger	68	68	71	72	279	-9	23,302.50	15,743.34
	Adam GROOM	Aus	69	68	72	70	279	-9	23,302.50	15,743.34
14	Søren KJELDSEN	Den	73	68	67	72	280	-8	19,110.00	12,910.85
	David DRYSDALE	Scot	69	70	66	75	280	-8	19,110.00	12,910.85
	Gareth PADDISON	NZ	69	72	68	71	280	-8	19,110.00	12,910.85
17	Maarten LAFEBER	NL	72	69	66	74	281	-7	16,510.00	11,154.27
	Francesco MOLINARI	It	69	70	69	73	281	-7	16,510.00	11,154.27
	Jonathan LOMAS	Eng	70	71	67	73	281	-7	16,510.00	11,154.27
	Joakim HAEGGMAN	Swe	73	68	68	72	281	-7	16,510.00	11,154.27
21	Gregory HAVRET	Fr	70	65	77	70	282	-6	14,495.00	9,792.93
	Andres ROMERO	Arg	69	70	71	72	282	-6	14,495.00	9,792.93
	Angel CABRERA	Arg	72	70	68	72	282	-6	14,495.00	9,792.93
	David LYNN	Eng	70	68	72	72	282	-6	14,495.00	9,792.93
25	Leif WESTERBERG	Swe	72	69	69	73	283	-5	12,350.00	8,343.75
	Paul BROADHURST	Eng	70	65	75	73	283	-5	12,350.00	8,343.75
	Gary EMERSON	Eng	71	70	70	72	283	-5	12,350.00	8,343.75
	Michael HOEY	N.Ire	72	71	72	68	283	-5	12,350.00	8,343.75
	David GILFORD	Eng	67	73	73	70	283	-5	12,350.00	8,343.75
	Sven STRÜVER	Ger	67	65	73	73	283	-5	12,350.00	8,343.75
	Gary MURPHY	Ire	67	72	66	78	283	-5	12,350.00	8,343.75
32	Johan AXGREN	Swe	73	68	71	72	284	-4	10,088.00	6,815.53
	Nicolas COLSAERTS	Bel	74	68	71	71	284	-4	10,088.00	6,815.53
	Jean-François LUCQUIN	Fr	72	71	73	284		-4	10,088.00	6,815.53
	Francois DELAMONTAGNE	Fr	66	77	70	71	284	-4	10,088.00	6,815.53
	Ivo GINER	Sp	68	72	73	71	284	-4	10,088.00	6,815.53
37	Andrew COLTART	Scot	73	70	69	73	285	-3	8,710.00	5,884.54
	Robert COLES	Eng	70	72	69	74	285	-3	8,710.00	5,884.54
	Robert ROCK	Eng	72	67	71	75	285	-3	8,710.00	5,884.54
	Sam TORRANCE	Scot	69	73	68	75	285	-3	8,710.00	5,884.54
	Miguel Angel MARTIN	Sp	69	70	71	75	285	-3	8,710.00	5,884.54
42	Andrew MARSHALL	Eng	71	70	74	71	286	-2	7,670.00	5,181.91
	Ian GARBUTT	Eng	69	73	70	74	286	-2	7,670.00	5,181.91
	Michele REALE	It	70	73	71	72	286	-2	7,670.00	5,181.91
45	Roger CHAPMAN	Eng	73	70	69	75	287	-1	6,890.00	4,654.93
	Niki ZITNY	Aut	69	74	73	71	287	-1	6,890.00	4,654.93
	Klas ERIKSSON	Swe	73	70	71	73	287	-1	6,890.00	4,654.93
48	Fredrik HENGE	Swe	69	73	70	76	288	0	5,850.00	3,952.30
	Sam LITTLE	Eng	70	73	71	74	288	0	5,850.00	3,952.30
	Gary EVANS	Eng	71	69	73	75	288	0	5,850.00	3,952.30
	David CARTER	Eng	72	70	77	69	288	0	5,850.00	3,952.30
	Carlos DE CORRAL	Sp	69	72	75	72	288	0	5,850.00	3,952.30
53	Mikko ILONEN	Fin	72	70	74	73	289	1	4,345.71	2,936.00
	Joakim BÄCKSTRÖM	Swe	69	70	75	75	289	1	4,345.71	2,936.00
	Julien VAN HAUWE	Fr	71	71	74	73	289	1	4,345.71	2,936.00
	Gordon BRAND JNR	Scot	75	68	68	78	289	1	4,345.71	2,936.00
	Ian WOOSNAM	Wal	73	67	75	74	289	1	4,345.71	2,936.00
	Costantino ROCCA	It	70	71	72	76	289	1	4,345.71	2,936.00
	José Manuel CARRILES	Sp	71	67	74	77	289	1	4,345.71	2,936.00
60	Mark ROE	Eng	70	70	72	78	290	2	3,380.00	2,283.55
	Johan EDFORS	Swe	73	70	72	75	290	2	3,380.00	2,283.55
	Gregory BOURDY	Fr	74	68	70	78	290	2	3,380.00	2,283.55
	Markus BRIER	Aut	72	69	74	75	290	2	3,380.00	2,283.55
	Rolf MUNTZ	NL	72	69	76	73	290	2	3,380.00	2,283.55
65	Garry HOUSTON	Wal	70	70	75	76	291	3	2,990.00	2,020.70
66	Darren FICHARDT	SA	76	67	70	80	293	5	2,795.00	1,888.32
	Sebastian FERNANDEZ	Arg	67	73	76	77	293	5	2,795.00	1,888.32
68	Benoit TEILLERIA	Fr	70	72	72	83	297	9	2,600.00	1,756.58
69	Dean ROBERTSON	Scot	68	73	76	83	300	12	2,470.00	1,668.75
70	Stephen GALLACHER	Scot	71	71	77	82	301	13	2,165.00	1,462.69
	Van PHILLIPS	Eng	74	69	80	78	301	13	2,165.00	1,462.69

Total Prize Fund
€1,301,950 £879,606

---

and my outlook is much more positive. We set goals for the tournament and the ones coming up. The main thing is to make sure I'm in contention – within three strokes of the lead – with nine holes to go, as many times as possible."

Qureshi's website on the subject of his mind-shaping approach makes for highly scientific reading as it...."seamlessly blends traditional magic with ultra-modern psychological techniques such as neuro-linguistic programming, spontaneous trance induction and physiological thought-reading."

But the man himself makes it all sound much simpler. He explained: "It's psychological magic – old fashioned mentalism. I've been using my magic to entertain - now I'm using it to do good. I've never picked up a golf club in my life but golfers are no different to other

Richard Finch

sportsmen and it's all about increasing their absolute self-belief. I told Steve not to go out the last day and try to shoot the lights out. I stressed if he concentrated on having a good steady round, he would win.

"I've tried to slow down his game, make him think more and to anchor certain trigger words about technique in his mind. Seve is his hero and I told him to try and visualise how he would think and what he would do in the circumstances."

The methodology certainly worked for Webster. He was coolly impressive on the final afternoon, going out in level par to maintain the one stroke lead a third round 66 – which had followed two opening 68s - had given him, then just as coolly harvesting four birdies in his next eight holes to move clear of the chasing pack. In the end, a third 68 of the week for an 18 under par total of 270 left him three clear at the finish.

Welshman Bradley Dredge was 16 under par after 71 holes but hit into the water hazard at the last to share second place with Dane Anders Hansen and rookie Richard Finch from England, who fired a record breaking 63 on day two and bravely came home in 32 on the final day for a 70.

But it was the new look Webster who finally emerged the 'Big Cheese', a fitting sobriquet considering that, aside from the €216,660 (£146,337) first prize, he also won his weight in Grana Padano parmesan.

Gordon Richardson

The Daily Telegraph Dunlop Masters

Warwickshire, England
May 12-15 • 2005

Marriott Forest of Arden

Par	Yards	Metres
72	7213	6586

Pos	Player	Score	To Par	
1	**Thomas BJÖRN**	282	-6	
2	Brian DAVIS	282	-6	
	David HOWELL	282	-6	
4	Michael CAMPBELL	283	-5	
5	Søren HANSEN	284	-4	
	Simon KHAN	284	-4	
	Steve WEBSTER	284	-4	
8	Darren CLARKE	285	-3	
	Robert-Jan DERKSEN	285	-3	
	Maarten LAFEBER	285	-3	

Round One Round Two Round Three Round Four

EUROPEAN TOUR ORDER OF MERIT
(After 21 tournaments)

Pos	Player	€	
1	**Retief GOOSEN**	946,479.00	
2	Ernie ELS	819,415.77	
3	Thomas BJÖRN	795,074.74	
4	Adam SCOTT	523,209.16	
5	Luke DONALD	488,731.80	
6	David HOWELL	485,196.20	
7	Steve WEBSTER	433,543.70	
8	Stephen DODD	431,043.56	
9	Ian POULTER	407,424.92	
10	Miguel Angel JIMÉNEZ	390,281.61	

Conquering The Demons

The Daily Telegraph Dunlop Masters

Warwickshire, England
May 12-15 • 2005

Thomas Björn must have felt somewhat like his beloved Liverpool Football Club – namely off the pace in Europe far too long. But, within 11 glorious days in May, both the Scandinavian and the Pride of Merseyside felt just champion again – Liverpool, thanks to an unforgettable victory over AC Milan in the Champions League Final, while Björn proved to be in a league of his own, too, at the Marriott Forest of Arden.

Niclas Fasth

"It's been a long time," sighed the Wentworth-based 34 year old before adding a telling postscript: "Too long." Three years after his last win on The European Tour International Schedule, Björn emerged triumphant again when he collected The Daily Telegraph Dunlop Masters title after a play-off against two Englishmen, Brian Davis and David Howell.

Björn's winning score of six under par 282 was testimony to both the strength of the course - a sparkling jewel in British parkland golf - and the demanding wind, which gusted up to 30mph for the first three days before relenting on the last. It was an ill wind for most, but it blew plenty of good

Björn's way, all of it most welcome after his public struggles throughout the previous two seasons.

In the summer of 2003, Björn had one hand on the claret jug in The Open Championship before coming a cropper in a bunker at Royal St George's, and a year later he was walking off The K Club after only six holes of the Smurfit European Open complaining that he could not play golf while battling inner demons. It was an admission which earned him the locker room nickname Van Helsing, but just like the famous doctor in the Dracula movies, Björn ultimately conquered them too.

David Howell

"The one thing we have come to expect at the Marriott Forest of Arden is a strong test on an outstanding course. We were not disappointed, as the greenkeepers had again done a magnificent job on what has become one of Britain's finest inland tests" – David Howell

Emanuele Canonica

Brian Davis

Søren Hansen

There was no masking Björn's relief as two towering and majestic five irons to the 18th green in the play-off brought the title aspirations of firstly Davis and then Howell to an end. He acknowledged that his road of doubt and self-discovery had had many potholes and that the learning process had been a difficult one, but now he felt a great deal of satisfaction at winning on British soil. "Some of my biggest letdowns have been in Britain, so it's nice to do something right," he said.

Björn is nothing if not honest and always his own fiercest critic. Had he been a schoolteacher he would have given himself 100 lines every day and written 'Could do Better' on his end-of-term reports. "When you've been successful you take a lot of things for granted and think success is going to come to you all the time," he said.

"I have been hard on myself in the past and have driven myself, perhaps a little too much. There are times when you don't get

what you think you deserve and that can be hard to take. But the harder you try, the more you drive yourself into the ground."

The lesson sunk in as decisively as any of the putts Björn holed throughout a testing week and he approached the tournament with the attitude that he would face good and bad with a smile on his face.

Whatever words he said firstly to Davis and then to Howell after his triumph and their respective loss would stay between them, but they were obviously of consolation and congratulation. Björn knows all about near misses and that losing in a play-off is not a sporting disaster. "I always try to win but when you haven't, you can't leave thinking that the world is coming to an end," he said.

Björn may have departed with a broad smile on his face, but it was almost matched by the one worn by Tour rookie Oliver Wilson as he drove home in a Jaguar XJS 2.7, courtesy

It's not just your office environment **we're improving.**

It's all very well talking about the environment, but what are we actually doing about it? Well how about this: we've reduced the waste we send to landfill by 92%, our Wellingborough Green Centre already recycles over 75% of the raw material of each machine and now we're – officially – CarbonNeutral®. (A company called Future Forests is helping us offset the CO_2 produced by our UK Head Office through tree planting.) Now we've produced a special green office guide so you can share what we've learned and make your own environment better for everyone. Visit www.ricoh.co.uk/environment today for your free copy.

Our earth,
Our tomorrow

How well do you share?

Ian Poulter

Final Results

Pos	Name		Rd1	Rd2	Rd3	Rd4	Total		€	£
1	Thomas BJÖRN	Den	73	68	73	68	282	-6	417,753.10	283,330.00
2	David HOWELL	Eng	69	72	72	69	282	-6	217,701.10	147,650.00
	Brian DAVIS	Eng	69	71	73	69	282	-6	217,701.10	147,650.00
4	Michael CAMPBELL	NZ	73	70	67	73	283	-5	125,327.40	85,000.00
5	Simon KHAN	Eng	71	77	69	67	284	-4	89,734.41	60,860.00
	Steve WEBSTER	Eng	72	71	70	71	284	-4	89,734.41	60,860.00
	Søren HANSEN	Den	70	71	76	67	284	-4	89,734.41	60,860.00
8	Maarten LAFEBER	NL	73	73	70	69	285	-3	56,313.78	38,193.33
	Robert-Jan DERKSEN	NL	71	75	70	69	285	-3	56,313.78	38,193.33
	Darren CLARKE	N.Ire	74	72	72	67	285	-3	56,313.78	38,193.33
11	Stephen DODD	Wal	70	77	75	65	287	-1	40,956.99	27,778.00
	Robert KARLSSON	Swe	74	73	73	67	287	-1	40,956.99	27,778.00
	Johan SKÖLD	Swe	74	74	72	67	287	-1	40,956.99	27,778.00
	Gary MURPHY	Ire	75	73	68	71	287	-1	40,956.99	27,778.00
	Barry LANE	Eng	70	76	73	68	287	-1	40,956.99	27,778.00
16	Roger CHAPMAN	Eng	73	73	76	66	288	0	32,534.99	22,066.00
	Mark ROE	Eng	75	73	71	69	288	0	32,534.99	22,066.00
	Ian POULTER	Eng	75	76	73	64	288	0	32,534.99	22,066.00
	David DRYSDALE	Scot	72	74	72	70	288	0	32,534.99	22,066.00
	Graeme MCDOWELL	N.Ire	74	75	73	66	288	0	32,534.99	22,066.00
21	Brett RUMFORD	Aus	72	74	74	69	289	1	28,323.99	19,210.00
	Ian WOOSNAM	Wal	74	71	75	69	289	1	28,323.99	19,210.00
	Marcus FRASER	Aus	73	72	76	68	289	1	28,323.99	19,210.00
24	Oliver WILSON	Eng	72	73	71	74	290	2	24,564.17	16,660.00
	Damien MCGRANE	Ire	72	77	70	71	290	2	24,564.17	16,660.00
	Andrew MCLARDY	SA	70	76	73	71	290	2	24,564.17	16,660.00
	Colin MONTGOMERIE	Scot	72	75	74	69	290	2	24,564.17	16,660.00
	Bradley DREDGE	Wal	74	73	72	71	290	2	24,564.17	16,660.00
	Patrik SJÖLAND	Swe	71	74	74	71	290	2	24,564.17	16,660.00
	Markus BRIER	Aut	74	73	72	71	290	2	24,564.17	16,660.00
31	Angel CABRERA	Arg	70	75	74	72	291	3	20,102.52	13,634.00
	Joakim HAEGGMAN	Swe	73	73	75	70	291	3	20,102.52	13,634.00
	Richard STERNE	SA	73	74	75	69	291	3	20,102.52	13,634.00
	Henrik STENSON	Swe	77	71	74	69	291	3	20,102.52	13,634.00
	Paul BROADHURST	Eng	73	73	70	75	291	3	20,102.52	13,634.00
36	Jean-François LUCQUIN	Fr	74	73	72	73	292	4	17,545.84	11,900.00
	Richard GREEN	Aus	72	73	74	73	292	4	17,545.84	11,900.00
	David LYNN	Eng	69	77	76	70	292	4	17,545.84	11,900.00
	Paul MCGINLEY	Ire	72	79	73	68	292	4	17,545.84	11,900.00
40	Christian CÉVAËR	Fr	72	74	73	74	293	5	15,540.60	10,540.00
	Fredrik ANDERSSON HED	Swe	74	73	73	73	293	5	15,540.60	10,540.00
	Mikko ILONEN	Fin	73	73	73	74	293	5	15,540.60	10,540.00
	Alessandro TADINI	It	72	74	72	75	293	5	15,540.60	10,540.00
44	Gonzalo FERNANDEZ-CASTANO	Sp	75	74	72	73	294	6	14,287.32	9,690.00
45	Scott DRUMMOND	Scot	70	75	75	75	295	7	12,783.39	8,670.00
	Nick O'HERN	Aus	74	76	72	73	295	7	12,783.39	8,670.00
	Philip GOLDING	Eng	73	74	80	68	295	7	12,783.39	8,670.00
	Stephen GALLACHER	Scot	71	78	75	71	295	7	12,783.39	8,670.00
	Robert COLES	Eng	74	76	71	74	295	7	12,783.39	8,670.00
50	Ignacio GARRIDO	Sp	78	73	74	71	296	8	9,775.54	6,630.00
	Gary ORR	Scot	76	74	76	70	296	8	9,775.54	6,630.00
	Lee WESTWOOD	Eng	76	75	74	71	296	8	9,775.54	6,630.00
	Simon DYSON	Eng	71	73	76	76	296	8	9,775.54	6,630.00
	Andrew MARSHALL	Eng	72	77	74	73	296	8	9,775.54	6,630.00
	Søren KJELDSEN	Den	75	75	76	70	296	8	9,775.54	6,630.00
	Jean-Francois REMESY	Fr	75	73	77	71	296	8	9,775.54	6,630.00
57	Peter BAKER	Eng	71	73	76	77	297	9	7,770.30	5,270.00
58	Mårten OLANDER	Swe	74	77	78	69	298	10	6,767.68	4,590.00
	Sam TORRANCE	Scot	76	74	74	74	298	10	6,767.68	4,590.00
	Terry PRICE	Aus	72	79	74	73	298	10	6,767.68	4,590.00
	Pierre FULKE	Swe	70	77	76	75	298	10	6,767.68	4,590.00
	Ian GARBUTT	Eng	74	77	74	73	298	10	6,767.68	4,590.00
	Stuart MANLEY	Wal	79	71	73	75	298	10	6,767.68	4,590.00
	Gregory BOURDY	Fr	75	75	75	73	298	10	6,767.68	4,590.00
65	Martin MARITZ	SA	74	77	75	73	299	11	5,150.71	3,493.33
	Richard FINCH	Eng	70	75	74	80	299	11	5,150.71	3,493.33
	Klas ERIKSSON	Swe	73	74	76	76	299	11	5,150.71	3,493.33
	Phillip ARCHER	Eng	75	75	75	74	299	11	5,150.71	3,493.33
	Jamie SPENCE	Eng	75	75	72	77	299	11	5,150.71	3,493.33
	Stuart LITTLE	Eng	72	78	74	75	299	11	5,150.71	3,493.33
71	Leif WESTERBERG	Swe	72	77	74	77	300	12	3,760.00	2,550.12
72	Emanuele CANONICA	It	74	74	84	69	301	13	3,757.00	2,548.09
73	Andrew COLTART	Scot	74	77	79	72	302	14	3,751.00	2,544.02
	Robert ROCK	Eng	72	76	77	77	302	14	3,751.00	2,544.02
	Mark FOSTER	Eng	76	74	79	73	302	14	3,751.00	2,544.02
76	Francesco MOLINARI	It	73	78	78	75	304	16	3,743.50	2,538.93
	Benoit TEILLERIA	Fr	74	77	78	75	304	16	3,743.50	2,538.93

of his four iron tee shot to the last on the final day which finished a mere 21 inches from the pin.

There were others smiling after another wonderful week in the Midlands, but Howell, for once, was not. He chastised himself for not winning after being in the lead with one hole to play, but the positive thing was that that was a sign of his own drive and determination.

Björn could fully understand Howell's disappointment. He had been down that road many times in the past himself, but had showed he had learned from the experience.

Martin Hardy

Michael Campbell

Total Prize Fund
€2,532,800 £1,717,808

Nissan Irish Open

Maynooth, Co. Kildare, Ireland
May 19-22 • 2005

Carton House Golf Club

Par	Yards	Metres
72	7301	6675

Pos	Player	Score	To Par	
1	**Stephen DODD**	279	-9	
2	David HOWELL	279	-9	
3	Angel CABRERA	281	-7	
	Nick DOUGHERTY	281	-7	
5	Padraig HARRINGTON	282	-6	
	Nick O'HERN	282	-6	
	Lee WESTWOOD	282	-6	
8	Francois DELAMONTAGNE	283	-5	
9	Philip GOLDING	284	-4	
	Steven O'HARA	284	-4	
	Richard STERNE	284	-4	
	Oliver WILSON	284	-4	

Round One Round Two Round Three Round Four

Changing Fortunes

EUROPEAN TOUR ORDER OF MERIT
(After 22 tournaments)

Pos	Player	€	
1	**Retief GOOSEN**	946,479.00	
2	Ernie ELS	819,415.77	
3	Thomas BJÖRN	795,074.74	
4	Stephen DODD	764,373.56	
5	David HOWELL	707,416.20	
6	Adam SCOTT	523,209.16	
7	Luke DONALD	488,731.80	
8	Steve WEBSTER	433,543.70	
9	Nick O'HERN	415,188.59	
10	Ian POULTER	407,424.92	

Mention of a quiet man among the loquacious Irish, will almost certainly prompt images of a much-loved Hollywood movie from 1952 and the boisterous blarney which director John Ford created to the backdrop of rural Mayo. Especially memorable was the climactic scene in which John Wayne and Victor McLaglen engaged in bruising fisticuffs, singularly lacking in finesse.

Another quiet man captured the limelight on the Montgomerie Course at Carton House Golf Club, Maynooth, Co. Kildare, where the Nissan Irish Open had its 50th staging. What is more, the demeanour of Stephen Dodd was a lot more in keeping with a royal and ancient game, especially when striking the killer blow against his closest rival, David Howell, in a sudden-death play-off.

Some locals would have remembered Dodd from an earlier visit to Slieve Russell Hotel Golf & Country Club in August 2001 when, with modest aspirations, he finished runner-up in the North West of Ireland Open for earnings of €38,880 (£24,352), which helped him retain his card at the end of that season. As a measure of how fortunes have changed for the softly-spoken Welshman, a winner's cheque on this occasion of €333,330 (£227,466) merely served to strengthen his position in the Top Ten of The European Tour Order of Merit.

The event had Colin Montgomerie behaving like a surrogate host, in his capacity as co-designer of the course with Stan Eby of European Golf Design. And, after practice rounds in hostile weather, the reaction of his playing colleagues ranged from tacit acceptance of a forbidding assignment, to dire predictions of a golfing armageddon, the latter being the view of Darren Clarke.

Much of their concern had to do with seriously tight fairways, shaped for the left-to-right shotmaking so favoured by the Scot, and with deep, difficult bunkers which were clearly half-shot hazards. Fortunately for the field, conditions improved dramatically when the tournament got underway, with the

result that Nick Dougherty and Klas Eriksson carded opening rounds of 68, Dodd was amongst a group of four players who posted a 69, while Clarke scored a rather tidy 70.

Still, as the tournament progressed, there was no doubting the demanding nature of Montgomerie's handiwork. And, with competition nearing an end, he was entirely unrepentent. "I'm glad there's been a bit of grief," he said on Sunday, by which stage the 513 yard 18th, which was reachable in two, had come to represent welcome respite at the end of an arduous journey.

This was also when Montgomerie chose to reveal that he had originally wanted the final green to be positioned on the far side of the River Rye, so that the second shot would involve a carry of at least 160 yards over water. "It would have been the ultimate risk-reward shot," he declared, with wicked glee.

Colin Montgomerie

Paul McGinley

Simon Khan

Brett Rumford of Australia poses with a propeller after winning 10,000 miles of air travel during the Red Bull Final 5 at the Nissan Irish Open

Meanwhile, Howell's commendable candour regarding his defeat in a play-off for The Daily Telegraph Dunlop Masters at the Marriott Forest of Arden the previous

" It has a bit of everything to be honest. The par threes are excellent, on the short par fours the greens are at a bit of an angle, and most of the par fives are just out of range. I would say it is an ideal, modern, links golf course " – Colin Montgomerie

Richard Green

Final Results

Pos	Name		Rd1	Rd2	Rd3	Rd4	Total		€	£
1	Stephen DODD	Wal	69	70	72	68	279	-9	333,330.00	227,466.90
2	David HOWELL	Eng	70	70	69	70	279	-9	222,220.00	151,644.60
3	Angel CABRERA	Arg	71	73	69	68	281	-7	112,600.00	76,839.00
	Nick DOUGHERTY	Eng	68	72	67	74	281	-7	112,600.00	76,839.00
5	Lee WESTWOOD	Eng	70	74	70	68	282	-6	71,600.00	48,860.38
	Padraig HARRINGTON	Ire	73	72	68	69	282	-6	71,600.00	48,860.38
	Nick O'HERN	Aus	73	73	70	66	282	-6	71,600.00	48,860.38
8	Francois DELAMONTAGNE	Fr	72	74	68	69	283	-5	50,000.00	34,120.38
9	Richard STERNE	SA	72	73	69	70	284	-4	39,000.00	26,613.89
	Steven O'HARA	Scot	74	73	70	67	284	-4	39,000.00	26,613.89
	Philip GOLDING	Eng	72	69	72	71	284	-4	39,000.00	26,613.89
	Oliver WILSON	Eng	72	71	66	75	284	-4	39,000.00	26,613.89
13	Jose-Filipe LIMA	Port	71	71	69	74	285	-3	30,100.00	20,540.47
	Colm MORIARTY	Ire	69	74	72	70	285	-3	30,100.00	20,540.47
	Simon DYSON	Eng	71	72	71	71	285	-3	30,100.00	20,540.47
	David CARTER	Eng	74	73	67	71	285	-3	30,100.00	20,540.47
17	Darren CLARKE	N.Ire	70	75	69	72	286	-2	27,000.00	18,425.00
18	Bradley DREDGE	Wal	72	68	75	72	287	-1	24,450.00	16,684.86
	Graeme STORM	Eng	71	75	73	68	287	-1	24,450.00	16,684.86
	José Maria OLAZÁBAL	Sp	74	71	68	74	287	-1	24,450.00	16,684.86
	Garry HOUSTON	Wal	77	71	70	69	287	-1	24,450.00	16,684.86
22	Maarten LAFEBER	NL	72	73	75	68	288	0	21,100.00	14,398.80
	Joakim HAEGGMAN	Swe	73	70	73	72	288	0	21,100.00	14,398.80
	Andrew MCLARDY	SA	72	71	68	77	288	0	21,100.00	14,398.80
	Terry PRICE	Aus	75	71	73	69	288	0	21,100.00	14,398.80
	Charl SCHWARTZEL	SA	74	72	73	69	288	0	21,100.00	14,398.80
	Richard FINCH	Eng	71	75	72	70	288	0	21,100.00	14,398.80
28	Christian CÉVAËR	Fr	73	73	68	75	289	1	16,181.82	11,042.60
	Paul MCGINLEY	Ire	72	69	74	74	289	1	16,181.82	11,042.60
	Carlos RODILES	Sp	73	73	70	73	289	1	16,181.82	11,042.60
	Joakim BÄCKSTRÖM	Swe	74	74	73	68	289	1	16,181.82	11,042.60
	Colin MONTGOMERIE	Scot	71	73	75	70	289	1	16,181.82	11,042.60
	Titch MOORE	SA	73	74	66	76	289	1	16,181.82	11,042.60
	Pelle EDBERG	Swe	72	68	73	76	289	1	16,181.82	11,042.60
	Peter HANSON	Swe	72	73	71	73	289	1	16,181.82	11,042.60
	Richard GREEN	Aus	73	74	68	74	289	1	16,181.82	11,042.60
	Sandy LYLE	Scot	73	72	73	71	289	1	16,181.82	11,042.60
	Stuart MANLEY	Wal	72	74	69	74	289	1	16,181.82	11,042.60
39	Mark FOSTER	Eng	71	73	71	75	290	2	12,800.00	8,734.82
	Peter LAWRIE	Ire	74	71	74	71	290	2	12,800.00	8,734.82
	Scott DRUMMOND	Scot	71	77	72	70	290	2	12,800.00	8,734.82
	Paul BROADHURST	Eng	72	75	72	71	290	2	12,800.00	8,734.82
43	Jonathan LOMAS	Eng	73	73	72	73	291	3	10,800.00	7,370.00
	Francesco MOLINARI	It	74	72	73	72	291	3	10,800.00	7,370.00
	Henrik STENSON	Swe	74	69	72	76	291	3	10,800.00	7,370.00
	Peter O'MALLEY	Aus	69	78	72	72	291	3	10,800.00	7,370.00
	Peter GUSTAFSSON	Swe	72	73	74	72	291	3	10,800.00	7,370.00
	David HIGGINS	Ire	73	75	70	73	291	3	10,800.00	7,370.00
49	Lee SLATTERY	Eng	72	72	73	75	292	4	8,000.00	5,459.26
	Brett RUMFORD	Aus	73	73	75	71	292	4	8,000.00	5,459.26
	Simon KHAN	Eng	70	76	74	72	292	4	8,000.00	5,459.26
	Simon WAKEFIELD	Eng	71	75	75	71	292	4	8,000.00	5,459.26
	Miguel Angel JIMÉNEZ	Sp	71	72	77	72	292	4	8,000.00	5,459.26
	Eduardo ROMERO	Arg	72	74	72	74	292	4	8,000.00	5,459.26
	Ian WOOSNAM	Wal	73	72	75	72	292	4	8,000.00	5,459.26
	Robert-Jan DERKSEN	NL	72	73	73	74	292	4	8,000.00	5,459.26
57	Miguel Angel MARTIN	Sp	72	76	73	72	293	5	5,600.00	3,821.48
	Gordon BRAND JNR	Scot	72	73	72	76	293	5	5,600.00	3,821.48
	Jean-Francois REMESY	Fr	71	72	73	77	293	5	5,600.00	3,821.48
	Søren HANSEN	Den	76	71	73	73	293	5	5,600.00	3,821.48
	Marc CAYEUX	Zim	71	73	74	75	293	5	5,600.00	3,821.48
	Trevor IMMELMAN	SA	74	74	74	71	293	5	5,600.00	3,821.48
	Ian GARBUTT	Eng	72	74	73	74	293	5	5,600.00	3,821.48
64	Rolf MUNTZ	NL	70	73	76	75	294	6	4,300.00	2,934.35
	Jimmy BOLGER	Ire	73	73	71	77	294	6	4,300.00	2,934.35
	Johan SKOLD	Swe	72	76	74	72	294	6	4,300.00	2,934.35
	Gary EMERSON	Eng	76	71	74	73	294	6	4,300.00	2,934.35
	Klas ERIKSSON	Swe	68	76	73	77	294	6	4,300.00	2,934.35
	Gary MURPHY	Ire	73	72	73	76	294	6	4,300.00	2,934.35
70	Raphaël JACQUELIN	Fr	76	72	70	77	295	7	3,650.00	2,490.79
71	Robert KARLSSON	Swe	72	75	75	74	296	8	3,000.00	2,047.22
72	Mattias ELIASSON	Swe	69	75	73	80	297	9	2,995.50	2,044.15
	John BICKERTON	Eng	73	73	73	78	297	9	2,995.50	2,044.15
74	Niki ZITNY	Aut	77	71	75	75	298	10	2,991.00	2,041.08

Total Prize Fund
€2,011,980 £1,372,991

weekend, would resonate painfully on Sunday evening. "You've got to stand up there and hit a decent shot and win the golf tournament," he said in self-reproach, after reaching the halfway stage in Ireland, a stroke behind leader Dodd.

Saturday brought a special treat for the home supporters in the pairing of Padraig Harrington and Clarke, whom Bob Torrance described as almost exact opposites, technically. "Darren is a touch and feel hands player whereas Padraig makes his legs and body swing his hands and arms," said the golfing guru from Largs.

As things happened, Harrington birdied four of the last six holes for a 68 to win this particular skirmish by a shot. But more spectacular happenings elsewhere brought to mind David Feherty's assertion that low scoring requires a vivid imagination. On that basis, Oliver Wilson must have been truly inspired when holing his second shots for eagle twos on both the 11th and 13th and then carding birdies at the 14th and 15th en route to a course record 66, equalling the effort of Titch Moore earlier in the day, and which was subsequently matched by Nick O'Hern on the final afternoon.

Ultimately, Dodd had to come from four behind the 54 hole leader Dougherty to force a play-off but it was not until 8.20pm when he and Howell went again to the 18th tee, due to the fact that 90 minutes was lost out of the afternoon because of a severe thunderstorm. In the circumstances, the dénouement was fortunately brief, with

Dodd delivering a textbook birdie four to become the champion.

As a postscript, it should be noted that neither he nor Howell got wet. Unlike the situation at Portmarnock in 1927, when, we are informed, Scotland's George Duncan had layers of brown paper wrapped around his body as protection against the elements, when winning the inaugural title.

Fittingly, Dodd's was a nicely-packaged victory too.

Dermot Gilleece
Sunday Independent (Ireland)

Gerard O'Toole, Chief Executive of Nissan Ireland (left), and Lee Mallaghan, President of Carton House Golf Club, pose for a photograph at the end of the third round, after announcing that the Nissan Irish Open will return to Carton House in 2006

BMW Championship

Surrey, England
May 26-29 • 2005

Wentworth Club

Par	Yards	Metres
72	7072	6468

1	**Angel CABRERA**	273	-15
2	Paul McGINLEY	275	-13
3	Nick O'HERN	277	-11
4	David HOWELL	279	-9
5	Peter HANSON	280	-8
	Peter HEDBLOM	280	-8
	Mårten OLANDER	280	-8
8	Michael CAMPBELL	281	-7
	Jamie DONALDSON	281	-7
10	Bradley DREDGE	282	-6

Round One   Round Two   Round Three   Round Four

EUROPEAN TOUR ORDER OF MERIT
(After 23 tournaments)

Pos		€
1	**Retief GOOSEN**	1,008,936.14
2	David HOWELL	907,416.20
3	Angel CABRERA	882,744.05
4	Ernie ELS	842,615.77
5	Thomas BJÖRN	837,874.74
6	Stephen DODD	787,573.56
7	Paul McGINLEY	680,468.75
8	Nick O'HERN	665,588.59
9	Luke DONALD	537,631.80
10	Adam SCOTT	523,209.16

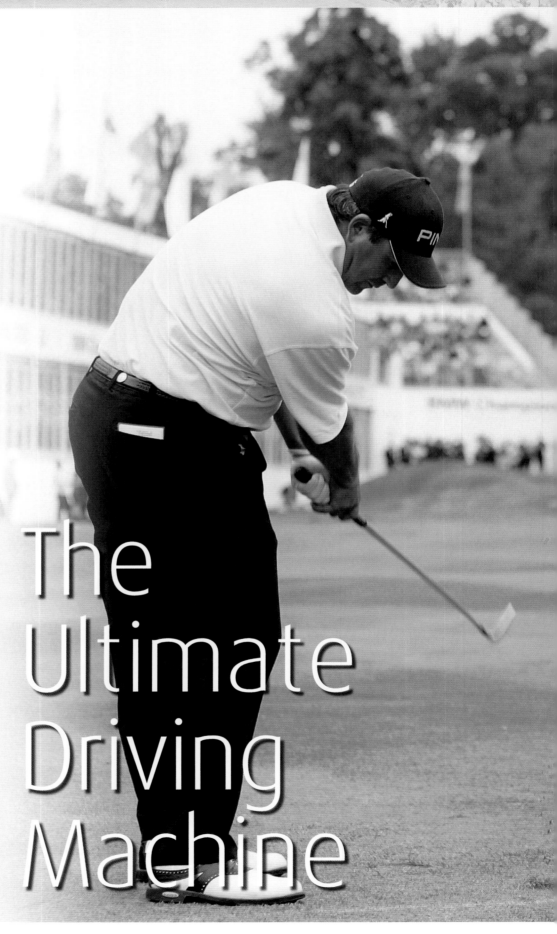

The Ultimate Driving Machine

Playing well across the demanding acres of Wentworth Club's West Course does not require rocket science. All you have to do is to putt like an Angel and drive like a Cabrera.

Ian Woosnam, The 2006 European Ryder Cup Captain, presented Jim Awtrey, the first Chief Executive Officer of The Professional Golfers' Association of America, with two vintage books on fishing at The European Tour Annual Dinner at which Awtrey was the guest speaker

To put it another way, Angel Cabrera has been threatening to win a truly prestigious title on The European Tour International Schedule and nowhere has he threatened more than in this exclusive corner of the Surrey hinterland. Quite how much he felt he was destined to win is difficult to say, given that despite nearly a decade in Europe, this amiable Argentine's English remains a work in progress.

However, you can often tell more from a man's eyes than you hear from his lips and Cabrera's broad and charming smile when he won the BMW Championship told the discerning observer all he or she needed to know about how much pleasure this victory brought, a deep satisfaction that could be filed high above the financial joy of a cheque for €666,660 (£458,652). It was a

win illuminated by play of the very highest calibre, a demonstration of power from the tee and subtlety around the greens that tickled the palms of the sporting gods and delighted everyone who saw it unravel over four days of high-octane competition.

Of course, such impressive play came as no surprise to those who have admired Cabrera's ability for some time. He has posted his intent to do well at this beautiful but demanding venue for years, never more so than in 2001 and 2004 when he finished second on both occasions. Even so, his weekend rounds of 66-67 on this occasion embroidered his CV like no other 36 holes he has ever completed. This was stupendous stuff, especially the 66, a six under par effort that was assembled despite the mischievousness of a viciously swirling wind.

Paul McGinley

Mårten Olander

Roger Chapman of England is presented with an Asprey Trophy commemorating his 600th appearance on The European Tour, which came in April's Jazztel Open de España en Andalucia

"I play good," was Cabrera's summation of that third round and as understatements go, it was a beauty. First to lead the applause was his friend and mentor Eduardo Romero, for it was Romero who encouraged, and financed, his compatriot as Cabrera struggled to gain his playing rights on The European Tour in the 1990s. It was Romero who recognised the raw talent lying within, and Romero who eased Cabrera's passage across the world when finally he made it on to the circuit.

This, of course, is a rich Argentine tradition, one that was finessed by the gauchos as they survived the harshness of the pampas and one that is now ingrained in the native spirit. Argentines are tough and self-disciplined, but they are also emotional and truly decent fellows. For fifty years now they have brought these attributes, and much more, to the European golf scene, adding colour, charm and vibrancy along the way.

The European Tour welcomed four Special Olympic Athletes to Wentworth Club for the BMW Championship, where they enjoyed a conducted tour of the complex which included meeting Sandy Lyle, former winner of the Open Championship and the Masters Tournament, with whom, from left, Graeme Andrew, Sharaine McPike, Siobhaun McPike and Shaun Buist are pictured

Sheer driving pleasure.

BMW Golfsport

www.bmw-golfsport.com

The Ultimate Driving Machine

HOLE	1									11	12	13	14	15	16	17	18	TOTAL
PAR	4	3								4	5	4	3	4	4	5	5	216
1 HEDBLOM	10	10																
4 CABRERA	4	4								5	7		8	8				
2 HOWELL	2	1								3	3	3	4	4	4	6	8	208
5 CAMPBELL	5																	

Nick O'Hern

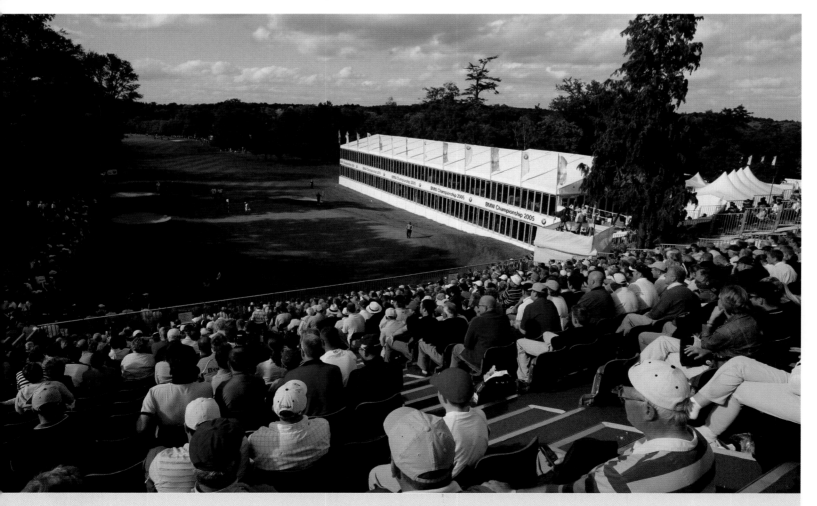

"Whenever I walk into Wentworth, something changes inside me, it is just a very special place. It is a pure shot-maker's course and it's the way I love to play golf. This golf course is a challenge; the rough is high, the fairways are tight and the greens are fast and firm, what more do you want?" – Andrew Oldcorn

Peter Hedblom

Tony Cerda and the great Roberto de Vicenzo were the first to make their mark in this way before Vicenté Fernandez, a gentle man with a gentle limp, carried on the tradition and then Romero dropped in to disarm us all with his play and his personality. Now Cabrera has picked up the torch. "I like playing in Europe," he said. "I feel comfortable here, the people are friendly, I have friends and I like it here."

And, of course, Europe likes him. It is not, however, easy for these guys. They may make an enviable living but there is a price to pay and that price is the loneliness of the long distance golfer, the removal, however temporary, of family and home, the routine of endless hotel rooms and the difficulty of enduring many lands where language is a barrier rather than a communication route. This, naturally, is not exclusive to Argentines, but the way that the golfers from this distant country deal with the problem is beyond

equal. These are mannered and gracious men as well as admirable players.

Mannered and gracious are also words that may be applied to the inaugural BMW Championship itself. The new sponsors of the "old" PGA Championship promised to bring a fresh and clear vision to Wentworth Club on this most important week for The European Tour. They said they would move everything up a gear and, without question, they succeeded brilliantly. It was good before, but it was even better this time, BMW's famous attention to detail adding an extra layer of gloss and class to the landscape.

All this helped to create a wonderful mood amongst the players, a sense that they were indeed somewhere special as well as playing for something very special. "The place has the feel of a Major about it this week, it is terrific," said Padraig Harrington as he

Jim O'Donnell, Managing Director of BMW UK and President of the BMW Championship, presents Steve Webster with a bottle of Moët & Chandon champagne for his hole-in-one on the fifth during the final round of the BMW Championship

Ian Poulter

Above, Retief Goosen presented Ernie Els with the Harry Vardon Trophy for finishing Number One on the 2004 European Tour Order of Merit, while Els presented Scott Drummond (below) with the 2004 Sir Henry Cotton Rookie of the Year Award

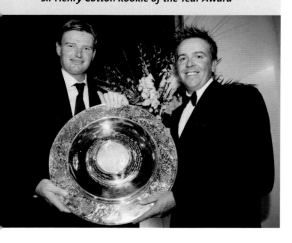

endorsed his own decision to return to the fold after a two year absence from the tournament during which time he learned how to keep the ball low while hitting it long, twin advantages that are necessary if the West Course is to be tackled properly.

It was expected that Harrington would provide Ireland's top challenge over the week but, although he played well to finish just outside the top ten, it was his compatriot Paul McGinley who so nearly stole all the honours. McGinley has been a terrific golfer for many years now and though he has much to celebrate, he has not won as many titles as the quality of his game deserves.

There are many reasons for this but that final veneer of luck is often the overriding one. On many occasions the Dubliner has been unfortunate to come up against an opponent in inspired form and it was the case again thus. His own last round of 67 was a wonderful effort and one worthy of victory, but the fact Cabrera was able to match it, having begun the day with a two

stroke cushion, proved the decisive factor in his winning 15 under par total of 273.

So a week that had begun with the Annual Tour Dinner, a glittering evening set amidst the baronial splendour of the Wentworth Club Ballroom, ended with a broad-shouldered golfer walking somewhat self-

José Maria Olazábal and Graeme McDowell

Luke Donald

Final Results

consciously forward to receive the newly created BMW Trophy, a hi-tech effort that looks as though it might well do 0-60 in under seven seconds if asked. As he held it high for the photographers to mark the moment, Cabrera, on the other hand, looked like he might struggle to complete a mile in under an hour.

Like his pal Romero, he is built for endurance. There is, however, one small but significant advantage for a man to this natural lack of acceleration: It might take longer to get there but he gets to smell more flowers along the way and Cabrera never enjoyed that aspect more than in a thrilling week at Wentworth Club. "Thank you very much," he said. "It is really the very best moment of my life."

He has never spoken better English.

Bill Elliott
The Observer / Golf Monthly

Pos	Name		Rd1	Rd2	Rd3	Rd4	Total		€	£
1	Angel CABRERA	Arg	70	70	66	67	273	-15	666,660.00	458,652.10
2	Paul MCGINLEY	Ire	72	64	72	67	275	-13	444,440.00	305,768.07
3	Nick O'HERN	Aus	68	69	76	64	277	-11	250,400.00	172,271.45
4	David HOWELL	Eng	70	72	66	71	279	-9	200,000.00	137,597.01
5	Mårten OLANDER	Swe	68	72	70	70	280	-8	143,200.00	98,519.46
	Peter HANSON	Swe	69	69	72	70	280	-8	143,200.00	98,519.46
	Peter HEDBLOM	Swe	68	65	73	74	280	-8	143,200.00	98,519.46
8	Michael CAMPBELL	NZ	71	68	71	71	281	-7	94,800.00	65,220.98
	Jamie DONALDSON	Wal	73	71	69	68	281	-7	94,800.00	65,220.98
10	Bradley DREDGE	Wal	75	68	69	70	282	-6	80,000.00	55,038.80
11	Retief GOOSEN	SA	70	70	72	71	283	-5	62,457.14	42,969.58
	Thongchai JAIDEE	Thai	72	67	71	73	283	-5	62,457.14	42,969.58
	Scott DRUMMOND	Scot	71	71	73	68	283	-5	62,457.14	42,969.58
	Colin MONTGOMERIE	Scot	71	73	73	66	283	-5	62,457.14	42,969.58
	Steve WEBSTER	Eng	71	72	71	69	283	-5	62,457.14	42,969.58
	Padraig HARRINGTON	Ire	70	68	74	71	283	-5	62,457.14	42,969.58
	Gary MURPHY	Ire	74	68	70	71	283	-5	62,457.14	42,969.58
18	Damien MCGRANE	Ire	69	71	72	72	284	-4	48,900.00	33,642.47
	Peter FOWLER	Aus	68	76	74	66	284	-4	48,900.00	33,642.47
	Paul BROADHURST	Eng	70	70	74	70	284	-4	48,900.00	33,642.47
	Luke DONALD	Eng	71	72	74	67	284	-4	48,900.00	33,642.47
22	Richard STERNE	SA	73	71	72	69	285	-3	42,800.00	29,445.76
	Peter LONARD	Aus	69	70	75	71	285	-3	42,800.00	29,445.76
	Thomas BJÖRN	Den	71	71	75	68	285	-3	42,800.00	29,445.76
	Ian WOOSNAM	Wal	75	69	71	70	285	-3	42,800.00	29,445.76
	José Maria OLAZÁBAL	Sp	72	69	71	73	285	-3	42,800.00	29,445.76
27	Søren KJELDSEN	Den	75	68	72	71	286	-2	36,200.00	24,905.06
	Andrew MARSHALL	Eng	72	72	70	72	286	-2	36,200.00	24,905.06
	Jonathan LOMAS	Eng	72	68	78	68	286	-2	36,200.00	24,905.06
	Niclas FASTH	Swe	71	73	74	68	286	-2	36,200.00	24,905.06
	Lee WESTWOOD	Eng	72	71	73	70	286	-2	36,200.00	24,905.06
	Graeme MCDOWELL	N.Ire	67	76	75	68	286	-2	36,200.00	24,905.06
33	Paul LAWRIE	Scot	73	70	70	74	287	-1	29,666.67	20,410.22
	Ian POULTER	Eng	71	69	73	74	287	-1	29,666.67	20,410.22
	Trevor IMMELMAN	SA	72	71	74	70	287	-1	29,666.67	20,410.22
	Richard GREEN	Aus	71	70	77	69	287	-1	29,666.67	20,410.22
	Nick FALDO	Eng	70	71	77	69	287	-1	29,666.67	20,410.22
	Ben CURTIS	USA	68	71	76	72	287	-1	29,666.67	20,410.22
39	Robert-Jan DERKSEN	NL	71	69	76	72	288	0	23,200.00	15,961.25
	Peter LAWRIE	Ire	67	75	75	71	288	0	23,200.00	15,961.25
	Thomas LEVET	Fr	72	72	73	71	288	0	23,200.00	15,961.25
	Philip GOLDING	Eng	71	73	74	70	288	0	23,200.00	15,961.25
	Ernie ELS	SA	73	69	75	71	288	0	23,200.00	15,961.25
	Stephen DODD	Wal	69	74	74	71	288	0	23,200.00	15,961.25
	Robert COLES	Eng	69	71	76	72	288	0	23,200.00	15,961.25
	David LYNN	Eng	71	73	74	70	288	0	23,200.00	15,961.25
	Steven O'HARA	Scot	69	72	73	74	288	0	23,200.00	15,961.25
	Alastair FORSYTH	Scot	69	72	75	72	288	0	23,200.00	15,961.25
49	Jose-Filipe LIMA	Port	67	73	78	71	289	1	16,400.00	11,282.95
	Marcus FRASER	Aus	68	72	78	71	289	1	16,400.00	11,282.95
	Stephen SCAHILL	NZ	71	73	73	72	289	1	16,400.00	11,282.95
	David CARTER	Eng	75	69	72	73	289	1	16,400.00	11,282.95
	Marcel SIEM	Ger	70	74	71	74	289	1	16,400.00	11,282.95
	Henrik STENSON	Swe	70	74	71	74	289	1	16,400.00	11,282.95
	Raphaël JACQUELIN	Fr	70	73	76	70	289	1	16,400.00	11,282.95
56	Kenneth FERRIE	Eng	72	69	76	73	290	2	12,300.00	8,462.22
	Miguel Angel JIMÉNEZ	Sp	70	73	76	71	290	2	12,300.00	8,462.22
	Pierre FULKE	Swe	74	69	73	74	290	2	12,300.00	8,462.22
	Lee SLATTERY	Eng	70	69	84	67	290	2	12,300.00	8,462.22
60	Søren HANSEN	Den	70	71	78	72	291	3	11,200.00	7,705.43
61	Andrew COLTART	Scot	70	73	80	69	292	4	10,800.00	7,430.24
62	Rolf MUNTZ	NL	74	69	77	73	293	5	10,000.00	6,879.85
	Phil EDWARDS	Eng	71	72	75	75	293	5	10,000.00	6,879.85
	Tony JOHNSTONE	Zim	72	72	76	73	293	5	10,000.00	6,879.85
65	Graeme STORM	Eng	73	71	82	70	296	8	8,800.00	6,054.27
	Patrik SJÖLAND	Swe	72	70	75	79	296	8	8,800.00	6,054.27
	Simon DYSON	Eng	70	73	76	77	296	8	8,800.00	6,054.27
68	Scott HENDERSON	Scot	73	72	78	75	297	9	7,800.00	5,366.28
	Alessandro TADINI	It	73	70	76	78	297	9	7,800.00	5,366.28
70	Matthew KING	Eng	72	71	82	77	302	14	7,300.00	5,022.79
71	Miles TUNNICLIFF	Eng	72	72	81	79	304	16	6,000.00	4,127.91
72	Darren CLARKE	N.Ire	71	69	W/D		140	-4		

George O'Grady, Executive Director of The European Tour, with The European Tour Wives' Association (ETWA) which announced under the slogan of 'GOLFERS GIVING BACK' a new initiative to support charitable causes throughout Europe by selling wristbands bearing the word 'GOLFAID' at European Tour events

Total Prize Fund
€4,006,000   £2,756,067

The Celtic Manor Wales Open

Newport, South Wales

June 2-5 • 2005

The Celtic Manor Resort		
Par	**Yards**	**Metres**
69	6743	6165

1	**Miguel Angel JIMÉNEZ**	262	-14	
2	Martin ERLANDSSON	266	-10	
	José Manuel LARA	266	-10	
4	Jean-François LUCQUIN	267	-9	
5	Joakim HAEGGMAN	268	-8	
	Alessandro TADINI	268	-8	
	Ian WOOSNAM	268	-8	
8	Jose-Filipe LIMA	270	-6	
	David LYNN	270	-6	
	Wade ORMSBY	270	-6	
	Oliver WILSON	270	-6	

| Round One | Round Two | Round Three | Round Four |

EUROPEAN TOUR ORDER OF MERIT
(After 24 tournaments)

Pos		€	
1	**Retief GOOSEN**	1,008,936.14	
2	David HOWELL	921,773.87	
3	Angel CABRERA	882,744.05	
4	Ernie ELS	842,615.77	
5	Thomas BJÖRN	837,874.74	
6	Stephen DODD	787,573.56	
7	Miguel Angel JIMÉNEZ	773,149.11	
8	Paul McGINLEY	690,910.69	
9	Nick O'HERN	665,588.59	
10	Luke DONALD	537,631.80	

Hail Caesar!

The Celtic Manor Wales Open

Newport, South Wales
June 2-5 • 2005

The year was 1990 and the venue, St Pierre on the outskirts of Chepstow. Welsh hearts pounded with pride as the Darling of the Valleys, Ian Woosnam, marched imperiously towards one of his 29 titles on The European Tour in the Epson Grand Prix of Europe. This was 'Woosie' in his pomp...powerful, accurate, fearless and indestructible.

Stephen Gallacher

Scant attention that day was paid to a 26 year old Spaniard with a sallow complexion and a mop of marmalade coloured curls, whose gait hinted more at farming stock rather than the graceful elegance of a matador. The man in question had not long succeeded at his fourth attempt to secure his playing credentials at The European Tour Qualifying School and his debut victory on Tour was more than two years in the future.

On that final day, however, as Woosnam swatted aside all-comers with that effortless swish of his to achieve victory with a total of 271, Miguel Angel Jiménez tied with four others for 41st place, 15 shots adrift, collecting a pay cheque for the princely sum of £2,400.

"The greens can be difficult unless you are driving it well and hitting it in the right part of the fairway. If you are not, you will not be able to access the pins because there are many different levels and shelves on the putting surfaces. It is a very good test" – Bradley Dredge

Christian Cévaër

By the season's end, £75,933 and 54th place on the Order of Merit represented a good return for his second full season on Tour.

Fast forward 15 years to The Celtic Manor Resort, that spectacular edifice perched on a rocky outcrop high above the M4 and the City of Newport and a glowing testimony to the vision and indefatigability of entrepreneur, Sir Terry Matthews.

The final day of The Celtic Manor Wales Open brought with it a sense of déjà vu. Once more there was Woosnam, just a single stroke off the lead, challenging for his 30th Tour title at the venerable age of 47. The crowds snaking along the edge of the fairways had come to hail Caesar at the Roman Road course. But, just like the great Emperor on the Ides of March, there was a Brutus lying in wait.

Both Jiménez and Woosnam went into the final day one shot behind long-time leader,

Alessandro Tadini of Italy, and when the Welshman chipped in at the first, it appeared that The European Ryder Cup Captain for 2006 might give the galleries their fervent wish.

Unknown to Woosnam, however, Jiménez was lurking menacingly with daggers drawn and a final round, course record-equalling 62, repelled all challengers. Unleashing his vast repertoire of stroke making and draining putts from every distance, the Spaniard cruised home in 29 to win by a four stroke margin from his fellow countryman, José Manuel Lara, and Swede Martin Erlandsson, as Woosnam finished tied fifth.

The wonder of golf is that it does not conform. Vigorous training regimens are optional, practice and diet likewise. Jiménez is certainly non-conformist. It is inconceivable that Tiger Woods's first task on signing his card would be to turn his golf bag upside down in search of a cigar cutter, prior to igniting a massive Havana.

Alessandro Tadini

1400 acres of breathing space

The Celtic Manor Resort is a world-class destination, set in 1400 acres of panoramic parkland in the beautiful Usk Valley, South Wales

A five star 330 room hotel serves as the luxurious setting for a complete golfing experience. The resort offers two very different and challenging championship courses along with a state of the art golf academy and Coldra Woods, an 18 hole golf course - the first of its kind in Europe, dedicated to tuition.

The Wentwood Hills course, venue for the 2010 Ryder Cup offers a perfect combination of wooded slopes and links-like features.

Roman Road, venue this year for The Celtic Manor Wales Open, offers long open fairways on the front nine and a back nine that twists and turns through trees and across streams.

Add to this The Forum Spa with 16 treatment rooms, 2 health clubs, a state of the art Convention Centre and Exhibition Hall, 4 restaurants, and outdoor activities which include tennis, fishing, walking trails, mountain biking and clay pigeon shooting, The Celtic Manor Resort offers something special for the discerning golfer.

THE CELTIC MANOR RESORT

The Celtic Manor Resort
Coldra Woods
The Usk Valley
South Wales
United Kingdom
NP18 1HQ

T: +44 (0) 1633 413000
F: +44 (0) 1633 412910

E: postbox@celtic-manor.com
www.celtic-manor.com

Paul Lawrie

Final Results

Pos	Name		Rd1	Rd2	Rd3	Rd4	Total		€	£
1	Miguel Angel JIMÉNEZ	Sp	63	67	70	62	262	-14	362,567.50	250,000.00
2	Martin ERLANDSSON	Swe	69	65	69	63	266	-10	188,941.20	130,280.00
	José Manuel LARA	Sp	68	65	67	66	266	-10	188,941.20	130,280.00
4	Jean-François LUCQUIN	Fr	65	66	69	67	267	-9	108,770.30	75,000.00
5	Joakim HAEGGMAN	Swe	68	66	68	66	268	-8	77,879.50	53,700.00
	Ian WOOSNAM	Wal	64	68	68	68	268	-8	77,879.50	53,700.00
	Alessandro TADINI	It	65	62	72	69	268	-8	77,879.50	53,700.00
8	David LYNN	Eng	63	66	72	69	270	-6	46,662.44	32,175.00
	Jose-Filipe LIMA	Port	65	70	67	68	270	-6	46,662.44	32,175.00
	Wade ORMSBY	Aus	67	68	70	65	270	-6	46,662.44	32,175.00
	Oliver WILSON	Eng	67	67	69	67	270	-6	46,662.44	32,175.00
12	Nick DOUGHERTY	Eng	65	72	65	69	271	-5	35,241.56	24,300.00
	Gary ORR	Scot	66	70	67	68	271	-5	35,241.56	24,300.00
	Anthony WALL	Eng	70	68	66	67	271	-5	35,241.56	24,300.00
15	Steve WEBSTER	Eng	68	71	68	65	272	-4	31,325.83	21,600.00
	Michael CAMPBELL	NZ	65	72	70	65	272	-4	31,325.83	21,600.00
17	Paul LAWRIE	Scot	67	68	69	69	273	-3	26,322.40	18,150.00
	Søren KJELDSEN	Den	69	69	68	67	273	-3	26,322.40	18,150.00
	Raphaël JACQUELIN	Fr	67	66	70	70	273	-3	26,322.40	18,150.00
	Peter SENIOR	Aus	63	72	72	66	273	-3	26,322.40	18,150.00
	Richard BLAND	Eng	66	70	69	68	273	-3	26,322.40	18,150.00
	Jan-Are LARSEN	Nor	67	68	69	69	273	-3	26,322.40	18,150.00
	Paul BROADHURST	Eng	70	68	70	65	273	-3	26,322.40	18,150.00
24	Stuart LITTLE	Eng	64	69	72	69	274	-2	21,645.28	14,925.00
	Robert COLES	Eng	68	69	72	65	274	-2	21,645.28	14,925.00
	Fredrik ANDERSSON HED	Swe	67	70	69	68	274	-2	21,645.28	14,925.00
	Terry PRICE	Aus	70	67	65	72	274	-2	21,645.28	14,925.00
	Francois DELAMONTAGNE	Fr	66	66	71	71	274	-2	21,645.28	14,925.00
	Richard STERNE	SA	67	72	70	65	274	-2	21,645.28	14,925.00
30	Richard FINCH	Eng	67	65	75	68	275	-1	17,765.81	12,250.00
	Andrew COLTART	Scot	65	74	66	70	275	-1	17,765.81	12,250.00
	Christian CÉVAËR	Fr	67	65	75	68	275	-1	17,765.81	12,250.00
	Søren HANSEN	Den	67	70	70	68	275	-1	17,765.81	12,250.00
	Jean-Francois REMESY	Fr	69	68	74	64	275	-1	17,765.81	12,250.00
	Gary MURPHY	Ire	68	71	69	67	275	-1	17,765.81	12,250.00
36	David HOWELL	Eng	71	67	72	66	276	0	14,357.67	9,900.00
	Kenneth FERRIE	Eng	65	68	73	70	276	0	14,357.67	9,900.00
	Henrik STENSON	Swe	67	69	71	69	276	0	14,357.67	9,900.00
	Bradley DREDGE	Wal	69	68	67	72	276	0	14,357.67	9,900.00
	Ignacio GARRIDO	Sp	66	71	70	69	276	0	14,357.67	9,900.00
	Jarmo SANDELIN	Swe	68	67	69	72	276	0	14,357.67	9,900.00
	Ben MASON	Eng	67	67	70	72	276	0	14,357.67	9,900.00
	Leif WESTERBERG	Swe	66	69	72	69	276	0	14,357.67	9,900.00
44	John BICKERTON	Eng	69	70	70	68	277	1	10,441.94	7,200.00
	Simon WAKEFIELD	Eng	69	68	70	70	277	1	10,441.94	7,200.00
	Niclas FASTH	Swe	68	69	67	73	277	1	10,441.94	7,200.00
	Paul MCGINLEY	Ire	68	70	71	68	277	1	10,441.94	7,200.00
	Peter LAWRIE	Ire	68	71	69	69	277	1	10,441.94	7,200.00
	Nicolas COLSAERTS	Bel	70	68	71	68	277	1	10,441.94	7,200.00
	Anders HANSEN	Den	67	69	70	71	277	1	10,441.94	7,200.00
	David GILFORD	Eng	69	70	71	67	277	1	10,441.94	7,200.00
	Sandy LYLE	Scot	68	70	74	65	277	1	10,441.94	7,200.00
	James HEATH	Eng	63	69	70	75	277	1	10,441.94	7,200.00
54	Ross FISHER	Eng	70	68	76	64	278	2	7,070.07	4,875.00
	Gordon BRAND JNR	Scot	71	68	72	67	278	2	7,070.07	4,875.00
	Carlos RODILES	Sp	68	68	71	71	278	2	7,070.07	4,875.00
	Emanuele CANONICA	It	67	68	76	67	278	2	7,070.07	4,875.00
	Benoit TEILLERIA	Fr	63	69	74	72	278	2	7,070.07	4,875.00
	Jamie DONALDSON	Wal	67	68	69	74	278	2	7,070.07	4,875.00
60	Stephen GALLACHER	Scot	66	68	76	69	279	3	5,329.74	3,675.00
	Graeme STORM	Eng	68	68	72	71	279	3	5,329.74	3,675.00
	David PARK	Wal	68	67	75	69	279	3	5,329.74	3,675.00
	Neil CHEETHAM	Eng	65	72	71	71	279	3	5,329.74	3,675.00
	Roger CHAPMAN	Eng	68	70	75	66	279	3	5,329.74	3,675.00
	Miguel Angel MARTIN	Sp	69	66	73	71	279	3	5,329.74	3,675.00
	Mårten OLANDER	Swe	67	67	72	73	279	3	5,329.74	3,675.00
	Marcus FRASER	Aus	71	68	69	71	279	3	5,329.74	3,675.00
68	Peter HEDBLOM	Swe	66	71	73	70	280	4	4,152.61	2,863.33
	Gary EMERSON	Eng	63	71	73	73	280	4	4,152.61	2,863.33
	Brad KENNEDY	Aus	69	67	75	69	280	4	4,152.61	2,863.33
71	Darren FICHARDT	SA	69	69	72	71	281	5	3,261.60	2,248.89
	Hernan REY	Arg	70	68	72	71	281	5	3,261.50	2,248.89
73	Adam GROOM	Aus	69	70	75	68	282	6	3,254.00	2,243.72
	David DRYSDALE	Scot	69	68	73	72	282	6	3,254.00	2,243.72
	Simon KHAN	Eng	67	72	69	74	282	6	3,254.00	2,243.72
76	Marco BERNARDINI	It	74	65	75	69	283	7	3,245.00	2,237.51
	André CRUSE	SA	67	72	78	66	283	7	3,245.00	2,237.51
	Andrew OLDCORN	Scot	66	73	72	72	283	7	3,245.00	2,237.51
79	Pelle EDBERG	Swe	72	66	78	72	288	12	3,239.00	2,233.38
80	Fernando ROCA	Sp	70	69	77	77	293	17	3,236.00	2,231.31

At 41, Jiménez has made one small concession to the advancing years by paying the occasional visit to any convenient Health Club or Spa when he is competing. "It's very important to be fit. I am fit – just look at my muscles!" he smiled mischievously, flexing biceps which would not have impressed many of the 'gym rats' who work out slavishly almost daily on Tour.

However, the man from Malaga places joie de vivre ahead of physical exertion. The cigars, the Rioja Reserva and the obligatory cups of extra strong coffee all go to create a toxic mix which might not work for many professionals, but provide Jiménez with the balance for an ideal lifestyle.

It was the absence of that very cocktail which persuaded him to abandon the US PGA Tour to return to play full-time on The European Tour. Victory in Wales was his seventh in his previous 39 starts and he remained very positive about the wisdom of that decision.

"I do concentrate more now on The European Tour" he observed. "This is my 17th season on Tour and I feel I want to give something back to The European Tour. It is my home Tour and I enjoy it very much."

Occasionally, his words in faltering English become lost, but there is no mistaking the sense of fun that he exudes. He is a courteous, likeable man but politeness should never be confused with weakness. That first Sunday in June, Jiménez was a general without equal.

Hail Miguel Angel, the new Caesar of the Roman Road.

Gordon Simpson

Total Prize Fund
€2,207,900 £1,522,406

The KLM Open

Hilversum, The Netherlands
June 9-12 • 2005

Hilversumsche Golf Club

Par	Yards	Metres
70	6660	6091

1	**Gonzalo FERNANDEZ-CASTANO**	**269**	**-11**	
2	Gary EMERSON	271	-9	
3	Paul BROADHURST	272	-8	
4	Markus BRIER	273	-7	
	Maarten LAFEBER	273	-7	
6	Robert COLES	274	-6	
7	John BICKERTON	275	-5	
	Peter SENIOR	275	-5	
9	Pierre FULKE	277	-3	
	David LYNN	277	-3	
	Damien McGRANE	277	-3	
	Steven O'HARA	277	-3	
	Andrew OLDCORN	277	-3	
	Johan SKOLD	277	-3	
	Alessandro TADINI	277	-3	

Round One	Round Two	Round Three	Round Four

EUROPEAN TOUR ORDER OF MERIT
(After 25 tournaments)

Pos		€	
1	**Retief GOOSEN**	**1,008,936.14**	
2	David HOWELL	921,773.87	
3	Angel CABRERA	882,744.05	
4	Ernie ELS	842,615.77	
5	Thomas BJÖRN	837,874.74	
6	Stephen DODD	787,573.56	
7	Miguel Angel JIMÉNEZ	773,149.11	
8	Paul McGINLEY	690,910.69	
9	Nick O'HERN	665,588.59	
10	Luke DONALD	537,631.80	

Shout of Triumph

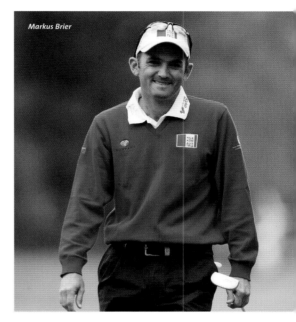

One of the great strengths of The European Tour is its ability to embrace both old and new elements of the game of golf under the same umbrella. A perfect example of that came in The KLM Open which, under various alter egos, had been in existence since 1912, but which was won this time by a young man who had not yet completed a full season as a professional.

KLM, national airline of The Netherlands, was now in its second consecutive year as title sponsor after having been in the same position from 1981 to 1990, but Gonzalo Fernandez-Castano would hardly remember much about those earlier days – for he was not born until 1980.

But that was there and then and this was here and now. A moment, an instant, a prolonged whisper of hope that was finally released and allowed to grow into a great shout of triumph.

On the face of it, Fernandez-Castano had, at best, a committed and eternally hopeful punter's hope of winning the tournament,

faced, as he was in the closing stages, by a pair of Englishmen who handsomely exceeded the average age of the field at the Hilversumsche Golf Club. Gary Emerson was 41 and Paul Broadhurst 39 - if not exactly greybeards yet, at least substantially seasoned performers.

And yet Fernandez-Castano was more than equal to the threat the pair were able to pose, especially on a final day when, it was thought, his lack of experience would find him out. That it did not was to his enormous credit.

Like most young Spaniards, Fernandez-Castano cited Severiano Ballesteros as a major influence in his golfing life and, although as a

Markus Brier

Paul Broadhurst

Peter Fowler

proud Madrileno the young pretender was born hundreds of miles away from El Gran Senor's stamping grounds in the north-east of that great country, his admiration for Seve was no less sincerely meant.

Comparisons between Fernandez-Castano and Ballesteros were inevitable, if invidious. Ballesteros turned professional at 17 and within two years was Europe's Number One. His young compatriot had a college education before taking the shilling the previous September when he was almost 24. For all that, this victory, completed with a final round of 67 for an 11 under par total of 269, came in his 16th appearance in a full European Tour International Schedule event - Ballesteros had had to wait until his 27th.

In the face of such a statistic, it might be thought that Fernandez-Castano careered through the tournament with all the desperate urgency of a man running late for his train. It was not like that at all, however.

Throughout the four days on the tough, ultra-demanding and tight Hilversumsche course, the young Spaniard kept commendably cool. The casual visitor to the club that day would, and could, never have known that this was an untried and relatively untested professional they were watching. To say that he played with a maturity far beyond his years would be to understate the case by a factor of about 50.

He thrust himself towards the top table early in the piece and with huge restraint combined with sensible aggression, he stayed there, and then some.

It has to be said - and he did, willingly – that he enjoyed several different shades of luck during the final day, played out in a tricky, troublesome breeze. Emerson, his playing partner, had said earlier in the week that he liked playing on tree-lined courses and he proved how fond of them he was by spending an inordinate amount of time

Gary Emerson

"This is a proper golf course, one that makes you think all the way round. The rough is very penal, but that doesn't make it in any way unfair. It's the Sunningdale of Holland and I can think of no greater praise than that. It is a privilege to play on" – *Gary Emerson*

Andrew Oldcorn

Final Results

Pos	Name		Rd1	Rd2	Rd3	Rd4	Total		€	£
1	Gonzalo FERNANDEZ-CASTANO	Sp	66	70	66	67	269	-11	250,000.00	168,704.62
2	Gary EMERSON	Eng	69	63	69	70	271	-9	166,660.00	112,465.25
3	Paul BROADHURST	Eng	66	67	69	70	272	-8	93,900.00	63,365.45
4	Maarten LAFEBER	NL	68	67	70	68	273	-7	69,300.00	46,764.92
	Markus BRIER	Aut	67	68	69	69	273	-7	69,300.00	46,764.92
6	Robert COLES	Eng	71	67	70	66	274	-6	52,500.00	35,427.97
7	John BICKERTON	Eng	74	67	69	65	275	-5	41,250.00	27,836.26
	Peter SENIOR	Aus	70	67	68	70	275	-5	41,250.00	27,836.26
9	Andrew OLDCORN	Scot	69	67	70	71	277	-3	26,592.86	17,945.35
	Alessandro TADINI	It	70	64	71	72	277	-3	26,592.86	17,945.35
	Damien MCGRANE	Ire	68	70	71	68	277	-3	26,592.86	17,945.35
	David LYNN	Eng	70	67	70	70	277	-3	26,592.86	17,945.35
	Johan SKOLD	Swe	68	70	72	67	277	-3	26,592.86	17,945.35
	Pierre FULKE	Swe	67	73	69	68	277	-3	26,592.86	17,945.35
	Steven O'HARA	Scot	70	65	72	70	277	-3	26,592.86	17,945.35
16	Rolf MUNTZ	NL	69	69	72	68	278	-2	19,470.00	13,138.72
	Carlos RODILES	Sp	73	68	67	70	278	-2	19,470.00	13,138.72
	Jamie SPENCE	Eng	73	69	71	65	278	-2	19,470.00	13,138.72
	Philip GOLDING	Eng	74	67	69	68	278	-2	19,470.00	13,138.72
	Andrew MARSHALL	Eng	72	69	68	69	278	-2	19,470.00	13,138.72
21	Miguel Angel MARTIN	Sp	69	67	70	73	279	-1	16,725.00	11,286.34
	Martin MARITZ	SA	69	70	71	69	279	-1	16,725.00	11,286.34
	Alastair FORSYTH	Scot	72	65	73	69	279	-1	16,725.00	11,286.34
	Guido VAN DER VALK	NL	66	70	72	71	279	-1	16,725.00	11,286.34
25	Ivo GINER	Sp	69	73	68	70	280	0	14,250.00	9,616.16
	Gregory BOURDY	Fr	71	69	68	72	280	0	14,250.00	9,616.16
	Marcus FRASER	Aus	68	69	71	72	280	0	14,250.00	9,616.16
	Bradley DREDGE	Wal	73	70	68	69	280	0	14,250.00	9,616.16
	David PARK	Wal	73	69	73	65	280	0	14,250.00	9,616.16
	Santiago LUNA	Sp	69	73	71	67	280	0	14,250.00	9,616.16
	Francesco MOLINARI	It	71	73	69	67	280	0	14,250.00	9,616.16
32	Stuart LITTLE	Eng	70	71	73	67	281	1	11,156.25	7,528.44
	Robert-Jan DERKSEN	NL	68	72	71	70	281	1	11,156.25	7,528.44
	Mark ROE	Eng	68	73	70	70	281	1	11,156.25	7,528.44
	José Manuel CARRILES	Sp	70	71	71	69	281	1	11,156.25	7,528.44
	Anthony WALL	Eng	69	71	68	73	281	1	11,156.25	7,528.44
	Christopher HANELL	Swe	69	74	70	68	281	1	11,156.25	7,528.44
	Michael JONZON	Swe	71	70	73	67	281	1	11,156.25	7,528.44
	Louis OOSTHUIZEN	SA	72	70	69	70	281	1	11,156.25	7,528.44
40	Graeme STORM	Eng	71	71	70	70	282	2	9,000.00	6,073.37
	Darren FICHARDT	SA	70	72	69	71	282	2	9,000.00	6,073.37
	José Manuel LARA	Sp	70	72	68	72	282	2	9,000.00	6,073.37
	Gordon BRAND JNR	Scot	74	67	69	72	282	2	9,000.00	6,073.37
	Richard BLAND	Eng	71	64	74	73	282	2	9,000.00	6,073.37
	Peter BAKER	Eng	69	71	73	69	282	2	9,000.00	6,073.37
46	Anders HANSEN	Den	71	73	69	70	283	3	7,950.00	5,364.81
47	Peter FOWLER	Aus	73	70	67	74	284	4	6,600.00	4,453.80
	Peter LAWRIE	Ire	70	70	74	70	284	4	6,600.00	4,453.80
	Ian GARBUTT	Eng	71	72	71	70	284	4	6,600.00	4,453.80
	Sebastian FERNANDEZ	Arg	72	69	75	68	284	4	6,600.00	4,453.80
	Raymond RUSSELL	Scot	67	70	73	74	284	4	6,600.00	4,453.80
	Simon WAKEFIELD	Eng	69	74	73	68	284	4	6,600.00	4,453.80
	David CARTER	Eng	71	73	70	70	284	4	6,600.00	4,453.80
	Gary ORR	Scot	72	70	75	67	284	4	6,600.00	4,453.80
55	Henrik NYSTROM	Swe	66	72	71	76	285	5	4,650.00	3,137.91
	Adam GROOM	Aus	66	71	78	70	285	5	4,650.00	3,137.91
	Stuart MANLEY	Wal	72	72	72	69	285	5	4,650.00	3,137.91
	Paul EALES	Eng	74	70	75	66	285	5	4,650.00	3,137.91
	Fredrik HENGE	Swe	68	71	73	73	285	5	4,650.00	3,137.91
	Roger CHAPMAN	Eng	70	70	75	70	285	5	4,650.00	3,137.91
61	Phillip ARCHER	Eng	70	74	69	73	286	6	3,825.00	2,581.18
	Leif WESTERBERG	Swe	73	68	75	70	286	6	3,825.00	2,581.18
	Robert ROCK	Eng	71	70	72	73	286	6	3,825.00	2,581.18
	Ben MASON	Eng	68	76	68	74	286	6	3,825.00	2,581.18
65	Benoit TEILLERIA	Fr	68	76	66	77	287	7	3,225.00	2,176.29
	Fredrik ANDERSSON HED	Swe	75	67	75	70	287	7	3,225.00	2,176.29
	Oliver WILSON	Eng	72	72	69	74	287	7	3,225.00	2,176.29
	Brad KENNEDY	Aus	71	70	75	71	287	7	3,225.00	2,176.29
69	Patrik SJÖLAND	Swe	73	68	75	72	288	8	2,521.75	1,701.72
	Kyron SULLIVAN	Wal	68	70	75	75	288	8	2,521.75	1,701.72
	Neil CHEETHAM	Eng	69	71	73	75	288	8	2,521.75	1,701.72
	Mark FOSTER	Eng	71	70	75	72	288	8	2,521.75	1,701.72
73	Cesar MONASTERIO	Arg	71	73	70	75	289	9	2,242.50	1,513.28
	Francois DELAMONTAGNE	Fr	72	72	74	71	289	9	2,242.50	1,513.28
75	Wade ORMSBY	Aus	71	73	75	71	290	10	2,232.00	1,506.19
	Sam LITTLE	Eng	72	72	71	75	290	10	2,232.00	1,506.19
	Jean-François LUCQUIN	Fr	69	73	77	71	290	10	2,232.00	1,506.19
	Pelle EDBERG	Swe	69	74	75	72	290	10	2,232.00	1,506.19
	Andrew MCLARDY	SA	73	69	76	72	290	10	2,232.00	1,506.19
80	Rafael GOMEZ	Arg	72	72	76	73	293	13	2,223.00	1,500.12
81	Jan-Are LARSEN	Nor	71	72	78	73	294	14	2,220.00	1,498.10
82	Tobias DIER	Ger	70	74	73	80	297	17	2,217.00	1,496.07

Total Prize Fund
€1,526,800   £1,030,313

wandering around in the forest on Sunday. It cost him six bogeys.

But if that was a factor in the winner being who he was, so was his own skill, allied to a few chunky dollops of good fortune. Compared with Emerson's profligacy off the tee, Fernandez-Castano was accuracy personified. Add in a couple of enormous putts for birdie on the eighth and ninth and another for par at the 11th and the plot became easier to comprehend.

Nobody knew it at the time, but the template for the day was set on the third hole, where Fernandez-Castano's seven-iron second shot from 161 yards would have ended up making an early acquaintance with the fourth tee had it not plunged full pitch into the hole without touching the sides for an outrageous eagle two. No wonder he won.

Even so, he only made it by two shots, which, if anything, flattered Emerson, who

although he intermittently produced some decent golf, would be the first to admit that he was always playing tag with his younger opponent without often threatening to catch him. A considerable consolation was that he had by far the biggest pay-day of his career - €166,660 (£112,465) – and in doing so, he won just under £1,000 less than he made in the whole of the previous season, which had included a victory in the BMW Russian Open.

"It's a dream come true," said Fernandez-Castano, who pocketed €250,000 (£168,704). "It was one of those days when everything came easy. I was really feeling the pressure on the back nine and by the time I got to the 18th I just wanted it to end."

He need not have worried - it had been over and done with long before that.

Mel Webb
The Times

Gordon Brand Jnr

Aa St Omer Open

Lumbres, France
June 16-19 • 2005

Aa Saint Omer Golf Club

Par	Yards	Metres
71	6880	6289

1	**Joakim BÄCKSTRÖM**	**280**	**-4**	
2	Paul DWYER	280	-4	
3	James HEATH	281	-3	
	Steven JEPPESEN	281	-3	
	Michael JONZON	281	-3	
6	Ross FISHER	282	-2	
	James HEPWORTH	282	-2	
	Ben MASON	282	-2	
	Alvaro SALTO	282	-2	
	Carl SUNESON	282	-2	

 Round One   Round Two   Round Three   Round Four

EUROPEAN TOUR ORDER OF MERIT
(After 26 tournaments)

Pos		€	
1	**Retief GOOSEN**	**1,008,936.14**	
2	David HOWELL	921,773.87	
3	Angel CABRERA	882,744.05	
4	Ernie ELS	842,615.77	
5	Thomas BJÖRN	837,874.74	
6	Stephen DODD	787,573.56	
7	Miguel Angel JIMÉNEZ	773,149.11	
8	Paul McGINLEY	690,910.69	
9	Nick O'HERN	665,588.59	
10	Luke DONALD	537,631.80	

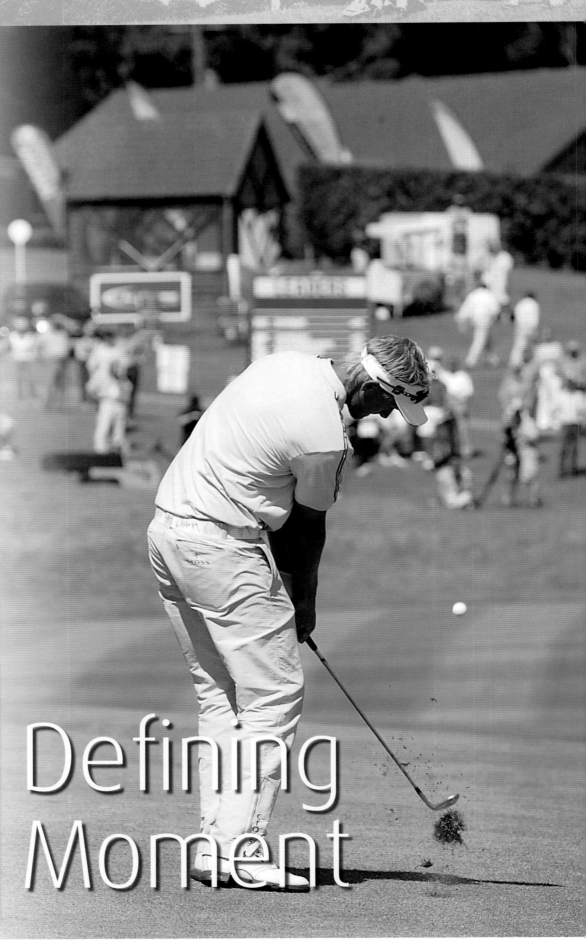

Defining Moment

The drama and the tension of the 2005 Aa St Omer Open was beautifully encapsulated in one adrenaline fuelled, fist pumping moment from the eventual champion, Joakim Bäckström of Sweden.

Playing the 72nd hole of the tournament, Bäckström landed his approach to the Aa Saint Omer Golf Club's 18th green around 20 feet from the pin. As he walked towards the putting surface, he shot a glance at the greenside scoreboard and saw his name in second place on three under par – one stroke behind clubhouse leader Paul Dwyer of England.

Bäckström, who had bogeyed the 17th to fall back to second place, was facing the biggest moment of his career to date. Make the birdie, and he was guaranteed a play-off for the €66,660 (£44,593) first prize as well as a full year's exemption to The 2006 European Tour. Given that tempting carrot, missing was never really an option.

Under extreme pressure, Bäckström came good. He saw the line of the putt and committed to it with a perfect stroke. As his ball disappeared below ground he clenched his fist, gritted his teeth and let the emotion of that most defining of moments wash over him.

In that split second, the Swede was overcome by the unique mix of ecstasy, relief and satisfaction that only top level sportsmen and women can experience when their years of dedication, hard work and sacrifice are rewarded.

It is an exceptional sight when those unforgettable moments occur and, considering what it meant to the Swede, he was able, at least in some part, to relate to some of the world's most revered sports people who have been captured in the ultimate moment of glory.

Be it Muhammad Ali's 1974 Rumble in the Jungle celebration after defeating George Foreman; Björn Borg's magic moment after that epic Wimbledon victory over John McEnroe in 1980; Ellen McArthur's salute to the world after circumnavigating the globe in record time in 2004; or Dennis Taylor finger wagging the Snooker World Championship trophy in 1985...... Bäckström now knew exactly what that feeling was.

It speaks volumes, too, for Bäckström that, after signing the scorecard that matched Dwyer's four round total of four under par 280, he did not relax, instead using the adrenaline of his brilliant birdie putt to defeat the Englishman at the first hole of their sudden-death shoot-out.

Bäckström teed off first, finding the left rough

Gary Orr

Carl Suneson

Paul Dwyer

The European Tour
is proud of its major role in the continued growth of the globalisation of golf

3 International Schedules

100 Tournaments

37 Countries

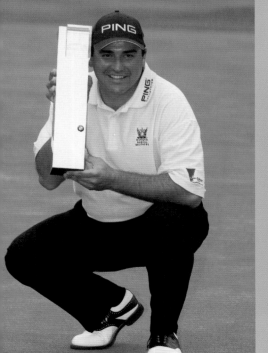

All the Main Events, Live Scoring & Latest Action...
www.europeantour.com

Final Results

"The course is tricky in parts with some cracking holes that are a real test. The first thing that strikes you is how undulating the ground is - the 18th is a great hole that highlights the nature of the course and perfect for a grandstand finish on Sunday afternoon" – Gary Orr

on the par four first before Dwyer put his ball in a similar spot on the opposite side of the fairway. The Englishman played his approach first, which came up 30 feet short of the flag, allowing Bäckström to force the issue by landing his own ball ten feet inside Dwyer's, but leaving both men with a tough task of making birdie.

Dwyer was the first to putt, leaving his ball three feet from the cup, while Bäckström

rolled his own effort to two feet. With every spectator around the green expecting a half in four and wondering what would unfold on the next play-off hole, Dwyer pushed his putt past the hole to allow Bäckström to tap-in for his maiden title on The European Tour.

The Swede celebrated once more, but without the unique intensity of that fist clenching moment that had guaranteed his place in the play-off, the moment that proved to be so crucial.

"That was the best putt I hit all day and it was always going in," Bäckström said of his birdie on the 72nd hole. "I think you could tell from the reaction how much that meant to me. It was probably the most important putt of my career and to make it under the pressure I was feeling made me very proud. I had looked at the leaderboard and knew that I had to make birdie on the last because I didn't want to finish second – no way.

"That feeling carried into the play-off and when Paul three putted I realised I had a two footer to win the tournament. I really can't put into words how I feel to win here."

He may have been lost for words, but Bäckström's vivid celebrations said it all.

Michael Gibbons

Steven Jeppesen

Pos	Name		Rd1	Rd2	Rd3	Rd4	Total		€	£
1	Joakim BÄCKSTRÖM	Swe	72	70	68	70	280	-4	66,660.00	44,593.10
2	Paul DWYER	Eng	73	68	71	68	280	-4	44,440.00	29,728.74
3	Michael JONZON	Swe	69	73	71	68	281	-3	20,666.67	13,825.25
	Steven JEPPESEN	Swe	73	70	70	68	281	-3	20,666.67	13,825.25
	James HEATH	Eng	70	66	73	72	281	-3	20,666.67	13,825.25
6	Ross FISHER	Eng	70	70	68	74	282	-2	10,592.00	7,085.66
	Ben MASON	Eng	71	74	70	67	282	-2	10,592.00	7,085.66
	James HEPWORTH	Eng	69	71	69	73	282	-2	10,592.00	7,085.66
	Carl SUNESON	Sp	74	69	65	74	282	-2	10,592.00	7,085.66
	Alvaro SALTO	Sp	74	69	69	70	282	-2	10,592.00	7,085.66
11	Martin ERLANDSSON	Swe	68	77	69	69	283	-1	6,386.67	4,272.45
	Denny LUCAS	Eng	70	73	71	69	283	-1	6,386.67	4,272.45
	Gary ORR	Scot	71	71	68	73	283	-1	6,386.67	4,272.45
	Roope KAKKO	Fin	72	71	73	67	283	-1	6,386.67	4,272.45
	David DIXON	Eng	76	69	70	68	283	-1	6,386.67	4,272.45
	Miguel CARBALLO	Arg	72	69	71	71	283	-1	6,386.67	4,272.45
17	Adam GROOM	Aus	71	70	68	75	284	0	4,913.33	3,286.84
	Stephen BROWNE	Ire	71	70	71	72	284	0	4,913.33	3,286.84
	Matthew MORRIS	Eng	70	72	72	70	284	0	4,913.33	3,286.84
	Iain PYMAN	Eng	72	71	66	75	284	0	4,913.33	3,286.84
	Sion E BEBB	Wal	70	72	68	74	284	0	4,913.33	3,286.84
	Gary CLARK	Eng	74	67	73	70	284	0	4,913.33	3,286.84
23	Neil CHEETHAM	Eng	68	76	70	71	285	1	4,040.00	2,702.61
	Tomas Jesus MUÑOZ	Sp	73	70	71	71	285	1	4,040.00	2,702.61
	Jan-Are LARSEN	Nor	70	73	73	69	285	1	4,040.00	2,702.61
	Mark MOULAND	Wal	73	71	72	69	285	1	4,040.00	2,702.61
	Sven STRÜVER	Ger	73	72	72	68	285	1	4,040.00	2,702.61
	Raphaël DE SOUSA	Swi	73	70	66	76	285	1	4,040.00	2,702.61
	Andres ROMERO	Arg	71	71	72	71	285	1	4,040.00	2,702.61
30	Kyron SULLIVAN	Wal	76	66	69	75	286	2	3,217.14	2,152.15
	Thomas NIELSEN	Den	72	72	72	70	286	2	3,217.14	2,152.15
	David ORR	Scot	72	73	68	73	286	2	3,217.14	2,152.15
	Sebastien DELAGRANGE	Fr	70	71	71	74	286	2	3,217.14	2,152.15
	David HIGGINS	Ire	75	69	71	71	286	2	3,217.14	2,152.15
	Cesar MONASTERIO	Arg	74	69	72	71	286	2	3,217.14	2,152.15
	Hennie OTTO	SA	68	73	75	70	286	2	3,217.14	2,152.15
37	Jamie LITTLE	Eng	69	74	73	71	287	3	2,400.00	1,605.51
	Phillip ARCHER	Eng	69	73	72	73	287	3	2,400.00	1,605.51
	Raphael EYRAUD	Fr	68	75	73	71	287	3	2,400.00	1,605.51
	Jesus Maria ARRUTI	Sp	72	71	72	72	287	3	2,400.00	1,605.51
	David DUPART	Fr	71	70	73	73	287	3	2,400.00	1,605.51
	Oskar BERGMAN	Swe	72	73	70	72	287	3	2,400.00	1,605.51
	Tom WHITEHOUSE	Eng	70	71	74	72	287	3	2,400.00	1,605.51
	David GRIFFITHS	Eng	70	74	70	73	287	3	2,400.00	1,605.51
	Sebastian FERNANDEZ	Arg	74	71	67	75	287	3	2,400.00	1,605.51
	Ariel CANETE	Arg	72	72	72	71	287	3	2,400.00	1,605.51
	Craig WILLIAMS	Wal	69	75	71	72	287	3	2,400.00	1,605.51
	Gareth DAVIES	Eng	73	72	71	71	287	3	2,400.00	1,605.51
49	Ivo GINER	Sp	69	72	73	74	288	4	1,720.00	1,150.62
	Birgir HAFTHORSSON	Ice	68	74	69	77	288	4	1,720.00	1,150.62
	Shaun P WEBSTER	Eng	71	68	75	74	288	4	1,720.00	1,150.62
	Jean VAN DE VELDE	Fr	71	71	73	73	288	4	1,720.00	1,150.62
	Julien QUESNE	Fr	75	69	71	73	288	4	1,720.00	1,150.62
54	Jeppe HULDAHL	Den	72	70	75	72	289	5	1,328.00	888.38
	Per G NYMAN	Swe	68	74	73	74	289	5	1,328.00	888.38
	Knud STORGAARD	Den	72	69	75	73	289	5	1,328.00	888.38
	Paul NILBRINK	Nor	73	69	72	75	289	5	1,328.00	888.38
	Rafael GOMEZ	Arg	72	69	72	76	289	5	1,328.00	888.38
59	Jean-Nicolas BILLOT	Fr	75	70	73	72	290	6	1,080.00	722.48
	Matthew BLACKEY	Eng	73	71	76	70	290	6	1,080.00	722.48
	Gabriel CANIZARES	Sp	71	72	75	72	290	6	1,080.00	722.48
	Massimo SCARPA	It	71	73	74	72	290	6	1,080.00	722.48
	Oliver WHITELEY	Eng	71	72	75	72	290	6	1,080.00	722.48
64	Carlos DE CORRAL	Sp	74	71	70	76	291	7	900.00	602.07
	Pelle EDBERG	Swe	70	69	78	74	291	7	900.00	602.07
	Garry HOUSTON	Wal	72	69	74	76	291	7	900.00	602.07
	Marcus HIGLEY	Eng	73	72	69	77	291	7	900.00	602.07
68	Lionel ALEXANDRE	Fr	74	71	69	78	292	8	725.00	485.00
	Edward RUSH	Eng	72	73	72	75	292	8	725.00	485.00
	Martin LEMESURIER	Eng	74	71	80	67	292	8	725.00	485.00
	Benoit TEILLERIA	Fr	72	72	75	73	292	8	725.00	485.00
72	Mark SANDERS	Eng	71	74	72	76	293	9	595.50	398.37
	Mattias NILSSON	Swe	70	75	76	72	293	9	595.50	398.37
74	Jeff HALL	Eng	74	71	76	73	294	10	589.50	394.35
	Jamie ELSON	Eng	69	73	73	79	294	10	589.50	394.35
76	Michael KIRK	SA	74	68	76	78	296	12	585.00	391.44
77	Gustavo ROJAS	Arg	74	71	77	76	298	14	582.00	389.34

Total Prize Fund
€404,140 £270,533

Pinehurst No.2

Par	Yards	Metres
70	7214	6598

	Player	Score		
1	**Michael CAMPBELL**	280	0	
2	Tiger WOODS	282	2	
3	Tim CLARK	285	5	
	Sergio GARCIA	285	5	
	Mark HENSBY	285	5	
6	Davis LOVE III	286	6	
	Rocco MEDIATE	286	6	
	Vijay SINGH	286	6	
9	Arron OBERHOLSER	287	7	
	Nick PRICE	287	7	

Round One   Round Two   Round Three   Round Four

EUROPEAN TOUR ORDER OF MERIT
(After 27 tournaments)

Pos		€	
1	**Michael CAMPBELL**	1,328,074.17	
2	Retief GOOSEN	1,111,069.64	
3	David HOWELL	922,598.47	
4	Ernie ELS	915,280.25	
5	Angel CABRERA	912,231.22	
6	Thomas BJÖRN	852,443.10	
7	Stephen DODD	787,573.56	
8	Miguel Angel JIMÉNEZ	773,973.71	
9	Paul McGINLEY	712,534.40	
10	Nick O'HERN	682,307.52	

To Win It,
You Have
To Be in It

US Open Championship

North Carolina, USA
June 16-19 • 2005

For many years now the song, as sung by some American observers, has been of a rather familiar refrain, namely that the American golf brand is stronger than its European counterpart and we are not just talking dollars.

Jonathan Lomas

This, of course, is utter tosh. The sub-plot to this bombast is that there are those who think that the US PGA Tour is inherently superior to The European Tour, a posture that fails to explain some inconvenient facts. One of these is the recent history of The Ryder Cup and another is the recent history of the US Open Championship.

On a gloriously sunny day in North Carolina, on a near-perfect Pinehurst No.2 golf course, Michael Campbell became the second player in five years nurtured by The European Tour to win this prestigious title. Retief Goosen won in 2001 and 2004 and played a major, if ultimately unavailing part, at Pinehurst this year. Going back a little further, we also have the two wins of Ernie Els.

Granted none of the above are Europeans, but all of them developed their games in Europe and could not possibly have reached the highest of standards playing on a Tour that, allegedly, does not have the strength in depth of its American counterpart.

Golf now is a truly global game, a fact emphasised by the make-up of the weekend field at Pinehurst. The winner was a Maori from New Zealand, the runner-up an African-American in Tiger Woods and, in addition, Sergio Garcia, from Spain, tied with a South African, Tim Clark, and an Australian, Mark Hensby, for joint third place. In the chasing pack there were South Africans, Japanese, Koreans, Australians, Argentines, a German, a Fijian, a Zimbabwean, a Canadian and players from Denmark, Sweden, France, England, Ireland and Scotland.

Paul McGinley finished back in joint 37th place but the Irishman brings a thoughtful approach to the game, both on and off the course. He said: "It's great for our Tour that

Peter Hedblom

Pinehurst was in perfect shape. The greens firm but not crazy. You've got to get the ball in the fairway and you've got to play away from some of the flags so you can't be too aggressive. But it's a great course, difficult but a wonderful design which tests your whole game – Ernie Els

Tiger Woods

Retief Goosen

Adam Scott

Cambo won. It makes you feel, without a doubt, that if he can do it, then so can you."

Campbell had to qualify at Walton Heath for his place at Pinehurst but McGinley felt that the performance of some of the others who got through at that event was equally as important. Jonathan Lomas and Nick Dougherty both played four rounds and Peter Hedblom had that great 66 in the second round - the lowest score of the Championship.

"There's nothing to be fearful of on the US PGA Tour," added McGinley. "We are every bit as good as they are."

Campbell, who had a brief and unsuccessful flirtation with the US PGA Tour in the late 1990s, playing while trying to recover from a wrist injury and trying to alter his swing

Sergio Garcia

Final Results

to accommodate the after-effects, is going to continue to play on The European Tour he loves best. There will be more commitments in America, naturally, but he is going to remain a Brighton boy, living in the seaside town he and his family have come to love.

Campbell's win wholly proves the point that former Executive Director of The European Tour, Ken Schofield, was always trying to make - that to win it you have first to be in it. The United States Golf Association was slow to recognise this truism although with the top 50 in the world now qualifying, and with regional qualifiers in the UK and Japan, that problem is largely rectified.

But Schofield often used to wonder how many Majors the likes of Neil Coles or Peter Butler might have won had they had the access to Championships that, say, Lou Graham, or Dave Stockton, had.

But, back in the present, everyone with the possible exception of Woods, has cause to be thankful for the manner of Campbell's win, and his demeanour afterwards. If, as the adage has it, Championships are won and lost on the back nine on Sunday, then that was where Campbell not only kept his nerve, he repulsed a challenge from the World Number One.

Bringing all the experience that 12 years on The European Tour had given him, he parred the difficult and dangerous 16th after Woods had bogeyed it, and then birdied the 17th with a superb 25 foot putt that gave him the opportunity to finish with a double bogey six, should he need to, and still win.

Carefully, craftily, he took five of those strokes and, strange though it may seem, all of Europe rejoiced when a New Zealand Maori won the US Open Championship.

David Davies

Pos	Name		Rd1	Rd2	Rd3	Rd4	Total		€	£
1	Michael CAMPBELL	NZ	71	69	71	69	280	0	964,791.80	645,410.44
2	Tiger WOODS	USA	70	71	72	69	282	2	577,225.80	386,142.96
3	Sergio GARCIA	Sp	71	69	75	70	285	5	263,906.80	176,544.00
	Tim CLARK	SA	76	69	70	70	285	5	263,906.80	176,544.00
	Mark HENSBY	Aus	71	68	72	74	285	5	263,906.80	176,544.00
6	Rocco MEDIATE	USA	67	74	74	71	286	6	154,872.20	103,603.84
	Davis LOVE III	USA	77	70	70	69	286	6	154,872.20	103,603.84
	Vijay SINGH	Fiji	70	70	74	72	286	6	154,872.20	103,603.84
9	Nick PRICE	Zim	72	71	72	72	287	7	124,379.00	83,205.00
	Arron OBERHOLSER	USA	76	67	71	73	287	7	124,379.00	83,205.00
11	Corey PAVIN	USA	73	72	70	73	288	8	102,133.50	68,323.58
	Peter HEDBLOM	Swe	77	66	70	75	288	8	102,133.50	68,323.58
	Bob ESTES	USA	70	73	75	70	288	8	102,133.50	68,323.58
	Retief GOOSEN	SA	68	70	69	81	288	8	102,133.50	68,323.58
15	Ernie ELS	SA	71	76	72	70	289	9	72,664.48	48,609.88
	Ryuji IMADA	USA	77	68	73	71	289	9	72,664.48	48,609.88
	David TOMS	USA	70	72	70	77	289	9	72,664.48	48,609.88
	John COOK	USA	71	76	70	72	289	9	72,664.48	48,609.88
	K J CHOI	Kor	69	70	74	76	289	9	72,664.48	48,609.88
	Fred COUPLES	USA	71	74	74	70	289	9	72,664.48	48,609.88
	Stewart CINK	USA	73	74	73	69	289	9	72,664.48	48,609.88
	Peter JACOBSEN	USA	72	73	69	75	289	9	72,664.48	48,609.88
23	Justin LEONARD	USA	76	71	70	73	290	10	49,173.87	32,895.52
	Fred FUNK	USA	73	71	76	70	290	10	49,173.87	32,895.52
	Olin BROWNE	USA	67	71	72	80	290	10	49,173.87	32,895.52
	Kenny PERRY	USA	75	70	71	74	290	10	49,173.87	32,895.52
	Paul CLAXTON	USA	72	72	72	74	290	10	49,173.87	32,895.52
28	Stephen ALLAN	Aus	72	69	73	77	291	11	36,683.53	24,539.94
	Adam SCOTT	Aus	70	71	74	76	291	11	36,683.53	24,539.94
	Jim FURYK	USA	71	70	75	75	291	11	36,683.53	24,539.94
	Geoff OGILVY	Aus	72	74	71	74	291	11	36,683.53	24,539.94
	Matt EVERY (Am)	USA	75	73	73	70	291	11		
33	Tim HERRON	USA	74	73	70	75	292	12	29,487.17	19,725.84
	Shigeki MARUYAMA	Jpn	71	74	72	75	292	12	29,487.17	19,725.84
	Bernhard LANGER	Ger	74	73	71	74	292	12	29,487.17	19,725.84
	Steve ELKINGTON	Aus	77	71	72	73	292	12	29,487.17	19,725.84
	Ted PURDY	USA	74	69	79	70	292	12	29,487.17	19,725.84
	Angel CABRERA	Arg	71	73	73	75	292	12	29,487.17	19,725.84
	Phil MICKELSON	USA	69	77	72	74	292	12	29,487.17	19,725.84
	Brandt JOBE	USA	68	73	79	72	292	12	29,487.17	19,725.84
	Lee WESTWOOD	Eng	68	72	73	79	292	12	29,487.17	19,725.84
42	Tom PERNICE	USA	74	73	73	73	293	13	21,623.71	14,465.47
	Peter LONARD	Aus	71	74	74	74	293	13	21,623.71	14,465.47
	Paul MCGINLEY	Ire	76	72	71	74	293	13	21,623.71	14,465.47
	Chad CAMPBELL	USA	77	71	72	73	293	13	21,623.71	14,465.47
	Colin MONTGOMERIE	Scot	72	75	72	74	293	13	21,623.71	14,465.47
	Mike WEIR	Can	75	72	75	71	293	13	21,623.71	14,465.47
	Rob RASHELL	USA	74	72	73	74	293	13	21,623.71	14,465.47
49	Jason GORE	USA	71	67	72	84	294	14	16,718.93	11,184.35
	Nick O'HERN	Aus	72	71	78	73	294	14	16,718.93	11,184.35
	J.L. LEWIS	USA	75	73	76	70	294	14	16,718.93	11,184.35
52	Nick DOUGHERTY	Eng	72	74	74	75	295	15	14,568.36	9,745.70
	Thomas BJÖRN	Den	71	74	75	75	295	15	14,568.36	9,745.70
	Thomas LEVET	Fr	75	73	73	74	295	15	14,568.36	9,745.70
	Richard GREEN	Aus	72	72	78	73	295	15	14,568.36	9,745.70
	Søren KJELDSEN	Den	74	71	77	73	295	15	14,568.36	9,745.70
57	Tommy ARMOUR III	USA	70	72	79	75	296	16	12,553.01	8,397.50
	Ian POULTER	Eng	77	69	74	76	296	16	12,553.01	8,397.50
	Jonathan LOMAS	Eng	72	74	75	75	296	16	12,553.01	8,397.50
	Keiichiro FUKABORI	Jpn	74	67	75	80	296	16	12,553.01	8,397.50
	Steve JONES	USA	69	74	74	79	296	16	12,553.01	8,397.50
	Lee JANZEN	USA	74	74	74	74	296	16	12,553.01	8,397.50
	Frank LICKLITER	USA	75	73	78	70	296	16	12,553.01	8,397.50
	Luke DONALD	Eng	69	73	74	80	296	16	12,553.01	8,397.50
	J.J. HENRY	USA	73	73	76	74	296	16	12,553.01	8,397.50
	Ryan MOORE (Am)	USA	75	73	75	73	296	16		
67	John MALLINGER	USA	74	72	73	78	297	17	11,175.92	7,476.28
	Michael ALLEN	USA	73	72	77	75	297	17	11,175.92	7,476.28
	Steve FLESCH	USA	72	71	78	76	297	17	11,175.92	7,476.28
	Bill GLASSON	USA	74	73	71	79	297	17	11,175.92	7,476.28
71	JP HAYES	USA	77	71	74	76	298	18	10,349.66	6,923.54
	Rory SABBATINI	SA	72	74	76	76	298	18	10,349.66	6,923.54
	Stephen AMES	T&T	71	75	76	76	298	18	10,349.66	6,923.54
	D.J. BRIGMAN	USA	74	73	75	76	298	18	10,349.66	6,923.54
75	Charles HOWELL III	USA	77	68	73	81	299	19	9,626.48	6,439.76
	John DALY	USA	74	72	77	76	299	19	9,626.48	6,439.76
	Omar URESTI	USA	75	73	75	76	299	19	9,626.48	6,439.76
78	Jeff MAGGERT	USA	72	75	75	78	300	20	9,110.27	6,094.44
	Bob TWAY	USA	71	75	79	75	300	20	9,110.27	6,094.44
80	Graeme MCDOWELL	N.Ire	74	74	72	81	301	21	8,697.15	5,818.07
	Chris NALLEN	USA	76	72	78	75	301	21	8,697.15	5,818.07
82	Craig BARLOW	USA	76	71	76	80	303	23	8,387.09	5,610.66
83	Jerry KELLY	USA	76	71	78	80	305	25	8,180.94	5,472.75

Ian Poulter

Total Prize Fund
€5,304,700   £3,548,653

Open de France

Le Golf National

Par	Yards	Metres
71	7214	6596

1	Jean-Francois REMESY	273	-11	
2	Jean VAN DE VELDE	273	-11	
3	Søren HANSEN	276	-8	
4	Francois DELAMONTAGNE	279	-5	
	Richard FINCH	279	-5	
	Gregory HAVRET	279	-5	
	Peter O'MALLEY	279	-5	
8	Bradley DREDGE	280	-4	
	Anders HANSEN	280	-4	
	Jonathan LOMAS	280	-4	
	José Maria OLAZÁBAL	280	-4	
	Eduardo ROMERO	280	-4	

Round One	Round Two	Round Three	Round Four

EUROPEAN TOUR ORDER OF MERIT
(After 28 tournaments)

Pos		€	
1	Michael CAMPBELL	1,328,074.17	
2	Retief GOOSEN	1,111,069.64	
3	David HOWELL	923,423.07	
4	Ernie ELS	915,280.25	
5	Angel CABRERA	912,231.22	
6	Thomas BJÖRN	852,443.10	
7	Stephen DODD	814,436.06	
8	Miguel Angel JIMÉNEZ	785,064.98	
9	Paul McGINLEY	722,801.07	
10	Nick O'HERN	682,307.52	

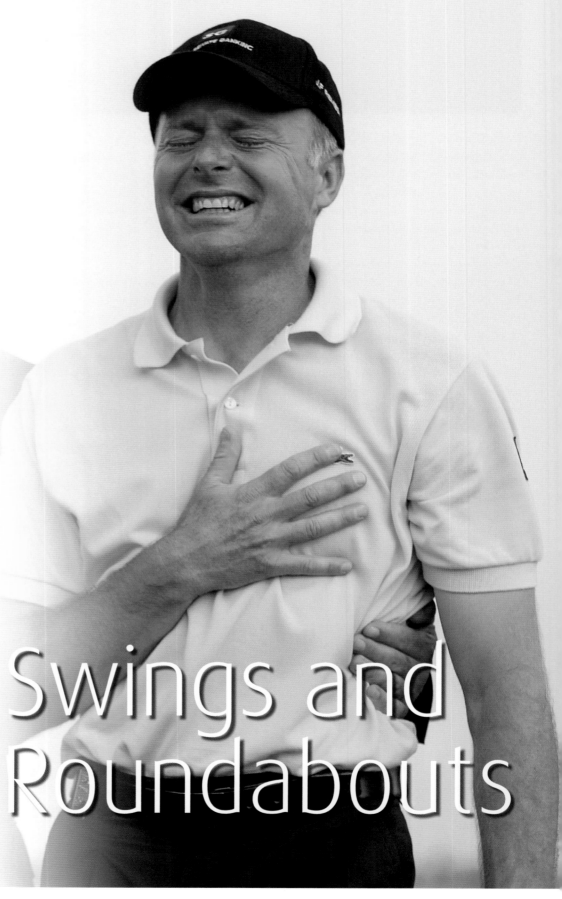

Swings and Roundabouts

Peter O'Malley

What goes around, comes around. Never were those old words of wisdom more appropriate than for Jean-Francois Remesy and Jean Van de Velde.

For Remesy, it all came around pretty quickly. He had been the first Frenchman to win the Open de France for 35 years when he ran away with the tournament in 2004. This time he was pushed to the limit before he ended another lengthy hiatus, for not since Marcel Dallemagne in both 1937 and 1938 had a Frenchman successfully defended his national title, while the last player to win the event back-to-back was Nick Faldo in 1988 and 1989.

For the man who was destined to finish second, Van de Velde, it was beginning to look as though things might never come around. Three years of misery had had nothing to do with the nightmares over his infamous finish at Carnoustie in 1999 when his hopes of winning the The Open Championship literally sunk in the Barry Burn. This time the

pain was physical after damaging his right knee in a skiing accident, forcing him to twice undergo major reconstructive surgery in 2002. Just limping, sometimes, left him weeping in agony.

By the end of 2004, Van de Velde was on the brink of giving up the professional game, perhaps resorting to commentating on golf at which he excels. The prospect of just talking about the game he loved, however, was not an appealing one and therefore drove him on to do something about his predicament. To protect his knee, his fitness level became that of an Olympic athlete as he made a fourth bid, in early 2005, to rescue his career.

Although his knee stood up to the rigours of tournament golf, and he had secured plenty

Jean Van de Velde

Open de France

Paris, France
June 23-26 • 2005

Eduardo Romero

of invitations by the week of the Open de France, Van de Velde was not really getting anywhere.

A lot of water had flowed under the bridge at the back of the 18th green at Le Golf National before Van de Velde set off on the quest to resurrect his career and Remesy set out to rewrite the French golfing history books.

Van de Velde could hardly have wished for a better start as he equalled the course record 64 in the first round. After play was halted for lightning, he had to wait until mid-afternoon the next day before beginning round two, only to find himself overtaken by the man who Søren Hansen – himself in the thick of things all week – called 'The Old Gangster', Argentine Eduardo Romero.

Romero carded a sublime second round 62 to smash the course record and prove there was plenty of life left in the player whose fourth of eight titles on The European Tour International Schedule was the Open de France at Le Golf National in 1991. Now, a chance to beat Des Smyth's record as the Tour's oldest winner had come round - Romero had already won at nearly 48 and now he was trying to win one month shy of his 51st birthday.

Saturday saw Remesy come up on the rails to join Van de Velde and Romero in a tie for the lead, the trio one shot clear of the field, but it was into Sunday's fourth round that the tournament drama really began following a three and a half hour thunderstorm delay. An outward half of 40 put paid to Romero's hopes and while Hansen battled gamely to secure third spot, at the head of affairs it came down to a head-to-head tussle between the two Frenchmen.

Showing admirable grace Van de Velde had joked, before the final round, that it would be fate if he came to the 18th with a three-shot lead, just like Carnoustie. How would he handle it this time he mused? As it turned out, the affable 39 year old did have

Gregory Havret

Final Results

Pos	Name		Rd1	Rd2	Rd3	Rd4	Total		€	£
1	Jean-Francois REMESY	Fr	68	69	67	69	273	-11	583,330.00	390,888.01
2	Jean VAN DE VELDE	Fr	64	70	70	69	273	-11	388,880.00	260,587.54
3	Søren HANSEN	Den	65	69	71	71	276	-8	219,100.00	146,818.38
4	Gregory HAVRET	Fr	70	70	67	72	279	-5	137,725.00	92,289.19
	Peter O'MALLEY	Aus	69	68	70	72	279	-5	137,725.00	92,289.19
	Francois DELAMONTAGNE	Fr	67	68	71	73	279	-5	137,725.00	92,289.19
	Richard FINCH	Eng	73	70	69	67	279	-5	137,725.00	92,289.19
8	Jonathan LOMAS	Eng	65	69	71	75	280	-4	72,100.00	48,314.03
	Bradley DREDGE	Wal	67	73	72	68	280	-4	72,100.00	48,314.03
	José Maria OLAZÁBAL	Sp	69	70	70	71	280	-4	72,100.00	48,314.03
	Anders HANSEN	Den	67	71	70	72	280	-4	72,100.00	48,314.03
	Eduardo ROMERO	Arg	70	62	72	76	280	-4	72,100.00	48,314.03
13	Stuart LITTLE	Eng	71	71	68	71	281	-3	52,675.00	35,297.39
	Philip GOLDING	Eng	69	69	68	75	281	-3	52,675.00	35,297.39
	Nick DOUGHERTY	Eng	72	68	69	72	281	-3	52,675.00	35,297.39
	Richard STERNE	SA	67	75	70	69	281	-3	52,675.00	35,297.39
17	Ignacio GARRIDO	Sp	72	66	75	69	282	-2	44,450.00	29,785.84
	David LYNN	Eng	73	68	70	71	282	-2	44,450.00	29,785.84
	Colin MONTGOMERIE	Scot	69	72	70	71	282	-2	44,450.00	29,785.84
	Martin ERLANDSSON	Swe	68	67	75	72	282	-2	44,450.00	29,785.84
21	Marcel SIEM	Ger	69	68	72	74	283	-1	38,500.00	25,798.76
	Robert-Jan DERKSEN	NL	71	69	69	74	283	-1	38,500.00	25,798.76
	Jarmo SANDELIN	Swe	68	72	72	71	283	-1	38,500.00	25,798.76
	Niclas FASTH	Swe	69	68	75	71	283	-1	38,500.00	25,798.76
	Wade ORMSBY	Aus	72	72	69	70	283	-1	38,500.00	25,798.76
26	Marc CAYEUX	Zim	68	72	71	73	284	0	33,250.00	22,280.74
	José Manuel LARA	Sp	72	71	71	70	284	0	33,250.00	22,280.74
	Miguel Angel MARTIN	Sp	72	70	71	71	284	0	33,250.00	22,280.74
	Søren KJELDSEN	Den	72	72	66	74	284	0	33,250.00	22,280.74
	Francesco MOLINARI	It	68	72	69	75	284	0	33,250.00	22,280.74
31	Andrew MCLARDY	SA	67	71	75	72	285	1	26,862.50	18,000.50
	Alessandro TADINI	It	70	73	69	73	285	1	26,862.50	18,000.50
	Phillip ARCHER	Eng	70	73	69	73	285	1	26,862.50	18,000.50
	Klas ERIKSSON	Swe	72	68	71	74	285	1	26,862.50	18,000.50
	Stephen DODD	Wal	73	70	69	73	285	1	26,862.50	18,000.50
	Markus BRIER	Aut	74	70	69	72	285	1	26,862.50	18,000.50
	Stephen GALLACHER	Scot	71	70	71	73	285	1	26,862.50	18,000.50
	Ben MASON	Eng	73	69	73	70	285	1	26,862.50	18,000.50
39	John BICKERTON	Eng	69	71	73	73	286	2	22,050.00	14,775.65
	Paul LAWRIE	Scot	71	70	69	76	286	2	22,050.00	14,775.65
	Miles TUNNICLIFF	Eng	71	69	72	74	286	2	22,050.00	14,775.65
	Garry HOUSTON	Wal	67	73	71	75	286	2	22,050.00	14,775.65
	Paul BROADHURST	Eng	71	72	69	74	286	2	22,050.00	14,775.65
44	Brian DAVIS	Eng	71	69	72	75	287	3	18,200.00	12,195.78
	Mark ROE	Eng	69	75	69	74	287	3	18,200.00	12,195.78
	Ricardo GONZALEZ	Arg	68	73	73	73	287	3	18,200.00	12,195.78
	Mads VIBE-HASTRUP	Den	70	74	69	74	287	3	18,200.00	12,195.78
	Steven O'HARA	Scot	74	70	75	68	287	3	18,200.00	12,195.78
	Stephen BROWNE	Ire	68	76	69	74	287	3	18,200.00	12,195.78
50	Brad KENNEDY	Aus	72	71	74	71	288	4	14,350.00	9,615.90
	Alastair FORSYTH	Scot	71	70	72	75	288	4	14,350.00	9,615.90
	Simon WAKEFIELD	Eng	71	73	72	72	288	4	14,350.00	9,615.90
	Sven STRÜVER	Ger	72	72	72	72	288	4	14,350.00	9,615.90
	Mattias ELIASSON	Swe	69	73	72	74	288	4	14,350.00	9,615.90
55	Henrik STENSON	Swe	70	71	71	77	289	5	10,266.67	6,879.67
	Peter HANSON	Swe	70	72	71	76	289	5	10,266.67	6,879.67
	Miguel Angel JIMÉNEZ	Sp	67	74	77	71	289	5	10,266.67	6,879.67
	Ian GARBUTT	Eng	72	71	68	78	289	5	10,266.67	6,879.67
	Pierre FULKE	Swe	72	72	74	71	289	5	10,266.67	6,879.67
	Paul MCGINLEY	Ire	70	71	73	75	289	5	10,266.67	6,879.67
	David CARTER	Eng	70	74	69	76	289	5	10,266.67	6,879.67
	Raymond RUSSELL	Scot	65	77	73	74	289	5	10,266.67	6,879.67
	Gonzalo FERNANDEZ-CASTANO	Sp	71	73	74	71	289	5	10,266.67	6,879.67
64	James KINGSTON	SA	72	71	73	74	290	6	8,400.00	5,628.82
65	Charl SCHWARTZEL	SA	66	73	71	81	291	7	7,700.00	5,159.75
	Andrew MARSHALL	Eng	68	74	73	76	291	7	7,700.00	5,159.75
	Anthony WALL	Eng	71	71	71	78	291	7	7,700.00	5,159.75
68	Mark FOSTER	Eng	70	70	74	78	292	8	6,107.40	4,092.55
	Thomas LEVET	Fr	72	72	72	76	292	8	6,107.40	4,092.55
	Peter LAWRIE	Ire	70	72	73	77	292	8	6,107.40	4,092.55
	Pelle EDBERG	Swe	69	74	71	78	292	8	6,107.40	4,092.55
	Scott DRUMMOND	Scot	69	72	74	77	292	8	6,107.40	4,092.55
73	Costantino ROCCA	It	72	71	74	76	293	9	5,241.00	3,511.98
	Gary MURPHY	Ire	75	68	77	73	293	9	5,241.00	3,511.98
	Jarrod MOSELEY	Aus	71	72	76	74	293	9	5,241.00	3,511.98
76	Kenneth FERRIE	Eng	70	73	75	76	294	10	5,235.00	3,507.96
77	Terry PRICE	Aus	70	71	76	78	295	11	5,232.00	3,505.95
78	Richard BLAND	Eng	70	74	79	73	296	12	5,227.50	3,502.94
	Eric MOREUL	Fr	70	74	71	81	296	12	5,227.50	3,502.94
80	Johan AXGREN	Swe	69	73	75	80	297	13	5,223.00	3,499.92
81	Brett RUMFORD	Aus	69	75	76	78	298	14	5,218.50	3,496.90
	Jan-Are LARSEN	Nor	73	71	74	80	298	14	5,218.50	3,496.90
83	Gordon BRAND JNR	Scot	72	71	73	83	299	15	5,214.00	3,493.89
84	Niki ZITNY	Aut	67	77	80	76	300	16	5,211.00	3,491.88
85	David DRYSDALE	Scot	72	70	80	79	301	17	5,208.00	3,489.87

Søren Hansen

the lead coming down the final hole, but only by one.

However, there was more than a little déjà vu as he pulled his drive into the water to open the door for Remesy, who took his chance to force a play-off with a par four as Van de Velde did well to make no more than a bogey five. Both protagonists returned to the 18th hole – the first extra hole – and both, incredibly, hit into the water, Remesy in front and Van de Velde in the reeds at the back. Remesy salvaged a double-bogey six which was good enough to win.

The year had turned full circle for Remesy but Van de Velde had, at least, gained on the roundabout of his career. After three years in the wilderness, his card, and his playing privileges for 2006, were assured.

Norman Dabell

Total Prize Fund
€3,578,430 £2,397,900

Smurfit European Open

Straffan, Co.Kildare, Ireland
June 30-July 3 • 2005

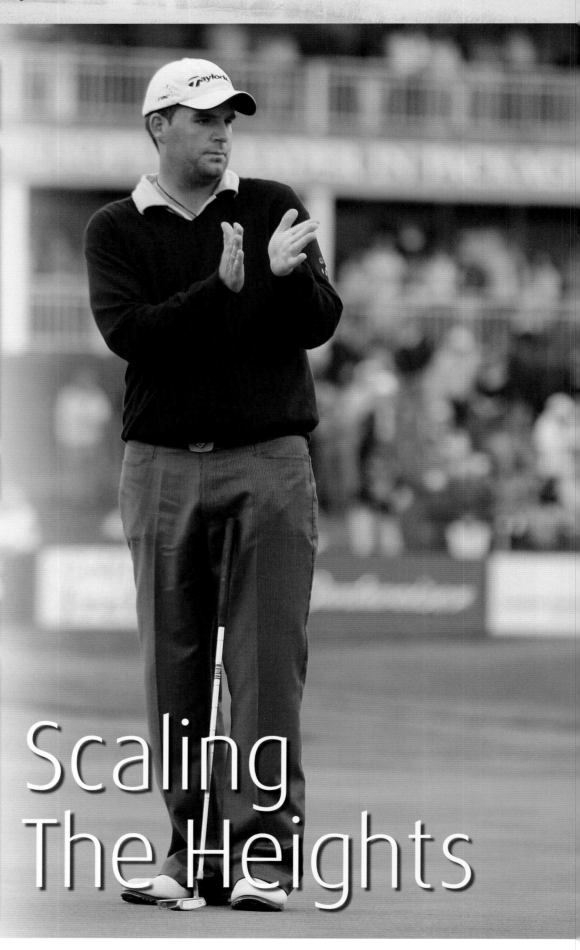

The K Club

Par	Yards	Metres
72	7350	6719

1	**Kenneth FERRIE**	**285**	**-3**	
2	Colin MONTGOMERIE	287	-1	
	Graeme STORM	287	-1	
4	Darren CLARKE	288	0	
	Peter HANSON	288	0	
6	Andrew COLTART	289	1	
	Brian DAVIS	289	1	
	Trevor IMMELMAN	289	1	
	José Manuel LARA	289	1	
	Damien McGRANE	289	1	
	Gary MURPHY	289	1	
	Jamie SPENCE	289	1	

Round One	Round Two	Round Three	Round Four

EUROPEAN TOUR ORDER OF MERIT
(After 29 tournaments)

Pos		€	
1	**Michael CAMPBELL**	**1,362,050.06**	
2	Retief GOOSEN	1,161,108.97	
3	Angel CABRERA	931,992.71	
4	David HOWELL	923,423.07	
5	Ernie ELS	915,280.25	
6	Thomas BJÖRN	878,156.15	
7	Stephen DODD	828,997.16	
8	Miguel Angel JIMÉNEZ	785,064.98	
9	Colin MONTGOMERIE	767,782.12	
10	Nick O'HERN	732,346.85	

Scaling
The Heights

T he price of success and failure mean different things to different people. To Kenneth Ferrie, victory in the Smurfit European Open on The K Club's Palmer Course meant more than most. It certainly meant fame and a small fortune, for his cheque for €577,816 (£383,330) represented, in one fell swoop, almost half what he had earned since he joined the professional ranks in 1999. It meant security, too, and above all, it meant a five year exemption on The European Tour International Schedule.

To Thomas Björn, however, the money was not quite as important. More than half a million euro is not to be sneezed at but with his wealth already assured, the Dane was after the title, not just because of its great prestige, but because he also knew a second win in his last five events would catapult him to Number One on The European Tour Order of Merit.

Almost exactly a year before, he had walked off the adjacent Smurfit Course after only six holes. He said: "I was going through a rough spell and I couldn't see my way out of it. I went home and just said to myself 'let's get back to what I'm good at' and it didn't take long to start playing well again. I put it behind me. I don't really think about it."

Andrew Coltart

Raphaël Jacquelin

Smurfit European Open

Straffan, Co.Kildare, Ireland
June 30-July 3 • 2005

Jamie Donaldson

Those were his words a year on and it did seem that his rehabilitation was complete as he moved, firstly into the joint lead with Jamie Donaldson of Wales at the halfway stage, before taking a four stroke lead on his own into the final day. Only Peter Hanson of Sweden and Angel Cabrera of Argentina matched Björn's third round 69.

There was no hint of weakness in Björn's mental or physical state. He looked a certainty – if there is such a thing in sport - to complete the job. He had, after all, returned to winning ways two months earlier with a nerveless display in a play-off to claim The Daily Telegraph Dunlop Masters at the Marriott Forest of Arden. But, as the old adage says, the show is never over until the fat lady sings.

What followed on that final Sunday was not just theatre; it was drama at its most compelling and gave some indication why the Palmer Course will prove a worthy setting for The 36th Ryder Cup at The K Club in September, 2006.

Trevor Immelman

The two principal actors as the end game approached were the Frenchman Raphaël Jacquelin and Björn, paired together in the final group. Jacquelin became a serious contender when he drew level with Björn with three holes to play, but that closing stretch proved a stretch too far for both players.

Björn took on the River Liffey for his second shot to the par five 16th and was extremely unlucky to see his ball narrowly fail to hold on to dry land. The Frenchman also bogeyed. Still, the title was there for the taking, but, incredibly, Björn put not one, but three balls into the tranquil waters of the river bordering the 17th fairway. He carded 11 for the hole. Jacquelin also found water, firstly the river at the 17th and then the lake at the 18th, and double bogeyed both.

All of this unfolded as Ferrie, following a fine final round of 70 for a three under par total of 285, walked from the recorder's hut to the locker room. Ferrie, gracious in victory, had finished two shots clear of Scotland's Colin Montgomerie and fellow north east of England golfer Graeme Storm.

It had been a momentous few days for the 26 year old whose first Tour victory had come in 2003 when he beat Sweden's Peter Hedblom and Ireland's Peter Lawrie in a play-off to win the Canarias Open de España. For, on the Monday before travelling to Ireland, he had secured his place in The Open Championship at St Andrews by winning a

" New tees and new greens have toughened it up so it is a real test. The greens are tricky and you have to be careful how you read them " – *Retief Goosen*

Ryder Cup Captains, Ian Woosnam of Europe (left) and Tom Lehman of the USA, pose with the trophy in their Team Captains' Cars, presented by Club Car, the Official Golf Car of The Ryder Cup, when played in Europe, for the past ten years

five-man play-off in the International Final Qualifying event at Sunningdale.

"I'm really, really pleased," he said. "To win the Open de España as your first event on Tour was great but to win again and take another step up is fantastic. To beat the quality of guys who were here today and to see the names of the players on the trophy makes me feel pretty good."

Ferrie survived where a number of others, including challengers like Jonathan Lomas, Andrew Coltart, Angel Cabrera and Jacquelin, fell victim to the windy conditions but no player was more disappointed than Björn. "It was the worst day of my golfing life," he said.

Simon Wakefield, however, had good reason

to celebrate. He won a Renault car worth €32,500 for the first hole-in-one of the tournament at the 173 yard eighth. Stephen Dodd and David Park also aced tee shots – Dodd at the third and Park at the eighth.

Darren Clarke, too, smiled broadly at his finish of birdie, birdie, birdie on the final day to share fourth place, but no player had more reason to rejoice than Ferrie. After experiencing a downturn in fortune in 2004 he had shed four stone in an attempt to return to the top.

Now, pound for pound, he could not have felt any better.

Colm Smith

Thomas Björn

Final Results

Pos	Name		Rd1	Rd2	Rd3	Rd4	Total		€	£
1	Kenneth FERRIE	Eng	75	70	70	70	285	-3	577,816.30	383,330.00
2	Colin MONTGOMERIE	Scot	73	75	70	69	287	-1	301,117.80	199,765.00
	Graeme STORM	Eng	69	71	74	73	287	-1	301,117.80	199,765.00
4	Darren CLARKE	N.Ire	69	71	75	73	288	0	160,172.10	106,260.00
	Peter HANSON	Swe	74	72	69	73	288	0	160,172.10	106,260.00
6	Trevor IMMELMAN	SA	66	76	74	73	289	1	83,206.27	55,200.00
	Jamie SPENCE	Eng	76	67	73	73	289	1	83,206.27	55,200.00
	Gary MURPHY	Ire	68	76	73	72	289	1	83,206.27	55,200.00
	José Manuel LARA	Sp	70	76	70	73	289	1	83,206.27	55,200.00
	Brian DAVIS	Eng	70	73	75	71	289	1	83,206.27	55,200.00
	Damien MCGRANE	Ire	70	71	74	74	289	1	83,206.27	55,200.00
	Andrew COLTART	Scot	75	68	71	75	289	1	83,206.27	55,200.00
13	Lee WESTWOOD	Eng	73	74	72	71	290	2	50,039.33	33,196.67
	Retief GOOSEN	SA	67	74	77	72	290	2	50,039.33	33,196.67
	Nick DOUGHERTY	Eng	74	70	79	67	290	2	50,039.33	33,196.67
	Graeme MCDOWELL	N.Ire	72	75	70	73	290	2	50,039.33	33,196.67
	Nick O'HERN	Aus	74	74	72	75	290	2	50,039.33	33,196.67
	Richard GREEN	Aus	72	73	70	75	290	2	50,039.33	33,196.67
19	Raphaël JACQUELIN	Fr	72	70	70	79	291	3	39,869.67	26,450.00
	Brett RUMFORD	Aus	69	71	75	76	291	3	39,869.67	26,450.00
	Peter HEDBLOM	Swe	73	70	75	73	291	3	39,869.67	26,450.00
	Jonathan LOMAS	Eng	68	72	72	79	291	3	39,869.67	26,450.00
	Jamie DONALDSON	Wal	69	70	82	70	291	3	39,869.67	26,450.00
	Gregory BOURDY	Fr	73	73	74	71	291	3	39,869.67	26,450.00
25	Michael CAMPBELL	NZ	74	72	71	75	292	4	33,975.89	22,540.00
	Niclas FASTH	Swe	70	74	72	76	292	4	33,975.89	22,540.00
	Steve WEBSTER	Eng	73	73	72	74	292	4	33,975.89	22,540.00
	Anthony WALL	Eng	73	72	76	71	292	4	33,975.89	22,540.00
	Søren HANSEN	Den	75	73	75	69	292	4	33,975.89	22,540.00
30	Maarten LAFEBER	NL	71	76	73	73	293	5	29,815.58	19,780.00
	Santiago LUNA	Sp	72	73	75	73	293	5	29,815.58	19,780.00
	Greg OWEN	Eng	72	72	76	73	293	5	29,815.58	19,780.00
33	Thomas BJÖRN	Den	70	69	69	86	294	6	25,713.05	17,058.33
	Peter FOWLER	Aus	74	72	76	72	294	6	25,713.05	17,058.33
	Mårten OLANDER	Swe	73	71	75	75	294	6	25,713.05	17,058.33
	Phillip ARCHER	Eng	74	72	71	77	294	6	25,713.05	17,058.33
	Fredrik HENGE	Swe	75	72	78	69	294	6	25,713.05	17,058.33
	Wade ORMSBY	Aus	74	70	74	76	294	6	25,713.05	17,058.33
39	Bradley DREDGE	Wal	75	72	75	73	295	7	22,188.34	14,720.00
	Markus BRIER	Aut	71	70	80	74	295	7	22,188.34	14,720.00
	Mikko ILONEN	Fin	72	72	75	76	295	7	22,188.34	14,720.00
	Terry PRICE	Aus	73	75	74	73	295	7	22,188.34	14,720.00
43	Rolf MUNTZ	NL	73	68	75	80	296	8	19,761.49	13,110.00
	Angel CABRERA	Arg	71	77	69	79	296	8	19,761.49	13,110.00
	Charl SCHWARTZEL	SA	73	68	79	76	296	8	19,761.49	13,110.00
46	Marcus FRASER	Aus	77	70	72	78	297	9	17,334.64	11,500.00
	Gary ORR	Scot	73	73	74	77	297	9	17,334.64	11,500.00
	Henrik NYSTROM	Swe	75	72	73	77	297	9	17,334.64	11,500.00
	Marcel SIEM	Ger	70	75	77	75	297	9	17,334.64	11,500.00
50	Paul EALES	Eng	73	71	76	78	298	10	14,561.10	9,660.00
	Roger CHAPMAN	Eng	69	74	78	77	298	10	14,561.10	9,660.00
	Ricardo GONZALEZ	Arg	74	71	76	77	298	10	14,561.10	9,660.00
	Stephen DODD	Wal	74	70	76	78	298	10	14,561.10	9,660.00
54	David CARTER	Eng	75	67	78	79	299	11	12,480.94	8,280.00
	Anders HANSEN	Den	70	70	80	79	299	11	12,480.94	8,280.00
56	Sven STRÜVER	Ger	71	74	75	80	300	12	10,863.04	7,206.67
	Mads VIBE-HASTRUP	Den	75	69	77	79	300	12	10,863.04	7,206.67
	Johan SKOLD	Swe	76	69	78	77	300	12	10,863.04	7,206.67
59	Paul LAWRIE	Scot	71	77	79	74	301	13	9,360.71	6,210.00
	Alastair FORSYTH	Scot	76	69	77	79	301	13	9,360.71	6,210.00
	David GRIFFITHS	Eng	73	75	76	77	301	13	9,360.71	6,210.00
	Stephen GALLACHER	Scot	76	71	74	80	301	13	9,360.71	6,210.00
	Søren KJELDSEN	Den	72	76	77	76	301	13	9,360.71	6,210.00
64	Jean VAN DE VELDE	Fr	74	72	74	82	302	14	8,147.28	5,405.00
	David PARK	Wal	75	70	80	77	302	14	8,147.28	5,405.00
66	Francois DELAMONTAGNE	Fr	67	74	81	81	303	15	7,107.20	4,715.00
	Gregory HAVRET	Fr	69	73	76	85	303	15	7,107.20	4,715.00
	Mark FOSTER	Eng	70	77	78	78	303	15	7,107.20	4,715.00
	Oliver WILSON	Eng	73	72	78	80	303	15	7,107.20	4,715.00
70	Leif WESTERBERG	Swe	75	71	78	82	306	18	6,330.91	4,200.00
71	Philip GOLDING	Eng	72	74	79	83	308	20	5,200.00	3,449.74
72	Tom LEHMAN	USA	75	71	79	84	309	21	5,197.00	3,447.15
73	Fernando ROCA	Sp	72	74	84	80	310	22	5,194.00	3,445.76
74	Costantino ROCCA	It	74	74	76	DISQ	224			

Total Prize Fund
€3,482,520   £2,310,343

The Barclays Scottish Open

Glasgow, Scotland
July 7-10 • 2005

Loch Lomond

Par	Yards	Metres
71	7113	6500

1	**Tim CLARK**	**265**	**-19**	
2	Darren CLARKE	267	-17	
	Maarten LAFEBER	267	-17	
4	Ian POULTER	268	-16	
5	Angel CABRERA	269	-15	
	Luke DONALD	269	-15	
	Nick DOUGHERTY	269	-15	
8	Alastair FORSYTH	270	-14	
	Peter HEDBLOM	270	-14	
	Miguel Angel JIMÉNEZ	270	-14	

Round One	Round Two	Round Three	Round Four

EUROPEAN TOUR ORDER OF MERIT
(After 30 tournaments)

Pos		€	
1	**Michael CAMPBELL**	**1,362,050.06**	
2	Retief GOOSEN	1,179,591.48	
3	Angel CABRERA	1,059,237.68	
4	Ernie ELS	980,679.89	
5	David HOWELL	923,423.07	
6	Thomas BJÖRN	878,156.15	
7	Miguel Angel JIMÉNEZ	864,918.88	
8	Stephen DODD	828,997.16	
9	Colin MONTGOMERIE	811,233.78	
10	Nick O'HERN	732,346.85	

Out
Of the
Shadows

The Barclays Scottish Open

Glasgow, Scotland
July 7-10 • 2005

Tim Clark emerged from the considerable shadows of compatriots Ernie Els and Retief Goosen to claim The Barclays Scottish Open at Loch Lomond. What is it about South Africans and the Bonnie Banks? Els was the winner in 2000 and 2003, while Goosen had his name engraved on the trophy in 2001, less than a month after winning his first US Open Championship.

Peter Hedblom

So it was that in a week of weather which must have reminded him of his home town of Durban, the diminutive Clark stood tall and joined them, striding to his first significant victory outside his homeland with a record equalling aggregate for the tournament at Loch Lomond of 19 under par 265.

In place of 'The Big Easy' came 'The Little Easy', the 29 year old Arizona-based golfer calmly holing a 25 foot birdie putt on the last green with a putter almost as long as himself, to finish two shots in front of Northern Ireland's Darren Clarke and Maarten Lafeber of The Netherlands, who gleefully accepted the one remaining place on offer for the upcoming Open Championship at St Andrews.

While winning his native South African Airways Open on two occasions was encouraging, this was the evidence Clark needed to convince himself that, on his day, he had all the attributes to prosper in the most exalted of company. For this was the strongest field ever assembled at Loch Lomond, headlined by four of the top seven on the Official World Golf Ranking – Phil Mickelson, Adam Scott, Els and Goosen.

For Clark this was the culmination of many years of toil away from the glare of publicity that has accompanied Els and Goosen

"Loch Lomond is one of my favourite venues– I love this place - and the course is in really great shape. I base my schedule around trying to test myself against the best field on the best golf courses and this is certainly the best tournament to play in this week of the year, anywhere in the world" – Adam Scott

Darren Clarke

Paul Lawrie

almost since the end of their schooldays in South Africa. At times it had not been an easy journey. But now, finally, Timothy Henry Clark - TC to his friends - had made it in the international arena.

Not blessed with the physical advantages bestowed on Els and Goosen, Clark had always to depend on fierce determination. Many back home in South Africa likened him to Gary Player, a fact quickly recognised by Player himself who made him one of his wild card selections for The International Team in The 2003 Presidents Cup.

A graduate of North Carolina State University, Clark was named College Golf All-American Freshman of the Year in 1996 and a year later he won the US Public Links Championship. However, unlike Els, he was not an instant success in the professional ranks. He had to serve his apprenticeship on the Nationwide Tour in 1999 and 2000 before qualifying for the US PGA Tour the following year.

Even then it was far from an easy ride. In his first main tour event in the United States, the AT&T Pebble Beach National

Pro-Am, he had to withdraw after the first round with a damaged wrist. That injury, which required surgery, cost him all but three events in 2001, resulting in a medical exemption for 2002.

He made his comeback in the South African Airways Open that year, but again obstacles reared up in his way. Although the event was held in his hometown of Durban, he was passed over for a sponsor's invitation, forcing him to play the qualifying tournament. To his enormous credit, he won it, and a few days later he won the Championship itself, the first qualifier to achieve such a feat. Finally, he had established himself, and at Loch Lomond in July 2005 he became a global figure in the game.

For a man who had gone through so much to get this far, his immediate reaction to victory was restrained, apart from a controlled punch in the air when his birdie putt dropped below ground on the last green.

There were no histrionics and no attempt at singing the Flower of Scotland at the following presentation ceremony as the Frenchman, Thomas Levet, had done the

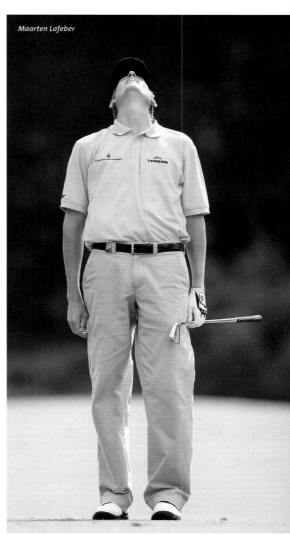
Maarten Lafeber

Commodities • FX • Derivatives • Equity Products • Loans • Bonds • Linkers • Emerging Markets • Fixed Income • Research • Private Equity

Whole in one

Ernie Els and Miguel Angel Jiménez

Final Results

Pos	Name		Rd1	Rd2	Rd3	Rd4	Total		€	£
1	Tim CLARK	SA	67	66	65	67	265	-19	592,388.00	400,000.00
2	Darren CLARKE	N.Ire	67	65	69	66	267	-17	308,708.20	208,450.00
	Maarten LAFEBER	NL	67	63	68	69	267	-17	308,708.20	208,450.00
4	Ian POULTER	Eng	69	67	67	65	268	-16	177,716.40	120,000.00
5	Angel CABRERA	Arg	64	67	68	70	269	-15	127,244.94	85,920.00
	Luke DONALD	Eng	68	67	67	67	269	-15	127,244.94	85,920.00
	Nick DOUGHERTY	Eng	66	69	67	67	269	-15	127,244.94	85,920.00
8	Alastair FORSYTH	Scot	68	64	67	71	270	-14	79,853.90	53,920.00
	Miguel Angel JIMÉNEZ	Sp	67	69	66	68	270	-14	79,853.90	53,920.00
	Peter HEDBLOM	Swe	67	68	68	67	270	-14	79,853.90	53,920.00
11	Ernie ELS	SA	70	66	67	68	271	-13	65,399.64	44,160.00
12	Gary ORR	Scot	68	65	71	68	272	-12	59,179.56	39,960.00
	Adam SCOTT	Aus	70	67	64	71	272	-12	59,179.56	39,960.00
14	Fredrik JACOBSON	Swe	71	67	69	66	273	-11	51,182.32	34,560.00
	Francesco MOLINARI	It	70	66	68	69	273	-11	51,182.32	34,560.00
	Trevor IMMELMAN	SA	74	66	65	68	273	-11	51,182.32	34,560.00
	Henrik STENSON	Swe	66	70	67	70	273	-11	51,182.32	34,560.00
18	Colin MONTGOMERIE	Scot	68	69	66	71	274	-10	43,451.66	29,340.00
	Anthony WALL	Eng	69	66	71	68	274	-10	43,451.66	29,340.00
	David LYNN	Eng	69	68	67	70	274	-10	43,451.66	29,340.00
	Simon DYSON	Eng	71	64	70	69	274	-10	43,451.66	29,340.00
22	Richard FINCH	Eng	68	71	68	68	275	-9	39,097.61	26,400.00
	Greg OWEN	Eng	67	66	72	70	275	-9	39,097.61	26,400.00
	Simon KHAN	Eng	67	67	70	71	275	-9	39,097.61	26,400.00
25	David DRYSDALE	Scot	67	69	70	70	276	-8	34,832.41	23,520.00
	Lee WESTWOOD	Eng	65	69	72	70	276	-8	34,832.41	23,520.00
	José Maria OLAZÁBAL	Sp	68	69	69	70	276	-8	34,832.41	23,520.00
	Paul BROADHURST	Eng	73	65	65	73	276	-8	34,832.41	23,520.00
	Richard BLAND	Eng	69	70	68	69	276	-8	34,832.41	23,520.00
30	Jonathan LOMAS	Eng	67	65	72	73	277	-7	27,763.25	18,746.67
	Phillip ARCHER	Eng	70	67	72	68	277	-7	27,763.25	18,746.67
	Mark ROE	Eng	68	71	70	68	277	-7	27,763.25	18,746.67
	Robert-Jan DERKSEN	NL	69	67	67	74	277	-7	27,763.25	18,746.67
	Niclas FASTH	Swe	69	70	69	69	277	-7	27,763.25	18,746.67
	Tom LEHMAN	USA	66	69	71	71	277	-7	27,763.25	18,746.67
	Thongchai JAIDEE	Thai	66	69	66	76	277	-7	27,763.25	18,746.67
	Richard STERNE	SA	65	68	74	70	277	-7	27,763.25	18,746.67
	Terry PRICE	Aus	69	68	67	73	277	-7	27,763.25	18,746.67
39	Ben MASON	Eng	72	65	68	73	278	-6	22,392.27	15,120.00
	Christopher HANELL	Swe	69	69	69	71	278	-6	22,392.27	15,120.00
	John BICKERTON	Eng	71	69	72	66	278	-6	22,392.27	15,120.00
	Klas ERIKSSON	Swe	68	70	68	72	278	-6	22,392.27	15,120.00
	Andrew MCLARDY	SA	71	69	69	69	278	-6	22,392.27	15,120.00
44	Eduardo ROMERO	Arg	70	67	71	71	279	-5	18,482.51	12,480.00
	Phil MICKELSON	USA	67	72	71	69	279	-5	18,482.51	12,480.00
	Robert ALLENBY	Aus	68	67	75	69	279	-5	18,482.51	12,480.00
	Scott HENDERSON	Scot	72	68	70	69	279	-5	18,482.51	12,480.00
	Retief GOOSEN	SA	71	67	71	70	279	-5	18,482.51	12,480.00
	Marcus FRASER	Aus	69	69	69	72	279	-5	18,482.51	12,480.00
50	Christian CÉVAÉR	Fr	71	69	72	68	280	-4	14,572.75	9,840.00
	Garry HOUSTON	Wal	70	69	69	72	280	-4	14,572.75	9,840.00
	Thomas LEVET	Fr	71	68	71	70	280	-4	14,572.75	9,840.00
	Philip GOLDING	Eng	70	66	72	72	280	-4	14,572.75	9,840.00
	Gregory BOURDY	Fr	66	72	71	71	280	-4	14,572.75	9,840.00
55	Ricardo GONZALEZ	Arg	68	70	72	71	281	-3	12,084.72	8,160.00
	Stephen GALLACHER	Scot	68	70	74	69	281	-3	12,084.72	8,160.00
57	Simon WAKEFIELD	Eng	70	68	67	77	282	-2	11,018.42	7,440.00
58	Paul LAWRIE	Scot	65	71	71	76	283	-1	9,774.40	6,600.00
	David GRIFFITHS	Eng	69	69	73	72	283	-1	9,774.40	6,600.00
	Jamie DONALDSON	Wal	71	65	75	72	283	-1	9,774.40	6,600.00
	Gonzalo FERNANDEZ-CASTANO	Sp	73	67	71	72	283	-1	9,774.40	6,600.00
	Scott DRUMMOND	Scot	72	67	71	73	283	-1	9,774.40	6,600.00
	Miguel Angel MARTIN	Sp	66	73	71	73	283	-1	9,774.40	6,600.00
64	Oliver WILSON	Eng	69	69	72	74	284	0	8,530.39	5,760.00
65	Peter GUSTAFSSON	Swe	69	70	72	74	285	1	8,174.95	5,520.00
66	Jamie SPENCE	Eng	73	67	74	72	286	2	7,641.81	5,160.00
	Stuart LITTLE	Eng	64	73	73	76	286	2	7,641.81	5,160.00
68	Raphaël JACQUELIN	Fr	72	68	69	78	287	3	6,782.84	4,580.00
	Louis OOSTHUIZEN	SA	70	70	73	74	287	3	6,782.84	4,580.00
	Rolf MUNTZ	NL	69	69	73	76	287	3	6,782.84	4,580.00
71	Kenneth FERRIE	Eng	67	71	79	71	288	4	5,331.00	3,599.67
72	David CARTER	Eng	68	68	79	74	289	5	5,328.00	3,597.64

Alastair Forsyth

previous year. However, before Clark and girlfriend Candice celebrated later that evening with friends in Glasgow, he had a few words which, for evermore, will make him a favourite among the Scottish fans.

Having taken in the All Blacks final thrashing of the British and Irish Lions before he set off on his third round on Saturday, the rugby loving Clark concluded his speech with a sentiment that generated a huge roar of approval. "By the way," he said, smiling broadly. "I think the Lions would have done much better if they had had a few Scots in the team!"

All week he had got it right on the course. Such a statement proved he was pretty adept off it, too.

Jock MacVicar
Scottish Daily Express

Total Prize Fund
€3,564,990 £2,407,197

134th Open Championship

St Andrews, Scotland
July 14-17 • 2005

The Old Course

Par	Yards	Metres
72	7279	6719

Pos				
1	**Tiger WOODS**	274	-14	
2	Colin MONTGOMERIE	279	-9	
3	Fred COUPLES	280	-8	
	José Maria OLAZÁBAL	280	-8	
5	Michael CAMPBELL	281	-7	
	Sergio GARCIA	281	-7	
	Retief GOOSEN	281	-7	
	Bernhard LANGER	281	-7	
	Geoff OGILVY	281	-7	
	Vijay SINGH	281	-7	

| Round One | Round Two | Round Three | Round Four |

EUROPEAN TOUR ORDER OF MERIT
(After 31 tournaments)

Pos		€	
1	**Michael CAMPBELL**	1,539,762.26	
2	Colin MONTGOMERIE	1,436,741.88	
3	Retief GOOSEN	1,357,303.68	
4	Angel CABRERA	1,062,510.69	
5	Ernie ELS	1,012,682.63	
6	David HOWELL	923,423.07	
7	Thomas BJÖRN	882,520.16	
8	Miguel Angel JIMÉNEZ	880,820.24	
9	Stephen DODD	833,361.17	
10	Nick O'HERN	799,677.29	

From A Jack To a King

134th Open Championship

St Andrews, Scotland
July 14-17 • 2005

The Old Course at St Andrews is always the most vibrant and historically relevant host of any Open Championship. Dismissed occasionally by the ill informed as an outdated relic, such critics miss the point of this grand, old place in the east neuk of Fife, their carping, the instinctive response of the sort of people who know the price of everything but the value of very little.

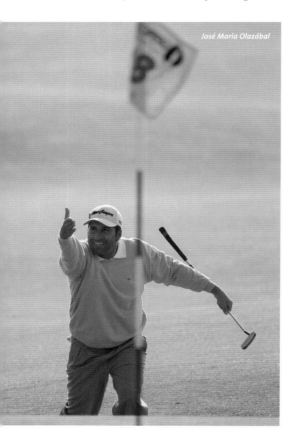
José María Olazábal

The Royal & Ancient Golf Club has no such qualms, which is why St Andrews hosts The Open at least twice as frequently as any of the other classic links on which this most significant of Major Championships is staged.

If the Masters Tournament is a test of nerve and putting, the US Open Championship a challenge to consistency and accuracy of strike, and the US PGA Championship invariably a challenge to a man's stamina, then The Open closes the deal by placing on trial a golfer's imagination above all else.

Given also that the yawning acres of St Andrews offer succour to even the most erratic of drivers on occasion, then here we have a place that might have been designed with just one player in mind. Step forward and receive our applause please, Eldrick Tiger Woods, who completed his second career Grand Slam at the Home of Golf.

His emphatic victory was no surprise to anyone who had spent even a few minutes considering the most likely outcome of this Open. The only way surprise could have embraced many of us would have been if he had finished second.

Mostly, however, it was no surprise to the man himself. His game plan, as ever, was devastatingly simple and based on a sporting blitzkrieg approach to a game that too often encourages caution rather than bravado. Put simply, Woods's intention was to go out and post the sort of score that would eat into all other psyches like a ravenous dog gnawing impatiently on a particularly succulent bone.

When he was handed the early first day tee time he so coveted, the scene was set. He did not let us, or himself, down, his opening 18 holes a flurry of controlled aggression as he returned a 66 that sent his name to the top of the giant yellow leaderboard so that every player returning to the 18th green and those standing on the first tee could not help but see that the challenge had been set by the most accomplished golfer in the world. Then, Woods retreated to his digs, put his feet up, and watched the pack try to do something about the inevitable.

Of course they tried. Hard. But they did not succeed, a multitude of skilled performers caught once again in the eye of the perfect storm that is Woods's golf. It only seems like yesterday many of us suspected that never again would he achieve the sort of numbing dominance he owned a few years ago. There was much talk about the improvement made by his rivals, that the likes of the Numbers Two, Three, Four and Five in the

"To have completed my first and second Grand Slams here at St Andrews is as special as it gets. To win at the Home of Golf is something you dream about. All players that want to win The Open Championship automatically think about St. Andrews. It doesn't get any sweeter than this - it's as good as it gets" – Tiger Woods

Colin Montgomerie

World, Vijay Singh, Ernie Els, Phil Mickelson and Retief Goosen, had the game and the ambition to take him on.

For a time, this was true. However, it was not a valid theory to put forward as this Open unfolded. By the end, Woods had reasserted his authority; the young King was on his throne.

The exception to this, for a while at least, was Colin Montgomerie who, alongside José Maria Olazábal, mounted the most relevant challenge to Woods over the second half of the Championship. Three behind after 54 holes, Montgomerie strode into the last day full of hope and draped in the dark blue of his native Scotland, his caddie Alastair McLean even carrying a towel emblazoned with the Saltire.

A two-minute silence honouring the casualties from the London bombings was observed at 12 noon during Thursday's first round

Imagine it.

Spending more time on the golf course.

Done.

Thanks to Unisys, you can leave work early.

Unisys has been supporting The PGA European Tour since 1989, a growing commitment that saw us become Official Sponsors in 1999.

Like many golf fans, you'd be forgiven for thinking that keeping track of scores and statistics was all Unisys was about.

But there's a good reason why we follow the Tour around Europe and the Middle East, week after week, meeting deadlines and working with whatever the landscape and the weather will throw at us.

We like to satisfy the needs of different clubs, organisers, TV networks and fans around the greens and around the world in the same dedicated way as we support our clients. Bringing the kind of thinking and technical innovation that is helping people transform the way they do business.

We make sense of information technology so you can work faster, smarter. And so you can spend more time on the golf course.

> Consulting.
> Systems Integration.
> Outsourcing.
> Infrastructure.
> Server Technology.

UNISYS

Imagine it. Done.

unisys.com

For a time he encouraged the great hope that had so energised the town of St Andrews the evening before. With supporters running alongside, their Saltires and Lion Rampants fluttering wildly in the breeze so that the Old Course seemed transformed, momentarily, into a medieval jousting field, Montgomerie was, for some considerable time, in his element, a happy mode helped by the fact that he was in the group ahead of Woods and paired with Goosen, a man he knows well.

For one delicious moment he even moved within a stroke of the American as the leaders began their circumference of The Loop. It was, however, a moment that flattered to deceive. After a flurry of birdies and bogeys, the former from Woods, the latter from Montgomerie and Olazábal, Woods walked off the 12th green a decisive four shots clear. Suddenly the Scottish banners dropped towards the ground in despair and anguish, suddenly the atmosphere turned eerily quiet, suddenly McLean's towel should have been plain white.

When Woods pulled off an exquisite flop shot recovery from rough beside the 14th green, his ball soaring up to the clouds before landing like a butterfly securing a berth on a silken scarf, the inevitable birdie, and a five shot lead, meant it really was game over. Off to the side, Olazábal nodded his approval, a gesture accepted by Woods with a tilt of his cap. One short game maestro instinctively acknowledging the brilliance of another.

Nick O'Hern

Jack Nicklaus (second left) stands with his son and caddie Steve , Luke Donald (far left) and Tom Watson (far right)

Thanks Jack

Jack Nicklaus is an RBS ambassador

For the inspiration

For the professionalism

For the way you changed the game

For the sheer mental strength

For being the one to beat

For taking the game of golf to a new level

Make it happen

RBS

The Royal Bank of Scotland Group

Bernhard Langer

Ian Poulter and Nick Faldo

This, it should be pointed out, is where Woods wins his Majors. His driving might grab the headlines but it is his short game abilities that make him such a phenomenal golfer. The devil, as ever, is in the detail and when you deconstruct Woods's Championship winning effort, it is not off the tee that he won this Open but close to or on the greens. It is here that his skill, nerve and imagination makes him the best in the world.

He amassed a total of 95 putts over the week while Montgomerie had 102 and Olazábal 104. He missed 18 greens over four days and scrambled par an astonishing 11 times. Montgomerie, meanwhile, missed 15 but only recovered at five of them, while Olazábal got up and down seven times out of 14.

With Woods's short game at its peak, in a sense, too, this was The Open that peaked early. It peaked on the course with Woods's opening round before peaking emotionally when Jack Nicklaus said goodbye late on a perfect Friday afternoon, the widest fairway in golf surrounded by thousands of adoring fans cheering and weeping in equal measure. After a wonderful birdie on the final hole of a stupendous Major career, Nicklaus walked off and into the embrace of his ever-loyal family.

Forty minutes later Woods and Olazábal came to the same green where the Spaniard holed out from the Valley of Sin for an eagle two before high-fiving with the Champion elect, the pair laughing and joking at the deliciousness of the moment.

For the watching R&A officials, it was perfect timing. From a Jack to a King...........

Bill Elliott
The Observer / Golf Monthly

Final Results

Pos	Name		Rd1	Rd2	Rd3	Rd4	Total		€	£
1	Tiger WOODS	USA	66	67	71	70	274	-14	1,047,362.40	720,000.00
2	Colin MONTGOMERIE	Scot	71	66	70	72	279	-9	625,508.10	430,000.00
3	Fred COUPLES	USA	68	71	73	68	280	-8	352,757.50	242,500.00
	José Maria OLAZÁBAL	Sp	68	70	68	74	280	-8	352,757.50	242,500.00
5	Sergio GARCIA	Sp	70	69	69	73	281	-7	177,712.20	122,166.68
	Bernhard LANGER	Ger	71	69	70	71	281	-7	177,712.20	122,166.68
	Geoff OGILVY	Aus	71	74	67	69	281	-7	177,712.20	122,166.68
	Vijay SINGH	Fiji	69	69	71	72	281	-7	177,712.20	122,166.68
	Retief GOOSEN	SA	68	73	66	74	281	-7	177,712.20	122,166.68
	Michael CAMPBELL	NZ	69	72	68	72	281	-7	177,712.20	122,166.68
11	Kenny PERRY	USA	71	71	68	72	282	-6	97,099.22	66,750.00
	Graeme MCDOWELL	N.Ire	69	72	74	67	282	-6	97,099.22	66,750.00
	Ian POULTER	Eng	70	72	71	69	282	-6	97,099.22	66,750.00
	Nick FALDO	Eng	74	69	70	69	282	-6	97,099.22	66,750.00
15	David FROST	SA	77	65	72	69	283	-5	67,330.44	46,285.71
	Nick O'HERN	Aus	73	69	71	70	283	-5	67,330.44	46,285.71
	Trevor IMMELMAN	SA	68	70	73	72	283	-5	67,330.44	46,285.71
	Darren CLARKE	N.Ire	73	70	67	73	283	-5	67,330.44	46,285.71
	John DALY	USA	71	69	70	73	283	-5	67,330.44	46,285.71
	Mark HENSBY	Aus	67	77	69	70	283	-5	67,330.44	46,285.71
	Sean O'HAIR	USA	73	67	70	73	283	-5	67,330.44	46,285.71
	Lloyd SALTMAN (Am)	Scot	73	71	68	71	283	-5		
23	Bart BRYANT	USA	69	70	71	74	284	-4	47,276.77	32,500.00
	Tadahiro TAKAYAMA	Jpn	72	72	70	70	284	-4	47,276.77	32,500.00
	Tom LEHMAN	USA	75	69	70	70	284	-4	47,276.77	32,500.00
	Tim CLARK	SA	71	69	70	74	284	-4	47,276.77	32,500.00
	Nick FLANAGAN	Aus	73	71	69	71	284	-4	47,276.77	32,500.00
	Scott VERPLANK	USA	68	70	72	74	284	-4	47,276.77	32,500.00
	Brad FAXON	USA	72	66	70	76	284	-4	47,276.77	32,500.00
	Scott DRUMMOND	Scot	74	71	69	70	284	-4	47,276.77	32,500.00
	Eric RAMSAY (AM)	Scot	68	74	74	68	284	-4		
32	Richard GREEN	Aus	72	68	72	73	285	-3	38,548.75	26,500.00
	Sandy LYLE	Scot	74	67	69	75	285	-3	38,548.75	26,500.00
34	Peter HANSON	Swe	72	72	71	71	286	-2	32,002.74	22,000.00
	Henrik STENSON	Swe	74	67	73	72	286	-2	32,002.74	22,000.00
	Thomas LEVET	Fr	69	71	75	71	286	-2	32,002.74	22,000.00
	Ernie ELS	SA	74	67	75	70	286	-2	32,002.74	22,000.00
	Joe OGILVIE	USA	74	70	73	69	286	-2	32,002.74	22,000.00
	Simon DYSON	Eng	70	71	72	73	286	-2	32,002.74	22,000.00
	Adam SCOTT	Aus	70	71	70	75	286	-2	32,002.74	22,000.00
41	Hiroyuki FUJITA	Jpn	72	68	74	73	287	-1	21,786.99	14,977.27
	Simon KHAN	Eng	69	70	78	70	287	-1	21,786.99	14,977.27
	Paul MCGINLEY	Ire	70	75	73	69	287	-1	21,786.99	14,977.27
	Bob TWAY	USA	69	71	72	75	287	-1	21,786.99	14,977.27
	Søren HANSEN	Den	72	72	66	77	287	-1	21,786.99	14,977.27
	Stuart APPLEBY	Aus	72	68	72	75	287	-1	21,786.99	14,977.27
	K J CHOI	Kor	75	68	71	73	287	-1	21,786.99	14,977.27
	Tim HERRON	USA	73	72	68	74	287	-1	21,786.99	14,977.27
	Maarten LAFEBER	NL	73	70	67	77	287	-1	21,786.99	14,977.27
	Steve WEBSTER	Eng	71	72	71	73	287	-1	21,786.99	14,977.27
	Tom WATSON	USA	75	70	70	72	287	-1	21,786.99	14,977.27
52	Justin LEONARD	USA	73	71	75	69	288	0	15,901.36	10,931.25
	Miguel Angel JIMÉNEZ	Sp	69	72	76	71	288	0	15,901.36	10,931.25
	Paul LAWRIE	Scot	72	71	75	70	288	0	15,901.36	10,931.25
	Fredrik JACOBSON	Swe	71	70	72	75	288	0	15,901.36	10,931.25
	Robert ALLENBY	Aus	70	68	79	71	288	0	15,901.36	10,931.25
	Luke DONALD	Eng	68	73	77	70	288	0	15,901.36	10,931.25
	Thongchai JAIDEE	Thai	73	68	75	72	288	0	15,901.36	10,931.25
	Bo VAN PELT	USA	72	67	73	76	288	0	15,901.36	10,931.25
60	John BICKERTON	Eng	75	70	71	73	289	1	14,546.70	10,000.00
	Tino SCHUSTER	Ger	68	74	74	73	289	1	14,546.70	10,000.00
	Phil MICKELSON	USA	74	67	72	76	289	1	14,546.70	10,000.00
	Mark CALCAVECCHIA	USA	70	73	73	73	289	1	14,546.70	10,000.00
	Greg NORMAN	Aus	72	71	70	76	289	1	14,546.70	10,000.00
	Edoardo MOLINARI (AM)	It	70	70	74	75	289	1		
66	Peter LONARD	Aus	68	70	77	75	290	2	14,110.30	9,700.00
67	Duffy WALDORF	USA	74	68	81	68	291	3	13,601.16	9,350.00
	Robert ROCK	Eng	73	71	75	72	291	3	13,601.16	9,350.00
	Chris DIMARCO	USA	75	69	71	76	291	3	13,601.16	9,350.00
	Chris RILEY	USA	68	73	75	75	291	3	13,601.16	9,350.00
	Pat PEREZ	USA	72	70	72	77	291	3	13,601.16	9,350.00
	David SMAIL	NZ	73	72	69	77	291	3	13,601.16	9,350.00
73	Patrik SJÖLAND	Swe	74	71	76	71	292	4	13,092.03	9,000.00
74	S K HO	Kor	73	71	72	77	293	5	12,801.10	8,800.00
	Ted PURDY	USA	72	72	77	72	293	5	12,801.10	8,800.00
	Scott GUTSCHEWSKI	USA	76	69	75	73	293	5	12,801.10	8,800.00
77	Steve FLESCH	USA	74	70	72	78	294	6	12,510.16	8,600.00
78	Rodney PAMPLING	Aus	74	71	71	80	296	8	12,291.96	8,450.00
	Graeme STORM	Eng	75	70	80	71	296	8	12,291.96	8,450.00
80	Matthew RICHARDSON (Am)	Eng	75	69	77	76	297	9		

Total Prize Fund
€5,607,610 £3,854,900

The Deutsche Bank Players' Championship of Europe

Hamburg, Germany
July 21-24 • 2005

Gut Kaden

Par	Yards	Metres
72	7290	6666

1	Niclas FASTH	274	-14	
2	Angel CABRERA	274	-14	
3	John DALY	276	-12	
	Stephen GALLACHER	276	-12	
5	Bradley DREDGE	277	-11	
	Bernhard LANGER	277	-11	
	Peter LAWRIE	277	-11	
	Graeme STORM	277	-11	
9	K J CHOI	278	-10	
	Henrik STENSON	278	-10	
	Richard STERNE	278	-10	

Round One   Round Two   Round Three   Round Four

EUROPEAN TOUR ORDER OF MERIT
(After 32 tournaments)

Pos		€	
1	Michael CAMPBELL	1,585,357.26	
2	Colin MONTGOMERIE	1,436,741.88	
3	Angel CABRERA	1,429,170.69	
4	Retief GOOSEN	1,365,078.28	
5	Ernie ELS	1,012,682.63	
6	Niclas FASTH	962,905.59	
7	David HOWELL	923,423.07	
8	Miguel Angel JIMÉNEZ	888,594.84	
9	Thomas BJÖRN	882,520.16	
10	Stephen DODD	833,361.17	

Over the Brow of The Hill

Deutsche Bank

The Deutsche Bank Players' Championship of Europe

Hamburg, Germany
July 21-24 • 2005

For 40 days and 40 nights it rained. Okay, it was more like 40 hours, but, nevertheless, the deluge felt biblical in its intensity. By the time it stopped, the course at Gut Kaden was like a stretch of the Norfolk Broads. As the first day of The Deutsche Bank Players' Championship of Europe was washed out, few could see a 72 hole tournament being completed by Sunday. It would not have been, but for the valiant efforts of Hermann Schulz and his greenkeeping staff.

Marcel Siem

John Daly said what many were thinking as we watched Niclas Fasth line up his putt for birdie and victory over Angel Cabrera on the third play-off hole on Sunday evening. "Considering all the rain that came down, the course has been unbelievably good," said Daly. "Hats off to all involved – to be able to play the ball down for all 36 holes today really was phenomenal."

Hats off, too, to Iron Man Fasth. After two draining rounds that Sunday, the Swede somehow found the resolve to grind down Cabrera – a rugged customer even before he had copper-plated his confidence with victory in the BMW Championship at Wentworth Club in May.

Though he had led by one shot after 36 holes, nothing came easy for Fasth on the final day at Gut Kaden. Indeed, he had to endure several crises before clinching the most lucrative of his three wins to date on The European Tour International Schedule.

Behind that choirboy's countenance, Fasth is hungry and tough, as he proved during a recent 18 month quest to perfect his technique. Though he had flirted with greatness in The 2001 Open Championship at Royal Lytham & St Annes, finishing second to David Duval, and shared in Europe's Ryder Cup victory in 2002, Fasth still yearned for improvement.

"The peak was playing in The Ryder Cup," he said. "That year I was swinging it well and the following year was okay. Yet I never really got to the next step. Last year it was obvious that if I wanted to get any further I needed to work really hard and change my technique. It pretty much involved working through everything. Now that the bulk of that technique work is over and done with, I deserve to relax, just play for a while and see what I get out of it."

Ironically, Fasth gave himself precious little opportunity to relax on the final day. He yielded the lead to Bradley Dredge as he completed the third round in level par 72, and this only by virtue of four birdies in the final six holes.

The birdie which saved his tournament came in unlikely circumstances on the 366 yard 13th. While his playing partners both laid up short of the stream which bisects the hole, Fasth aimed left for the adjacent

" It's a great course, different because of the contrast between the two nines. While the front is very open and links-like, there are a lot of trees on the back. The greens are perfect, though they can be tough to read. I love coming to Germany: The people are warm and welcoming and everything, from the food to the hotels, is great " – John Daly

162

Angel Cabrera

Stephen Gallacher

David Park

12th fairway, yet his ball ran through that fairway and into the rough. With the pin tight at the back left-hand side of the green, the margin for error was miniscule as Fasth aimed his nine iron approach over trees, but the shot was close to perfection. His ball landed in the rough about five yards short of the flag, but he chipped in for the first of a hat-trick of birdies.

In the final round, he needed to birdie three of the last five holes to hunt down Cabrera. The Argentine had looked invincible as he swept to 15 under par with his fifth birdie

Passion: Best of Golf.
Performance: Deutsche Bank Players' Championship of Europe.

For the 11th year in a row, Deutsche Bank has brought the world's best golf players to Germany – and to our clients. As the title sponsor of Deutsche Bank Players' Championship of Europe, the most spectacular golf event in Continental Europe held in July at Gut Kaden near Hamburg, we have continued our strong commitment: Deutsche Bank and golf – a successful partnership in which drive, persistence and precision are always to the fore.

www.db.com

Deutsche Bank
Players' Championship

A Passion to Perform.   **Deutsche Bank** ◪

Padraig Harrington

Final Results

Pos	Name		Rd1	Rd2	Rd3	Rd4	Total		€	£
1	Niclas FASTH	Swe	68	66	72	68	274	-14	550,000.00	377,594.24
2	Angel CABRERA	Arg	69	70	68	67	274	-14	366,660.00	251,724.92
3	John DALY	USA	74	64	73	65	276	-12	185,790.00	127,551.34
	Stephen GALLACHER	Scot	68	71	68	69	276	-12	185,790.00	127,551.34
5	Graeme STORM	Eng	70	71	69	67	277	-11	109,230.00	74,990.22
	Bradley DREDGE	Wal	66	69	69	73	277	-11	109,230.00	74,990.22
	Bernhard LANGER	Ger	72	68	69	68	277	-11	109,230.00	74,990.22
	Peter LAWRIE	Ire	71	65	70	71	277	-11	109,230.00	74,990.22
9	K J CHOI	Kor	67	71	69	71	278	-10	66,880.00	45,915.46
	Henrik STENSON	Swe	65	72	69	72	278	-10	66,880.00	45,915.46
	Richard STERNE	SA	70	70	67	71	278	-10	66,880.00	45,915.46
12	Steven O'HARA	Scot	68	70	69	73	280	-8	54,945.00	37,721.66
	Nick DOUGHERTY	Eng	69	70	68	73	280	-8	54,945.00	37,721.66
14	Michael CAMPBELL	NZ	65	71	71	74	281	-7	45,595.00	31,302.56
	Emanuele CANONICA	It	70	69	69	73	281	-7	45,595.00	31,302.56
	Pierre FULKE	Swe	67	73	74	67	281	-7	45,595.00	31,302.56
	Anthony WALL	Eng	71	71	68	71	281	-7	45,595.00	31,302.56
	Thomas LEVET	Fr	68	74	73	66	281	-7	45,595.00	31,302.56
	Wade ORMSBY	Aus	66	73	69	73	281	-7	45,595.00	31,302.56
20	Marcel SIEM	Ger	67	71	72	72	282	-6	39,600.00	27,186.79
21	David LYNN	Eng	70	72	72	69	283	-5	35,805.00	24,581.39
	Andrew COLTART	Scot	69	73	72	69	283	-5	35,805.00	24,581.39
	Alastair FORSYTH	Scot	68	74	69	72	283	-5	35,805.00	24,581.39
	Fredrik HENGE	Swe	68	74	71	70	283	-5	35,805.00	24,581.39
	Joakim BÄCKSTRÖM	Swe	67	73	69	74	283	-5	35,805.00	24,581.39
	Mark ROE	Eng	68	69	74	72	283	-5	35,805.00	24,581.39
27	Richard BLAND	Eng	70	70	74	70	284	-4	29,370.00	20,163.53
	Ian POULTER	Eng	69	73	74	68	284	-4	29,370.00	20,163.53
	Peter HANSON	Swe	71	69	74	70	284	-4	29,370.00	20,163.53
	Graeme MCDOWELL	N.Ire	69	72	70	73	284	-4	29,370.00	20,163.53
	David PARK	Wal	72	68	68	76	284	-4	29,370.00	20,163.53
	Robert COLES	Eng	71	71	73	69	284	-4	29,370.00	20,163.53
	Louis OOSTHUIZEN	SA	69	73	74	68	284	-4	29,370.00	20,163.53
34	Marc CAYEUX	Zim	69	72	74	70	285	-3	23,760.00	16,312.07
	Francois DELAMONTAGNE	Fr	71	71	73	70	285	-3	23,760.00	16,312.07
	David CARTER	Eng	73	69	69	74	285	-3	23,760.00	16,312.07
	Sam LITTLE	Eng	75	67	70	73	285	-3	23,760.00	16,312.07
	Lian-Wei ZHANG	PRC	69	72	72	72	285	-3	23,760.00	16,312.07
	Brian DAVIS	Eng	71	67	72	75	285	-3	23,760.00	16,312.07
40	José Manuel LARA	Sp	72	70	72	72	286	-2	20,790.00	14,273.06
	Padraig HARRINGTON	Ire	70	71	76	69	286	-2	20,790.00	14,273.06
	Joakim HAEGGMAN	Swe	71	70	71	74	286	-2	20,790.00	14,273.06
43	Ian GARBUTT	Eng	72	69	73	73	287	-1	18,480.00	12,687.17
	Anders HANSEN	Den	69	69	75	74	287	-1	18,480.00	12,687.17
	Maarten LAFEBER	NL	70	71	76	70	287	-1	18,480.00	12,687.17
	Alessandro TADINI	It	66	72	79	70	287	-1	18,480.00	12,687.17
47	Paul MCGINLEY	Ire	70	72	72	74	288	0	16,170.00	11,101.27
	David DRYSDALE	Scot	69	72	74	73	288	0	16,170.00	11,101.27
	David GRIFFITHS	Eng	70	71	74	73	288	0	16,170.00	11,101.27
50	Mark FOSTER	Eng	73	69	69	79	290	2	14,850.00	10,195.04
51	Peter FOWLER	Aus	69	73	73	76	291	3	14,190.00	9,741.93
52	Damien MCGRANE	Ire	71	71	74	76	292	4	13,200.00	9,062.26
	Jean-Francois REMESY	Fr	74	67	75	76	292	4	13,200.00	9,062.26
54	Stuart MANLEY	Wal	73	69	70	81	293	5	12,210.00	8,382.59
55	Barry LANE	Eng	73	70			143	-1	7,774.60	5,337.53
	Raphaël JACQUELIN	Fr	73	70			143	-1	7,774.60	5,337.53
	Steve WEBSTER	Eng	71	72			143	-1	7,774.60	5,337.53
	Costantino ROCCA	It	72	71			143	-1	7,774.60	5,337.53
	Ian WOOSNAM	Wal	68	75			143	-1	7,774.60	5,337.53
	Klas ERIKSSON	Swe	75	68			143	-1	7,774.60	5,337.53
	David FROST	SA	69	74			143	-1	7,774.60	5,337.53
	Darren FICHARDT	SA	76	67			143	-1	7,774.60	5,337.53
	Scott DRUMMOND	Scot	72	71			143	-1	7,774.60	5,337.53
	Titch MOORE	SA	72	71			143	-1	7,774.60	5,337.53
	Jean-François LUCQUIN	Fr	74	69			143	-1	7,774.60	5,337.53
	Miguel Angel JIMÉNEZ	Sp	74	69			143	-1	7,774.60	5,337.53
	Paul CASEY	Eng	73	70			143	-1	7,774.60	5,337.53
	Retief GOOSEN	SA	70	73			143	-1	7,774.60	5,337.53
	Tobias DIER	Ger	72	71			143	-1	7,774.60	5,337.53
	Christopher HANELL	Swe	70	73			143	-1	7,774.60	5,337.53
	Terry PRICE	Aus	70	73			143	-1	7,774.60	5,337.53
	Simon HURD	Eng	68	75			143	-1	7,774.60	5,337.53
	Jonathan LOMAS	Eng	71	72			143	-1	7,774.60	5,337.53
	Peter HEDBLOM	Swe	73	70			143	-1	7,774.60	5,337.53

in eight holes on the 17th, but he bogeyed the last after blocking his second shot into the rough.

Fasth had his own problems at the final hole, pulling his approach deep into a greenside trap. But boy would the Swede be grateful for a tutorial in bunker play he had received from Tony Johnstone at the Marriott Forest of Arden in May, as he played his escape to tap-in range.

In the play-off, Fasth and Cabrera both parred the 18th twice before the crunch came as they stood over similar 12 foot putts for birdie. Cabrera missed and Fasth stroked his home – later revealing that the putt had looked identical to his play-off clincher over Miles Tunnicliff in the Holden New Zealand Open in February.

Fasth paid humble tribute to caddie Dave McNeilly, who had linked up with him exactly 12 months earlier after six years on Padraig Harrington's bag – a spell which included victory with the Irishman at Gut Kaden in 2003.

"It was good timing and good luck for me," said Fasth of Harrington's decision to part with McNeilly. "Dave's a very skilled and experienced caddie. At that time I wasn't even playing very well, so I was lucky he saw the potential in me."

McNeilly added: "I joined up with Niclas for one reason – because he's so incredibly strong mentally. You should see how hard this guy works. I've seen the pain and agony he's gone through. He had a horrible time last year, he worked through it and now he's come over the brow of the hill."

Karl MacGinty
Irish Independent

Steven O'Hara

Total Prize Fund
€3,319,780 £2,279,146

Scandinavian Masters by Carlsberg

Sweden
July 28-31 • 2005

Kungsängen Golf Club

Par	Yards	Metres
71	6482	5929

Pos	Player	Score		
1	**Mark HENSBY**	262	-22	
2	Henrik STENSON	262	-22	
3	Marc CAYEUX	265	-19	
	Bradley DREDGE	265	-19	
5	Pierre FULKE	268	-16	
	Adam SCOTT	268	-16	
7	Gary EMERSON	269	-15	
	Martin ERLANDSSON	269	-15	
	Barry LANE	269	-15	
	Henrik NYSTROM	269	-15	

Round One | Round Two | Round Three | Round Four

EUROPEAN TOUR ORDER OF MERIT
(After 33 tournaments)

Pos	Player	€	
1	**Michael CAMPBELL**	1,585,357.26	
2	Colin MONTGOMERIE	1,436,741.88	
3	Angel CABRERA	1,429,170.69	
4	Retief GOOSEN	1,365,078.28	
5	Ernie ELS	1,012,682.63	
6	Niclas FASTH	962,905.59	
7	David HOWELL	923,423.07	
8	Miguel Angel JIMÉNEZ	888,594.84	
9	Thomas BJÖRN	882,520.16	
10	Stephen DODD	833,361.17	

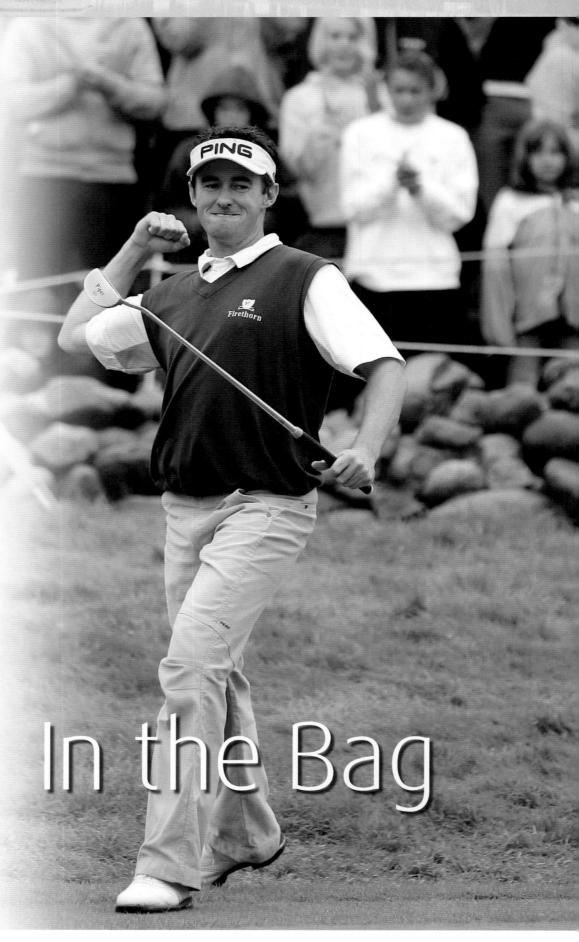

In the Bag

It is an observable fact that Sweden boasts more knapsacks per head of the population than arguably any other nation in the western world. To walk along the streets of Stockholm or Malmö is to come under heavy risk, at every turn, of getting forcibly bodychecked by otherwise law abiding citizens.

They love the things. No matter that the presence of the shoulder-borne hampers make those who wear them take on the silhouette of a latter-day Quasimodo. They are not just fond of them. They are utterly besotted.

Short people regularly get their ears clipped if somebody makes a sudden turn to look in the window of a shoe shop or the like. Tall people get it around the chest. Very tall people are prone to getting punched in the stomach, no matter that the wearers of the strappy satchels are probably living exemplars of peace and love. To be safe from assault it is necessary to be Jimmy Krankie, Ronnie Corbett or a Hobbit.

Be that as it may, these back-packers' friends have uses beyond the transportation of a couple of rounds of ham sandwiches, a banana and a bottle of water. They came in useful, for example, during the Scandinavian Masters by Carlsberg at the end of July. Waterproofs and galoshes were de rigueur from start to finish - and nothing carries such kit quite as well as the ubiquitous sack on the back.

It was, not to overstate the case, damp at Kungsängen Golf Club. When it was not throwing the wet stuff down from the skies, it was making the going underfoot soft to heavy. The walkways, not to mention the fairways, made one circuit of the course not so much a pleasant stroll as a full-scale, cross-country yomp.

It left the amateur side of the pre-tournament Pro-Am disappointed when torrential rain meant that it had to be called

Richard Finch

Bradley Dredge

Martin Erlandsson

Scandinavian Masters by Carlsberg

Sweden
July 28-31 • 2005

Damien McGrane

off. Fortunately though, when it came to the business end of the tournament, things improved.

That did not mean, however, that the players had it easy. Wet ground may make a golf course more vulnerable in the sense that flagsticks can be attacked at will in the knowledge that the greens will hold, but it wreaks havoc with the effective length of the course. No run on the ball makes it play long with all the attendant problems that clubbing for second and subsequent shots bring.

It was, therefore, going to be a tournament for those with finesse alongside a gentle and imaginative touch, and nobody provided more of those skills during the week than Mark Hensby and Henrik Stenson. The Australian guest and the local Swedish favourite lasted the pace better than anybody else and proved it by tying for the lead after 72 holes with matching final rounds of 65 and 22 under par totals of 262.

As the pair marched out to the first play-off hole, Hensby's caddie, Fanny Sunesson, told her boss that the next few minutes were either going to make a lot of Swedes happy or that she would be left as the only happy Swede in the place.

Well, she was after steering Hensby to victory at the second extra hole, a three putt bogey by Stenson bringing matters to a close. Sunesson had enjoyed more than her fair share of success as Nick Faldo's bag-carrier during the Englishman's glory years, but this one tasted just as sweet for one of the best caddies in the world.

Hensby, 34, was playing in the tournament as a sponsor's invitee having had a stellar year in the three Major Championships that had been played thus far, finishing in a tie for fifth in the Masters Tournament, a tie for third in the US Open Championship and a tie for 15th in The Open Championship.

"It was quite amazing, really, how well the course played in the tournament compared to what it was like on Tuesday after the rainstorms came. I think the greenkeeping staff did a wonderful job. It was the right decision to move a few tees forward to make the course playable" - Barry Lane

Adam Scott

Final Results

How well the winner of the John Deere Classic on the US PGA Tour the previous year took his chance.

So impressed was he in his first outing on a regulation European Tour event that he immediately announced his intention of taking up Membership. "It's much more relaxing over here," he said. "You get to visit different cities and it's something I really enjoy."

Others played their part in yet another successful European Tour event in Scandinavia. Talented Zimbabwean Marc Cayeux and seasoned campaigner Barry Lane grabbed the headlines on the first day while the consistent Welshman Bradley Dredge put himself in the picture on the second and third.

But in the end it was left to the visitor from Melbourne to steal the day. He departed from Kungsängen as happy as Larry. And Larry? He left, too. Bearing, it hardly needs to be said, his knapsack.

Mel Webb
The Times

Pos	Name		Rd1	Rd2	Rd3	Rd4	Total		€	£
1	Mark HENSBY	Aus	65	68	64	65	262	-22	266,660.00	184,976.31
2	Henrik STENSON	Swe	67	66	64	65	262	-22	177,770.00	123,315.23
3	Marc CAYEUX	Zim	63	69	68	65	265	-19	90,080.00	62,486.56
	Bradley DREDGE	Wal	66	63	66	70	265	-19	90,080.00	62,486.56
5	Pierre FULKE	Swe	67	63	70	68	268	-16	61,920.00	42,952.57
	Adam SCOTT	Aus	70	65	65	68	268	-16	61,920.00	42,952.57
7	Henrik NYSTROM	Swe	66	65	69	69	269	-15	38,960.00	27,025.71
	Martin ERLANDSSON	Swe	69	65	69	66	269	-15	38,960.00	27,025.71
	Gary EMERSON	Eng	69	67	66	67	269	-15	38,960.00	27,025.71
	Barry LANE	Eng	64	66	65	74	269	-15	38,960.00	27,025.71
11	Jean-François REMESY	Fr	66	65	69	70	270	-14	25,546.67	17,721.18
	Damien MCGRANE	Ire	68	66	64	72	270	-14	25,546.67	17,721.18
	Lian-Wei ZHANG	PRC	66	69	68	67	270	-14	25,546.67	17,721.18
	Paul BROADHURST	Eng	67	68	67	68	270	-14	25,546.67	17,721.18
	Richard FINCH	Eng	71	64	65	70	270	-14	25,546.67	17,721.18
	Wilhelm SCHAUMAN	Swe	70	68	66	66	270	-14	25,546.67	17,721.18
17	Jamie DONALDSON	Wal	68	69	67	67	271	-13	21,600.00	14,983.46
18	Alexander NOREN (AM)	Swe	69	66	69	68	272	-12		
	Johan SKOLD	Swe	67	70	70	65	272	-12	18,986.67	13,170.64
	Peter O'MALLEY	Aus	66	68	67	71	272	-12	18,986.67	13,170.64
	Joakim HAEGGMAN	Swe	67	65	69	72	272	-12	18,986.67	13,170.64
	Andrew MCLARDY	SA	66	71	65	70	272	-12	18,986.67	13,170.64
	Jarrod MOSELEY	Aus	67	68	67	70	272	-12	18,986.67	13,170.64
	Henrik BJORNSTAD	Nor	67	65	70	70	272	-12	18,986.67	13,170.64
25	Stuart LITTLE	Eng	69	66	68	70	273	-11	15,920.00	11,043.36
	Johan EDFORS	Swe	67	67	69	70	273	-11	15,920.00	11,043.36
	Peter LAWRIE	Ire	67	70	69	67	273	-11	15,920.00	11,043.36
	Mårten OLANDER	Swe	68	70	69	66	273	-11	15,920.00	11,043.36
	Simon WAKEFIELD	Eng	71	65	68	69	273	-11	15,920.00	11,043.36
	Raymond RUSSELL	Scot	68	67	72	66	273	-11	15,920.00	11,043.36
31	David LYNN	Eng	70	65	71	68	274	-10	12,680.00	8,795.84
	Robert KARLSSON	Swe	65	69	71	69	274	-10	12,680.00	8,795.84
	Peter GUSTAFSSON	Swe	71	64	71	68	274	-10	12,680.00	8,795.84
	Fredrik WIDMARK	Swe	68	70	69	67	274	-10	12,680.00	8,795.84
	Mattias ELIASSON	Swe	67	69	70	68	274	-10	12,680.00	8,795.84
	Mark ROE	Eng	70	65	67	72	274	-10	12,680.00	8,795.84
	Andrew MARSHALL	Eng	66	70	71	67	274	-10	12,680.00	8,795.84
	Sam LITTLE	Eng	69	69	69	67	274	-10	12,680.00	8,795.84
	David PALM (AM)	Swe	71	67	68	68	274	-10		
	David PALM (AM)	Swe	70	65	72	67	274	-10		
40	Hernan REY	Arg	69	69	71	66	275	-9	10,240.00	7,103.27
	Gordon BRAND JNR	Scot	69	66	71	69	275	-9	10,240.00	7,103.27
	Johan AXGREN	Swe	70	66	71	68	275	-9	10,240.00	7,103.27
	Sam WALKER	Eng	67	70	71	67	275	-9	10,240.00	7,103.27
	Ignacio GARRIDO	Sp	74	62	68	71	275	-9	10,240.00	7,103.27
	Stephen SCAHILL	NZ	71	67	65	72	275	-9	10,240.00	7,103.27
46	Benoit TEILLERIA	Fr	70	67	70	69	276	-8	8,160.00	5,660.42
	Terry PRICE	Aus	72	65	68	71	276	-8	8,160.00	5,660.42
	Steven O'HARA	Scot	67	70	68	71	276	-8	8,160.00	5,660.42
	Robert-Jan DERKSEN	NL	72	66	69	69	276	-8	8,160.00	5,660.42
	Peter HEDBLOM	Swe	68	68	70	70	276	-8	8,160.00	5,660.42
	Scott DRUMMOND	Scot	71	66	71	68	276	-8	8,160.00	5,660.42
	Joakim BÄCKSTRÖM	Swe	68	69	70	69	276	-8	8,160.00	5,660.42
53	Leif WESTERBERG	Swe	69	67	69	72	277	-7	6,560.00	4,550.53
	Ian GARBUTT	Eng	66	70	69	72	277	-7	6,560.00	4,550.53
	Martin MARITZ	SA	73	65	67	72	277	-7	6,560.00	4,550.53
56	Jose-Filipe LIMA	Port	68	67	71	72	278	-6	5,097.14	3,535.78
	Rolf MUNTZ	NL	71	67	68	72	278	-6	5,097.14	3,535.78
	Gary ORR	Scot	68	69	69	72	278	-6	5,097.14	3,535.78
	Markus BRIER	Aut	70	66	71	71	278	-6	5,097.14	3,535.78
	Ben MASON	Eng	69	69	72	68	278	-6	5,097.14	3,535.78
	Fredrik HENGE	Swe	67	70	71	70	278	-6	5,097.14	3,535.78
	Jesper PARNEVIK	Swe	71	66	67	74	278	-6	5,097.14	3,535.78
63	Andrew OLDCORN	Scot	66	68	75	70	279	-5	4,080.00	2,830.21
	Per-Ulrik JOHANSSON	Swe	66	70	76	67	279	-5	4,080.00	2,830.21
	Richard BLAND	Eng	66	70	70	73	279	-5	4,080.00	2,830.21
	Oliver WILSON	Eng	68	69	73	69	279	-5	4,080.00	2,830.21
67	Peter FOWLER	Aus	67	70	72	71	280	-4	3,520.00	2,441.75
	Darren FICHARDT	SA	72	66	68	74	280	-4	3,520.00	2,441.75
	Andrew COLTART	Scot	69	67	76	68	280	-4	3,520.00	2,441.75
70	Pelle EDBERG	Swe	66	70	78	67	281	-3	3,120.00	2,164.28
	Stuart MANLEY	Wal	68	70	73	70	281	-3	3,120.00	2,164.28
72	Arjun ATWAL	Ind	71	66	71	74	282	-2	2,575.67	1,786.68
	Peter HANSON	Swe	69	68	69	76	282	-2	2,575.67	1,786.68
	Oskar BERGMAN	Swe	72	66	70	74	282	-2	2,575.67	1,786.68
75	Simon HURD	Eng	69	68	72	74	283	-1	2,394.00	1,660.67
76	Phillip ARCHER	Eng	68	70	77	72	287	3	2,389.50	1,657.54
	Gary MURPHY	Ire	68	70	77	72	287	3	2,389.50	1,657.54

Joakim Haeggman

Total Prize Fund
€1,611,970   £1,118,188

Johnnie Walker Championship at Gleneagles

Perthshire, Scotland
August 4-7 · 2005

The Gleneagles Hotel

Par	Yards	Metres
72	7136	6526

Pos	Player	Score	To Par	
1	**Emanuele CANONICA**	281	-7	
2	Nicolas COLSAERTS	283	-5	
	Bradley DREDGE	283	-5	
	Barry LANE	283	-5	
	David LYNN	283	-5	
6	Francesco MOLINARI	284	-4	
	Wade ORMSBY	284	-4	
8	Richard BLAND	285	-3	
	Raphaël JACQUELIN	285	-3	
	Sam LITTLE	285	-3	
	Gary ORR	285	-3	
	Steve WEBSTER	285	-3	

Round One	Round Two	Round Three	Round Four

EUROPEAN TOUR ORDER OF MERIT
(After 34 tournaments)

Pos		€	
1	**Michael CAMPBELL**	1,585,357.26	
2	Colin MONTGOMERIE	1,436,741.88	
3	Angel CABRERA	1,429,170.69	
4	Retief GOOSEN	1,365,078.28	
5	Ernie ELS	1,012,682.63	
6	Niclas FASTH	962,905.59	
7	David HOWELL	923,423.07	
8	Miguel Angel JIMÉNEZ	888,594.84	
9	Thomas BJÖRN	882,520.16	
10	Stephen DODD	833,361.17	

Reaching The Summit

In the 16 years since he made his debut on The European Tour as an amateur in the 1989 Volvo Open at Is Molas, Emanuele Canonica has been a magnet for those golf fans who admire raw length off the tee in a player.

Unlike Tiger Woods, who has the stature of a natural athlete, the Italian is only five feet four inches tall but he is built like a pocket battleship with the power to match. He can recall with pride, for example, the day he sent a screaming drive some 475 metres down a fairway.

Yet no matter how much the manufacturers of modern golf clubs and balls place huge emphasis on length in their advertising campaigns, Canonica's career statistics before his arrival in Scotland for the Johnnie Walker Championship at Gleneagles only proved one of golf's prime truisms: that length is not everything.

The 34 year old from Pavia could happily

boast that he won the Reuters Statistics Driving Distance category three years in a row from 1998 to 2000 and again in 2002. But, failing to match his strength with accuracy, he had also previously missed 113 cuts in 230 tournament appearances and only recorded 16 top ten finishes.

It was a record which almost persuaded him to quit the game in 2004. He explained. "I started to play well but the results didn't come. That was the end of last year, but I talked with some friends and they said to try a couple more years. Also my wife and a couple of footballers I know - Gianluca Vialli and Marco Simone - told me they thought I needed to go on, and try and stay there. I thought a couple of years

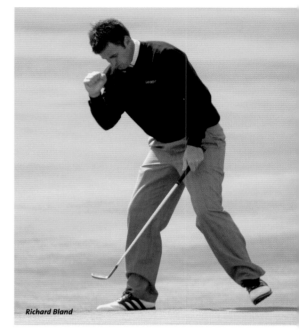

Richard Bland

Emanuele Canonica of Italy (centre) poses with the trophy with the runners-up - Nicolas Colsaerts (left), Barry Lane (second left), Bradley Dredge (second right) and David Lynn (far right)

Johnnie Walker Championship at Gleneagles

Perthshire, Scotland
August 4-7 • 2005

Steve Webster

" The course was superb. The rough was punishing and, as the tournament progressed and the greens started to run, it was vital to hit the immaculate fairways to impart spin and get close to the flags. Therefore, good shots were rewarded while the poor ones were severely punished, just as it should be "
– David Lynn

might be a bit much, so I thought I would play maybe one."

After those words of encouragement there was little form to note in the first half of 2005 from Canonica - except a fifth place in his native Telecom Italia Open - to suggest that he could finally end the long wait for his maiden victory on The European Tour, even less that he would achieve that milestone in the majestic setting of The Gleneagles Hotel.

With its status as a luxury resort confirmed by the staging, a month earlier, of the G8 summit of world leaders, and its place in world golf assured by its choice as the venue for The 2014 Ryder Cup, the Perthshire complex's PGA Centenary Course had been prepared to perfection and presented a stiff test.

Indeed the rough in parts was so deep that, had he ventured in, Canonica would have

Paul Broadhurst

Robert Karlsson

been looking for his ball in grass reaching up to his waist. Yet, after years of searching for a winning formula, he finally devised a strategy that was to clinch the €338,442 (£233,330) first prize cheque with a two shot winning margin.

"I didn't hit a lot of drivers," he said after his final round one under par 71 saw off the challenge of Englishmen Barry Lane and David Lynn, Welshman Bradley Dredge and the third round leader Nicolas Colsaerts of Belgium. I hit a lot of one irons, three irons and four irons. Where I hit a one iron, a lot of guys can't hit the driver. I hit it 240-250 metres off the tee. I put the ball on the fairway and that was one of the keys to the week."

Canonica's short game, too, held up under pressure, never more so than at the par

five 16th hole in the final round when his second shot rolled back towards the small lake in front of the green. Faced with a delicate uphill lob shot from an awkward lie, he worked his approach to within five feet for the birdie that took him away from his pursuers.

Nevertheless his winning total of 281, after a weekend when the weather conditions were benign, was still only seven under par and reflected the difficulty the field had experienced on a course where accuracy counted for everything.

That had been expected to play into the hands of the pre-tournament favourite and the Johnnie Walker Championship Chairman Colin Montgomerie, who was devastated to disappoint his army of Scottish fans when, halfway through the first round, he jarred his hand trying to extract his ball from the rough and had to retire.

It provided an opportunity for England's Mark Foster, who opened with a marvellous four under par 68, to lead. He shared pole position with compatriot Steve Webster at halfway before, he too, fell victim to the long grass with a third round 77.

In fact, Canonica was the only player to break par on all four days to earn the ultimate reward for finally discovering his personal key to success.

Graham Otway

Final Results

Pos	Name		Rd1	Rd2	Rd3	Rd4	Total		€	£
1	Emanuele CANONICA	It	70	71	69	71	281	-7	338,442.83	233,330.00
2	Bradley DREDGE	Wal	70	72	69	72	283	-5	135,095.01	93,137.50
	David LYNN	Eng	70	71	73	69	283	-5	135,095.01	93,137.50
	Barry LANE	Eng	73	74	66	70	283	-5	135,095.01	93,137.50
	Nicolas COLSAERTS	Bel	70	71	67	75	283	-5	135,095.01	93,137.50
6	Francesco MOLINARI	It	75	69	71	69	284	-4	65,997.29	45,500.00
	Wade ORMSBY	Aus	73	73	66	72	284	-4	65,997.29	45,500.00
8	Richard BLAND	Eng	71	71	68	75	285	-3	41,832.13	28,840.00
	Sam LITTLE	Eng	71	68	75	71	285	-3	41,832.13	28,840.00
	Raphaël JACQUELIN	Fr	75	66	76	68	285	-3	41,832.13	28,840.00
	Steve WEBSTER	Eng	71	67	74	73	285	-3	41,832.13	28,840.00
	Gary ORR	Scot	77	71	69	68	285	-3	41,832.13	28,840.00
13	Robert COLES	Eng	74	72	69	71	286	-2	30,561.82	21,070.00
	Jonathan LOMAS	Eng	70	71	73	72	286	-2	30,561.82	21,070.00
	Santiago LUNA	Sp	75	68	71	72	286	-2	30,561.82	21,070.00
	Paul BROADHURST	Eng	71	73	69	73	286	-2	30,561.82	21,070.00
17	Robert-Jan DERKSEN	NL	73	71	73	70	287	-1	24,943.59	17,196.67
	Damien MCGRANE	Ire	70	72	69	76	287	-1	24,943.59	17,196.67
	Ian GARBUTT	Eng	71	69	72	75	287	-1	24,943.59	17,196.67
	Jose-Filipe LIMA	Port	75	70	76	66	287	-1	24,943.59	17,196.67
	Oliver WILSON	Eng	76	71	70	70	287	-1	24,943.59	17,196.67
	Gregory BOURDY	Fr	70	69	74	74	287	-1	24,943.59	17,196.67
23	Paul CASEY	Eng	71	73	70	74	288	0	21,728.34	14,980.00
	Carlos RODILES	Sp	74	72	70	72	288	0	21,728.34	14,980.00
	Jamie SPENCE	Eng	71	73	70	74	288	0	21,728.34	14,980.00
26	Fredrik HENGE	Swe	72	76	71	70	289	1	18,682.31	12,880.00
	Robert KARLSSON	Swe	70	71	74	74	289	1	18,682.31	12,880.00
	Andrew MCLARDY	SA	76	70	72	71	289	1	18,682.31	12,880.00
	Sandy LYLE	Scot	73	72	70	74	289	1	18,682.31	12,880.00
	Ben MASON	Eng	71	73	75	70	289	1	18,682.31	12,880.00
	Paul LAWRIE	Scot	74	68	75	72	289	1	18,682.31	12,880.00
	Raymond RUSSELL	Scot	75	71	71	72	289	1	18,682.31	12,880.00
33	Christopher DOAK	Scot	72	74	69	75	290	2	15,483.98	10,675.00
	Mark FOSTER	Eng	68	70	77	75	290	2	15,483.98	10,675.00
	Mattias ELIASSON	Swe	71	72	77	70	290	2	15,483.98	10,675.00
	David GILFORD	Eng	75	70	73	72	290	2	15,483.98	10,675.00
37	Gary MURPHY	Ire	71	76	72	72	291	3	12,793.32	8,820.00
	Johan AXGREN	Swe	75	72	70	74	291	3	12,793.32	8,820.00
	Peter FOWLER	Aus	76	71	70	74	291	3	12,793.32	8,820.00
	Peter BAKER	Eng	74	74	73	70	291	3	12,793.32	8,820.00
	Philip GOLDING	Eng	73	73	72	73	291	3	12,793.32	8,820.00
	Miles TUNNICLIFF	Eng	75	69	75	72	291	3	12,793.32	8,820.00
	Richard FINCH	Eng	74	73	74	70	291	3	12,793.32	8,820.00
	Sebastian FERNANDEZ	Arg	73	73	75	70	291	3	12,793.32	8,820.00
	Johan SKOLD	Swe	71	74	68	78	291	3	12,793.32	8,820.00
46	Simon WAKEFIELD	Eng	71	72	75	74	292	4	9,341.16	6,440.00
	Andrew COLTART	Scot	74	69	74	75	292	4	9,341.16	6,440.00
	Terry PRICE	Aus	76	72	72	72	292	4	9,341.16	6,440.00
	Jarrod MOSELEY	Aus	75	72	70	75	292	4	9,341.16	6,440.00
	Stuart LITTLE	Eng	74	74	73	71	292	4	9,341.16	6,440.00
	Kenneth FERRIE	Eng	76	70	73	73	292	4	9,341.16	6,440.00
	Malcolm MACKENZIE	Eng	73	72	73	74	292	4	9,341.16	6,440.00
	Anders HANSEN	Den	73	74	68	77	292	4	9,341.16	6,440.00
54	Mark ROE	Eng	70	74	78	71	293	5	6,345.89	4,375.00
	Philip WALTON	Ire	74	73	70	76	293	5	6,345.89	4,375.00
	Andrew MARSHALL	Eng	74	72	72	75	293	5	6,345.89	4,375.00
	Gregory HAVRET	Fr	75	73	70	75	293	5	6,345.89	4,375.00
	Gary EMERSON	Eng	72	71	73	77	293	5	6,345.89	4,375.00
	Paul EALES	Eng	74	71	75	73	293	5	6,345.89	4,375.00
	Graeme STORM	Eng	72	73	72	76	293	5	6,345.89	4,375.00
	Alastair FORSYTH	Scot	74	74	69	76	293	5	6,345.89	4,375.00
62	Mark SANDERS	Eng	75	73	72	74	294	6	4,473.96	3,084.44
	David DRYSDALE	Scot	79	69	73	73	294	6	4,473.96	3,084.44
	Martin ERLANDSSON	Swe	72	70	74	78	294	6	4,473.96	3,084.44
	Darren FICHARDT	SA	70	76	73	75	294	6	4,473.96	3,084.44
	Roger CHAPMAN	Eng	71	73	79	71	294	6	4,473.96	3,084.44
	Andrew OLDCORN	Scot	74	73	73	74	294	6	4,473.96	3,084.44
	Richard GREEN	Aus	77	71	70	76	294	6	4,473.96	3,084.44
	Stuart MANLEY	Wal	76	71	73	74	294	6	4,473.96	3,084.44
	Matthew MORRIS	Eng	73	73	73	75	294	6	4,473.96	3,084.44
71	Christian CÉVAËR	Fr	73	72	72	78	295	7	3,044.50	2,098.95
	David GRIFFITHS	Eng	76	71	69	79	295	7	3,044.50	2,098.95
73	Peter GUSTAFSSON	Swe	74	71	75	76	296	8	3,031.00	2,089.64
	Michael KIRK	SA	70	77	75	74	296	8	3,031.00	2,089.64
	Simon DYSON	Eng	79	69	76	72	296	8	3,031.00	2,089.64
	Leif WESTERBERG	Swe	77	68	74	77	296	8	3,031.00	2,089.64
	Fernando ROCA	Sp	72	75	73	76	296	8	3,031.00	2,089.64
	Simon HURD	Eng	73	75	75	73	296	8	3,031.00	2,089.64
	José Manuel LARA	Sp	74	72	76	74	296	8	3,031.00	2,089.64
80	Jarmo SANDELIN	Swe	75	71	71	80	297	9	3,019.00	2,081.37
81	Peter LAWRIE	Ire	72	76	71	79	298	10	3,016.00	2,079.30
82	José Manuel CARRILES	Sp	73	75	78	73	299	11	3,011.50	2,076.19
	Rolf MUNTZ	NL	72	76	78	73	299	11	3,011.50	2,076.19
84	Ignacio GARRIDO	Sp	72	76	73	79	300	12	3,007.00	2,073.09
85	Stephen BROWNE	Ire	75	73	79	74	301	13	3,004.00	2,071.02
86	Jamie DONALDSON	Wal	75	70	DISQ		145	2		

Total Prize Fund
€2,076,060   £1,431,282

Le Meridien Moscow Country Club

Par	Yards	Metres
72	7154	6542

1	**Mikael LUNDBERG**	273	-15	
2	Andrew BUTTERFIELD	273	-15	
3	David DRYSDALE	276	-12	
	Jarrod MOSELEY	276	-12	
5	Fredrik WIDMARK	277	-11	
6	Jesus Maria ARRUTI	278	-10	
	Benn BARHAM	278	-10	
	Sebastien DELAGRANGE	278	-10	
	Michele REALE	278	-10	
	Shaun P WEBSTER	278	-10	

Round One   Round Two   Round Three   Round Four

EUROPEAN TOUR ORDER OF MERIT
(After 35 tournaments)

Pos		€	
1	**Michael CAMPBELL**	1,585,357.26	
2	Colin MONTGOMERIE	1,436,741.88	
3	Angel CABRERA	1,429,170.69	
4	Retief GOOSEN	1,365,078.28	
5	Ernie ELS	1,012,682.63	
6	Niclas FASTH	962,905.59	
7	David HOWELL	923,423.07	
8	Miguel Angel JIMÉNEZ	888,594.84	
9	Thomas BJÖRN	882,520.16	
10	Stephen DODD	833,361.17	

Eureka
Moment

It was just two weeks before The Cadillac Russian Open that Mikael Lundberg of Sweden experienced the Archimedean moment that would allow him to re-align his career onto the most positive of trajectories, and one which would also lead to a thrilling play-off victory over Englishman Andrew Butterfield at Le Meridien Moscow Country Club.

The legend of Archimedes is well known. Around 250 BC, the fabled Greek mathematician had been charged by King Hieron II of Syracuse to determine whether or not his Highness had been fooled by a fraudulent goldsmith who had been commissioned to craft a gold crown as a tribute to the Gods. Upon entering the public baths in Syracuse, Archimedes realised that a body, when immersed wholly or partly in fluid, shows a loss of weight equal to the weight of fluid it displaces, which was the exact formula he required to confirm the King's suspicions.

Archimedes leapt straight out of the bath and ran naked down the streets proclaiming, "Eureka! I've found it!" The goldsmith soon confessed his crime and was dealt with by the King.

The mathematical nature of the technical analysis that golfers and their coaches now devote to extrapolating theories of the modern golf swing, and the reaction Archimedes experienced upon unearthing his significant breakthrough, makes a comparison between the two irresistible.

Lundberg's 'eureka' moment came two weeks earlier on the practice range at Kungsängen Golf Club during the Scandinavian Masters by Carlsberg, and, while the Swede resisted the temptation of cavorting around the driving range naked, he felt the same kind of euphoria that Archimedes had when he leapt out of his bath.

What Lundberg had discovered cured an ailment that had plagued his swing for four years, and had been the main debilitating

factor in him falling from his best position of 63rd on The 2001 European Tour Order of Merit, to 261st in 2004.

"At the end of 2001, not long after the Volvo Masters, something started happening in my swing that was causing me to hit this strange pull-draw shot and I had been fighting it ever since," he explained. "There was something wrong with the rotation in my forearms in my backswing. Then, I was standing on the range in Sweden hitting balls and it just happened. I fixed it. I felt it immediately and I turned round to my coach straight away and said: 'This is it!' I knew I had solved the problem and it felt so good to have done it after fighting against it for so long – it was amazing."

Lundberg set out for Russia excited by the fact he had cured his swing, but was unable to predict when he could configure all the contributing factors – a healthy

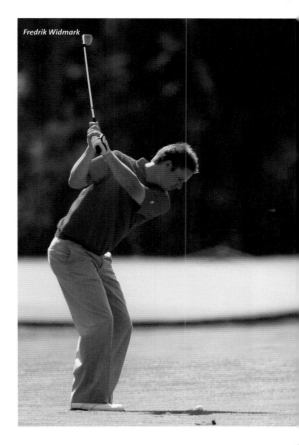

Fredrik Widmark

Andrew Butterfield

Spanish golfer Sergio Garcia during the Omega European Masters, Crans Montana, Switzerland, September 2, 2005. 54114504, Andrew Redington/Getty Images

Portrait of Swedish golfer Henrik Stenson, Doha, Qatar, March 11, 2005.
52374787, Ross Kinnaird/Getty Images

View of "Maidens," the 174-yard par 3 11th hole on the Ailsa Course, Turnberry, Scotland, July 10, 2005.
53451852, David Cannon/Getty Images

Your definitive source

Find a wealth of high-quality editorial imagery, captured
by world-class photographers specialising in golf.
Creative promotional assignments. Global coverage.

News. Sport. Entertainment. Archival. Features.
gettyimages.co.uk/editorial
Call us: +44 (0)20 7428 5294

gettyimages®

> "*This is my first time in Russia and the golf course is outstanding. When you consider the weather problems the course must endure over the winter, its condition is excellent and the layout is first class. It's pretty impressive all round*" – Roger Chapman

Final Results

Pos	Name		Rd1	Rd2	Rd3	Rd4	Total		€	£
1	Mikael LUNDBERG	Swe	67	68	69	69	273	-15	67,599.75	46,951.77
2	Andrew BUTTERFIELD	Eng	70	68	69	66	273	-15	45,063.80	31,299.30
3	David DRYSDALE	Scot	67	72	70	67	276	-12	22,836.11	15,860.94
	Jarrod MOSELEY	Aus	70	70	68	68	276	-12	22,836.11	15,860.94
5	Fredrik WIDMARK	Swe	67	67	71	72	277	-11	17,198.06	11,945.01
6	Sebastien DELAGRANGE	Fr	72	67	66	73	278	-10	10,740.68	7,460.00
	Jesus Maria ARRUTI	Sp	67	70	70	71	278	-10	10,740.68	7,460.00
	Michele REALE	It	71	70	71	66	278	-10	10,740.68	7,460.00
	Benn BARHAM	Eng	73	69	68	68	278	-10	10,740.68	7,460.00
	Shaun P WEBSTER	Eng	68	68	73	69	278	-10	10,740.68	7,460.00
11	Johan EDFORS	Swe	72	67	70	70	279	-9	7,219.94	5,014.65
	Ben MASON	Eng	68	68	71	72	279	-9	7,219.94	5,014.65
13	Toni KARJALAINEN	Fin	72	72	67	69	280	-8	5,978.76	4,152.58
	Martin WIEGELE	Aut	70	69	72	69	280	-8	5,978.76	4,152.58
	Jamie SPENCE	Eng	70	74	66	70	280	-8	5,978.76	4,152.58
	Roger CHAPMAN	Eng	70	72	69	69	280	-8	5,978.76	4,152.58
	Oliver WHITELEY	Eng	71	70	70	69	280	-8	5,978.76	4,152.58
18	Cesar MONASTERIO	Arg	72	69	68	72	281	-7	4,883.60	3,391.93
	Michael JONZON	Swe	72	68	70	71	281	-7	4,883.60	3,391.93
	Tom WHITEHOUSE	Eng	66	75	69	71	281	-7	4,883.60	3,391.93
	Kyron SULLIVAN	Wal	70	70	70	71	281	-7	4,883.60	3,391.93
	Peter WHITEFORD	Scot	70	69	67	75	281	-7	4,883.60	3,391.93
23	Leif WESTERBERG	Swe	74	68	71	69	282	-6	4,218.39	2,929.91
	Andrew COLTART	Scot	72	72	71	67	282	-6	4,218.39	2,929.91
	Michael HOEY	N.Ire	71	73	68	70	282	-6	4,218.39	2,929.91
	Bertrand CORNUT	Fr	69	72	67	74	282	-6	4,218.39	2,929.91
	Mark PILKINGTON	Wal	71	70	68	73	282	-6	4,218.39	2,929.91
28	Denny LUCAS	Eng	71	67	73	72	283	-5	3,609.97	2,507.32
	David ORR	Scot	71	69	73	70	283	-5	3,609.97	2,507.32
	Marc WARREN	Scot	74	64	76	69	283	-5	3,609.97	2,507.32
	Stuart MANLEY	Wal	75	67	69	72	283	-5	3,609.97	2,507.32
	Anders S HANSEN	Den	72	71	69	71	283	-5	3,609.97	2,507.32
33	Edward RUSH	Eng	71	69	74	70	284	-4	2,925.50	2,031.92
	Ariel CANETE	Arg	75	69	70	70	284	-4	2,925.50	2,031.92
	Iain PYMAN	Eng	67	72	72	73	284	-4	2,925.50	2,031.92
	Benoit TEILLERIA	Fr	70	72	69	73	284	-4	2,925.50	2,031.92
	Ivo GINER	Sp	70	71	71	72	284	-4	2,925.50	2,031.92
	Tomas Jesus MUÑOZ	Sp	72	70	74	68	284	-4	2,925.50	2,031.92
	Hernan REY	Arg	69	70	76	69	284	-4	2,925.50	2,031.92
	Carlos DE CORRAL	Sp	73	70	70	71	284	-4	2,925.50	2,031.92
41	Roope KAKKO	Fin	72	69	73	71	285	-3	2,393.13	1,662.16
	Van PHILLIPS	Eng	70	70	72	73	285	-3	2,393.13	1,662.16
	Johan AXGREN	Swe	71	71	72	71	285	-3	2,393.13	1,662.16
	Steven JEPPESEN	Swe	73	66	71	75	285	-3	2,393.13	1,662.16
	Terry PILKADARIS	Aus	71	71	67	75	285	-3	2,393.13	1,662.16
46	Stephen BROWNE	Ire	69	73	71	73	286	-2	1,987.51	1,380.44
	Martin LEMESURIER	Eng	75	68	72	71	286	-2	1,987.51	1,380.44
	Rafael GOMEZ	Arg	73	71	71	71	286	-2	1,987.51	1,380.44
	Sven STRÜVER	Ger	71	71	71	73	286	-2	1,987.51	1,380.44
	Marcus HIGLEY	Eng	71	72	70	73	286	-2	1,987.51	1,380.44
51	José Manuel CARRILES	Sp	68	75	72	72	287	-1	1,541.34	1,070.54
	Mark MOULAND	Wal	75	66	71	75	287	-1	1,541.34	1,070.54
	Titch MOORE	SA	70	73	71	73	287	-1	1,541.34	1,070.54
	Jan-Are LARSEN	Nor	70	73	68	76	287	-1	1,541.34	1,070.54
	David DIXON	Eng	69	71	71	76	287	-1	1,541.34	1,070.54
	Craig WILLIAMS	Wal	68	70	77	72	287	-1	1,541.34	1,070.54
57	Andres ROMERO	Arg	74	69	70	75	288	0	1,176.28	816.99
	Gareth DAVIES	Eng	74	70	69	75	288	0	1,176.28	816.99
	Peter KAENSCHE	Nor	72	72	77	67	288	0	1,176.28	816.99
	Diego BORREGO	Sp	73	71	71	73	288	0	1,176.28	816.99
	Paul EALES	Eng	75	69	73	71	288	0	1,176.28	816.99
62	Sam LITTLE	Eng	73	68	74	74	289	1	1,034.32	718.39
	Jeppe HULDAHL	Den	69	74	74	72	289	1	1,034.32	718.39
64	Julien VAN HAUWE	Fr	72	68	83	67	290	2	953.19	662.05
	Paul DWYER	Eng	74	69	73	74	290	2	953.19	662.05
66	Daniel VANCSIK	Arg	71	73	78	69	291	3	872.07	605.70
	Mads VIBE-HASTRUP	Den	73	71	73	74	291	3	872.07	605.70
68	Niels KRAAIJ	NL	72	71	71	78	292	4	811.23	563.44
69	Massimo FLORIOLI	It	70	73	81	74	298	10	770.67	535.27
70	Matt ZAPOL	Eng	71	71	79	W/D	221	5	746.33	518.37

Benn Barham

swing, a solid short game, a hot putter and a sound mind – into an equation which would add up to victory on The European Tour International Schedule.

He did not have to wait long.

After posting a four round aggregate of 15 under par 273 at Le Meridien Moscow Country Club following rounds of 67-68-69-69, Lundberg went back to the 18th tee and into a play-off with Butterfield, who had stormed into contention with a stunning back nine of six under par 30 during his final round 66.

After halving the first three sudden-death holes, all played on the 18th, the players moved to the par five 17th, where Lundberg's newly calculated swing underwent the stiffest of examinations. After a perfect drive, the Swede was left a testing three wood into the small green, which he executed brilliantly, leaving the ball some 25 feet from the cup. With Butterfield unable to get up and down for birdie, Lundberg was left two putts to secure a cheque for €67,599 (£46,951) and a one year exemption to The 2006 European Tour. The Swede played the percentages and concentrated on getting the weight of his first putt just right, leaving himself a 15 inch tap-in for the title, over which he wasted very little time.

The re-alignment of his career was complete, and it did not take a mathematician, never mind Archimedes, to work out what victory meant to Lundberg. "This is incredible, a dream come true," he said.

Eureka indeed.

Michael Gibbons

Marc Warren

Total Prize Fund
€405,610 £281,721

US PGA Championship

Springfield, New Jersey, USA
August 11-14 • 2005

Baltusrol Golf Club

Par	Yards	Metres
70	7392	6759

1	Phil MICKELSON	276	-4
2	Thomas BJÖRN	277	-3
	Steve ELKINGTON	277	-3
4	Davis LOVE III	278	-2
	Tiger WOODS	278	-2
6	Michael CAMPBELL	279	-1
	Retief GOOSEN	279	-1
	Geoff OGILVY	279	-1
	Pat PEREZ	279	-1
10	Steve FLESCH	280	0
	Dudley HART	280	0
	Ted PURDY	280	0
	Vijay SINGH	280	0
	David TOMS	280	0

Round One · Round Two · Round Three · Round Four

Major Media Mania

EUROPEAN TOUR ORDER OF MERIT
(After 36 tournaments)

Pos		€
1	Michael CAMPBELL	1,748,819.96
2	Retief GOOSEN	1,528,540.98
3	Colin MONTGOMERIE	1,438,364.34
4	Angel CABRERA	1,429,170.69
5	Thomas BJÖRN	1,346,543.46
6	Ernie ELS	1,012,682.63
7	Niclas FASTH	964,528.05
8	David HOWELL	925,045.53
9	Miguel Angel JIMÉNEZ	906,685.26
10	Stephen DODD	834,983.63

178

US PGA Championship

Springfield, New Jersey, USA
August 11-14 • 2005

I t used to be that the media, that portmanteau word for television, radio, newspapers, magazines and now, the internet, went to the season's premier sporting occasions with the simple intention of watching events unfold and, at the end, reporting on who won.

Sergio Garcia

But, as the 2005 golf season progressed, that intention changed subtly and it became increasingly obvious that by the time of the US PGA Championship at Baltusrol Golf Club, large chunks of the media came not to see who won, but whether or not Tiger Woods would win.

It was evident not just in the air time devoted to Woods - his playing partners might just as well have not existed as far as the television producers were concerned - or in the casual chat around the water cooler, but also in the accent of the coverage by the world's press and, perhaps most tellingly, by the questions asked of the other competitors.

For instance, the very first interview of the week, on Monday, was exactly eight questions old when Ian Poulter was asked: "Does the spectre of Tiger loom over the proceedings at all?" Next in the interview room was Darren Clarke, who was informed that the odds on Woods, the favourite, were 2/1, and what did he think of that?

Lee Janzen, who won the US Open Championship at Baltusrol in 1993, followed and his question was: "Can you speak about the dynamic of the rest of the people in the field, what happens to them when they see Tiger playing so well?" Janzen forbore to say: "Look mate, I've got enough to worry about....."

"I think this is one of the best, fairest and toughest set-ups we've had in years. There's no tricked-up greens and no tricked-up pin placements, and I now understand why this course gets so many Major Championships - it's just a terrific test of golf" – Phil Mickelson

Even Phil Mickelson got a Woods question, convoluted though it was. He was asked how he would rate a player who won three Majors and came second in a fourth in the same season. Not surprisingly, he was a little taken aback that Woods was the player to whom his questioner was referring and that he had already given him the 2005 US PGA Championship. "Let's answer that one a little later," said Mickelson, with mightily impressive restraint.

Woods, himself, provided the answer. Even for him, an eight shot deficit after 18 holes is a major disadvantage, and his 75 to the 67s of six players meant he was always pressing, not an ideal situation. In an honest summation, he said: "I didn't hit it well off the tee, I didn't hit my irons close and when I did, I didn't make the putts. I just didn't have it."

Trevor Immelman

He did not have it in the second round either, not in the way of form or luck. Needing, as he thought, to pick up three shots over the two par five final holes to get back into the tournament, he got an atrocious bounce at the 17th, leading to a bogey six, and had to birdie the last simply to stay in the Championship. A third round 66 gave a glimpse of the expected Woods, but starting the final round six shots behind, and with 18 players ahead of him, was too much, even for the World Number One.

So there you are: all that about a golfer who finished tied fourth in a Major Championship and only the barest of

Thomas Björn

BALANCE GOLF

OSCAR JACOBSON

when clothes talk people listen

WPS
WaterProof
WeatherProtectiveSystem

BEST IN TEST: **Svensk Golf**

when a hole in the ground becomes heaven

FOR MORE INFORMATION CALL OSCAR JACOBSON ON (GB) +44 (0) 2074020797 (SWE) +46 (0) 33-23 33 00 OR VISIT WWW.OSCARJACOBSON.COM

Lee Westwood

Final Results

mentions about the man who actually won. That's Tiger-Media-Mania for you.

Of course, the second, and most important answer to the question asked of Mickelson, came from Mickelson himself. During the course of a final round when everyone but Woods went backwards, Mickelson held on better than anyone else and was a hugely popular winner with the fans, a true people's champion. Mickelson smiles, you see; he waves to the spectators; he gives the impression of enjoying himself and, when he is done, he spends hours signing autographs.

And he can play. He came to the 72nd hole – the fourth hole he needed to complete on Monday morning after lightning storms brought a premature end to play on Sunday night - needing a birdie four to win his

Vijay Singh

second Major Championship. He had been denied a birdie at the long 17th by a putt which, a foot from the hole, looked to be in, dead centre, and now he had to get past the three under par totals of 277 already respectively posted by Thomas Björn and Steve Elkington.

The American missed the green at this second successive par five but produced a magnificent flop shot from the greenside rough, to two feet, to do the needful. He was engulfed by his family, wife, three children, mother, father and seemingly, as they say in Gilbert and Sullivan operettas; "his sisters and his cousins and his aunts."

He was embraced, too, by the media - at long last.

There is little room left to extol the exploits of Björn, but that is the way of things when media mania with one pre-determined player takes hold. But the man from Denmark certainly gave every indication in this event that he will, at some point, claim a Major title his superb game deserves.

He seems to have overcome the 'demons' he has been afflicted by in the past and he was generous in defeat. "Phil Mickelson led from start to finish and he was the best player here this week," he said. "He's going to go on now and contend for more Majors and he deserves greatness."

Well said Thomas, and let's see what the media make of that.

David Davies

Pos	Name		Rd1	Rd2	Rd3	Rd4	Total		€	£
1	Phil MICKELSON	USA	67	65	72	72	276	-4	949,138.40	659,229.18
2	Steve ELKINGTON	Aus	68	70	68	71	277	-3	464,023.30	322,289.88
	Thomas BJÖRN	Den	71	71	63	72	277	-3	464,023.30	322,289.88
4	Davis LOVE III	USA	68	68	68	74	278	-2	232,011.60	161,144.91
	Tiger WOODS	USA	75	69	66	68	278	-2	232,011.60	161,144.91
6	Geoff OGILVY	Aus	69	69	72	69	279	-1	163,462.70	113,533.90
	Retief GOOSEN	SA	68	70	69	72	279	-1	163,462.70	113,533.90
	Michael CAMPBELL	NZ	73	68	69	69	279	-1	163,462.70	113,533.90
	Pat PEREZ	USA	68	71	67	73	279	-1	163,462.70	113,533.90
10	David TOMS	USA	71	72	69	68	280	0	106,920.00	74,261.86
	Ted PURDY	USA	69	75	70	66	280	0	106,920.00	74,261.86
	Vijay SINGH	Fiji	70	67	69	74	280	0	106,920.00	74,261.86
	Dudley HART	USA	70	73	66	71	280	0	106,920.00	74,261.86
	Steve FLESCH	USA	70	71	69	70	280	0	106,920.00	74,261.86
15	Stuart APPLEBY	Aus	67	70	69	75	281	1	83,151.02	57,752.99
	Charles HOWELL III	USA	70	71	68	72	281	1	83,151.02	57,752.99
17	Joe OGILVIE	USA	74	68	69	71	282	2	66,926.43	46,484.11
	Zach JOHNSON	USA	70	70	73	69	282	2	66,926.43	46,484.11
	Lee WESTWOOD	Eng	68	68	71	75	282	2	66,926.43	46,484.11
	Bo VAN PELT	USA	70	70	68	74	282	2	66,926.43	46,484.11
	Tim CLARK	SA	71	73	70	68	282	2	66,926.43	46,484.11
	Trevor IMMELMAN	SA	67	72	72	71	282	2	66,926.43	46,484.11
23	Paul MCGINLEY	Ire	72	70	72	69	283	3	45,753.34	31,778.23
	Sergio GARCIA	Sp	72	70	71	70	283	3	45,753.34	31,778.23
	Kenny PERRY	USA	69	70	70	74	283	3	45,753.34	31,778.23
	Shingo KATAYAMA	Jpn	71	66	74	72	283	3	45,753.34	31,778.23
	Tom PERNICE Jnr	USA	69	73	69	72	283	3	45,753.34	31,778.23
28	Vaughn TAYLOR	USA	75	69	71	69	284	4	33,666.02	23,382.92
	Arron OBERHOLSER	USA	74	68	69	73	284	4	33,666.02	23,382.92
	Chad CAMPBELL	USA	71	71	70	72	284	4	33,666.02	23,382.92
	Jesper PARNEVIK	Swe	68	69	72	75	284	4	33,666.02	23,382.92
	Stewart CINK	USA	71	72	66	75	284	4	33,666.02	23,382.92
	Bob ESTES	USA	71	72	73	68	284	4	33,666.02	23,382.92
34	Fredrik JACOBSON	Swe	72	69	73	71	285	5	25,891.74	17,983.25
	Jerry KELLY	USA	70	65	74	76	285	5	25,891.74	17,983.25
	Scott VERPLANK	USA	71	72	71	71	285	5	25,891.74	17,983.25
	Jim FURYK	USA	72	71	69	73	285	5	25,891.74	17,983.25
	Ben CURTIS	USA	67	73	67	78	285	5	25,891.74	17,983.25
	Jason BOHN	USA	71	68	68	78	285	5	25,891.74	17,983.25
40	John ROLLINS	USA	68	71	73	74	286	6	18,090.42	12,564.80
	Patrick SHEEHAN	USA	73	71	71	71	286	6	18,090.42	12,564.80
	Adam SCOTT	Aus	74	69	72	71	286	6	18,090.42	12,564.80
	Ben CRANE	USA	68	76	72	70	286	6	18,090.42	12,564.80
	Steve SCHNEITER	Can	72	72	72	70	286	6	18,090.42	12,564.80
	K J CHOI	Kor	71	70	73	72	286	6	18,090.42	12,564.80
	Miguel Angel JIMÉNEZ	Sp	72	72	69	73	286	6	18,090.42	12,564.80
47	Mike WEIR	Can	72	72	71	72	287	7	12,469.27	8,660.60
	Henrik STENSON	Swe	74	67	75	71	287	7	12,469.27	8,660.60
	Ian POULTER	Eng	69	74	69	75	287	7	12,469.27	8,660.60
	Greg OWEN	Eng	68	69	70	80	287	7	12,469.27	8,660.60
	Fred FUNK	USA	69	75	67	76	287	7	12,469.27	8,660.60
	José María OLAZÁBAL	Sp	76	67	72	72	287	7	12,469.27	8,660.60
	Bernhard LANGER	Ger	68	72	72	75	287	7	12,469.27	8,660.60
	J.L. LEWIS	USA	72	72	70	73	287	7	12,469.27	8,660.60
	Todd HAMILTON	USA	73	70	70	74	287	7	12,469.27	8,660.60
	Heath SLOCUM	USA	68	75	73	71	287	7	12,469.27	8,660.60
	Yong-Eun YANG	Kor	71	67	76	73	287	7	12,469.27	8,660.60
	Ryan PALMER	USA	73	70	73	71	287	7	12,469.27	8,660.60
59	Mark HENSBY	Aus	69	70	75	74	288	8	10,824.12	7,517.95
	Paul CASEY	Eng	70	74	72	72	288	8	10,824.12	7,517.95
	Steve WEBSTER	Eng	72	70	75	71	288	8	10,824.12	7,517.95
	Peter HANSON	Swe	73	71	72	72	288	8	10,824.12	7,517.95
	Scott MCCARRON	USA	72	72	74	70	288	8	10,824.12	7,517.95
	Carlos FRANCO	Par	70	70	76	72	288	8	10,824.12	7,517.95
	Sean O'HAIR	USA	71	71	76	70	288	8	10,824.12	7,517.95
66	Ron PHILO JR.	USA	71	73	73	72	289	9	10,343.18	7,183.91
	Woody AUSTIN	USA	72	71	68	78	289	9	10,343.18	7,183.91
	Luke DONALD	Eng	69	73	73	74	289	9	10,343.18	7,183.91
	Chris RILEY	USA	72	68	72	77	289	9	10,343.18	7,183.91
70	Mark CALCAVECCHIA	USA	70	69	77	74	290	10	10,099.81	7,014.88
	Fred COUPLES	USA	72	72	70	76	290	10	10,099.81	7,014.88
72	Joe DURANT	USA	73	71	73	74	291	11	9,937.56	6,902.19
	Stephen AMES	T&T	67	72	74	78	291	11	9,937.56	6,902.19
74	John DALY	USA	71	69	78	74	292	12	9,775.31	6,789.50
	Rory SABBATINI	SA	67	69	76	80	292	12	9,775.31	6,789.50
76	Mike SMALL	USA	74	68	80	73	295	15	9,653.63	6,704.98
77	Kevin SUTHERLAND	USA	74	70	75	77	296	16	9,572.51	6,648.64
78	Darrell KESTNER	USA	72	70	78	79	299	19	9,491.39	6,592.29
79	Hal SUTTON	USA	69	73	80	78	300	20	9,410.26	6,535.95

Total Prize Fund
€5,299,720 £3,690,949

WGC – NEC Invitational

Akron, Ohio, USA
August 18-21 • 2005

Firestone Country Club

Par	Yards	Metres
70	7360	6731

1	Tiger WOODS	274	-6	
2	Chris DiMARCO	275	-5	
3	Paul McGINLEY	276	-4	
	Ryan PALMER	276	-4	
	Vijay SINGH	276	-4	
6	Luke DONALD	277	-3	
	David HOWELL	277	-3	
	Kenny PERRY	277	-3	
9	Zach JOHNSON	278	-2	
	Colin MONTGOMERIE	278	-2	
	José Maria OLAZÁBAL	278	-2	
	David TOMS	278	-2	

Round One   Round Two   Round Three   Round Four

EUROPEAN TOUR ORDER OF MERIT
(After 37 tournaments)

Pos		€
1	Michael CAMPBELL	1,775,372.89
2	Retief GOOSEN	1,557,910.12
3	Colin MONTGOMERIE	1,546,989.94
4	Angel CABRERA	1,466,988.49
5	Thomas BJÖRN	1,413,328.09
6	Paul McGINLEY	1,091,083.70
7	David HOWELL	1,085,972.33
8	Ernie ELS	1,012,682.63
9	Niclas FASTH	1,009,587.56
10	Vijay SINGH	973,096.17

Crucial And Critical

On paper there were several players for whom victory in the World Golf Championships – NEC Invitational would have provided not only a joyous day in their own respective golfing careers but also an interestingly different story for the watching media.

However, golf is not played on paper. It is contested on grass and when the particular lush green pasture in question belongs to Firestone Country Club in Akron, viewing anyone other than Tiger Woods as a potential champion becomes an increasingly fruitless exercise.

The World Number One's six under par total of 274, despite being the highest winning aggregate in the tournament's history, gave Woods his fourth victory in this corner of Ohio and his tenth overall in WGC competition, including the World Cup team event. It also meant he has won at least one WGC event in each season since the series began in 1999.

All of which, unquestionably, makes rather impressive reading. Yet this particular chapter might have had a different ending if one of a handful of challengers had possessed the belief, allied to that all important stroke of luck, to push them over the winning line.

Consider Chris DiMarco: The People's Choice. The combative New Yorker muscled his way into the hearts of the golfing world in April when he battled Woods all the way in a titanic tussle for the Masters Tournament at Augusta National, and he emerged as his main challenger again in Ohio.

Despite springing from the pack with a final round 68, the 37 year old had to be content with the runners-up position again after misclubbing at the 17th, which led to a bogey five. It proved to be, ultimately, the one shot he finished behind the eventual champion.

Consider Paul McGinley: The Ex-Pats' Choice. The European Tour Member was hugely popular amongst the many tricolour-waving Irish supporters and would have been an appropriately sequential winner, too, considering the last time the event was held at Firestone in an odd numbered year – 2003 – fellow Irishman Darren Clarke was victorious.

Nevertheless, as with DiMarco, it was not to be. A three putt for double bogey five on the 12th looked to have extinguished all hope but, showing grit and determination, he battled back with birdies at the 14th and 16th before he, too, saw his chance finally evaporate with a bogey five at the 17th to finish tied third.

Consider Kenny Perry: The Sentimental Choice. One of the gentlemen of the game, he started the final round in a tie for the

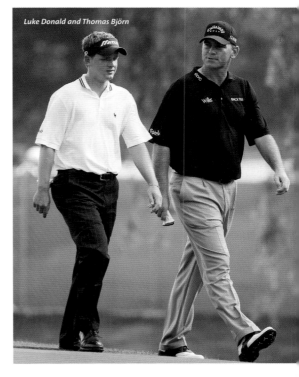

Luke Donald and Thomas Björn

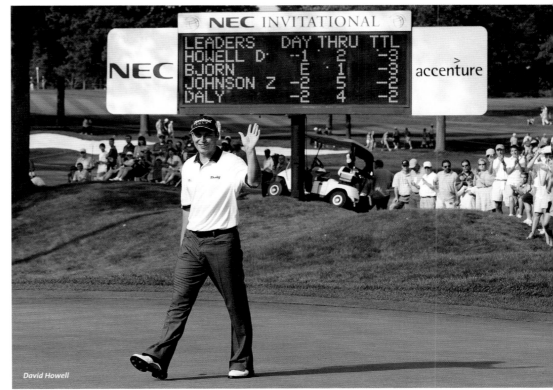

David Howell

WGC – NEC Invitational

Akron, Ohio, USA
August 18-21 • 2005

José Maria Olazábal

lead with Woods having taken the 'Phil Mickelson' route to the top. Just as the left-hander had done the week before the US PGA Championship in consulting Baltusrol Country Club head professional Doug Steffen for advice on how to play the course, Perry sought the wise counsel of Akron veteran Fuzzy Zoeller in the run-up to the event.

"Just remember, everything breaks towards the ball," Zoeller had told him. "You know, the huge water tower at the course that looks like a golf ball." Perry heeded the advice, especially during a superb third round 64, but the pressure of accompanying Woods on the final afternoon eventually told as his 74, for a share of sixth place, proved.

Finally, consider Stuart Appleby: The New Sponsors' Choice. On the final afternoon a press conference revealed that from next year, the tournament will be called the WGC – Bridgestone Invitational, and the

new sponsors would have loved nothing better than to have the Australian – the highest ranked golfer in the world playing their ball at that time - as the defending champion in 2006.

It might well have happened had it not been for an unfortunate incident at the 13th hole in the final round. Over the green, Appleby was granted a free drop from a cart path but could only look on in horror as caddie Joe Damiano picked the ball up as it was still rolling. The eagle eye of European Tour Chief Referee John Paramor confirmed a two stroke penalty and, with the wind knocked from his sails, Appleby could do no better than a share of 13th.

Therefore, with every other possibility considered, the answer remained Woods. Despite not producing the fireworks often associated with his final rounds, he retained the ability to produce the crucial shot at the critical time.

" *This is one of the greatest golf courses we play. It's straightforward and there are no hidden agendas. Every hole is like a bowling alley and you've got to somehow fit the ball down there. You have the opportunity to be aggressive as well as conservative. Every year the rough is up, the greens are fast and perfect, and it's always a lot of fun* " – *Tiger Woods*

Phil Mickelson and Colin Montgomerie

Final Results

Pos	Name		Rd1	Rd2	Rd3	Rd4	Total		€	£
1	Tiger WOODS	USA	66	70	67	71	274	-6	1,046,024.00	716,332.13
2	Chris DIMARCO	USA	67	70	70	68	275	-5	603,475.60	413,268.69
3	Ryan PALMER	USA	72	68	67	69	276	-4	284,572.30	194,879.16
	Vijay SINGH	Fiji	66	71	72	67	276	-4	284,572.30	194,879.16
	Paul MCGINLEY	Ire	71	66	67	72	276	-4	284,572.30	194,879.16
6	David HOWELL	Eng	70	68	70	69	277	-3	160,926.80	110,204.96
	Kenny PERRY	USA	70	69	64	74	277	-3	160,926.80	110,204.96
	Luke DONALD	Eng	69	67	74	67	277	-3	160,926.80	110,204.96
9	David TOMS	USA	71	67	69	71	278	-2	108,625.60	74,388.36
	Zach JOHNSON	USA	70	70	69	69	278	-2	108,625.60	74,388.36
	José Maria OLAZÁBAL	Sp	72	68	66	72	278	-2	108,625.60	74,388.36
	Colin MONTGOMERIE	Scot	70	72	68	68	278	-2	108,625.60	74,388.36
13	Henrik STENSON	Swe	66	71	72	70	279	-1	75,957.46	52,016.75
	Davis LOVE III	USA	67	73	69	70	279	-1	75,957.46	52,016.75
	Sergio GARCIA	Sp	68	70	67	74	279	-1	75,957.46	52,016.75
	Rodney PAMPLING	Aus	71	70	71	67	279	-1	75,957.46	52,016.75
	Stuart APPLEBY	Aus	68	70	67	74	279	-1	75,957.46	52,016.75
18	Thomas BJÖRN	Den	70	67	72	71	280	0	66,784.63	45,735.07
19	Paul CASEY	Eng	75	68	67	71	281	1	61,956.83	42,428.92
	Trevor IMMELMAN	SA	73	71	71	66	281	1	61,956.83	42,428.92
	Kenneth FERRIE	Eng	71	70	73	67	281	1	61,956.83	42,428.92
	Justin LEONARD	USA	72	66	71	72	281	1	61,956.83	42,428.92
	Jay HAAS	USA	76	69	67	69	281	1	61,956.83	42,428.92
24	Padraig HARRINGTON	Ire	75	68	69	70	282	2	55,519.75	38,020.72
	Jim FURYK	USA	72	73	68	69	282	2	55,519.75	38,020.72
	Lee WESTWOOD	Eng	73	72	63	74	282	2	55,519.75	38,020.72
27	John DALY	USA	71	69	69	74	283	3	52,301.22	35,816.62
28	Rory SABBATINI	SA	73	69	67	75	284	4	48,438.97	33,171.70
	Bart BRYANT	USA	74	73	67	70	284	4	48,438.97	33,171.70
	Fred COUPLES	USA	71	74	70	69	284	4	48,438.97	33,171.70
	Nick O'HERN	Aus	68	73	72	71	284	4	48,438.97	33,171.70
	Darren CLARKE	N.Ire	76	68	72	68	284	4	48,438.97	33,171.70
33	Ian POULTER	Eng	73	69	69	74	285	5	45,059.51	30,857.39
	Niclas FASTH	Swe	72	72	70	71	285	5	45,059.51	30,857.39
	Chad CAMPBELL	USA	72	72	69	72	285	5	45,059.51	30,857.39
36	Peter LONARD	Aus	74	71	68	73	286	6	41,840.97	28,653.29
	Stephen AMES	T&T	74	71	68	73	286	6	41,840.97	28,653.29
	Adam SCOTT	Aus	70	76	67	73	286	6	41,840.97	28,653.29
	Woody AUSTIN	USA	73	68	77	68	286	6	41,840.97	28,653.29
	Mike WEIR	Can	71	69	70	76	286	6	41,840.97	28,653.29
41	Stewart CINK	USA	72	72	73	70	287	7	37,817.80	25,898.17
	Fred FUNK	USA	74	71	69	73	287	7	37,817.80	25,898.17
	Geoff OGILVY	Aus	74	74	70	69	287	7	37,817.80	25,898.17
	Angel CABRERA	Arg	75	74	67	71	287	7	37,817.80	25,898.17
	Tom LEHMAN	USA	73	71	75	68	287	7	37,817.80	25,898.17
46	Brent GEIBERGER	USA	70	76	69	73	288	8	35,001.59	23,969.59
	Thomas LEVET	Fr	72	71	72	73	288	8	35,001.59	23,969.59
	Shigeki MARUYAMA	Jpn	75	70	71	72	288	8	35,001.59	23,969.59
49	Steve ELKINGTON	Aus	72	76	75	66	289	9	33,995.79	23,280.80
	Marc CAYEUX	Zim	71	75	71	72	289	9	33,995.79	23,280.80
51	Scott VERPLANK	USA	73	73	67	77	290	10	32,386.52	22,178.75
	K J CHOI	Kor	71	76	69	74	290	10	32,386.52	22,178.75
	Phil MICKELSON	USA	69	72	75	74	290	10	32,386.52	22,178.75
	Tim CLARK	SA	71	75	72	72	290	10	32,386.52	22,178.75
	Nick DOUGHERTY	Eng	67	81	71	71	290	10	32,386.52	22,178.75
	Sean O'HAIR	USA	70	74	73	73	290	10	32,386.52	22,178.75
57	Miguel Angel JIMÉNEZ	Sp	76	75	73	67	291	11	30,978.41	21,214.46
58	Craig PARRY	Aus	79	71	73	70	293	13	29,369.14	20,112.41
	Mark HENSBY	Aus	70	76	71	76	293	13	29,369.14	20,112.41
	Ben CRANE	USA	74	75	71	73	293	13	29,369.14	20,112.41
	Thongchai JAIDEE	Thai	73	76	72	72	293	13	29,369.14	20,112.41
	Stephen GALLACHER	Scot	74	74	75	70	293	13	29,369.14	20,112.41
	Retief GOOSEN	SA	77	73	73	70	293	13	29,369.14	20,112.41
	Chris RILEY	USA	69	81	74	69	293	13	29,369.14	20,112.41
65	Kazuhiko HOSOKAWA	Jpn	70	78	71	75	294	14	27,759.88	19,010.36
66	Tim PETROVIC	USA	80	73	69	73	295	15	27,357.56	18,734.85
67	Richard GREEN	Aus	76	78	69	73	296	16	26,955.24	18,459.33
68	Michael CAMPBELL	NZ	72	74	78	74	298	18	26,552.93	18,183.82
69	Stephen DODD	Wal	74	78	77	73	302	22	26,150.61	17,908.31
70	Jyoti RANDHAWA	Ind	79	77	75	73	304	24	25,748.29	17,632.80
71	Ted PURDY	USA	72	71	DISQ		143	3	25,144.82	17,219.53
	Graeme MCDOWELL	N.Ire	RETD						25,144.82	17,219.53

Nowhere was that more apparent than on Firestone's signature hole, the 667 yard, par five, 16th. After hitting his tee shot way right into the trees, he had no choice but to chip back into the fairway, leaving 193 yards, over water, to the flag. His seven iron approach finished 18 feet behind the pin, but his curling birdie putt dropped to the bottom of the cup as if drawn by a magnet.

Nick Dougherty

The resultant roar might have been partly to blame for McGinley missing his par effort on the adjacent 17th green, but it also sent a resounding rumble around the rest of the field signifying that the destination of the €1,046,024 (£716,332) first prize was all but decided.

Two hours earlier, as well as announcing the sponsorship deal which will take them to 2010, Bridgestone representatives admitted they would be delighted if the tournament could remain in their spiritual Akron home for that spell too.

It was a decision questioned by some who felt a World Golf Championship event might benefit from actually travelling around the world but, not surprisingly, it was a sentiment backed wholeheartedly by Woods. "We move the American Express tournament around, that's fine, but let's keep this one right here," he joked.

Having won four times in six years at Firestone, it was not hard to follow his reasoning.

Scott Crockett

Total Prize Fund
€5,986,080 £4,099,349

BMW International Open

Munich, Germany
August 25-28 • 2005

Golfclub München Nord-Eichenried

Par	Yards	Metres
72	6963	6366

Pos	Name	Score		
1	David HOWELL	265	-23	
2	John DALY	266	-22	
	Brett RUMFORD	266	-22	
4	Niclas FASTH	267	-21	
	Søren KJELDSEN	267	-21	
6	Paul McGINLEY	268	-20	
7	Simon DYSON	269	-19	
8	Simon KHAN	270	-18	
9	Bradley DREDGE	271	-17	
	Raphaël JACQUELIN	271	-17	

Round One	Round Two	Round Three	Round Four

EUROPEAN TOUR ORDER OF MERIT
(After 38 tournaments)

Pos	Name	€	
1	Michael CAMPBELL	1,775,372.89	
2	Retief GOOSEN	1,557,910.12	
3	Colin MONTGOMERIE	1,546,989.94	
4	Angel CABRERA	1,499,668.49	
5	Thomas BJÖRN	1,435,628.09	
6	David HOWELL	1,419,302.33	
7	Paul McGINLEY	1,161,083.70	
8	Niclas FASTH	1,101,987.56	
9	Ernie ELS	1,012,682.63	
10	Vijay SINGH	973,096.17	

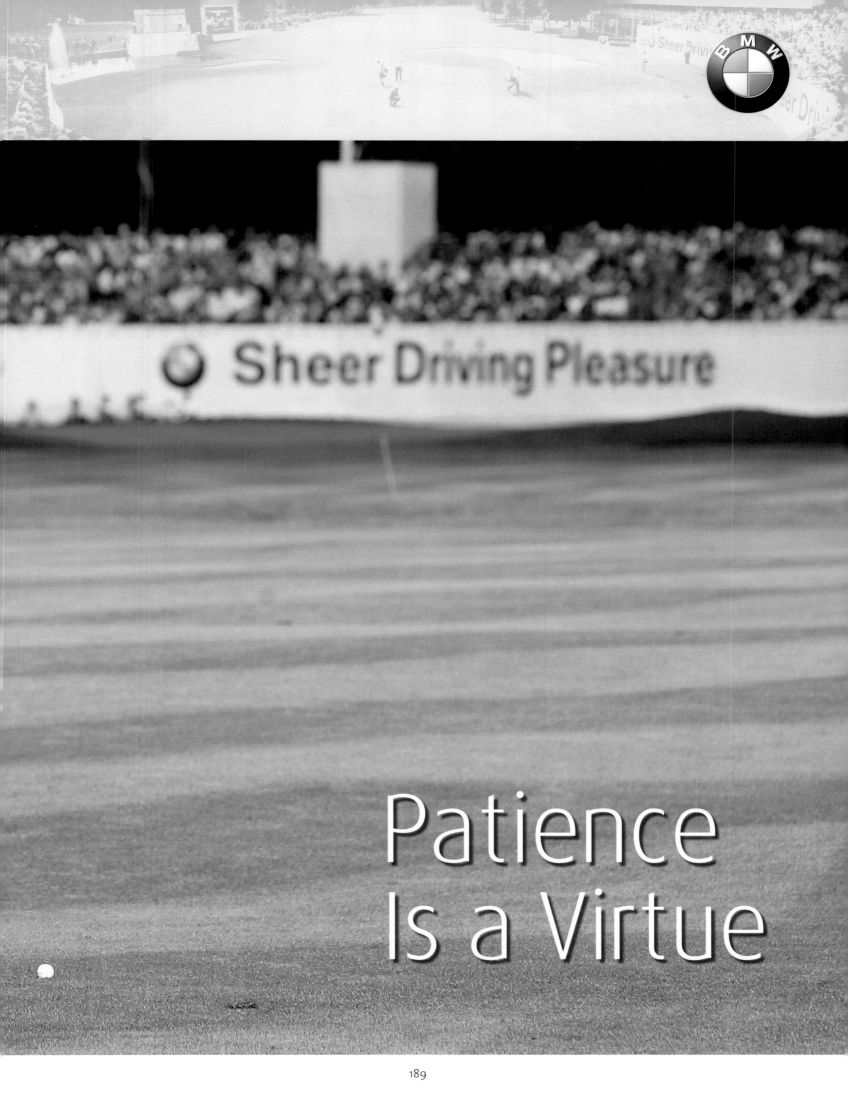

Patience
Is a Virtue

BMW International Open

Munich, Germany
August 25-28 • 2005

P atience is a virtue and never more so than in the life of a tournament professional, as David Howell proved with his long overdue second European Tour International Schedule victory in the BMW International Open at Golfclub München Nord-Eichenried. It was a result that owed everything to his unwavering perseverance on and off the course.

Phillip Archer

When the affable Englishman stepped onto the winner's rostrum at the 1999 Dubai Desert Classic, having won the Australian PGA Championship by seven strokes three months earlier, no-one was surprised.

After all, he had turned professional in 1995 after helping Great Britain and Ireland to victory over a Tiger Woods-led United States in the Walker Cup at Royal Porthcawl, and a glittering, trophy-laden career seemingly stretched before him. However, Tour win number two took more than six years to arrive following that day in the desert.

Howell explained: "In 1999 I wasn't ready to be one of the better players in the world. Although I'd won a couple of events and

shown I could play if it was my week, I didn't really have the game."

Things started to click into place in 2004 when he finished in the money in 24 out of 26 European Tour events and climbed to a career-highest tenth in the Order of Merit. Moreover making 19 cuts in 21 events before The 2004 Ryder Cup helped Howell secure his debut in the biennial contest at Oakland Hills Country Club and he played a crucial role. In that match he also won the RBS Shot of the Year Award for a stunning tee shot at the 17th which helped square the Saturday morning fourball match against Jim Furyk and Chad Campbell, and enabled partner Paul Casey to win the last to clinch a vital comeback point as Europe strode to a record 18½-9½ victory.

Søren Kjeldsen

" *Golfclub München Nord-Eichenried is a flat course which favours the long hitters. When the rough is as wet and long as it was after heavy rain this year, accuracy off the tee is essential* "
– Luke Donald

Eddie Jordan, the former F1 motor racing chief, relaxes with fellow Irishman Paul McGinley

His confidence buoyed, he notched three top ten finishes in his first five European Tour starts in 2005, then tied 11th on a fine debut in the Masters Tournament at Augusta National. Still, however, the second win eluded him as he agonisingly lost out in sudden death play-offs in successive weeks in May, firstly to Thomas Björn in The Daily Telegraph Dunlop Masters and secondly to Stephen Dodd in the Nissan Irish Open.

When he suffered a freak stomach muscle strain after playfully swinging Vijay Singh's 25 pound practice three wood and had to withdraw from the US Open Championship at Pinehurst No.2 in June, frustration could easily have turned to despair at the two months the injury cost him on the sidelines.

But he stayed patient and a tie for sixth place in the World Golf Championships – NEC Invitational at Firestone Country Club in August, in his second comeback

tournament, boosted his confidence for the trip to Munich.

There, 177 tournaments after Dubai and following seven second place finishes, he finally got his hands on silverware again, a closing 65 sweeping Howell to a 23 under par total of 265, one stroke clear of John Daly and Brett Rumford, to claim the handsome €333,330 (£225,782) first prize.

Howell said: "It has been ten years of hard work to get where I am now. My coach Clive Tucker takes a lot of the credit. Over the last three years he has turned my game around. I've gone from 150th to 22nd in the Official World Golf Ranking.

"I've also been working hard in the gym with Paul Hoskins in Ascot. Paul Morrissey, an osteopath in Croydon has been helping me too and I've employed one of the travelling physios, Dale Richardson, over the past two years. All of that has been a big help and an

Simon Dyson

RUMFORD STAYS ALIVE FOR THE FINAL 5

How often have you got a good round going only for it to fall apart over the closing holes? The final five holes are where golfers of all standards tend to make errors due to fatigue in both body and mind. As Red Bull has been especially developed for periods of increased mental and physical exertion, it has been proven to benefit golfers in this area as it increases endurance, concentration and reaction speed.

From the grassroots of the game to Tour professionals, Red Bull is used by golfers to improve performance.

European Ryder Cup and World Cup winner, Paul Casey, says: "Mental focus is probably more important than being physically fit towards the end of a round. Red Bull really assists me in keeping sharp and alert and able to do my job late in the day, which is very, very important."

The Red Bull Final 5 is a competition that rewards the player with the best score over the final five holes, when the pressure to perform is highest and concentration levels are most affected by tiredness. The Final 5 competition demonstrates to golfers that fatigue affects performance and their enjoyment of a round could suffer as a result. First seen on the Challenge Tour in 2003, the Red Bull Final 5 is now played at all levels in the game, from the top Tour professionals to juniors getting their first taste of golf.

In 2004 the Red Bull Final 5 was played on The European Tour for the first time. At The Daily Telegraph Dunlop Masters, the BMW Championship and at The Barclays Scottish Open, many of the world's best players demonstrated their ability under pressure during the final holes of a major tournament and the statistics were revealing. Ernie Els, the 2004 European Tour Order of Merit winner, was comfortably the best player of the Final 5 holes across the season.

In 2005, The Red Bull Final 5 was played on The European Tour at the Nissan Irish Open. The players had to battle out over four rounds to determine who the best player was over the closing holes. Brett Rumford ended the Final 5 victorious with a fabulous last round showing. The Australian's eagle three on the par 5 14th and birdie on the 15th made him five under par over the Final 5 holes for the tournament and winner of the competition on countback. Rumford won 10,000 air miles on a private jet to travel to and from European Tour events

that season. The eight-seater jet had room for family, friends and maybe even his caddie. Rumford said: "It was unreal, brilliant! I couldn't believe it. I got excited about it at the beginning of the week when all the players were buzzing about the Red Bull Final 5." However, a quiet performance over the Final 5 in the early stages meant the young golfer thought he had no chance.

"I drained a 45 foot putt for eagle on the 15th and thought 'that's a great start for the Final 5.' After the birdie at the next I kept telling myself 'I've got to focus.' But when I missed a 12-footer for birdie at the last I thought my chance had gone."

Irishman Padraig Harrington missed an eagle putt on the last that would have given him the Red Bull Final 5 title at six under par. "I patted him on the back for missing that putt! said a delighted Rumford after receiving the trophy.

In 2006, the Final 5 club competition becomes a national leaderboard challenge. UK club golfers will be invited to continually submit their best Final 5 scores across the season, to be included on a leaderboard. At the end of the year those in the top 40 on the leaderboard will be flown to the majestic Pinehurst resort in North Carolina, USA, to contest the Final 5 Grand Final on Pinehurst No.2, host of the 2005 US Open.

For more information on the Red Bull Final 5 please visit the website:
www.redbullfinal5.co.uk

Final Results

investment in my golf - we've covered all the bases and it's bearing fruit.

"The difference between winning and finishing second was simply that I hit the ball better in Munich. Often I would shoot 67 having hit only 12 greens. I hit all 18 on Friday in Germany which, statistically, was the best round of golf I've ever played.

Robert Coles

Ricardo Gonzalez

"Ironically, I only shot 68 which was a little frustrating, but I stayed patient and on Sunday I finally holed some putts. I got lucky on the tenth, holing from 45 feet, and the 30 footer I knocked in at the 14th after earlier birdies at the 11th and 13th, was crucial.

"I've spent years looking at guys playing the Major Championships and the World Golf Championships. They were the best players and I didn't begrudge them their place. Now, however, after ten years of hard work, I've got myself in the same position. I'm looking forward to the next ten years being the best of my career."

Gordon Richardson

Total Prize Fund
€2,000,000 £1,354,710

Omega European Masters

Crans Montana, Switzerland
September 1-4 • 2005

Crans-sur-Sierre

Par	Yards	Metres
71	6857	6239

1	**Sergio GARCIA**	**270**	**-14**	
2	Peter GUSTAFSSON	271	-13	
3	Paul CASEY	272	-12	
4	Luke DONALD	273	-11	
	Garry HOUSTON	273	-11	
6	Pierre FULKE	274	-10	
7	Philip GOLDING	275	-9	
	Stuart LITTLE	275	-9	
9	Paul BROADHURST	276	-8	
	Emanuele CANONICA	276	-8	
	Steven O'HARA	276	-8	
	Jamie SPENCE	276	-8	

Round One   Round Two   Round Three   Round Four

EUROPEAN TOUR ORDER OF MERIT
(After 39 tournaments)

Pos		€	
1	**Michael CAMPBELL**	1,775,372.89	
2	Retief GOOSEN	1,557,910.12	
3	Colin MONTGOMERIE	1,546,989.94	
4	Angel CABRERA	1,499,668.49	
5	Thomas BJÖRN	1,435,628.09	
6	David HOWELL	1,419,302.33	
7	Paul McGINLEY	1,161,083.70	
8	Niclas FASTH	1,101,987.56	
9	Ernie ELS	1,012,682.63	
10	Miguel Angel JIMÉNEZ	986,653.67	

Guardian
Angel

On the surface, Sergio Garcia appeared at peace with the world as he and his close-knit entourage decanted in Crans Montana for the 2005 Omega European Masters. After all, this is the picture postcard Swiss village where the Spaniard has purchased a cosy holiday home and where the sponsors, whose expensive products adorn his wrist, can command their famous client's undivided attention for the week.

Yet, underneath the bonhomie lay a deeply troubled soul. Very few people were aware that one of the golfer's closest and dearest friends, a lovely girl named Maria Garcia-Estrada, was suffering from terminal cancer and lay gravely ill at her home in Tenerife.

In the days when he was still known as El Niño, the pair travelled together as part of the Spanish Boys and Girls teams, sharing transport, hotels, meals and many laughs along the way.

Even when stardom came calling, Garcia remained close to his former team-mate, herself an extremely talented golfer who represented the Spanish national team in the 1990s and won numerous individual titles. Both she and Garcia were part of the Spanish junior side which captured the Topolino Trophy and World Championship in 1994.

Cancer struck suddenly in February, 2004, when Maria was diagnosed with Sarcoma-Carcinosarcoma, a rare but potent strain of the disease. She spent months in a London hospital undergoing treatment where, among her many callers, was Garcia himself.

Earlier in 2005, as she battled the disease with great courage, Garcia, his family and friends, wore blue wristbands with her initials emblazoned on them as a gesture of support and, in fact, he sported the band when winning the Booz Allen Classic on the US PGA Tour in the summer.

Pierre Fulke

Paul Casey

Omega European Masters

Crans Montana, Switzerland
September 1-4 • 2005

"This is such a wonderful place and so beautiful with the mountains all around and the course has improved every year I've been coming here. The greens are fast and roll nicely and the shaping of the fairways is better" – Sergio Garcia

Ian Woosnam

Meanwhile, Crans-sur-Sierre had never looked more beautiful, or the course better conditioned, as the first two days unfolded in the still Swiss air. The sun blazed down relentlessly as Luke Donald and Garcia held sway centre stage, 12 months after the former had won the title from under the nose of the man in whose home he had been staying.

Once again, Donald and his girlfriend, Diane, were house guests and Garcia the chalet host for the week as jokes abounded as to whether the pair were still on speaking terms, whether Sergio would treble the rent, or if he would withdraw the invitation entirely if Donald prevailed for a second time!

Sure enough, the first round saw the two friends locked on 66, one stroke behind

Philip Golding

Final Results

leaders David Carter, Garry Houston and Jarmo Sandelin, while the Spaniard's second round 65 carried him to the front, 11 under par, three ahead of the field and seven clear of Donald.

Then the bombshell struck.

Garcia awoke on Saturday morning to the devastating news that Maria had passed away at the age of 24. The shock was intense and, for once in his life, Garcia felt no motivation to play golf. He was, as he put it later, in a spin. He said: "When I found out, it hit me hard. In my head, I felt very down. She was a wonderful person and didn't deserve to go that way."

Certainly it appeared that the tournament leader was out of sorts during a third round littered with errors. His double bogey at the 17th was out of character and dropped him out of the lead. However, professional pride resurfaced in time and he promptly holed his 111 yard second shot at the last for an eagle two – much to the consternation of Welshman Houston, who had briefly held pole position.

A third round 66 brought Donald back into focus in a tie for third with Anders Hansen, one behind Houston and two behind Garcia, who signed for a 71. So, to another gloriously still Sunday and, after a day of fluctuating fortunes, Garcia arrived at the 16th level on 13 under par with Swede Peter Gustafsson, who had picked his way quietly through the field with a closing 64.

Intuitively, Garcia felt the spirit of his friend by his side. Having missed the green at the tricky par three he played the most exquisite chip. The ball moved towards the hole at pace, held its line perfectly, and dropped in for a birdie two. It was the defining moment. Two simple pars at the 17th and 18th and the title belonged to Garcia.

There was little joy, only a cursory, melancholy handshake with Houston, who tied for fourth with Donald, just behind Paul Casey, after a splendid week's work. Moments later, as he accepted the trophy, Garcia dedicated his victory to Maria. Gazing towards the azure heavens, he said: "I guess my friend was looking down and watching me at the 16th. My chip had the perfect line and I was fortunate it went in.

"She was a wonderful golfer and such a lovely, caring person. It is so sad. We are here one day and the next, we are gone."

Gone, perhaps, but for as long as Garcia gulps in the clean fresh air in Crans Montana, certainly not forgotten.

Gordon Simpson

Garry Houston

Pos	Name		Rd1	Rd2	Rd3	Rd4	Total		€	£
1	Sergio GARCIA	Sp	66	65	71	68	270	-14	283,330.00	193,277.94
2	Peter GUSTAFSSON	Swe	69	70	68	64	271	-13	188,880.00	128,847.41
3	Paul CASEY	Eng	67	72	67	66	272	-12	106,420.00	72,596.05
4	Luke DONALD	Eng	66	72	66	69	273	-11	78,540.00	53,577.28
	Garry HOUSTON	Wal	65	69	69	70	273	-11	78,540.00	53,577.28
6	Pierre FULKE	Swe	69	67	70	68	274	-10	59,500.00	40,588.85
7	Philip GOLDING	Eng	68	73	66	68	275	-9	46,750.00	31,891.24
	Stuart LITTLE	Eng	69	70	69	67	275	-9	46,750.00	31,891.24
9	Jamie SPENCE	Eng	71	70	70	65	276	-8	33,150.00	22,613.79
	Paul BROADHURST	Eng	67	69	71	69	276	-8	33,150.00	22,613.79
	Emanuele CANONICA	It	71	68	69	68	276	-8	33,150.00	22,613.79
	Steven O'HARA	Scot	70	69	70	67	276	-8	33,150.00	22,613.79
13	Henrik STENSON	Swe	70	68	69	70	277	-7	26,690.00	18,207.00
	Miguel Angel JIMÉNEZ	Sp	71	69	67	70	277	-7	26,690.00	18,207.00
15	Damien MCGRANE	Ire	68	71	74	65	278	-6	24,480.00	16,699.41
	Bradley DREDGE	Wal	72	68	67	71	278	-6	24,480.00	16,699.41
17	Christian CÉVAËR	Fr	67	71	70	71	279	-5	20,881.67	14,244.75
	Jarmo SANDELIN	Swe	65	73	71	70	279	-5	20,881.67	14,244.75
	Maarten LAFEBER	NL	69	74	65	71	279	-5	20,881.67	14,244.75
	Francesco MOLINARI	It	73	66	69	71	279	-5	20,881.67	14,244.75
	Robert KARLSSON	Swe	70	68	71	70	279	-5	20,881.67	14,244.75
	Andrew MCLARDY	SA	69	73	68	69	279	-5	20,881.67	14,244.75
23	Peter LAWRIE	Ire	68	69	75	68	280	-4	17,170.00	11,712.78
	Marc CAYEUX	Zim	75	68	71	66	280	-4	17,170.00	11,712.78
	Mattias ELIASSON	Swe	72	68	71	69	280	-4	17,170.00	11,712.78
	Ricardo GONZALEZ	Arg	74	67	70	69	280	-4	17,170.00	11,712.78
	Ian GARBUTT	Eng	73	68	70	69	280	-4	17,170.00	11,712.78
	Simon KHAN	Eng	70	72	66	72	280	-4	17,170.00	11,712.78
	Oliver WILSON	Eng	67	72	67	74	280	-4	17,170.00	11,712.78
30	Tino SCHUSTER	Ger	70	70	72	69	281	-3	14,365.00	9,799.31
	Darren FICHARDT	SA	68	70	68	75	281	-3	14,365.00	9,799.31
	Johan AXGREN	Swe	68	74	69	70	281	-3	14,365.00	9,799.31
	Anders HANSEN	Den	67	70	67	77	281	-3	14,365.00	9,799.31
34	Anthony WALL	Eng	72	71	71	68	282	-2	12,240.00	8,349.71
	José Manuel LARA	Sp	73	68	72	69	282	-2	12,240.00	8,349.71
	Miles TUNNICLIFF	Eng	72	69	69	72	282	-2	12,240.00	8,349.71
	Jean VAN DE VELDE	Fr	70	65	75	72	282	-2	12,240.00	8,349.71
	Leif WESTERBERG	Swe	67	70	69	76	282	-2	12,240.00	8,349.71
	Peter O'MALLEY	Aus	68	71	71	72	282	-2	12,240.00	8,349.71
40	Jan-Are LARSEN	Nor	68	72	70	73	283	-1	9,860.00	6,726.15
	Raymond RUSSELL	Scot	71	72	73	67	283	-1	9,860.00	6,726.15
	Johan SKOLD	Swe	72	71	71	69	283	-1	9,860.00	6,726.15
	Gary EMERSON	Eng	70	70	69	74	283	-1	9,860.00	6,726.15
	Peter HANSON	Swe	72	69	71	71	283	-1	9,860.00	6,726.15
	Peter HEDBLOM	Swe	66	76	70	71	283	-1	9,860.00	6,726.15
	Ian WOOSNAM	Wal	72	67	73	71	283	-1	9,860.00	6,726.15
	Stuart MANLEY	Wal	70	72	67	74	283	-1	9,860.00	6,726.15
48	Wade ORMSBY	Aus	70	73	76	65	284	0	7,140.00	4,870.66
	Peter SENIOR	Aus	68	73	71	72	284	0	7,140.00	4,870.66
	Roger CHAPMAN	Eng	72	70	70	72	284	0	7,140.00	4,870.66
	Andrea MAESTRONI	It	68	75	68	73	284	0	7,140.00	4,870.66
	Joakim BÄCKSTRÖM	Swe	73	70	69	72	284	0	7,140.00	4,870.66
	Stephen SCAHILL	NZ	69	71	73	71	284	0	7,140.00	4,870.66
	Graeme STORM	Eng	71	65	74	74	284	0	7,140.00	4,870.66
	Charl SCHWARTZEL	SA	74	68	68	74	284	0	7,140.00	4,870.66
56	Jose-Filipe LIMA	Port	76	65	71	73	285	1	4,954.29	3,379.64
	Edoardo MOLINARI (AM)	It	72	71	67	75	285	1		
	Robert ROCK	Eng	69	71	73	72	285	1	4,954.29	3,379.64
	André BOSSERT	Swi	69	70	74	72	285	1	4,954.29	3,379.64
	David CARTER	Eng	65	72	76	72	285	1	4,954.29	3,379.64
	Santiago LUNA	Sp	69	72	72	72	285	1	4,954.29	3,379.64
	Martin ERLANDSSON	Swe	72	64	70	79	285	1	4,954.29	3,379.64
	Lee SLATTERY	Eng	71	72	72	70	285	1	4,954.29	3,379.64
64	Mårten OLANDER	Swe	72	71	75	68	286	2	4,080.00	2,783.24
	Gordon BRAND JNR	Scot	70	71	70	75	286	2	4,080.00	2,783.24
	Michael JONZON	Swe	67	73	72	74	286	2	4,080.00	2,783.24
67	Fredrik ANDERSSON HED	Swe	72	69	74	72	287	3	3,740.00	2,551.30
68	Richard BLAND	Eng	67	76	73	73	289	5	3,570.00	2,435.33
69	Simon DYSON	Eng	74	68	70	78	290	6	3,315.00	2,261.38
	Brett RUMFORD	Aus	75	68	73	74	290	6	3,315.00	2,261.38
71	Mark FOSTER	Eng	71	72	73	75	291	7	3,110.00	2,121.53
72	Barry LANE	Eng	72	70	75	75	292	8	2,548.50	1,738.50
	Tobias DIER	Ger	71	72	74	75	292	8	2,548.50	1,738.50
74	Patrik SJÖLAND	Swe	68	75	73	78	294	10	2,544.00	1,735.43
75	Mads VIBE-HASTRUP	Den	71	72	75	77	295	11	2,541.00	1,733.38
76	Phillip ARCHER	Eng	73	69	83	73	298	14	2,538.00	1,731.34
77	Marcus KNIGHT	Swi	70	72	77	81	300	16	2,535.00	1,729.29
78	Nicolas COLSAERTS	Bel	71	72	76	82	301	17	2,532.00	1,727.24

Total Prize Fund
€1,717,790 £1,171,814

Linde German Masters

Cologne, Germany
September 8-11 • 2005

Gut Lärchenhof

Par	Yards	Metres
72	7289	6662

1	**Retief GOOSEN**	**268**	**-20**	
2	Nick DOUGHERTY	269	-19	
	David LYNN	269	-19	
	José Maria OLAZÁBAL	269	-19	
	Henrik STENSON	269	-19	
6	David HOWELL	270	-18	
7	Paul CASEY	271	-17	
	Anthony WALL	271	-17	
9	Angel CABRERA	272	-16	
10	Kenneth FERRIE	273	-15	
	Ricardo GONZALEZ	273	-15	

Round One   Round Two   Round Three   Round Four

EUROPEAN TOUR ORDER OF MERIT
(After 40 tournaments)

Pos		€	
1	**Retief GOOSEN**	**2,057,910.12**	
2	Michael CAMPBELL	1,796,372.89	
3	Angel CABRERA	1,566,868.49	
4	Colin MONTGOMERIE	1,546,989.94	
5	David HOWELL	1,524,302.33	
6	Thomas BJÖRN	1,472,478.09	
7	Paul McGINLEY	1,161,083.70	
8	Niclas FASTH	1,148,427.56	
9	Henrik STENSON	1,053,657.53	
10	Ernie ELS	1,012,682.63	

Twists and Turns

Linde German Masters

Cologne, Germany
September 8-11 • 2005

It was in the third hour of trying to negotiate a passage between Cologne and Gut Lärchenhof, where the final round of the Linde German Masters was being played on a humid day in September, that a line in one of the most significant songs of the 20th Century came unbidden to mind.

David Lynn

However, the fabled Dylan's opus had somehow become changed by the situation so that it now asked: "How many roads must a man drive down, before he admits he is lost?" Okay, the original was better, but this fitted with a gruesome reality that transcended lyrical niceties.

The trouble with Gut Lärchenhof - and, in truth, it is but a minor quibble in the greater scheme of things - is that when the good burghers of Cologne are holding their annual marathon, it makes getting there a proposition that requires a stoicism of the most heroic kind.

For the record, the foot race was won by one Joseph Kadon, of Kenya, in two hours, 11 minutes and 55 seconds. He was lucky. He covered 26 miles and 385 yards approximately 32 minutes quicker than it took to negotiate the nominal 14.1 miles from Cologne city centre to the golf course.

But it did not end there. Having got within a handful of miles of the destination and seemingly set fair for an imminent arrival, another roped-off strasse hove into view. It might have been in Bickendorf, Ossendorf, Mungersdorf - they were all in the vicinity - or, for all that it was possible to tell, Milford Haven. The point was that this time, it was so that the competitors in a cycle race could pedal past at suicidal speeds.

This contest was won, after intensive research and as far as it was possible to ascertain, by some bloke on a bike. Nice for him and his supporters, no doubt. For those fired with the simple ambition of getting to the golf course, it was just another teeth-grinding moment among many.

To be fair, when landfall was finally reached, shortly, it seemed at the time, before darkness fell, the suburban diversions were rendered worthwhile by a thunderous, jaw-quivering, nerve-jangling finish to the tournament that tuned up the senses like a harmonic 11th on a Fender Stratocaster.

The fact was that Retief Goosen, he of the impassive, South African face and a game bestowed upon him by the gods, won with a closing 67 for a 20 under par total of 268. However, not for the first time, his equilibrium had been knocked out of kilter at a pivotal moment. And not for the first

"This is a great course. The rough is formidable but fair and it's set up beautifully. The greens are so good that even if you put yourself in trouble, you can get yourself out if you get a good roll on the ball. I love it" – Paul Casey

time - nor yet the last it is safe to speculate - he survived it to win.

All manner of twists and turns had preceded the end game of this most intriguing of tournaments, but ultimately it was all distilled into a handful of soul-searching minutes.

With one hole to play, Goosen seemed totally in control of himself and the situation, then wobbled so shockingly that he was left to suffer a few minutes' agony before taking his 12th title on The European Tour International Schedule.

Goosen had dismissed all manner of challenges throughout a tense final day and

was two ahead of the field on the final tee. He then cast his drive into a water hazard and took a penalty drop, before hitting a shot that was brushed with perfection to five feet, only to miss the putt. The resulting bogey left him to wait, watch and wonder if it had all been enough.

It had seemed over but was no longer so. The last two men on the course, Nick Dougherty and Henrik Stenson, could force a play-off with birdies. Fortunately for Goosen, a combination of adrenalin and the occasion proved too much for both young men, Dougherty's second shot leaving him with a 50 foot putt, which he narrowly missed, and Stenson flying the green with his own second.

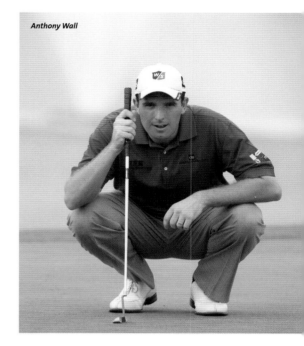

Anthony Wall

Bernhard Langer

Professionalism never fails to impress.

Lead**Ing.**

Linde

Kenneth Ferrie

Final Results

Pos	Name		Rd1	Rd2	Rd3	Rd4	Total		€	£
1	Retief GOOSEN	SA	67	68	66	67	268	-20	500,000.00	340,650.51
2	David LYNN	Eng	68	67	67	67	269	-19	199,582.50	135,975.76
	Nick DOUGHERTY	Eng	71	64	66	68	269	-19	199,582.50	135,975.76
	José Maria OLAZÁBAL	Sp	68	65	70	66	269	-19	199,582.50	135,975.76
	Henrik STENSON	Swe	71	66	64	68	269	-19	199,582.50	135,975.76
6	David HOWELL	Eng	72	66	66	66	270	-18	105,000.00	71,536.61
7	Anthony WALL	Eng	71	62	68	70	271	-17	82,500.00	56,207.33
	Paul CASEY	Eng	67	67	71	66	271	-17	82,500.00	56,207.33
9	Angel CABRERA	Arg	70	68	67	67	272	-16	67,200.00	45,783.43
10	Ricardo GONZALEZ	Arg	67	71	71	64	273	-15	57,600.00	39,242.94
	Kenneth FERRIE	Eng	68	72	66	67	273	-15	57,600.00	39,242.94
12	Scott DRUMMOND	Scot	68	68	68	71	275	-13	46,440.00	31,639.62
	Marc CAYEUX	Zim	66	69	72	68	275	-13	46,440.00	31,639.62
	Bernhard LANGER	Ger	67	69	71	68	275	-13	46,440.00	31,639.62
	Pierre FULKE	Swe	68	69	69	69	275	-13	46,440.00	31,639.62
	Niclas FASTH	Swe	69	71	65	70	275	-13	46,440.00	31,639.62
17	Stephen DODD	Wal	69	70	70	67	276	-12	36,850.00	25,105.94
	Thomas BJÖRN	Den	71	70	69	66	276	-12	36,850.00	25,105.94
	Simon KHAN	Eng	69	69	69	69	276	-12	36,850.00	25,105.94
	Simon DYSON	Eng	72	68	67	69	276	-12	36,850.00	25,105.94
	Thomas LEVET	Fr	71	66	67	72	276	-12	36,850.00	25,105.94
	Philip GOLDING	Eng	71	66	68	71	276	-12	36,850.00	25,105.94
23	Jose-Filipe LIMA	Port	71	69	65	72	277	-11	32,100.00	21,869.76
	Fredrik ANDERSSON HED	Swe	69	70	66	72	277	-11	32,100.00	21,869.76
	Andrew COLTART	Scot	73	68	67	69	277	-11	32,100.00	21,869.76
26	Christian CÉVAËR	Fr	71	71	70	66	278	-10	28,500.00	19,417.08
	Charl SCHWARTZEL	SA	67	72	72	67	278	-10	28,500.00	19,417.08
	Lee SLATTERY	Eng	72	66	71	69	278	-10	28,500.00	19,417.08
	Graeme STORM	Eng	69	69	70	70	278	-10	28,500.00	19,417.08
	Richard GREEN	Aus	70	70	66	72	278	-10	28,500.00	19,417.08
31	Paul BROADHURST	Eng	69	68	73	69	279	-9	24,060.00	16,392.10
	Jonathan LOMAS	Eng	73	65	71	70	279	-9	24,060.00	16,392.10
	Mårten OLANDER	Swe	71	68	72	68	279	-9	24,060.00	16,392.10
	José Manuel LARA	Sp	67	74	66	72	279	-9	24,060.00	16,392.10
	Bradley DREDGE	Wal	66	75	68	70	279	-9	24,060.00	16,392.10
36	Michael CAMPBELL	NZ	71	69	73	67	280	-8	21,000.00	14,307.32
	Barry LANE	Eng	66	72	70	72	280	-8	21,000.00	14,307.32
	Peter SENIOR	Aus	66	72	72	70	280	-8	21,000.00	14,307.32
	Søren HANSEN	Den	71	71	70	68	280	-8	21,000.00	14,307.32
40	Ian WOOSNAM	Wal	75	67	68	71	281	-7	19,200.00	13,080.98
	Graeme MCDOWELL	N.Ire	71	70	70	70	281	-7	19,200.00	13,080.98
42	Mark HENSBY	Aus	71	71	68	72	282	-6	17,100.00	11,650.25
	John BICKERTON	Eng	72	70	71	69	282	-6	17,100.00	11,650.25
	Damien MCGRANE	Ire	71	70	70	71	282	-6	17,100.00	11,650.25
	Steve WEBSTER	Eng	69	72	68	73	282	-6	17,100.00	11,650.25
	Andrew MARSHALL	Eng	71	64	71	72	282	-6	17,100.00	11,650.25
47	Carlos RODILES	Sp	72	67	74	70	283	-5	13,200.00	8,993.17
	Peter HANSON	Swe	69	73	70	71	283	-5	13,200.00	8,993.17
	Stuart LITTLE	Eng	69	71	70	73	283	-5	13,200.00	8,993.17
	Robert KARLSSON	Swe	68	73	71	71	283	-5	13,200.00	8,993.17
	Miles TUNNICLIFF	Eng	74	68	73	68	283	-5	13,200.00	8,993.17
	Mikael LUNDBERG	Swe	71	71	72	69	283	-5	13,200.00	8,993.17
	Raymond RUSSELL	Scot	72	70	70	71	283	-5	13,200.00	8,993.17
	Gonzalo FERNANDEZ-CASTANO	Sp	71	67	73	72	283	-5	13,200.00	8,993.17
55	Alastair FORSYTH	Scot	69	71	74	70	284	-4	9,300.00	6,336.10
	Louis OOSTHUIZEN	SA	70	70	74	70	284	-4	9,300.00	6,336.10
	Markus BRIER	Aut	66	73	72	73	284	-4	9,300.00	6,336.10
	Ignacio GARRIDO	Sp	73	67	71	73	284	-4	9,300.00	6,336.10
	Robert-Jan DERKSEN	NL	75	65	72	72	284	-4	9,300.00	6,336.10
	Niki ZITNY	Aut	67	72	76	69	284	-4	9,300.00	6,336.10
61	Sven STRÜVER	Ger	70	68	73	74	285	-3	7,650.00	5,211.95
	Joakim BÄCKSTRÖM	Swe	71	66	72	76	285	-3	7,650.00	5,211.95
	Joakim HAEGGMAN	Swe	70	71	71	73	285	-3	7,650.00	5,211.95
	Brett RUMFORD	Aus	70	72	69	74	285	-3	7,650.00	5,211.95
65	Ian POULTER	Eng	72	70	74	70	286	-2	6,900.00	4,700.98
66	Peter O'MALLEY	Aus	71	71	72	73	287	-1	6,300.00	4,292.20
	Andrew OLDCORN	Scot	68	73	74	72	287	-1	6,300.00	4,292.20
	André BOSSERT	Swi	69	73	72	73	287	-1	6,300.00	4,292.20
69	David CARTER	Eng	71	71	74	72	288	0	5,700.00	3,883.42
70	Jean-François REMESY	Fr	74	68	71	77	290	2	4,985.00	3,396.29
	Marcel SIEM	Ger	71	70	75	74	290	2	4,985.00	3,396.29
72	Raphaël JACQUELIN	Fr	71	71	74	75	291	3	4,497.00	3,063.81

For most of the day, Goosen's main opponent was Anthony Wall, who had led with distinction in mid-tournament and had fought the good fight, but who was undone by bogeys on each of the last three holes to finish three strokes behind. There were other challenges, too, from David Lynn and José Maria Olazábal, who both finished alongside Dougherty and Stenson, a stroke behind Goosen.

Wall had been a revelation. He had long been a player whose skills had not been matched by his results but here one was almost equalled by the other. He had a glittering 62 in the second round and refused to go away in the third. He had no reason to be unhappy and yet, inevitably, he was. He had been close to breasting the tape first, like good old Joseph Kadon, but unlike the fleet-footed Kenyan, he had flagged with the winning post in sight.

Goosen went within a whisker of an implosion of a comparable magnitude. He is a precious man to his nearest and dearest, no doubt, but he does not half conjure up the collywobbles when they are least needed. The curious thing about this most modest of champions is that he does it so quietly, so gently and so unassumingly, that nobody quite realises he has put them through the wringer until he has allayed their fears and won.

Yet again he prevailed, and it made the long odyssey through the semi-detached suburbs of one of the great cities of Europe worthwhile. You can't say fairer than that, can you?

Mel Webb
The Times

Total Prize Fund
€3,009,000   £2,050,032

HSBC World Match Play Championship

Surrey, England
September 15-18 • 2005

Wentworth Club

Par	Yards	Metres
72	7072	6468

Champion - Michael Campbell

Runner-Up - Paul McGinley

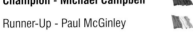

Round One	Round Two	Round Three	Round Four

EUROPEAN TOUR ORDER OF MERIT
(After 41 tournaments)

Pos		€	
1	**Michael CAMPBELL**	**2,398,201.22**	
2	Retief GOOSEN	2,261,211.06	
3	Angel CABRERA	1,770,169.43	
4	Colin MONTGOMERIE	1,609,370.47	
5	David HOWELL	1,586,682.86	
6	Paul McGINLEY	1,562,307.52	
7	Thomas BJÖRN	1,534,858.62	
8	Niclas FASTH	1,148,427.56	
9	Luke DONALD	1,095,346.19	
10	Henrik STENSON	1,053,657.53	

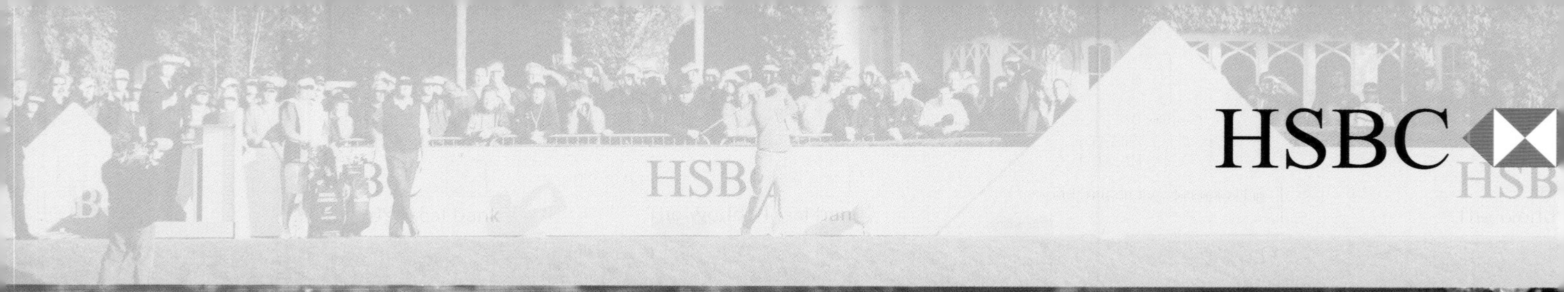

HSBC

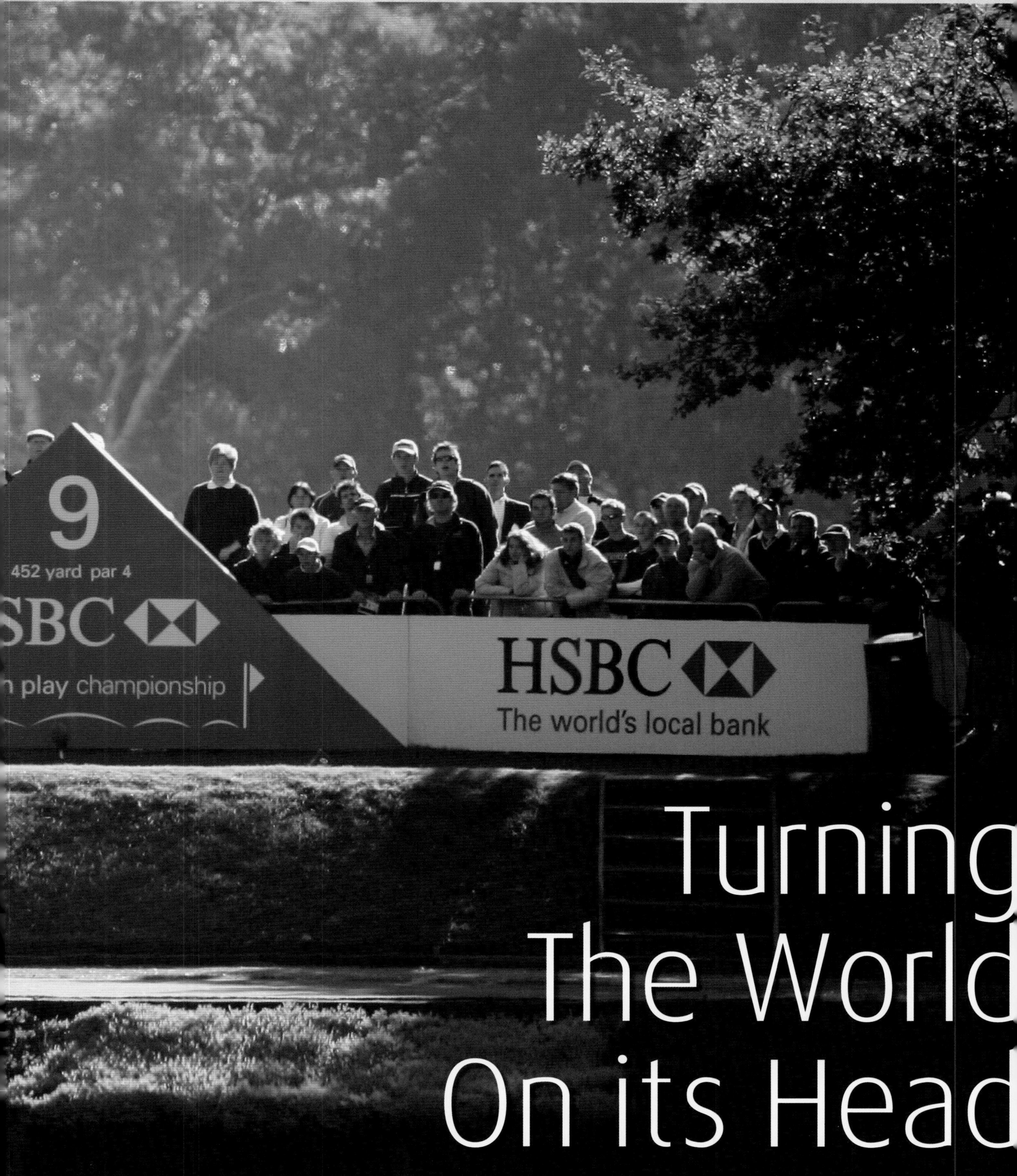
9
452 yard par 4
SBC
n play championship
HSBC
The world's local bank

Turning The World On its Head

HSBC World Match Play Championship

Surrey, England
September 15-18 • 2005

Y ou could argue that Michael Campbell won the HSBC World Match Play Championship crown and the £1 million first prize standing on his head. To be fair, it was not quite that easy for the New Zealander who defeated Ireland's Paul McGinley 2 and 1 in the 36 hole final, but he did energise himself during four stamina-sapping days at Wentworth Club by indulging in upside-down yoga exercises.

David Howell

The reigning US Open Champion had to battle through 140 holes in total on the West Course before he could finally lift the coveted trophy and declare: "I am so proud to be part of history now and to match my famous compatriot Bob Charles in winning the World Match Play Championship – in fact I was born in 1969, the year he beat Gene Littler in the final. It has been a magical four months."

Victory completed a remarkable turnaround for a man who missed the cut in his first five tournaments in 2005. The changes have come in every aspect of Campbell's life, not only on the golf course, but off it too, hence the yoga. "When my wife Julie and I looked at me, we found things deep down that weren't good. I've worked on certain things and changed my whole routine around," he said.

A lot of the talk earlier in the week had been about players such as Phil Mickelson, Vijay Singh and Tiger Woods, who had turned down their respective invitations to the Surrey hinterland. But the thousands who once again flocked to the fairways and the millions more who watched on BBC Television were more interested in two men who unashamedly deemed it a privilege to be playing in the event.

" The West Course was in absolutely magnificent order. Chris Kennedy, Graham Matheson and the team have done an incredible job. It was unusual to see the course running so fast for this event and the greens, in particular, were as quick as we have had in Europe all year " – Paul McGinley

Just how much both Campbell and McGinley wanted to see their names inscribed alongside a veritable Who's Who on the gleaming Mark McCormack Trophy was underlined as they scrapped for every advantage in an enthralling final. "We play for prestige and the honour of being part of something special," said Campbell. "I'm financially set for my family and myself.

Competing and winning around the world - that's my goal."

Winning was what 38 year old McGinley had set his heart on, too, and gaining enough points from second place to move to the top of The Ryder Cup European Points List was only a minor consolation. The Irishman could not hide his emotion as he declared: "It hurts like you can't believe to lose out here. I am bitterly disappointed after playing so well all week only to finish as poorly as I did in the final."

After requiring 73 holes to see off two Australians – Geoff Ogilvy at the 36th hole

in the first round and Steve Elkington at the 37th in round two - Campbell admitted he would need his 'A' game for the semi-final clash with number one seed Retief Goosen, who had thumped debutant Kenneth Ferrie 8 and 7 in round one before demolishing another first-timer Mark Hensby 12 and 11 in round two, to equal the record winning margin he set against Jeff Maggert last year. Campbell did find his 'A' game and more beside, posting a clutch of birdies and eagles on his way to easily dispatching an out of sorts Goosen 7 and 6.

Meanwhile, in the bottom half of the draw, McGinley marched purposefully to the final,

Luke Donald

Paul McGinley

CONTINUING THE
TRADITION

Angel Cabrera **BMW** CHAMPION, *Michael Campbell* **HSBC WORLD MATCH PLAY** CHAMPION, and *Eduardo Romero* **TRAVIS PERKINS SENIOR MASTERS** CHAMPION, join the list of illustrious names who have won at Wentworth. Names such as Ernie Els, Colin Montgomerie, Vijay Singh, Severiano Ballesteros, Nick Faldo, Greg Norman, Gary Player, Jack Nicklaus and Arnold Palmer. Thrilling the tens of thousands who followed the matches around the courses and the millions watching on TV, unpredictable, dramatic and gripping. Breathtaking golf by the best players in the world. That's what makes Wentworth so special.

Angel Cabrera

Final Results

outgunning Ryder Cup team-mates Thomas Björn 6 and 5 in round one and Luke Donald 9 and 8 in round two, before gaining some revenge over Angel Cabrera, who had pipped him for the BMW Championship title at Wentworth Club in May, with a 4 and 3 semi-final victory.

Perhaps fittingly, for a grey autumn Sunday, the finalists appeared on the first tee as the Men in Black. It might have set a sombre tone for the match but nothing could have been further from the truth as the duo produced absorbing, screw-tightening tension.

McGinley gained the early ascendancy when Campbell missed a five foot putt at the first, but after Campbell won the long fifth with an eagle three, he was never behind again. The New Zealander took the lead with a birdie at the short tenth and lunched one

hole to the good, while his birdie at the opening hole of the afternoon round allied to McGinley's double bogey at the third, put the Antipodean three up.

McGinley, cheered on by a large flag-waving Irish contingent including former Celtic manager Martin O'Neill, showed his character by pulling back to all square with three wins in four holes to the afternoon turn. But as both players were to agree later, the key moment arrived at the 12th hole, their 30th overall.

When Campbell's second shot came within a foot of the out of bounds fence, McGinley looked a strong favourite to go one up. But Campbell somehow contrived the unlikeliest of winning birdie fours and the dye was set. There was still virtually nothing in it, but when McGinley fired his five iron approach into the trees at the 15th and then hooked his drive deep into the woods at the 16th to lose both holes, it looked all over. When Campbell rolled a 40 yard chip down to a foot for a half at the 17th, it was.

He had become the fourth man to capture the US Open and the World Match Play Championship in the same year – following in the footsteps of Gary Player (1965), Hale Irwin (1974) and Ernie Els (1994).

José Maria Olazábal

John Whitbread
Surrey Herald

First Round Losers each received:
€88,795 (£60,000)
For The European Tour Order of Merit, the First Round Losers each received:
€62,380 (£42,151)

Losing Quarter Finalists each received:
€118,394 (£80,000)
For The European Tour Order of Merit, the losing Quarter Finalists each received:
€119,525 (£80,764)

Losing Semi Finalists each received:
€177,591 (£120,000)
For The European Tour Order of Merit, the losing Semi Finalists each received:
€203,300 (£137,372)

The Winner received:
€1,479,930 (£1,000,000)
For The European Tour Order of Merit, the Winner received:
€601,828 (£406,660)

The Runner-Up received:
€591,972 (£400,000)
For The European Tour Order of Merit, the Runner-Up received:
€401,223 (£271,110)

Seve Trophy

Billingham, Tees Valley, England
September 22-25 • 2005

Team Spirit

The Wynyard Golf Club

Par	Yards	Metres
71	7097	6490

INDIVIDUAL PLAYER PERFORMANCES

CONTINENTAL EUROPE	PLD	WON	LOST	HVD	PTS
José Maria Olazábal (Captain)	4	2	2	0	2
Thomas Björn	5	2	2	1	2½
Emanuele Canonica	5	2	2	1	2½
Niclas Fasth	5	2	3	0	2
Peter Hanson	4	1	2	1	1½
Miguel Angel Jiménez	5	1	3	1	1½
Maarten Lafeber	4	1	3	0	1
Thomas Levet	5	1	3	1	1½
Jean-Francois Remesy	4	1	2	1	1½
Henrik Stenson	5	3	0	2	4

GREAT BRITAIN & IRELAND	PLD	WON	LOST	HVD	PTS
Colin Montgomerie (Captain)	4	2	2	0	2
Paul Casey	5	4	1	0	4
Stephen Dodd	4	1	2	1	1½
Nick Dougherty	5	2	1	2	3
Bradley Dredge	4	1	3	0	1
Padraig Harrington	5	2	2	1	2½
David Howell	5	4	1	0	4
Graeme McDowell	4	2	1	1	2½
Paul McGinley	5	3	1	1	3½
Ian Poulter	5	1	2	2	2

Round One	Round Two	Round Three	Round Four

EUROPEAN TOUR ORDER OF MERIT
(After 41 tournaments)

Pos		€	
1	**Michael CAMPBELL**	2,398,201.22	
2	Retief GOOSEN	2,261,211.06	
3	Angel CABRERA	1,770,169.43	
4	Colin MONTGOMERIE	1,609,370.47	
5	David HOWELL	1,586,682.86	
6	Paul McGINLEY	1,562,307.52	
7	Thomas BJÖRN	1,534,858.62	
8	Niclas FASTH	1,148,427.56	
9	Luke DONALD	1,095,346.19	
10	Henrik STENSON	1,053,657.53	

Like every great drama, the Seve Trophy works because it has both a strong plot and sub-plot. On the one hand you have 20 competitors, representing either Great Britain and Ireland or Continental Europe, treating the event on its own merits, and giving the matches a thrilling edge. As for sub-plot, it is impossible not to watch the machinations of the captains and how their partnerships gel, and not glean one or two pointers in terms of The Ryder Cup.

Nick Dougherty

The fourth Seve Trophy at The Wynyard Club in the Tees Valley was arguably the most compelling edition yet because, not only did it work well on both those levels, it was also notable for the way the event so obviously captured the imagination of the good people of the north east of England. Down the road there was a football derby between Middlesborough and Sunderland competing for attention on the final day but thousands of spectators, including an encouragingly large number of under-18s, forgot tribal allegiances for an afternoon and turned up to watch the golf instead.

In turn they were rewarded with an event that showed off the present and future of European golf to fine effect. Anyone who chose to watch Nick Dougherty and Henrik Stenson going at it hammer and tongs in the final day's singles, for example, could not help but think that here were two young players who will surely go on to make a huge impression in years to come.

There was Paul Casey, pleasingly emerging from a troubled year to show just what an accomplished player he really is, and his partner, David Howell. Those of us with an affinity for European golf cannot help but take pleasure in the way Howell, an unassuming man, has developed way beyond his own expectations to fully understand that it is no fluke that he is now among the elite. He is there on merit.

The bare bones of the plot are that Great Britain and Ireland simply could not cope with the fast start made by the visitors in the opening day's five fourballs, as they relished the role of underdogs like so many European sides in the past. The truth of the matter is that partnerships as strong as Thomas Björn and Stenson, and Spanish maestros Miguel Angel Jiménez and José Maria Olazábal, could beat anyone in the world on a given day, and did so on this. Continental Europe led 4-1, and, as you can imagine, Colin Montgomerie, the Great Britain and Ireland captain, was not happy. You do not get to be one of the top players in the world for nigh on 20 years by readily accepting such an outcome.

Montgomerie handled it beautifully. In front of the press he gave full credit to the opposition - before dropping a hint or two that behind the privacy of closed doors he had let his team know full well they had not delivered as he would have liked. Montgomerie's parting words resonated throughout the rest of the contest. "How do you deliver a positive rollicking?" he asked. "There's an art to that, and we'll see if I've managed it."

We saw it all right. We saw it in the way Ian Poulter, visibly upset with his performance on

"The course is a very challenging one, with a lot of fine holes, including a very testing finish"
- José Maria Olazábal

HEREDEROS DEL
MARQUES DE RISCAL
www.marquesderiscal.com

Jean-Francois Remesy

Thomas Levet

day one, wrenched six birdies in one brilliant nine hole passage of play in the Friday fourballs. Indeed, the home team were so transformed that European captain Olazábal, standing in for the injured Seve Ballesteros who assumed the role of Tournament Host for the week, was grateful for just a 3-2 loss on the second day.

But momentum is everything in team golf. It had swung towards Great Britain and Ireland and these players are so hungry for success, it is hard to stop them once in their stride. They kept striving. They won both the greensomes and foursomes series held on the third day, before turning in as complete a performance as you could imagine to win the singles matches by a score of 7-3 for a 16½-11½ victory.

How nice, too, that the winning point should be claimed by the Welshman Bradley Dredge, which meant every player in the victorious side had contributed at least a point to the cause. It emphasised the strength in depth of British and Irish golf these days, and a comeback worthy of the man after whom the tournament was named.

As Olazábal, whose wit and competitive zeal contributed so much to the occasion, said: "My eyes were sore from seeing all the British and Irish red on the leaderboards. I have never seen a team hole so many putts in my life. They were brilliant."

During those four days we saw why so many people believe the inspirational Montgomerie and the delightful Olazábal will both be Ryder Cup Captains in the

future. We also saw why Europe has enjoyed so much success in The Ryder Cup. Maybe it is because these players go from tournament to tournament together, dine together, creating obvious bonds as they go, that they can so readily change from individuals to embrace the concept of team golf.

Certainly its value, whether at The Ryder Cup or the Seve Trophy, is inestimable.

Derek Lawrenson
Daily Mail

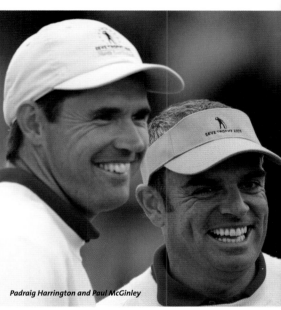

Padraig Harrington and Paul McGinley

Final Results

CONTINENTAL EUROPE Captain: José Maria Olazábal		GREAT BRITAIN & IRELAND Captain: Colin Montgomerie	
Thursday September 22: Fourballs			
Thomas Björn & Henrik Stenson (2 holes)	1	Ian Poulter & Nick Dougherty	0
Maarten Lafeber & Emanuele Canonica	0	Colin Montgomerie & Graeme McDowell (4 & 2)	1
Miguel Angel Jiménez & José Maria Olazábal (4 & 2)	1	Stephen Dodd & Bradley Dredge	0
Niclas Fasth & Peter Hanson (3 & 2)	1	David Howell & Paul Casey	0
Jean-Francois Remesy & Thomas Levet (1 hole)	1	Paul McGinley & Padraig Harrington	0
	4		**1**
Friday September 23: Fourballs			
Niclas Fasth & Peter Hanson	0	Paul McGinley & Padraig Harrington (3 & 1)	1
Miguel Angel Jiménez & José Maria Olazábal	0	David Howell & Paul Casey (5 & 4)	1
Thomas Björn & Henrik Stenson (3 & 2)	1	Colin Montgomerie & Graeme McDowell	0
Maarten Lafeber & Emanuele Canonica (2 holes)	1	Stephen Dodd & Bradley Dredge	0
Jean-Francois Remesy & Thomas Levet	0	Ian Poulter & Nick Dougherty (5 & 4)	1
	6		**4**
Saturday September 24: Morning Greensomes			
Thomas Levet & José Maria Olazábal	0	Paul McGinley & Padraig Harrington (3 & 2)	1
Niclas Fasth & Peter Hanson	0	David Howell & Paul Casey (2 holes)	1
Miguel Angel Jiménez & Emanuele Canonica (halved)	½	Stephen Dodd & Graeme McDowell (halved)	½
Thomas Björn & Henrik Stenson (halved)	½	Ian Poulter & Nick Dougherty (halved)	½
	7		**7**
Saturday September 24: Afternoon Foursomes			
Thomas Levet & Jean-Francois Remesy (halved)	½	Paul McGinley & Padraig Harrington (halved)	½
Miguel Angel Jiménez & Emanuele Canonica	0	David Howell & Paul Casey (2 & 1)	1
Niclas Fasth & Henrik Stenson (1 hole)	1	Ian Poulter & Bradley Dredge	0
Thomas Björn & Maarten Lafeber	0	Colin Montgomerie & Nick Dougherty (1 hole)	1
	8½		**9½**
Sunday September 25: Singles			
José Maria Olazábal (2 & 1)	1	Colin Montgomerie	0
Niclas Fasth	0	Paul Casey (4 & 3)	1
Peter Hanson (halved)	½	Ian Poulter (halved)	½
Thomas Björn	0	David Howell (6 & 5)	1
Jean-Francois Remesy	0	Stephen Dodd (2 & 1)	1
Thomas Levet	0	Bradley Dredge (2 & 1)	1
Maarten Lafeber	0	Graeme McDowell (5 & 4)	1
Miguel Angel Jiménez	0	Paul McGinley (1 hole)	1
Emanuele Canonica (2 & 1)	1	Padraig Harrington	0
Henrik Stenson (halved)	½	Nick Dougherty (halved)	½
	11½		**16½**

dunhill links championship

Scotland
September 29- October 2 • 2005

Old Course, St Andrews
Par	Yards	Metres
72	7279	6655

Carnoustie
Par	Yards	Metres
72	7112	6504

Kingsbarns
Par	Yards	Metres
72	7099	6492

1	**Colin MONTGOMERIE**	279	-9	
2	Kenneth FERRIE	280	-8	
3	Anders HANSEN	281	-7	
	Padraig HARRINGTON	281	-7	
	Robert KARLSSON	281	-7	
	Henrik STENSON	281	-7	
7	Darren CLARKE	282	-6	
	Pierre FULKE	282	-6	
	Stephen GALLACHER	282	-6	
	Ricardo GONZALEZ	282	-6	
	Titch MOORE	282	-6	
	Lee WESTWOOD	282	-6	

Round One	Round Two	Round Three	Round Four

EUROPEAN TOUR ORDER OF MERIT
(After 42 tournaments)

Pos		€	
1	**Michael CAMPBELL**	2,398,201.22	
2	Colin MONTGOMERIE	2,271,785.57	
3	Retief GOOSEN	2,261,211.06	
4	Angel CABRERA	1,770,169.43	
5	David HOWELL	1,613,709.40	
6	Paul McGINLEY	1,584,564.67	
7	Thomas BJÖRN	1,534,858.62	
8	Kenneth FERRIE	1,302,668.64	
9	Henrik STENSON	1,242,445.83	
10	Niclas FASTH	1,170,684.71	

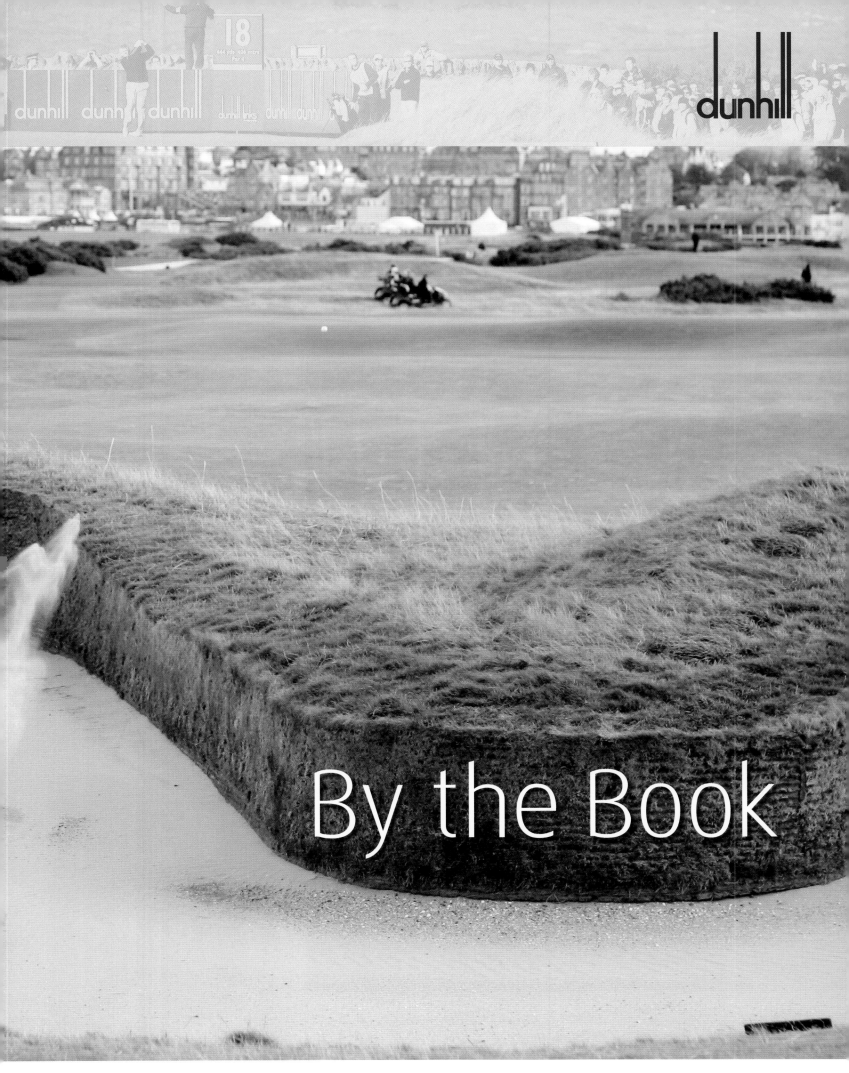

By the Book

dunhill links championship

Scotland
September 29- October 2 • 2005

When, nearly three months after finishing runner-up to Tiger Woods in The 134th Open Championship at St Andrews, Colin Montgomerie returned to the Old Course Hotel for the dunhill links championship, he was so determined not to change anything that he even requested the same room.

Kenneth Ferrie

It was not the only thing which the Scot did not want to alter as he plotted how to go one better and win his first European Tour event in 19 months. Always a golfer who thrived on self-belief, the sight of the ancient links where he had pushed the World Number One all the way in the summer was sufficient to convince Montgomerie that, at 42 years and 101 days old, he could win on home turf for the first time since the Scottish Open at Loch Lomond in 1999.

As well as retaining confidence and the swing which served him so well during the Open, Montgomerie and his caddie, Alastair McLean, also remembered to bring the yardage book which served them so well. "Alastair used the Open yardage book, as opposed to the dunhill links yardage book, because it had all of the wind directions and also every club I hit in the Open," the Scot would reveal on Sunday evening.

"At the tenth hole, for example, I knew exactly what I'd done in windy conditions at the Open. During the final round of the

Kingsbarns

"Whenever I get the chance to play Carnoustie, Kingsbarns and St Andrews in the one week then you can sign me up. I just love visiting Scotland and playing links golf" – Rich Beem

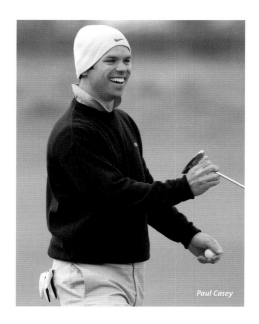

Paul Casey

dunhill, we had exactly the same second shot on that hole. So we hit exactly the same club and the same ball. In the end I think it was worth a shot of a difference."

Since Montgomerie would go on to win by a stroke from Kenneth Ferrie, the decision to rely on the shots which had served him so well in July undoubtedly played a significant role in assisting the seven-time Order of Merit winner to secure his 29th European Tour International Schedule victory in 18 years as a professional.

Like many who have won at St Andrews before him – notably Bobby Jones, as well as past dunhill links champions such as Stephen Gallacher and Lee Westwood – it took time for the Old Course to work its charm on Montgomerie. But, after opening up with a 70 at Carnoustie to trail the first round leaders Rich Beem, David Howell and Alessandro Tadini by three strokes, Montgomerie arrived on the first tee at St Andrews on Friday morning feeling so relaxed and assured, he sensed something special was at hand.

Already the course record holder at Carnoustie and Muirfield, Montgomerie went on to match David Frost's lengthened Old Course record of 65 thanks to an

Rurik Gobel (centre) and Henrik Stenson (right) are presented with the Team Competition Trophy by Johann Rupert, Chairman of the dunhill links championship committee

astonishing opening surge. Six under par after the first six holes – he made four birdies and an eagle – the Scot compiled one of the great rounds of his career. It was an error free performance which mocked the prevailing wisdom that he could not produce his best golf in strong winds. "To shoot 65 with no bogeys in such conditions was as good as I've ever done," he said.

Since the average professional score that day at St Andrews was 73.3, Montgomerie's 65 was arguably even more impressive than the 64s he carded in calmer conditions at Carnoustie and Muirfield. Having played in professional competition at St Andrews every year since 1988, Montgomerie wryly recalled how, when Scotland were losing Dunhill Cup ties to Paraguay, India and China, the famous links course was far from his favourite venue. "I'm glad I was able to overcome that," he smiled. "Because I remember when your sports editors made up some interesting headlines!"

On Saturday at Kingsbarns, he slipped back with a 73 in blustery conditions while

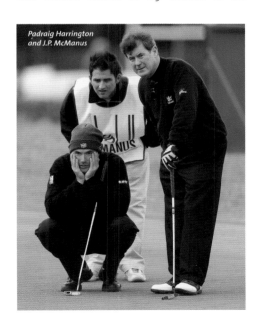

Padraig Harrington and J.P. McManus

Team Results

Pos	Name	Rd1	Rd2	Rd3	Rd4	Total		€	£
1	Henrik STENSON and Rurik Gobel	67	64	62	66	259	-29	41,400.94	28,558.68
2	Warren ABERY and Chad Morse	63	65	70	64	262	-26	17,940.41	12,375.43
	Kenneth FERRIE and Jonathan Edwards	64	65	60	73	262	-26	17,940.41	12,375.43
	Rich BEEM and John Tyson	62	65	70	65	262	-26	17,940.41	12,375.43
5	Anders HANSEN and Peter Schmeichel	66	63	70	64	263	-25	6,210.14	4,283.80
	Padraig HARRINGTON and J.P. McManus	64	66	67	66	263	-25	6,210.14	4,283.80
7	Francesco MOLINARI and Edoardo Molinari	66	63	70	65	264	-24	4,140.09	2,855.87
8	Andrew MARSHALL and Eric Watson	64	67	69	66	266	-22	4,140.09	2,855.87
	Matthew RICHARDSON and Johnathan Joseph	65	69	65	67	266	-22	4,140.09	2,855.87
10	Simon DYSON and Mark Pears	66	67	66	68	267	-21	4,140.09	2,855.87
	Søren KJELDSEN and Gerry Tvedt	66	66	68	67	267	-21	4,140.09	2,855.87
12	Nick O'HERN and Steve Waugh	67	66	66	69	268	-20	4,140.09	2,855.87
	Christian CÉVAËR and Allan Taylor	62	68	69	69	268	-20	4,140.09	2,855.87
14	Colin MONTGOMERIE and Michael Douglas	68	63	69	69	269	-19	4,140.09	2,855.87
	Bradley DREDGE and Eric J. Gleacher	62	69	68	70	269	-19	4,140.09	2,855.87
	Martin DOYLE and Michael Wang	66	69	64	70	269	-19	4,140.09	2,855.87
17	Ricardo GONZALEZ and Andrew Strauss	67	67	66	70	270	-18	4,140.09	2,855.87
	Ignacio GARRIDO and Ladina King	69	64	67	70	270	-18	4,140.09	2,855.87
19	Søren HANSEN and Alan G. Quasha	68	67	64	72	271	-17	4,140.09	2,855.87
20	Pierre FULKE and Phillip H. Morse	66	64	70	73	273	-15	4,140.09	2,855.87

Invest in your game.

PROQUIP

WINNING WEATHERWEAR™

ProQuip Ltd, North Berwick, Scotland. Sales: 01620 892219 www.proquipgolf.com

Ian Poulter and Mark Roe

Ferrie, who came from behind to thwart Montgomerie in the Smurfit European Open at The K Club at the beginning of July, forged ahead thanks to a timely 67 at St Andrews, which meant he took a five shot lead into the final day.

In all his previous 28 European Tour successes, Montgomerie had never won coming from five shots behind on the final day, but all that was about to change. Ferrie lost his way midway through the front nine on Sunday and when the duo turned for home on The Loop, they were level.

Montgomerie, however, suffered a mini-collapse of his own when he three putted the 11th and carded a double bogey on the 12th to briefly hand the initiative back to the Englishman. But, if there was a turning point in the winning of the first prize of €662,415 (£449,741), it came on the 15th when Montgomerie holed a 45 foot putt for birdie and Ferrie three putted for bogey.

It left the pair level again and the Scot needing to birdie the 18th, after Ferrie could only make par, to win. When he drove left of the green and putted from 90 feet away to within four feet of the cup, Montgomerie somehow managed to prevent any negative images of Doug Sanders missing a similar putt in the 1970 Open Championship from entering his thoughts.

He knew the putt broke from left to right and that it needed to be struck more firmly than you might think from a first guess. "I was trying to remember all the ones just like it that I'd holed over the years," he said. "This was one I wasn't going to miss."

While the main focus lay on a third Scottish victory in five stagings of the dunhill links championship – Paul Lawrie won in 2001 and Stephen Gallacher in 2004 - it also turned out to be a rewarding week for Sweden's Henrik Stenson and South African stockbroker Rurik Gobel who, on 29 under par 259, won the team prize, finishing three shots ahead of three teams including Ferrie and his amateur partner, the former Olympic gold medal triple jumper, Jonathan Edwards.

Michael Douglas and Catherine Zeta-Jones

Mike Aitken
The Scotsman

Pos	Name		Rd1	Rd2	Rd3	Rd4	Total		€	£
1	Colin MONTGOMERIE	Scot	70	65	73	71	279	-9	662,415.10	449,741.39
2	Kenneth FERRIE	Eng	68	68	67	77	280	-8	441,607.30	299,825.72
3	Henrik STENSON	Swe	69	74	65	73	281	-7	188,788.30	128,176.29
	Padraig HARRINGTON	Ire	70	70	71	70	281	-7	188,788.30	128,176.29
	Anders HANSEN	Den	69	71	72	69	281	-7	188,788.30	128,176.29
	Robert KARLSSON	Swe	70	74	69	68	281	-7	188,788.30	128,176.29
7	Pierre FULKE	Swe	71	66	72	73	282	-6	88,101.21	59,815.61
	Ricardo GONZALEZ	Arg	69	68	71	74	282	-6	88,101.21	59,815.61
	Darren CLARKE	N.Ire	68	75	69	70	282	-6	88,101.21	59,815.61
	Lee WESTWOOD	Eng	71	71	69	71	282	-6	88,101.21	59,815.61
	Stephen GALLACHER	Scot	74	73	67	68	282	-6	88,101.21	59,815.61
	Titch MOORE	SA	72	68	73	69	282	-6	88,101.21	59,815.61
13	Søren KJELDSEN	Den	70	72	69	72	283	-5	61,074.67	41,466.15
	Maarten LAFEBER	NL	72	70	73	68	283	-5	61,074.67	41,466.15
	Miles TUNNICLIFF	Eng	71	71	72	69	283	-5	61,074.67	41,466.15
16	Simon KHAN	Eng	69	72	74	69	284	-4	53,655.63	36,429.06
	Raymond RUSSELL	Scot	73	70	72	69	284	-4	53,655.63	36,429.06
	Paul BROADHURST	Eng	70	71	73	70	284	-4	53,655.63	36,429.06
19	Carlos RODILES	Sp	70	73	69	73	285	-3	46,998.35	31,909.15
	Nick O'HERN	Aus	68	75	70	72	285	-3	46,998.35	31,909.15
	David CARTER	Eng	72	71	71	71	285	-3	46,998.35	31,909.15
	Gary ORR	Scot	72	71	70	72	285	-3	46,998.35	31,909.15
23	Bradley DREDGE	Wal	68	73	73	72	286	-2	41,334.70	28,063.86
	Peter GUSTAFSSON	Swe	73	68	71	74	286	-2	41,334.70	28,063.86
	Paul CASEY	Eng	68	70	72	76	286	-2	41,334.70	28,063.86
	Peter HANSON	Swe	73	71	71	71	286	-2	41,334.70	28,063.86
	Johan AXGREN	Swe	73	70	72	71	286	-2	41,334.70	28,063.86
28	Scott DRUMMOND	Scot	71	72	69	75	287	-1	33,120.75	22,487.07
	Jean VAN DE VELDE	Fr	72	74	70	71	287	-1	33,120.75	22,487.07
	Andrew MARSHALL	Eng	70	70	74	73	287	-1	33,120.75	22,487.07
	Brian DAVIS	Eng	68	71	77	71	287	-1	33,120.75	22,487.07
	Mark FOSTER	Eng	70	70	73	74	287	-1	33,120.75	22,487.07
	Rich BEEM	USA	67	73	75	72	287	-1	33,120.75	22,487.07
	Peter HEDBLOM	Swe	70	69	76	72	287	-1	33,120.75	22,487.07
	Sam LITTLE	Eng	73	71	71	72	287	-1	33,120.75	22,487.07
	Martin DOYLE	Aus	73	72	66	76	287	-1	33,120.75	22,487.07
37	Christian CÉVAËR	Fr	69	74	72	73	288	0	27,026.54	18,349.45
	Brett RUMFORD	Aus	68	70	78	72	288	0	27,026.54	18,349.45
	David HOWELL	Eng	67	74	76	71	288	0	27,026.54	18,349.45
	Anthony WALL	Eng	69	72	73	74	288	0	27,026.54	18,349.45
41	Mark MURLESS	SA	71	76	69	73	289	1	22,257.15	15,111.31
	Alessandro TADINI	It	67	72	73	77	289	1	22,257.15	15,111.31
	Warren ABERY	SA	69	71	75	74	289	1	22,257.15	15,111.31
	Roger CHAPMAN	Eng	71	72	71	75	289	1	22,257.15	15,111.31
	Barry LANE	Eng	72	70	74	73	289	1	22,257.15	15,111.31
	Richard STERNE	SA	74	71	71	73	289	1	22,257.15	15,111.31
	Niclas FASTH	Swe	70	72	75	72	289	1	22,257.15	15,111.31
	Paul MCGINLEY	Ire	74	71	72	72	289	1	22,257.15	15,111.31
49	Nick DOUGHERTY	Eng	68	74	73	75	290	2	17,885.21	12,143.02
	Simon DYSON	Eng	69	73	73	75	290	2	17,885.21	12,143.02
	Darren FICHARDT	SA	71	73	72	74	290	2	17,885.21	12,143.02
52	Richard GREEN	Aus	70	71	70	80	291	3	13,380.79	9,084.78
	Phillip ARCHER	Eng	70	73	71	77	291	3	13,380.79	9,084.78
	Ian POULTER	Eng	71	73	72	75	291	3	13,380.79	9,084.78
	Mark ROE	Eng	70	74	72	75	291	3	13,380.79	9,084.78
	Alastair FORSYTH	Scot	73	74	68	76	291	3	13,380.79	9,084.78
	Andrew COLTART	Scot	70	76	71	74	291	3	13,380.79	9,084.78
	Ignacio GARRIDO	Sp	74	66	75	76	291	3	13,380.79	9,084.78
	David PARK	Wal	70	72	74	75	291	3	13,380.79	9,084.78
	Terry PILKADARIS	Aus	74	65	76	76	291	3	13,380.79	9,084.78
61	Markus BRIER	Aut	72	70	75	76	293	5	10,532.40	7,150.89
	Joakim BÄCKSTRÖM	Swe	70	75	71	77	293	5	10,532.40	7,150.89
63	José Manuel LARA	Sp	70	70	77	77	294	6	9,737.50	6,611.20
	James KINGSTON	SA	70	75	70	79	294	6	9,737.50	6,611.20
65	Eduardo ROMERO	Arg	69	74	74	83	300	12	9,141.33	6,206.43
66	Santiago LUNA	Sp	71	76	71		218	2	7,393.86	5,020.00
	Peter BAKER	Eng	69	75	74		218	2	7,393.86	5,020.00
	Francesco MOLINARI	It	69	73	76		218	2	7,393.86	5,020.00
	Edward LOAR	USA	71	74	73		218	2	7,393.86	5,020.00
	Charl SCHWARTZEL	SA	74	72	72		218	2	7,393.86	5,020.00
	Jamie DONALDSON	Wal	72	70	76		218	2	7,393.86	5,020.00
	Martin MARITZ	SA	75	70	73		218	2	7,393.86	5,020.00

Total Prize Fund
€3,986,410 £2,706,542

WGC – American Express Championship

San Francisco, USA
October 6-9 • 2005

Harding Park

Par	Yards	Metres
70	7086	6478

Pos	Name	Score		
1	**Tiger WOODS**	270	-10	
2	John DALY	270	-10	
3	Sergio GARCIA	272	-8	
	Colin MONTGOMERIE	272	-8	
	Henrik STENSON	272	-8	
6	David HOWELL	275	-5	
	Graeme McDOWELL	275	-5	
	Vijay SINGH	275	-5	
	David TOMS	275	-5	
10	Stephen AMES	276	-4	

Round One	Round Two	Round Three	Round Four

EUROPEAN TOUR ORDER OF MERIT
(After 43 tournaments)

Pos	Name	€	
1	**Colin MONTGOMERIE**	2,565,089.47	
2	Michael CAMPBELL	2,434,069.44	
3	Retief GOOSEN	2,261,211.06	
4	Angel CABRERA	1,834,027.30	
5	David HOWELL	1,769,207.50	
6	Paul McGINLEY	1,629,762.77	
7	Thomas BJÖRN	1,561,189.62	
8	Henrik STENSON	1,535,749.73	
9	Kenneth FERRIE	1,338,536.86	
10	Sergio GARCIA	1,272,251.44	

My Life.
My Tournament.

All around the course, the sponsor's slogan proclaimed: 'My Life. My Card.' For Tiger Woods, it could as easily have read: 'My Life. My Tournament.' For, after a thrilling week in San Francisco, the World Number One picked up his fourth World Golf Championships – American Express Championship in six years.

The main challenge to the American came from European Tour Members but ultimately it was the greatest player of a generation, playing in front of an adoring crowd at Harding Park, who emerged triumphant, defeating John Daly in a play-off to win the Gene Sarazen Trophy. It was also, remarkably, his tenth individual WGC success.

Woods first played Harding Park as a 12 year old and a few years later spent his college days at Stanford University, some 20 miles south of the city. He described the area as "my second home" and the huge crowds which lined the fairways were filled with old college friends. Roars reverberated after his every shot but he had to draw on every ounce of his considerable experience to eventually claim the title.

The World Golf Championships were designed to bring the best players in the world together and in San Francisco the theory worked to perfection. Part of the success came from the course itself, a once treasured but long-neglected municipal outlet which was spectacularly reborn two years ago. Harding Park had last hosted a US PGA Tour event in 1969 but had subsequently fallen into disrepair. However, it was rebuilt and proved itself a worthy test for the world's best golfers over four days of absorbing competition.

The leaderboard was packed with names such as Sergio Garcia and David Howell, Colin Montgomerie and Henrik Stenson, Daly and Woods, all battling for one of the sport's biggest prizes.

Montgomerie, who only a few days earlier had won the dunhill links championship at St Andrews, was riding the crest of a wave and started with a course record 64.

Sergio Garcia

John Daly and Colin Montgomerie

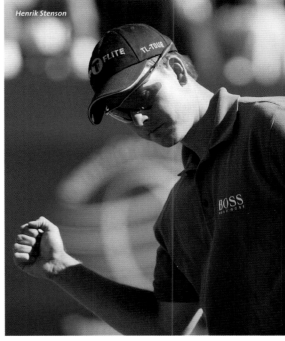

Henrik Stenson

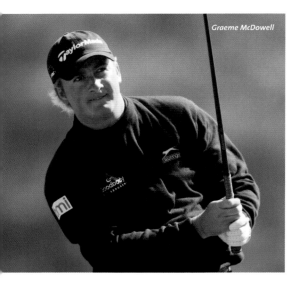

Graeme McDowell

He continued to lead at the halfway stage, although Howell, with a second successive 67, and Daly were only one shot behind, and it was not until Daly passed him midway through the third round that the Scot finally relinquished pole position.

Montgomerie battled hard during the final round but the course was unyielding. A birdie on the 17th took him within a stroke of the leaders but it was not to be his day. His consolation was a return to the summit of European golf as he overhauled Michael Campbell in his quest to win an eighth Order of Merit title.

Montgomerie was joined in a tie for third place by Garcia and Stenson. Garcia, who was finishing in the top ten for the fifth time in six WGC - American Express Championships, enjoyed four sub-70 rounds.

Meanwhile Stenson further underlined his growing reputation on the world stage, conducting himself with a calmness that belied his relative inexperience at this level. For the first two days he played in the company of Phil Mickelson, outplaying his more famous partner by three strokes - 137 to 140 - and in the final round he was not intimidated by Woods in any shape or form.

"This is a hidden secret. It's just amazing. There are so many great public golf courses we need to find. The older the better, because they seem to be more friendly towards driving and playing shots " – John Daly

Final Results

Two birdies in the last three holes provided further evidence that he has the ability and belief to win at this level.

Even so, the battle for the title became a duel between Daly and Woods. Thanks to his spectacular driving and all round excellence from tee to green, Daly led going into the final round and kept his nose in front as Woods made a characteristic charge on the back nine. Then, as he stood on the threshold of a famous win, his putter betrayed him.

If ever there was a tournament which reinforced the old idiom that 'you drive for show but putt for dough' this was it as Daly consistently launched massive tee-shots only for his putter to go cold. It occurred on the penultimate green when three putts cost him the outright lead and again, most cruelly of all, when he again three putted

the second play-off hole – missing finally from three feet - to gift Woods the title.

There was no immediate celebration from Woods. He knew in his heart what it would have meant to Daly, winner of the 1991 US PGA Championship at The 1995 Open Championship, to add this title to his career record and how cruel the game can be.

Woods, however, is the ultimate competitor and, once the dust had settled and the thrilling realisation of another victory had set it, the 29 year old would have been forgiven for recalling a previous slogan employed by the sponsors: 'That'll Do Nicely!'

Rod Williams

Pos	Name		Rd1	Rd2	Rd3	Rd4	Total		€	£
1	Tiger WOODS	USA	67	68	68	67	270	-10	1,078,120.00	734,629.35
2	John DALY	USA	67	67	67	69	270	-10	621,992.30	423,824.62
3	Sergio GARCIA	Sp	67	69	67	69	272	-8	293,303.90	199,856.84
	Henrik STENSON	Swe	70	67	67	68	272	-8	293,303.90	199,856.84
	Colin MONTGOMERIE	Scot	64	69	69	70	272	-8	293,303.90	199,856.84
6	Vijay SINGH	Fiji	67	70	69	69	275	-5	155,498.10	105,956.17
	David HOWELL	Eng	67	67	74	67	275	-5	155,498.10	105,956.17
	David TOMS	USA	68	68	70	69	275	-5	155,498.10	105,956.17
	Graeme MCDOWELL	N.Ire	69	70	68	68	275	-5	155,498.10	105,956.17
10	Stephen AMES	T&T	72	64	71	69	276	-4	116,105.20	79,113.91
11	Luke DONALD	Eng	70	71	68	68	277	-3	95,372.14	64,986.43
	Shigeki MARUYAMA	Jpn	74	69	67	67	277	-3	95,372.14	64,986.43
	Stuart APPLEBY	Aus	71	65	69	72	277	-3	95,372.14	64,986.43
	Davis LOVE III	USA	71	68	71	67	277	-3	95,372.14	64,986.43
15	Fred COUPLES	USA	74	69	66	69	278	-2	72,427.54	49,352.02
	Jim FURYK	USA	68	67	71	72	278	-2	72,427.54	49,352.02
	Chad CAMPBELL	USA	67	70	70	71	278	-2	72,427.54	49,352.02
18	Bradley DREDGE	Wal	69	69	72	69	279	-1	63,857.87	43,512.66
	Charl SCHWARTZEL	SA	72	66	74	67	279	-1	63,857.87	43,512.66
	Tim CLARK	SA	69	69	72	69	279	-1	63,857.87	43,512.66
	Mike WEIR	Can	73	67	70	69	279	-1	63,857.87	43,512.66
	Ian POULTER	Eng	67	70	72	70	279	-1	63,857.87	43,512.66
	Stephen DODD	Wal	70	68	70	71	279	-1	63,857.87	43,512.66
	Angel CABRERA	Arg	69	66	72	72	279	-1	63,857.87	43,512.66
25	Billy MAYFAIR	USA	69	67	73	71	280	0	54,735.32	37,296.57
	Mark CALCAVECCHIA	USA	67	68	74	71	280	0	54,735.32	37,296.57
	Yasuharu IMANO	Jpn	69	68	72	71	280	0	54,735.32	37,296.57
	Brandt JOBE	USA	68	71	71	70	280	0	54,735.32	37,296.57
29	Phil MICKELSON	USA	71	69	73	68	281	1	49,759.38	33,905.97
	Adam SCOTT	Aus	68	70	69	74	281	1	49,759.38	33,905.97
	Fred FUNK	USA	67	68	75	71	281	1	49,759.38	33,905.97
32	Vaughn TAYLOR	USA	71	72	66	73	282	2	47,271.41	32,210.67
	Jason BOHN	USA	70	68	70	74	282	2	47,271.41	32,210.67
	Kenny PERRY	USA	76	69	69	68	282	2	47,271.41	32,210.67
35	Paul MCGINLEY	Ire	73	65	72	73	283	3	45,198.10	30,797.92
	Sean O'HAIR	USA	68	67	71	77	283	3	45,198.10	30,797.92
37	Ben CRANE	USA	70	68	76	70	284	4	42,710.13	29,102.62
	Niclas FASTH	Swe	70	70	73	71	284	4	42,710.13	29,102.62
	Olin BROWNE	USA	67	74	73	70	284	4	42,710.13	29,102.62
	Peter LONARD	Aus	73	71	69	71	284	4	42,710.13	29,102.62
41	Miguel Angel JIMÉNEZ	Sp	69	70	73	73	285	5	40,222.16	27,407.32
	Rodney PAMPLING	Aus	67	71	76	71	285	5	40,222.16	27,407.32
43	K J CHOI	Kor	70	71	72	73	286	6	38,148.86	25,994.58
	Simon YATES	Scot	73	68	70	75	286	6	38,148.86	25,994.58
	Zach JOHNSON	USA	68	69	74	75	286	6	38,148.86	25,994.58
46	Michael CAMPBELL	NZ	71	68	72	76	287	7	35,868.22	24,440.55
	Kenneth FERRIE	Eng	74	67	71	75	287	7	35,868.22	24,440.55
	Justin LEONARD	USA	75	72	71	69	287	7	35,868.22	24,440.55
	Stewart CINK	USA	70	72	75	70	287	7	35,868.22	24,440.55
50	Joe OGILVIE	USA	71	74	68	75	288	8	34,831.57	23,734.18
51	Nick DOUGHERTY	Eng	71	74	72	72	289	9	33,587.58	22,886.53
	Lee WESTWOOD	Eng	71	75	75	68	289	9	33,587.58	22,886.53
	José María OLAZÁBAL	Sp	72	72	76	69	289	9	33,587.58	22,886.53
	Richard GREEN	Aus	69	74	76	70	289	9	33,587.58	22,886.53
	Jyoti RANDHAWA	Ind	70	70	74	75	289	9	33,587.58	22,886.53
56	Nick O'HERN	Aus	75	69	71	75	290	10	31,928.93	21,756.33
	Mark HENSBY	Aus	72	74	71	73	290	10	31,928.93	21,756.33
	Bart BRYANT	USA	71	76	71	72	290	10	31,928.93	21,756.33
59	Gavin COLES	Aus	71	74	75	71	291	11	31,099.61	21,191.23
60	Thongchai JAIDEE	Thai	73	72	73	74	292	12	30,684.95	20,908.68
61	Tom LEHMAN	USA	73	74	72	74	293	13	30,270.29	20,626.13
62	Euan WALTERS	Aus	74	72	75	73	294	14	29,648.30	20,202.31
	Scott VERPLANK	USA	72	69	76	77	294	14	29,648.30	20,202.31
64	S K HO	Kor	72	77	71	75	295	15	28,818.97	19,637.20
	Chris DIMARCO	USA	71	75	73	76	295	15	28,818.97	19,637.20
66	Ted PURDY	USA	71	75	75	76	297	17	28,196.98	19,213.38
67	Padraig HARRINGTON	Ire	74	72	80	73	299	19	27,782.32	18,930.83
68	Neil CHEETHAM	Eng	77	78	72	76	303	23	27,367.66	18,648.28
69	Warren ABERY	SA	80	77	75	74	306	26	26,953.00	18,365.73
70	Thomas BJÖRN	Den	71	67	74	W/D			26,331.00	17,941.90
	Steve ELKINGTON	Aus	73	W/D					26,331.00	17,941.90

Total Prize Fund
€6,144,040 £4,186,539

Angel Cabrera

Abama Open de Canarias

Tenerife, Spain
October 6-9 • 2005

Abama Golf Club

Par	Yards	Metres
71	6857	6271

1	**John BICKERTON**	**274**	**-10**	
2	Michael KIRK	279	-5	
	Stuart LITTLE	279	-5	
4	Johan AXGREN	280	-4	
	Mark ROE	280	-4	
	Marc WARREN	280	-4	
7	Lee SLATTERY	281	-3	
	Fredrik WIDMARK	281	-3	
9	José Manuel CARRILES	282	-2	
	Stephen SCAHILL	282	-2	

☼	☼	☂	☂
Round One	Round Two	Round Three	Round Four

EUROPEAN TOUR ORDER OF MERIT
(After 44 tournaments)

Pos		€	
1	**Colin MONTGOMERIE**	**2,565,089.47**	
2	Michael CAMPBELL	2,434,069.44	
3	Retief GOOSEN	2,261,211.06	
4	Angel CABRERA	1,834,027.30	
5	David HOWELL	1,769,207.50	
6	Paul McGINLEY	1,629,762.77	
7	Thomas BJÖRN	1,561,189.62	
8	Henrik STENSON	1,535,749.73	
9	Kenneth FERRIE	1,338,536.86	
10	Sergio GARCIA	1,272,251.44	

Fighting For The Future

Some things are worth the wait and in the case of John Bickerton his long overdue maiden victory in the dual ranking Abama Open de Canarias could not have come at a more opportune time.

While the world's elite were contesting the World Golf Championships – American Express Championship in San Francisco, there was serious work on the agenda for many of The European Tour regulars. Tenerife may be a popular tourist destination, but for a number of the 132 players teeing up at the spectacular Abama Golf Club this was no holiday.

The reason, of course, was the fact that the race to keep their cards for the 2006 campaign had entered the home straight. Pale faces and furrowed brows could be seen all along the range as players hovering around 115th position on The European Tour Order of Merit fought for their futures.

England's Mark Roe, for example, would have loved to have been at home celebrating the fifth birthday of his twin

daughters, Alexandra and Emily. He was, however, on the cusp of keeping his card and arrived on the island in 117th place in the Order of Merit.

So Roe, the winner of three European Tour titles between 1989 and 1994, teed up in the 500th event of his European Tour career, coincidently in the same week as Spain's Santiago Luna reached this notable milestone. By the end of the week Roe was enjoying celebrations of his own after finishing fourth and climbing to 107th place – a finger touch away from safety.

Bickerton was another player who arrived seeking something special. The Englishman started the week at 118th in the Order of Merit. He needed a top five finish to virtually eliminate the prospect of returning to the Qualifying School. He may not have played

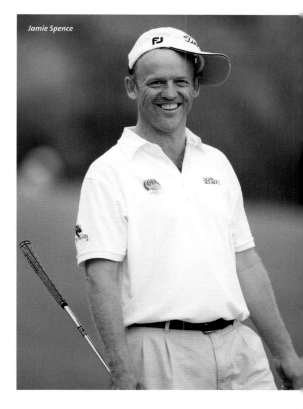

Jamie Spence

Michael Kirk

Mark Roe

"Abama is a golf course that makes you think from the first tee, you cannot go out there and just hit driver, you've got to think about placing the ball in a position where you can make a score. If you miss a green, it never leaves you an easy chip" – John Bickerton

Final Results

as many tournaments as Roe but after 286 attempts including five runners-up finishes, had good reason to consider whether he would claim that elusive first win on The European Tour.

In 1999 he reached a career high of 20th on the Order of Merit. He had remained in the top 80 for each of the next five years. Now he too, was fighting for his future.

The 35 year old from Droitwich, a graduate of the European Challenge Tour in 1998, made steady progress over the first three days until finally taking a one stroke lead with one round to play. He birdied three of the first ten holes of the final round and with four successive sub-70 rounds he cruised to a five stroke victory. While the cheque for €75,000 (£51,104) was obviously welcome, the all important one year exemption represented far greater riches.

Others had reason to celebrate, such as South African Michael Kirk, whose share of second place ensured he had done enough to graduate to The European Tour from the Challenge Tour. Left-handed Englishman Stuart Little had no worries about his future as he was already enjoying the best season of his career, and his share of second place with Kirk represented his best finish on The European Tour since joining in 1992.

Together they celebrated, although none more so than Bickerton and, of course, Roe's wife, Julia, and their twin daughters whose birthday celebrations were made all the happier by their father's successful journey from the family home in Surrey to Tenerife.

Mitchell Platts

Stuart Little

Pos	Name		Rd1	Rd2	Rd3	Rd4	Total		€	£
1	John BICKERTON	Eng	69	68	69	68	274	-10	75,000.00	51,104.89
2	Michael KIRK	SA	69	66	75	69	279	-5	39,085.00	26,632.46
	Stuart LITTLE	Eng	68	67	72	72	279	-5	39,085.00	26,632.46
4	Mark ROE	Eng	69	68	71	72	280	-4	19,110.00	13,021.53
	Johan AXGREN	Swe	72	67	71	70	280	-4	19,110.00	13,021.53
	Marc WARREN	Scot	68	71	72	69	280	-4	19,110.00	13,021.53
7	Lee SLATTERY	Eng	69	72	71	69	281	-3	12,375.00	8,432.31
	Fredrik WIDMARK	Swe	70	73	67	71	281	-3	12,375.00	8,432.31
9	José Manuel CARRILES	Sp	72	70	66	74	282	-2	9,540.00	6,500.54
	Stephen SCAHILL	NZ	70	66	73	73	282	-2	9,540.00	6,500.54
11	Peter BAKER	Eng	69	68	72	74	283	-1	7,026.43	4,787.80
	Jamie SPENCE	Eng	69	69	72	73	283	-1	7,026.43	4,787.80
	David CARTER	Eng	74	71	70	68	283	-1	7,026.43	4,787.80
	Martin MARITZ	SA	74	71	72	66	283	-1	7,026.43	4,787.80
	Gareth DAVIES		74	71	73	65	283	-1	7,026.43	4,787.80
	Gareth PADDISON	NZ	74	68	68	73	283	-1	7,026.43	4,787.80
	Gregory BOURDY	Fr	69	71	72	71	283	-1	7,026.43	4,787.80
18	Hernan REY	Arg	72	69	73	70	284	0	5,265.00	3,587.56
	Benoit TEILLERIA	Fr	72	72	69	71	284	0	5,265.00	3,587.56
	Ivo GINER	Sp	72	72	72	68	284	0	5,265.00	3,587.56
	Phillip ARCHER	Eng	70	72	71	71	284	0	5,265.00	3,587.56
	Roger CHAPMAN	Eng	69	72	71	72	284	0	5,265.00	3,587.56
	Patrik SJÖLAND	Swe	69	76	72	67	284	0	5,265.00	3,587.56
	Ignacio GARRIDO	Sp	70	70	73	71	284	0	5,265.00	3,587.56
25	Jesus Maria ARRUTI	Sp	70	74	70	71	285	1	4,140.00	2,820.99
	Simon HURD	Eng	69	72	67	77	285	1	4,140.00	2,820.99
	Gordon BRAND JNR	Scot	70	74	68	73	285	1	4,140.00	2,820.99
	Kariem BARAKA	Ger	71	68	70	76	285	1	4,140.00	2,820.99
	Mikko ILONEN	Fin	72	69	68	76	285	1	4,140.00	2,820.99
	Sam WALKER	Eng	80	65	69	71	285	1	4,140.00	2,820.99
	Daniel VANCSIK	Arg	72	67	70	76	285	1	4,140.00	2,820.99
	Manuel QUIROS	Sp	73	68	75	69	285	1	4,140.00	2,820.99
	Marcus FRASER	Aus	71	72	74	68	285	1	4,140.00	2,820.99
34	Andrew MARSHALL	Eng	72	73	73	68	286	2	3,240.00	2,207.73
	Santiago LUNA	Sp	70	72	71	73	286	2	3,240.00	2,207.73
	Michael JONZON	Swe	74	68	73	71	286	2	3,240.00	2,207.73
	Carl SUNESON	Sp	71	71	71	73	286	2	3,240.00	2,207.73
	Paul DWYER	Eng	76	67	72	71	286	2	3,240.00	2,207.73
	Sion E BEBB	Wal	72	72	69	73	286	2	3,240.00	2,207.73
40	Michael HOEY	N.Ire	72	73	72	70	287	3	2,790.00	1,901.10
	Lars BROVOLD	Nor	73	70	74	70	287	3	2,790.00	1,901.10
	Denny LUCAS	Eng	72	70	76	69	287	3	2,790.00	1,901.10
	Carlos GARCIA	Sp	73	70	72	72	287	3	2,790.00	1,901.10
44	Alvaro VELASCO	Sp	71	73	70	74	288	4	2,295.00	1,563.81
	Ilya GORONESKOUL	Fr	71	72	73	72	288	4	2,295.00	1,563.81
	Titch MOORE	SA	68	68	76	76	288	4	2,295.00	1,563.81
	Miguel Angel MARTIN	Sp	71	71	76	70	288	4	2,295.00	1,563.81
	Niki ZITNY	Aut	76	68	74	70	288	4	2,295.00	1,563.81
	Mark FOSTER	Eng	72	70	72	74	288	4	2,295.00	1,563.81
	Garry HOUSTON	Wal	73	65	77	73	288	4	2,295.00	1,563.81
51	Magnus P. ATLEVI	Swe	74	71	72	72	289	5	1,710.00	1,165.19
	Carlos RODILES	Sp	74	69	72	74	289	5	1,710.00	1,165.19
	Jarrod MOSELEY	Aus	73	67	73	76	289	5	1,710.00	1,165.19
	Ben MASON	Eng	71	70	73	75	289	5	1,710.00	1,165.19
	Leif WESTERBERG	Swe	71	72	73	73	289	5	1,710.00	1,165.19
	David DIXON	Eng	71	70	73	75	289	5	1,710.00	1,165.19
57	Stephen BROWNE	Ire	74	68	73	75	290	6	1,350.00	919.89
	Ariel CANETE	Arg	72	73	73	72	290	6	1,350.00	919.89
	Johan SKÖLD	Swe	66	76	76	72	290	6	1,350.00	919.89
60	Ricardo GONZALEZ	Arg	69	74	73	75	291	7	1,260.00	858.56
61	Gary CLARK	Eng	73	72	71	76	292	8	1,147.50	781.90
	Miguel CARBALLO	Arg	71	72	74	75	292	8	1,147.50	781.90
	David HIGGINS	Ire	77	68	81	66	292	8	1,147.50	781.90
	Pedro LINHART	Sp	74	70	78	70	292	8	1,147.50	781.90
65	Richard MCEVOY	Eng	71	73	77	72	293	9	1,012.50	689.92
	Alvaro SALTO	Sp	71	73	72	77	293	9	1,012.50	689.92
67	Rafael GOMEZ	Arg	71	69	77	77	294	10	922.50	628.59
	Edward RUSH	Eng	71	69	81	73	294	10	922.50	628.59
69	Robert ROCK	Eng	71	73	82	71	297	13	855.00	582.60
70	Matthew MORRIS	Eng	76	69	72	91	308	24	820.00	558.75
71	Andres ROMERO	Arg	66	72	73	DISQ	211	-3		

Total Prize Fund
€450,675   £307,089

Open de Madrid

Madrid, Spain
October 13-16 • 2005

Club de Campo

Par	Yards	Metres
71	6967	6371

1	**Raphaël JACQUELIN**	**261**	**-23**	
2	Paul LAWRIE	264	-20	
3	Darren CLARKE	266	-18	
	Anders HANSEN	266	-18	
5	Ian WOOSNAM	267	-17	
6	José Manuel LARA	268	-16	
	Jose-Filipe LIMA	268	-16	
8	Gregory BOURDY	269	-15	
	David LYNN	269	-15	
	Colin MONTGOMERIE	269	-15	

Round One	Round Two	Round Three	Round Four

EUROPEAN TOUR ORDER OF MERIT
(After 45 tournaments)

Pos		€	
1	**Colin MONTGOMERIE**	**2,587,556.14**	
2	Michael CAMPBELL	2,434,069.44	
3	Retief GOOSEN	2,261,211.06	
4	Angel CABRERA	1,834,027.30	
5	David HOWELL	1,769,207.50	
6	Paul McGINLEY	1,629,762.77	
7	Thomas BJÖRN	1,561,189.62	
8	Henrik STENSON	1,535,749.73	
9	Kenneth FERRIE	1,338,536.86	
10	Sergio GARCIA	1,272,251.44	

Past and Present

Andrew Marshall

While the crowds who thronged to Club de Campo ended up admiring a current star of the game in the shape of Frenchman Raphaël Jacquelin who, after 238 European Tour events, eventually claimed a title his golf has deserved, they began the week with a glimpse back at glorious history.

Step forward Seve Ballesteros, Sandy Lyle and Ian Woosnam. Between them, three of European golf's greatest ambassadors of the past 30 years had amassed 11 Harry Vardon Trophies for topping The European Tour Order of Merit and eight Major Championship titles. How appropriate it was that autumn in Madrid reflected the autumn of their careers.

Of course, for Ballesteros, the Open de Madrid represented a comeback. After almost two years out of the game because of a chronic back condition, the question on everybody's lips was how would he cope back in the competitive arena? Also, how would he cope with a demanding Club de Campo course soaked by October rain?

On a damp morning in the Spanish capital, Ballesteros was unusually tense. He had ruled Club de Campo in the past. But two years without hitting a competitive shot took

its toll. Within a few holes he was battling to achieve a score; his optimism diminished by a flurry of errant drives and uncharacteristically indifferent chips and putts.

On the tenth hole however, everyone knew who they were watching when, from his knees, he hit a remarkable five-wood recovery from the trees on his way to a mouthwatering four. Only he would have dared play such a shot in a tournament. Seve was back.

That par settled him. A more composed nine holes followed and only a couple over par the next day, Ballesteros, while missing the cut, had at least a degree of respectability to take away with him. While he was still far from achieving his desired goal of winning on his comeback, a milestone had been passed. There had been no pain, no breakdown and no cricket score. Ballesteros would not be going back to Pedrena contemplating

Paul Lawrie

Open de Madrid

Christopher Hanell

retirement, rather he would be considering his playing schedule for 2006.

Lyle went back to Perthshire to do just the same. Madrid was a watershed for the Scot, too. While it proved the end of his season, he hoped it was not the end of an era. With no exemption for 2006 and therefore no card, the 1985 Open Champion and the master of Augusta National in 1988, had again to think about sitting down during the winter and writing letters requesting invitations.

Woosnam had no such problems. The 2006 European Ryder Cup Captain had plenty on his plate before going to Madrid, and not just matters pertaining to The K Club. Having builders in both his homes in Jersey and Barbados had been stressful and his game had suffered, causing him to miss seven cuts in his previous nine tournaments. However, he was determined to show his potential Ryder Cup players he could still cut it with the best of them. Contending strongly at Club de Campo before finishing fifth gave him a ticket to ride and reasons to be cheerful.

This, however, will go down in the record

"With the trees closing in on you and dangerous ground never far away, being accurate off the tee was so important" – Raphaël Jacquelin

David Carter

Final Results

Pos	Name		Rd1	Rd2	Rd3	Rd4	Total		€	£
1	Raphaël JACQUELIN	Fr	64	64	64	69	261	-23	166,660.00	114,727.47
2	Paul LAWRIE	Scot	68	66	66	64	264	-20	111,110.00	76,487.27
3	Darren CLARKE	N.Ire	64	67	68	67	266	-18	56,300.00	38,756.49
	Anders HANSEN	Den	67	69	66	64	266	-18	56,300.00	38,756.49
5	Ian WOOSNAM	Wal	69	65	68	65	267	-17	42,400.00	29,187.83
6	José Manuel LARA	Sp	67	69	68	64	268	-16	32,500.00	22,372.75
	Jose-Filipe LIMA	Port	66	66	67	69	268	-16	32,500.00	22,372.75
8	Gregory BOURDY	Fr	69	68	67	65	269	-15	22,466.67	15,465.88
	David LYNN	Eng	69	69	65	66	269	-15	22,466.67	15,465.88
	Colin MONTGOMERIE	Scot	72	66	65	66	269	-15	22,466.67	15,465.88
11	Miguel Angel JIMÉNEZ	Sp	72	64	66	68	270	-14	18,400.00	12,666.42
12	Stuart LITTLE	Eng	67	66	68	70	271	-13	14,828.57	10,207.87
	Andrew MARSHALL	Eng	70	68	65	68	271	-13	14,828.57	10,207.87
	James KINGSTON	SA	71	66	68	66	271	-13	14,828.57	10,207.87
	José Maria OLAZÁBAL	Sp	67	69	70	65	271	-13	14,828.57	10,207.87
	Robert-Jan DERKSEN	NL	67	69	66	69	271	-13	14,828.57	10,207.87
	David PARK	Wal	68	67	67	69	271	-13	14,828.57	10,207.87
	Wade ORMSBY	Aus	70	70	65	66	271	-13	14,828.57	10,207.87
19	Alastair FORSYTH	Scot	66	71	67	68	272	-12	11,825.00	8,140.24
	Mark ROE	Eng	63	72	69	68	272	-12	11,825.00	8,140.24
	Garry HOUSTON	Wal	68	71	68	65	272	-12	11,825.00	8,140.24
	Ricardo GONZALEZ	Arg	72	67	64	69	272	-12	11,825.00	8,140.24
23	Robert KARLSSON	Swe	63	76	65	69	273	-11	10,100.00	6,952.76
	Fernando ROCA	Sp	69	68	70	66	273	-11	10,100.00	6,952.76
	Mark FOSTER	Eng	69	69	68	67	273	-11	10,100.00	6,952.76
	Gonzalo FERNANDEZ-CASTANO	Sp	67	71	65	70	273	-11	10,100.00	6,952.76
	Ignacio GARRIDO	Sp	74	65	66	68	273	-11	10,100.00	6,952.76
	Oliver WILSON	Eng	69	68	70	66	273	-11	10,100.00	6,952.76
	Brad KENNEDY	Aus	68	72	66	67	273	-11	10,100.00	6,952.76
30	Christopher HANELL	Swe	69	68	70	68	275	-9	8,450.00	5,816.92
	François DELAMONTAGNE	Fr	67	69	72	67	275	-9	8,450.00	5,816.92
	Gregory HAVRET	Fr	69	68	70	68	275	-9	8,450.00	5,816.92
	Gary EMERSON	Eng	67	64	73	71	275	-9	8,450.00	5,816.92
34	Ian GARBUTT	Eng	69	64	74	69	276	-8	6,900.00	4,749.91
	Phillip ARCHER	Eng	70	67	66	73	276	-8	6,900.00	4,749.91
	Steve WEBSTER	Eng	72	68	69	67	276	-8	6,900.00	4,749.91
	Damien MCGRANE	Ire	68	66	71	71	276	-8	6,900.00	4,749.91
	Simon WAKEFIELD	Eng	73	67	69	67	276	-8	6,900.00	4,749.91
	Johan SKÖLD	Swe	69	68	68	71	276	-8	6,900.00	4,749.91
	Ivo GINER	Sp	75	60	68	73	276	-8	6,900.00	4,749.91
	Stuart MANLEY	Wal	68	70	68	70	276	-8	6,900.00	4,749.91
	Carlos DE CORRAL	Sp	71	66	68	71	276	-8	6,900.00	4,749.91
43	Marcel SIEM	Ger	70	66	70	71	277	-7	5,900.00	4,061.51
44	Martin ERLANDSSON	Swe	67	69	69	73	278	-6	5,000.00	3,441.96
	Scott DRUMMOND	Scot	70	67	74	67	278	-6	5,000.00	3,441.96
	Maarten LAFEBER	NL	67	70	70	71	278	-6	5,000.00	3,441.96
	Francesco MOLINARI	It	72	67	68	71	278	-6	5,000.00	3,441.96
	Miguel Angel MARTIN	Sp	69	67	72	70	278	-6	5,000.00	3,441.96
	Stephen GALLACHER	Scot	69	67	71	71	278	-6	5,000.00	3,441.96
	Markus BRIER	Aut	69	69	71	69	278	-6	5,000.00	3,441.96
	Brett RUMFORD	Aus	66	71	67	74	278	-6	5,000.00	3,441.96
52	Graeme STORM	Eng	66	68	73	72	279	-5	3,437.50	2,366.35
	Fredrik ANDERSSON HED	Swe	69	71	68	71	279	-5	3,437.50	2,366.35
	David DRYSDALE	Scot	72	67	70	70	279	-5	3,437.50	2,366.35
	Simon KHAN	Eng	68	69	72	70	279	-5	3,437.50	2,366.35
	Gary MURPHY	Ire	70	69	68	72	279	-5	3,437.50	2,366.35
	Anthony WALL	Eng	68	69	70	72	279	-5	3,437.50	2,366.35
	Philip GOLDING	Eng	74	65	70	70	279	-5	3,437.50	2,366.35
	Richard BLAND	Eng	73	66	71	69	279	-5	3,437.50	2,366.35
60	Alessandro TADINI	It	69	70	73	68	280	-4	2,700.00	1,858.66
	Mattias ELIASSON	Swe	70	67	71	72	280	-4	2,700.00	1,858.66
	Alvaro SALTO	Sp	69	71	71	69	280	-4	2,700.00	1,858.66
63	Santiago LUNA	Sp	69	69	68	75	281	-3	2,400.00	1,652.14
	Johan AXGREN	Swe	70	70	70	71	281	-3	2,400.00	1,652.14
	Emanuele CANONICA	It	69	68	75	69	281	-3	2,400.00	1,652.14
66	Miles TUNNICLIFF	Eng	71	69	73	69	282	-2	2,006.00	1,380.92
	Neil CHEETHAM	Eng	70	67	70	75	282	-2	2,006.00	1,380.92
	Peter HEDBLOM	Swe	68	70	70	74	282	-2	2,006.00	1,380.92
	Christian CÉVAËR	Fr	66	70	74	72	282	-2	2,006.00	1,380.92
	David CARTER	Eng	70	70	70	72	282	-2	2,006.00	1,380.92
	Jorge MAZARIO (AM)	Sp	69	71	72	70	282	-2		
72	Søren KJELDSEN	Den	69	68	70	74	284	0	1,500.00	1,032.59
73	José Manuel CARRILES	Sp	70	69	75	71	285	1	1,495.50	1,029.49
	Costantino ROCCA	It	71	69	74	71	285	1	1,495.50	1,029.49
75	Rolf MUNTZ	NL	72	67	72	75	286	2	1,491.00	1,026.39

Total Prize Fund
€1,005,980   £692,519

books as the birth of Raphael Jacquelin's career. Imperious and almost unassailable in his determination to break into The European Tour winner's circle, the Frenchman finally pulled it off. At the age of 31, Jacquelin had finally savoured the success his supreme talent deserved.

On the opening day, Robert Karlsson and Mark Roe led with respective 63s. Jacquelin was only a stroke behind, shooting the first of three wonderful and consecutive 64s, and even Spaniard Ivo Giner, whose spectacular second round 60 would have gone in the record book but for the preferred lies in operation all week, had to take a back seat.

Jacquelin was determined. He wanted to lose his label as the best player never to win on The European Tour. His wife, Fanny, was expecting their second child at any time, and he knew quite frankly this was his time and that he could allow no-one to take it away.

His third 64 virtually shut the door, his 21 under par total of 192 giving him a seven shot cushion going into the final round. The enormity of his achievement was measured by the fact that it represented the biggest third round lead of the 2005 season.

Nevertheless in the final round he had to withstand the fiercest test from a Scot who had already beaten a Frenchman from a long way back, six years previously in The Open Championship at Carnoustie.

Ten shots behind Jean Van de Velde in 1999, Paul Lawrie had come back to triumph and at eight adrift this time, the 36 year old Aberdonian gave it his very best shot again, pushing Jacquelin all the way with a closing 64. The Lyon-heart would not be beaten, though, and held off Lawrie with a closing 69 of his own.

Seve Ballesteros had not had to wait quite so long for his first European Tour win but if autumn in Madrid had proved a milestone for the Spaniard, it had, too, for Raphaël Jacquelin.

Norman Dabell

Wade Ormsby

Mallorca Classic

Majorca, Spain
October 20-23 • 2005

Pula Golf Club

Par	Yards	Metres
70	6676	6105

1	José Maria OLAZÁBAL	270	-10	
2	Paul BROADHURST	275	-5	
	Sergio GARCIA	275	-5	
	José Manuel LARA	275	-5	
5	Bradley DREDGE	276	-4	
	Miles TUNNICLIFF	276	-4	
	Simon WAKEFIELD	276	-4	
8	Mattias ELIASSON	277	-3	
	Miguel Angel JIMÉNEZ	277	-3	
	Jean VAN DE VELDE	277	-3	

Round One	Round Two	Round Three	Round Four

EUROPEAN TOUR ORDER OF MERIT
(After 46 tournaments)

Pos		€	
1	Colin MONTGOMERIE	2,587,556.14	
2	Michael CAMPBELL	2,434,069.44	
3	Retief GOOSEN	2,261,211.06	
4	Angel CABRERA	1,834,027.30	
5	David HOWELL	1,769,207.50	
6	Paul McGINLEY	1,629,762.77	
7	Thomas BJÖRN	1,561,189.62	
8	Henrik STENSON	1,535,749.73	
9	Sergio GARCIA	1,384,104.74	
10	Kenneth FERRIE	1,338,536.86	

Sweet
And Special

Those who are few more popular players in the world of golf than José Maria Olazábal and, hence, few more popular winners. A man as gracious in victory as he is in defeat, the Spaniard had gone more than three years since his previous victory by the time he arrived at the Pula Golf Club for the Mallorca Classic, but he was right to feel confident about his chances of bringing an end to the drought.

For one thing, the double Masters Tournament Champion had come into a rich vein of form. He had been playing well in the United States and in Europe and had a look about him that spoke volumes for his inner belief. For another, he was about to put to good use his intimate knowledge of a tricky and testing par 70 layout that he had been involved in redesigning over the previous two years.

Jonathan Lomas

On the face of it, the Pula course did not look too difficult. At 6,676 yards, it was short by modern standards and seemingly at the mercy of the big-hitters. Not so. It was a set-up that demanded accuracy and good course management; an attractive course that could not be bludgeoned into submission.

Which would explain why only 20 players from a field of 120 managed to break par by the end of a tournament which, midway through the final day, had become a cakewalk for Olazábal, a battle for second place for others, and a fight for survival for those trying to hold on to their European Tour cards for another year.

He might be 39, but Olazábal proved that his ambition still burns as strongly as ever. The way he fought back from a crippling and career-threatening injury in the 1990s before going on to win the 1999 Masters Tournament is both a heart-warming and an inspirational tale. But he takes inspiration, too, from the likes of Colin Montgomerie and Vijay Singh, who have both proved that there is competitive life after 40.

In fact, in the final round, Olazábal was paired with Paul Broadhurst, another fortysomething and a former Ryder Cup team-mate of the Spaniard, who had also rediscovered his zest for the game and who was having his best season on The European Tour for almost a decade. Olazábal started the day one shot ahead of the Englishman and Søren Hansen of Denmark, but finished it with victory by five strokes over Broadhurst and two of his Spanish compatriots, Sergio Garcia and José Manuel Lara.

Paul Broadhurst

After the first day, Olazábal had been four shots in arrears of Jonathan Lomas, who posted a 65, but subsequent rounds of 65-70-66 gave him a ten under par total of 270, a well-deserved victory, and a first prize of €250,000 (£170,744).

Mallorca Classic

Peter Hanson

In the final round, Chema, as he is affectionately known, knew he had to make the most of the easier outward half because birdies were harder to come by on the back nine, and by the turn he had done just that to effectively see off the challenge of the field. Out in 31, with birdies at the fourth, fifth, sixth and ninth, Olazábal extended his lead and now it was not so much a matter of whether the Spaniard would win, but by how much.

He had come close to victory earlier in the season, losing a play-off to Phil Mickelson in the BellSouth Classic on the US PGA Tour in April, finishing tied third in The Open Championship at St Andrews in July, and sharing second place at the Linde German Masters in September. But nothing matches the sweet taste of victory and Olazábal was able to revel in it once more. "It is a very special victory and the last three holes were very emotional," he said. "I am very happy because it happened on a course I've been involved with."

With victory in the bag - his 23rd on The European Tour and his 30th worldwide - Olazábal once again turned his attention towards The Ryder Cup and his desire to play at The K Club in September 2006. "I've not been a part of The Ryder Cup for the past two matches and it hurts," he said. "But I've been climbing the world rankings and I am moving in the right direction. It would be nice to get back into the Team."

While Olazábal was celebrating victory, one player celebrating survival was Sam Little who finished 116th on the Order of Merit at the end of the tournament, therefore securing the final automatic card for The 2006 European Tour. The Englishman needed to finish 24th at worst to pass Scotland's David Drysdale, who had missed the cut, and got up and down from a greenside bunker at the last hole for a par that secured him a six-way tie for 21st place.

It was the end of a long season, but the

" It is a very nice looking course. Although it is quite short, it is not easy to score low here. It is tough and the greens are difficult to read " – *Miguel Angel Jiménez*

Miles Tunnicliff

234

José Manuel Lara

Final Results

Pos	Name		Rd1	Rd2	Rd3	Rd4	Total		€	£
1	José Maria OLAZÁBAL	Sp	69	65	70	66	270	-10	250,000.00	170,744.03
2	Sergio GARCIA	Sp	69	69	71	66	275	-5	111,853.33	76,393.13
	José Manuel LARA	Sp	68	69	70	68	275	-5	111,853.33	76,393.13
	Paul BROADHURST	Eng	67	66	72	70	275	-5	111,853.33	76,393.13
5	Miles TUNNICLIFF	Eng	69	68	70	69	276	-4	53,700.00	36,675.82
	Bradley DREDGE	Wal	72	67	67	70	276	-4	53,700.00	36,675.82
	Simon WAKEFIELD	Eng	69	71	67	69	276	-4	53,700.00	36,675.82
8	Jean VAN DE VELDE	Fr	70	71	66	70	277	-3	33,700.00	23,016.30
	Miguel Angel JIMÉNEZ	Sp	67	71	72	67	277	-3	33,700.00	23,016.30
	Mattias ELIASSON	Swe	68	68	70	71	277	-3	33,700.00	23,016.30
11	Robert-Jan DERKSEN	NL	70	68	71	69	278	-2	23,950.00	16,357.28
	David PARK	Wal	68	70	72	68	278	-2	23,950.00	16,357.28
	Fredrik ANDERSSON HED	Swe	70	71	69	68	278	-2	23,950.00	16,357.28
	Andrew COLTART	Scot	71	73	71	63	278	-2	23,950.00	16,357.28
	John BICKERTON	Eng	67	71	70	70	278	-2	23,950.00	16,357.28
	Graeme STORM	Eng	70	71	69	68	278	-2	23,950.00	16,357.28
17	Christopher HANELL	Swe	73	69	69	68	279	-1	19,050.00	13,010.70
	Robert COLES	Eng	70	70	74	65	279	-1	19,050.00	13,010.70
	Wade ORMSBY	Aus	70	66	70	73	279	-1	19,050.00	13,010.70
	Søren HANSEN	Den	70	69	66	74	279	-1	19,050.00	13,010.70
21	Sam LITTLE	Eng	67	73	68	72	280	0	16,275.00	11,115.44
	Paul LAWRIE	Scot	70	71	71	68	280	0	16,275.00	11,115.44
	Stephen SCAHILL	NZ	70	69	69	72	280	0	16,275.00	11,115.44
	Marcus FRASER	Aus	71	70	71	68	280	0	16,275.00	11,115.44
	Simon KHAN	Eng	69	69	72	72	280	0	16,275.00	11,115.44
	Markus BRIER	Aut	71	73	68	68	280	0	16,275.00	11,115.44
27	David LYNN	Eng	70	68	72	71	281	1	14,025.00	9,578.74
	Christian CÉVAËR	Fr	72	68	71	70	281	1	14,025.00	9,578.74
	Gregory HAVRET	Fr	69	66	73	73	281	1	14,025.00	9,578.74
	Miguel Angel MARTIN	Sp	69	71	73	68	281	1	14,025.00	9,578.74
31	Andrew OLDCORN	Scot	71	71	69	71	282	2	11,190.00	7,642.50
	Santiago LUNA	Sp	69	69	71	73	282	2	11,190.00	7,642.50
	Klas ERIKSSON	Swe	68	72	69	73	282	2	11,190.00	7,642.50
	Ricardo GONZALEZ	Arg	71	71	74	66	282	2	11,190.00	7,642.50
	Jonathan LOMAS	Eng	65	74	72	71	282	2	11,190.00	7,642.50
	Robert KARLSSON	Swe	72	69	69	72	282	2	11,190.00	7,642.50
	Benoit TEILLERIA	Fr	69	69	77	67	282	2	11,190.00	7,642.50
	Alastair FORSYTH	Scot	69	70	76	67	282	2	11,190.00	7,642.50
	François DELAMONTAGNE	Fr	73	71	72	66	282	2	11,190.00	7,642.50
	Gonzalo FERNANDEZ-CASTANO	Sp	68	72	70	72	282	2	11,190.00	7,642.50
41	Carlos DEL MORAL	Sp	69	70	76	68	283	3	8,550.00	5,839.45
	Jarmo SANDELIN	Swe	71	73	69	70	283	3	8,550.00	5,839.45
	Jamie SPENCE	Eng	72	70	72	69	283	3	8,550.00	5,839.45
	Jean-François LUCQUIN	Fr	71	69	71	72	283	3	8,550.00	5,839.45
	Jean-François REMESY	Fr	69	70	74	70	283	3	8,550.00	5,839.45
	Mark ROE	Eng	69	72	72	70	283	3	8,550.00	5,839.45
	Peter HANSON	Swe	69	73	70	71	283	3	8,550.00	5,839.45
48	Damien MCGRANE	Ire	72	71	68	73	284	4	6,600.00	4,507.64
	Maarten LAFEBER	NL	70	73	71	70	284	4	6,600.00	4,507.64
	Mark FOSTER	Eng	66	72	75	71	284	4	6,600.00	4,507.64
	Scott DRUMMOND	Scot	69	69	75	71	284	4	6,600.00	4,507.64
	Jesus Maria ARRUTI	Sp	68	70	69	77	284	4	6,600.00	4,507.64
	Brad KENNEDY	Aus	69	70	72	73	284	4	6,600.00	4,507.64
54	Johan SKÖLD	Swe	71	73	69	72	285	5	5,100.00	3,483.18
	Robert ROCK	Eng	70	70	72	73	285	5	5,100.00	3,483.18
	Ian GARBUTT	Eng	73	71	73	68	285	5	5,100.00	3,483.18
	Alessandro TADINI	It	70	71	68	76	285	5	5,100.00	3,483.18
58	Garry HOUSTON	Wal	71	73	73	69	286	6	4,200.00	2,868.50
	Søren KJELDSEN	Den	69	75	70	72	286	6	4,200.00	2,868.50
	Peter HEDBLOM	Swe	70	73	69	74	286	6	4,200.00	2,868.50
	Marcel SIEM	Ger	71	72	77	66	286	6	4,200.00	2,868.50
	Raymond RUSSELL	Scot	74	70	72	70	286	6	4,200.00	2,868.50
63	Matthew BLACKEY	Eng	72	71	73	71	287	7	3,375.00	2,305.04
	Stephen GALLACHER	Scot	73	71	71	72	287	7	3,375.00	2,305.04
	Alfredo GARCIA	Sp	75	69	73	70	287	7	3,375.00	2,305.04
	Jose-Filipe LIMA	Port	68	68	75	76	287	7	3,375.00	2,305.04
	José Manuel CARRILES	Sp	69	74	74	70	287	7	3,375.00	2,305.04
	Niki ZITNY	Aut	70	72	75	70	287	7	3,375.00	2,305.04
69	Pelle EDBERG	Swe	70	71	72	75	288	8	2,613.33	1,784.84
	Jamie DONALDSON	Wal	73	70	71	74	288	8	2,613.33	1,784.84
	Nick DOUGHERTY	Eng	71	73	76	68	288	8	2,613.33	1,784.84
72	Mårten OLANDER	Swe	68	71	80	70	289	9	2,247.00	1,534.66
73	Phillip ARCHER	Eng	71	73	75	71	290	10	2,241.00	1,530.55
	Andrea MAESTRONI	It	73	68	71	78	290	10	2,241.00	1,530.55
	Fredrik HENGE	Swe	68	74	72	76	290	10	2,241.00	1,530.55
76	Simon DYSON	Eng	77	65	78	71	291	11	2,232.00	1,524.40
	Ivo GINER	Sp	70	73	78	70	291	11	2,232.00	1,524.40
	Simon HURD	Eng	69	74	75	73	291	11	2,232.00	1,524.40
79	Emanuele CANONICA	It	70	69	74	79	292	12	2,226.00	1,520.30
80	Gary MURPHY	Ire	66	74	78	76	294	14	2,223.00	1,518.26

€16,275 (£11,115) that Little won was enough to push him €586 (£400) ahead of Drysdale and therefore spare himself a return to the Qualifying School. Unwittingly, Drysdale had been the architect of his own downfall. At the dunhill links championship three weeks earlier, the Scot had had to pull out with an injury an hour before he was due to tee off and was replaced by, none other than Little, who went on to win €33,120 (£22,487) for his share of 28th place, to revive his season.

What Jarmo Sandelin would have given for such a change in fortune. A Ryder Cup player alongside Olazábal at Brookline in 1999, the Swede had endured a tough season and a share of 41st place in the Mallorca Classic meant he could do no better than 140th on the Order of Merit, necessitating a return to the Qualifying School - alongside Drysdale et al - for the first time since 1993.

Peter Dixon
The Times

Total Prize Fund
€1,522,370 £1,039,738

Volvo Masters

Sotogrande, Spain
October 27-30 • 2005

Club de Golf Valderrama

Par	Yards	Metres
71	6952	6356

1	Paul McGINLEY	274	-10	
2	Sergio GARCIA	276	-8	
3	Luke DONALD	277	-7	
	Colin MONTGOMERIE	277	-7	
	José Maria OLAZÁBAL	277	-7	
6	Paul BROADHURST	278	-6	
7	Niclas FASTH	279	-5	
	Simon KHAN	279	-5	
	Lee WESTWOOD	279	-5	
10	Stephen DODD	280	-4	
	Kenneth FERRIE	280	-4	
	Padraig HARRINGTON	280	-4	
	Ian POULTER	280	-4	

Round One   Round Two   Round Three   Round Four

EUROPEAN TOUR ORDER OF MERIT
(Final after 47 tournaments)

Pos		€	
1	Colin MONTGOMERIE	2,794,222.84	
2	Michael CAMPBELL	2,496,269.44	
3	Paul McGINLEY	2,296,422.77	
4	Retief GOOSEN	2,261,211.06	
5	Angel CABRERA	1,866,277.30	
6	Sergio GARCIA	1,828,544.74	
7	David HOWELL	1,798,307.50	
8	Henrik STENSON	1,585,749.73	
9	Thomas BJÖRN	1,561,189.62	
10	José Maria OLAZÁBAL	1,489,016.29	

VOLVO

Masters of
Destiny

Volvo Masters

Sotogrande, Spain
October 27-30 • 2005

Oh, to be sure, greed is a terrible but delicious sin. And, of all the courses in all of the world, Club de Golf Valderrama will expose a player's frailties. It is a fickle temptress, beguiling and bewitching. It gives and takes like no other course on this planet, and those on whom it bestows its favours know they have been chosen and that they are special.

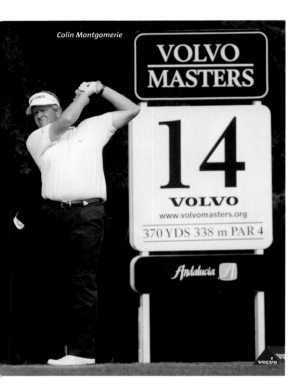

Colin Montgomerie

Sometimes, though, it pays to be hungry. Like Paul McGinley. On the driving range on the eve of the tournament he sat forlornly on a chair in his stockinged feet while his caddie Darren Reynolds went in search of new shoes with longer spikes. There, the Irishman watched Ian Poulter, the winner in 2004, hit perfect shot after perfect shot towards the 11th fairway that runs to the back and right of the practice ground.

Was McGinley searching for inspiration, as he immersed himself in chitchat with his 2004 Ryder Cup team-mate from Oakland Hills, or simply wondering if fate would conspire to reward him in a similar manner? Remember, 12 months previously, Poulter, like McGinley, had arrived at Valderrama winless only to discover that his best had been saved until last. Would it now be McGinley's turn?

Three runners-up finishes – in the TCL Classic in China, where he lost in a play-off to Paul Casey; in the BMW Championship at Wentworth Club, where Angel Cabrera came out on top; and in the HSBC World Match Play Championship, also at Wentworth, where he lost 2 and 1 to Michael Campbell in the final - had made 2005 his finest season if you simply surveyed the Order of Merit. It had not, however, satisfied his appetite. He was hungry for a win.

Colin Montgomerie, too, was hungry. He came to Valderrama wanting the lot. He wanted that newly crafted Waterford Crystal trophy which would be presented to the winner along with an equally handsome cheque for €666,660 (£450,595). He wanted his 'A' game to tame the Valderrama course where he had tasted success in 1993 and

Robert Karlsson

"Valderrama is a very special place. I think it is a great test of golf; it tests every single part of your game and that's what a great golf course should do. It's tight, not very long, but you have to position the ball off the tee. I really enjoy this golf course" – Sergio Garcia

again in 2002. More than anything, however, he wanted to leave the Volvo Masters for the eighth time as the Master of European Golf with his clutches on the famous Harry Vardon Trophy.

"I'll be giving everything I know in the game to achieve this goal," remarked Montgomerie before a shot was struck. "I'll be trying on every shot, every putt. That's all I can do. I can't predict the future. I can't predict what other people can do. I have no control over what other people do. But I have control of what I do, and I will be in full control of what I'm doing."

By the end of the first day, it seemed Montgomerie could indeed predict the future as he was utterly in control of all that was occurring on the cork tree-lined fairways and small, slick greens. An opening round of four under par 67, installed the Scot as the leader alongside Poulter and one ahead of Luke Donald, Sergio Garcia and José Maria Olazábal. Michael Campbell, the US Open Champion and Montgomerie's only challenger for the Order of Merit, was five shots behind. And McGinley? He carded 74, a round which included a triple bogey and a double bogey in his first seven holes, and he was back in 40th place in the 55-strong field.

As destiny beckoned, Montgomerie again played beautifully on Friday, and his 66 for 133 gave him the outright lead by two shots ahead of Garcia and Poulter. And McGinley? He had recovered his equilibrium with a 68 for 142, yet he was now nine shots behind the leader.

In Saturday's third round McGinley — without a victory on The European Tour since The Celtic Manor Resort Wales Open in 2001 — posted a 65 which, by two shots, was the best round of the day. Garcia's 68 to Montgomerie's 70 meant the pair would tee-off in the final round tied for the lead on ten under par 203 — four ahead of

Niclas Fasth in action on the driving range with his four year old son Adam

Paul Broadhurst, Lee Westwood, Poulter... and McGinley.

Meanwhile Campbell, following a third round 68, had received from George O'Grady, the Executive Director of The European Tour, a silver card to mark the Honorary Life Membership of The European Tour awarded to him following his win in the US Open Championship. He was also 24 hours away from the possibility of receiving another significant prize in the shape of the Harry Vardon Trophy as he would start the final round six shots behind Montgomerie, a margin acknowledged by the Scot himself that was nothing at Valderrama. Even so it required a Campbell charge and that did not materialise as Montgomerie's challenge for the title stayed alive until, like Garcia and Olazábal for whom there was much vocal support, they were overhauled by the magnificent McGinley.

Padraig Harrington

DRIVING INFORMATION FURTHER
REUTERS AND THE EUROPEAN TOUR

Reuters has been an official sponsor of the PGA European Tour's official statistics for over four years. Our global brand is synonymous with fast, relevant and above all, accurate information and is perfectly linked to this sport – where numbers mean everything.

REUTERS

Ewen Murray of Sky Sports chats with Sergio Garcia at the Reuters Statistics Awards 2005 at Valderrama

Final Results

Pos	Name		Rd1	Rd2	Rd3	Rd4	Total		€	£
1	Paul MCGINLEY	Ire	74	68	65	67	274	-10	666,660.00	450,595.13
2	Sergio GARCIA	Sp	68	67	68	73	276	-8	444,440.00	300,396.75
3	José Maria OLAZÁBAL	Sp	68	72	68	69	277	-7	206,666.70	139,685.91
	Colin MONTGOMERIE	Scot	67	66	70	74	277	-7	206,666.70	139,685.91
	Luke DONALD	Eng	68	73	72	64	277	-7	206,666.70	139,685.91
6	Paul BROADHURST	Eng	71	69	67	71	278	-6	140,000.00	94,625.92
7	Simon KHAN	Eng	75	68	67	69	279	-5	103,200.00	69,752.82
	Niclas FASTH	Swe	70	70	71	68	279	-5	103,200.00	69,752.82
	Lee WESTWOOD	Eng	71	69	67	72	279	-5	103,200.00	69,752.82
10	Ian POULTER	Eng	67	68	72	73	280	-4	72,100.00	48,732.35
	Stephen DODD	Wal	71	72	70	67	280	-4	72,100.00	48,732.35
	Padraig HARRINGTON	Ire	72	74	67	67	280	-4	72,100.00	48,732.35
	Kenneth FERRIE	Eng	72	72	70	66	280	-4	72,100.00	48,732.35
14	Michael CAMPBELL	NZ	72	69	68	72	281	-3	62,200.00	42,040.95
15	Bradley DREDGE	Wal	70	68	73	71	282	-2	56,550.00	38,222.11
	Nick DOUGHERTY	Eng	71	70	76	65	282	-2	56,550.00	38,222.11
	Paul CASEY	Eng	70	72	71	69	282	-2	56,550.00	38,222.11
	Charl SCHWARTZEL	SA	72	71	70	69	282	-2	56,550.00	38,222.11
19	Barry LANE	Eng	76	70	69	68	283	-1	50,000.00	33,794.97
	Henrik STENSON	Swe	70	69	73	71	283	-1	50,000.00	33,794.97
	Gregory HAVRET	Fr	72	70	75	66	283	-1	50,000.00	33,794.97
22	Pierre FULKE	Swe	76	73	67	68	284	0	43,585.71	29,459.56
	Peter HANSON	Swe	71	75	71	67	284	0	43,585.71	29,459.56
	Steve WEBSTER	Eng	69	73	74	68	284	0	43,585.71	29,459.56
	Søren KJELDSEN	Den	71	74	73	66	284	0	43,585.71	29,459.56
	Graeme MCDOWELL	N.Ire	72	71	69	72	284	0	43,585.71	29,459.56
	Thongchai JAIDEE	Thai	72	72	70	70	284	0	43,585.71	29,459.56
	David LYNN	Eng	73	73	68	70	284	0	43,585.71	29,459.56
29	Stephen GALLACHER	Scot	73	69	73	70	285	1	36,480.00	24,656.81
	Raphaël JACQUELIN	Fr	70	74	74	67	285	1	36,480.00	24,656.81
	Robert KARLSSON	Swe	69	73	70	73	285	1	36,480.00	24,656.81
	Miguel Angel JIMÉNEZ	Sp	73	72	70	70	285	1	36,480.00	24,656.81
	Nick O'HERN	Aus	72	67	70	76	285	1	36,480.00	24,656.81
34	Søren HANSEN	Den	72	75	68	72	287	3	32,250.00	21,797.76
	Angel CABRERA	Arg	73	72	71	71	287	3	32,250.00	21,797.76
	Maarten LAFEBER	NL	70	75	72	70	287	3	32,250.00	21,797.76
	Gonzalo FERNANDEZ-CASTANO	Sp	73	71	73	70	287	3	32,250.00	21,797.76
38	David HOWELL	Eng	71	72	71	74	288	4	29,100.00	19,668.67
	Jean-François REMESY	Fr	74	76	69	69	288	4	29,100.00	19,668.67
	Robert-Jan DERKSEN	NL	73	71	71	73	288	4	29,100.00	19,668.67
41	Anders HANSEN	Den	73	74	71	72	290	6	25,950.00	17,539.59
	Richard GREEN	Aus	71	75	72	72	290	6	25,950.00	17,539.59
	Peter LAWRIE	Ire	76	73	71	70	290	6	25,950.00	17,539.59
	Richard STERNE	SA	74	72	74	70	290	6	25,950.00	17,539.59
45	Graeme STORM	Eng	76	75	67	73	291	7	22,800.00	15,410.51
	José Manuel LARA	Sp	75	73	69	74	291	7	22,800.00	15,410.51
	Damien MCGRANE	Ire	75	73	71	72	291	7	22,800.00	15,410.51
48	Jean VAN DE VELDE	Fr	78	73	73	68	292	8	21,000.00	14,193.89
49	Paul LAWRIE	Scot	72	76	71	74	293	9	19,200.00	12,977.27
	Simon DYSON	Eng	72	78	72	71	293	9	19,200.00	12,977.27
	Richard FINCH	Eng	79	74	68	72	293	9	19,200.00	12,977.27
52	Peter GUSTAFSSON	Swe	78	74	72	70	294	10	17,500.00	11,828.24
53	Peter HEDBLOM	Swe	76	73	75	74	298	14	16,800.00	11,355.11
54	Emanuele CANONICA	It	82	79	73	78	312	28	16,300.00	11,017.16
55	Darren CLARKE	N.Ire	76	75	WD		151	9	15,800.00	10,679.21

Donald had set the target with a 64 – the lowest score of the week – but by then McGinley was on the move. He had birdied the tenth hole to take the lead. He had not given a shot back to this toughest of courses since the first hole of the second round and that is the way it would remain to the end.

McGinley's focus was there to be seen by all when, at the 17th, he left himself a third shot of a little over 100 yards from where he struck a wonderful sand wedge over the water to six feet. Then he confidently holed the putt. Game, set and match.

For Montgomerie there was victory in defeat. First he walked straight from the 18th green to shake hands and congratulate McGinley. Then he took hold of the Harry Vardon Trophy and declared: "This is so very important. I didn't need this trophy. I had seven already. But I wanted it."

McGinley, of course, had 'wanted' a big win like this since he became a professional in 1991. Now it was his and he had satisfied that hunger. He said: "What pleases me most is the size of this title. I always knew I had a big one in me. Is it better than The Ryder Cup putt? Well it's different. This was selfish. This was for Paul McGinley."

Philip Reid
The Irish Times

Michael Campbell receives his Honorary Life Membership Card from George O'Grady, the Executive Director of The European Tour

Total Prize Fund
€3,928,500 £2,655,271

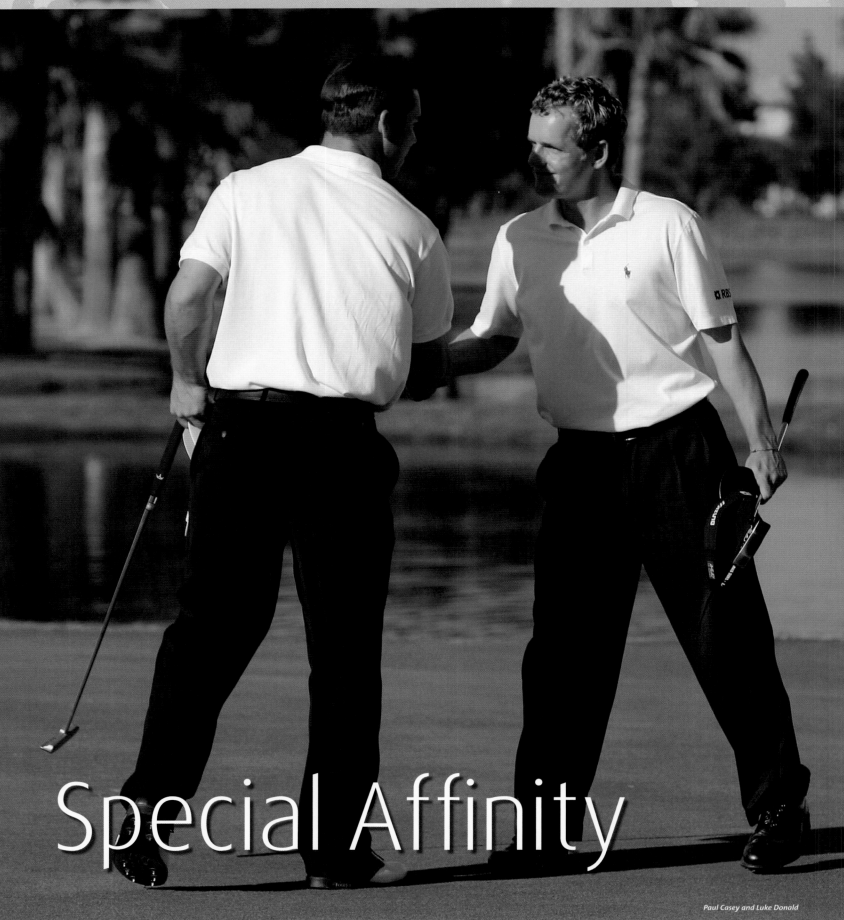

Special Affinity

Paul Casey and Luke Donald

It is a measure of the universal appeal of the sport, that when the World Golf Championships – Algarve World Cup in Portugal took place at the Victoria Clube de Golfe in November, 2005, the event was being hosted by a different nation for the 24th time.

For the WGC – Algarve World Cup in Portugal retains a special affinity with the World Cup, first played as the Canada Cup in 1953, which over the years has visited Argentina, Australia, Canada, China, Colombia, England, France, Greece, Indonesia, Ireland, Italy, Japan, Malaysia, Mexico, New Zealand, Philippines, Puerto Rico, Singapore, South Africa, Spain, Thailand, the United States and Venezuela.

The competition became part of the World Golf Championships in 2000 although, in a sense, there was an historical flavour about the 2004 edition as this was the 50th occasion of an event which has held an esteemed position within the world of golf for decades because of the distinct way in which it has promoted the sport.

Victory in the 2004 tournament, staged at the Real Club de Golf de Sevilla in Spain, went to England with Paul Casey and Luke Donald (pictured left) compiling a 31 under par total of 257 to edge out Spain (Sergio Garcia and Miguel Angel Jiménez) by one shot and Ireland (Padraig Harrington and Paul McGinley) by three shots. All six of those players, of course, had been part of Europe's glorious Ryder Cup experience two months earlier.

This was England's second success – David Carter and Nick Faldo triumphed in New Zealand in 1998 – while the United States hold the record for the most number of wins in the World Cup with 23, although South Africa enjoyed their fifth victory, and the second since the event became part of the World Golf Championships, in 2003.

Unquestionably the World Golf

Championships have become a truly global experience since their launch in February, 1999. They feature the game's leading players competing against one another in a variety of formats. The World Cup joined the Accenture Match Play, the NEC Invitational and the American Express Championship in a line-up which sees the events rotating through a variety of outstanding venues.

Clearly this was the case when the 2005 WGC – Algarve World Cup in Portugal unfolded at the Victoria Clube de Golfe. Designed by Arnold Palmer, and the most recent of the five courses at Vilamoura - an outstanding complex a short distance from Faro International Airport – Victoria Clube de Golfe is recognised as one of the most sophisticated golf courses in Europe. One extraordinary fact is that the Palmer design team masterly created 18 greens with totally different shapes and sizes. Palmer said: "Victoria is truly one of the finest courses Palmer Design has had the pleasure of creating among the hundreds we have designed over the last quarter of a century."

Palmer, too, has an affinity with the World Cup. He won the title with Sam Snead in 1960 and 1962 and with Jack Nicklaus in 1963, 1964, 1966 and 1967, and in those days, when there was also an individual prize, he won that as well in 1967. There is something very special about this competition and the tradition continues.

Mitchell Platts

Victoria Clube de Golfe

Miguel Angel Jiménez and Sergio Garcia

The European Tour Qualifying School

San Roque Club, Cadiz, Spain
November 10-15 • 2005

Rich Ability

Sweden's Peter Gustafsson is presented with the trophy for winning The 2004 European Tour Qualifying School Finals by George O'Grady, Executive Director of The European Tour

When Spain's Gonzalo Fernandez-Castano and Sweden's Joakim Bäckström won The KLM Open and the Aa St Omer Open in mid-summer on The 2005 European Tour International Schedule, they highlighted another vintage year in the history of The European Tour Qualifying School Finals.

San Roque (New Course)

Par	Yards	Metres
72	7105	6497

San Roque (Old Course)

Par	Yards	Metres
72	7103	6494

For in 2004 both players graduated from the Qualifying School Finals at their first attempts, finishing seventh and eighth respectively behind the eventual winner, Peter Gustafsson of Sweden. What is more they brought to 14 the number of players who have moved on from the School to win the very next year on The European Tour.

Bäckström said: "I really enjoyed the Qualifying School Finals as it was the first time I had made it through all three stages and by the time I reached the Finals I was determined to relax and enjoy it. It is a long week – six days of golf really is a lot – but it is probably the best way to see who are the best players."

Fernandez-Castano said: "The Qualifying School Finals are a marathon and you have to be tough and very strong minded to get through it. You can never take it easy

during the whole six rounds, so it is very demanding. "For me, having only turned professional two months before the Finals, it was an awesome feeling to have a place on The European Tour."

In order to fulfil the goal to graduate from The European Tour Qualifying School Finals the players must progress through 108 holes on the Old and New Courses at the San Roque Club in southern Spain. It is widely considered one of the toughest examinations of skill, stamina and mental fortitude in sport.

Few events can rival the drama and tension. At the outset more than 800 players begin the quest each year to join The European Tour where they can stand shoulder to shoulder with the greats of the game. Following Stage One, which in 2005 was held at six venues across England, France, Germany and Italy, and Stage Two, held at Costa Ballena Club de Golf, Cadiz, Emporda Golf Club, Girona, and PGA Golf de Catalunya, Girona, Spain, 168 players remained to contest the Finals.

The pressure, with the ultimate dream of Membership of The European Tour at stake, has always been immense but then rewards, as Bäckström and Fernandez-Castano moved on to demonstrate, are enormous. What is more it has always been that way since the very first Qualifying School Finals at Foxhills

and Walton Heath in England in 1976. In the 28 years since then, the Finals have also been staged at Downshire, England; Dom Pedro and Quinta do Lago, Portugal; La Manga, Murcia, Spain; La Grande Motte and Golf Massane, Montpellier, France; San Roque, Guadalmina and Club de Golf Sotogrande, Spain, before featuring at Emporda Golf Club and Golf Platja de Pals, Spain, in 2002 and 2003.

In November 2005, the Finals returned to San Roque where they were staged between 1995 and 2001 and again in 2004. The event was played on the venue's Old Course, designed by Dave Thomas, and the New Course, a layout designed by Seve Ballesteros and Perry Dye, which opened in November 2003.

Uniquely, the Qualifying School is one tournament where the goal is not necessarily to triumph but simply to finish in the upper echelons. The higher you finish can maximise playing opportunities but, in reality, anyone finishing the six rounds with a card can consider themselves a worthy winner.

The Graduates of 2004 proved ample evidence of their rich ability when they took their place on The 2005 European Tour International Schedule: the Graduates of 2005 followed suit.

Mitchell Platts

Final Results (2004)

Pos	Name & Country		PQ	Rd1	Rd2	Rd3	Rd4	Rd5	Rd6	Agg	Par	€	£
1	Peter GUSTAFSSON*	Swe	EX	71	70	72	73	69	68	423	-9	15,764.54	11,000.00
2	Simon WAKEFIELD*	Eng	EX	69	69	71	73	69	75	426	-6	12,468.32	8,700.00
3	Francois DELAMONTAGNE*	Fr	EX	72	67	69	74	69	76	427	-5	10,031.98	7,000.00
4	Francesco MOLINARI	It	281*	79	71	70	70	70	69	429	-3	7,882.27	5,500.00
5	Stuart MANLEY	Wal	280	73	69	71	72	72	72	429	-3	7,882.27	5,500.00
6	Fernando ROCA*	Sp	277	76	70	77	74	69	66	432	0	5,159.30	3,600.00
7	Joakim BACKSTROM	Swe	276*	71	68	74	76	73	70	432	0	5,159.30	3,600.00
8	Gonzalo FERNANDEZ-CASTANO	Sp	282*	73	71	74	74	69	71	432	0	5,159.30	3,600.00
9	Adam MEDNICK*	Swe	EX	77	71	72	68	69	75	432	0	5,159.30	3,600.00
10	Richard FINCH	Eng	278	80	70	73	69	73	68	433	1	3,439.54	2,400.00
11	Pelle EDBERG	Swe	281*	71	73	76	68	71	74	433	1	3,439.54	2,400.00
12	Lars BROVOLD**	Nor	279*	79	61	69	77	70	77	433	1	3,439.54	2,400.00
13	Johan SKOLD	Swe	EX	76	75	71	75	68	70	435	3	2,937.94	2,050.00
14	Sven STRÜVER*	Ger	EX	75	69	70	73	75	73	435	3	2,937.94	2,050.00
15	Ben MASON*	Eng	273	76	73	73	73	73	68	436	4	2,522.33	1,760.00
16	Simon HURD	Eng	274	76	73	70	72	75	70	436	4	2,522.33	1,760.00
17	Philip WALTON*	Ire	EX	76	74	69	73	73	71	436	4	2,522.33	1,760.00
18	Niki ZITNY	Aut	273	74	72	75	71	70	74	436	4	2,522.33	1,760.00
19	Jan-Are LARSEN	Nor	EX	78	72	68	71	70	77	436	4	2,522.33	1,760.00
20	Stephen BROWNE	Ire	EX	73	77	74	73	70	70	437	5	2,149.71	1,500.00
21	André CRUSE	SA	273	79	69	73	74	71	71	437	5	2,149.71	1,500.00
22	Titch MOORE	SA	EX	74	69	78	73	72	71	437	5	2,149.71	1,500.00
23	Ian GARBUTT*	Eng	EX	74	73	73	73	72	72	437	5	2,149.71	1,500.00
24	Andrea MAESTRONI	It	281	73	69	71	79	73	72	437	5	2,149.71	1,500.00
25	Jarrod MOSELEY*	Aus	EX	73	78	70	73	74	70	438	6	1,845.17	1,287.50
26	Sam LITTLE*	Eng	EX	75	73	72	77	68	73	438	6	1,845.17	1,287.50
27	Andrew MCLARDY	SA	EX	74	74	73	72	70	75	438	6	1,845.17	1,287.50
28	Stuart LITTLE*	Eng	275	74	70	74	74	71	75	438	6	1,845.17	1,287.50
29	Dean ROBERTSON*	Scot	EX	74	71	72	72	73	76	438	6	1,845.17	1,287.50
30	Gregory BOURDY*	Fr	EX	78	70	68	70	73	79	438	6	1,845.17	1,287.50
31	Neil CHEETHAM*	Eng	EX	72	74	74	76	74	69	439	7	1,616.26	1,127.78
32	Mark SANDERS	Eng	278	75	72	69	82	71	70	439	7	1,616.26	1,127.78
33	Benoit TEILLERIA	Fr	276	72	72	73	79	72	71	439	7	1,616.26	1,127.78
34	Matthew BLACKEY*	Eng	EX	77	76	68	74	71	73	439	7	1,616.26	1,127.78
35	Martin ERLANDSSON*	Swe	EX	72	76	73	73	72	73	439	7	1,616.26	1,127.78
36	Marco BERNARDINI	It	275*	75	70	70	78	73	73	439	7	1,616.26	1,127.78
37	Michael JONZON*	Swe	EX	76	71	70	73	75	74	439	7	1,616.26	1,127.78
38	Hernan REY	Arg	281	75	69	71	75	75	74	439	7	1,616.26	1,127.78
39	David GRIFFITHS	Eng	278	72	70	70	73	79	75	439	7	1,616.26	1,127.78
40	Michael HOEY	N.Ire	EX	79	73	74	72	74	68	440	8	716.57	500.00
41	Adam GROOM	Aus	EX	74	73	70	80	71	72	440	8	716.57	500.00
42	André BOSSERT*	Swi	EX	71	73	75	77	71	73	440	8	716.57	500.00
43	Cesar MONASTERIO*	Arg	EX	74	72	72	77	72	73	440	8	716.57	500.00
44	Oliver WHITELEY	Eng	280*	71	73	74	74	75	73	440	8	716.57	500.00
45	Fredrik WIDMARK*	Swe	280	74	76	74	74	68	74	440	8	716.57	500.00
46	Birgir HAFTHORSSON	Ice	278*	75	69	69	80	73	74	440	8	716.57	500.00
47	Ariel CANETE*	Arg	EX	72	74	72	77	75	71	441	9	716.57	500.00
48	Johan KOK*	SA	277	76	76	69	77	71	72	441	9	716.57	500.00
49	Stuart DAVIS*	Eng	275	74	76	74	71	73	73	441	9	716.57	500.00
50	Paul STREETER*	Eng	273	76	70	75	73	71	76	441	9	716.57	500.00
51	Gianluca BARUFFALDI	It	276*	73	72	74	72	74	76	441	9	716.57	500.00
52	Van PHILLIPS*	Eng	EX	76	71	73	76	76	70	442	10	716.57	500.00
53	Sebastien DELAGRANGE*	Fr	267	82	70	68	77	71	74	442	10	716.57	500.00
54	Carlos DE CORRAL	Sp	279*	73	74	72	75	74	74	442	10	716.57	500.00
55	Liam BOND	Eng	283*	78	70	72	77	75	71	443	11	716.57	500.00
56	Diego BORREGO*	Sp	EX	72	74	75	76	74	72	443	11	716.57	500.00
57	Darren LENG	Eng	279	76	72	70	79	74	72	443	11	716.57	500.00
58	Paul MARANTZ*	Aus	265	71	74	75	75	76	72	443	11	716.57	500.00
59	Richard MCEVOY*	Eng	EX	74	72	74	77	72	74	443	11	716.57	500.00
60	David HIGGINS	Ire	EX	75	72	74	74	74	74	443	11	716.57	500.00
61	Bertrand CORNUT	Fr	282	78	68	77	74	71	75	443	11	716.57	500.00
62	Lee S JAMES	Eng	278	76	72	71	74	75	75	443	11	716.57	500.00
63	José Manuel CARRILES*	Sp	EX	75	71	76	72	72	77	443	11	716.57	500.00
64	David ORR	Scot	277	76	69	73	79	68	78	443	11	716.57	500.00
65	Knud STORGAARD*	Den	275	80	72	72	74	72	74	444	12	716.57	500.00
66	Colm MORIARTY	Ire	282*	75	74	77	72	72	74	444	12	716.57	500.00
67	Johan EDFORS*	Swe	EX	80	71	71	72	74	76	444	12	716.57	500.00
68	Mark MOULAND*	Wal	274	69	72	77	75	75	76	444	12	716.57	500.00
69	Julien VAN HAUWE	Fr	279	77	74	70	74	78	72	445	13	716.57	500.00
70	Andres ROMERO	Arg	271	78	70	74	75	73	75	445	13	716.57	500.00
71	Sam OSBORNE (AM)	Eng	276	76	70	75	75	73	76	445	13		
72	Roope KAKKO	Fin	275	75	76	74	70	75	76	446	14	716.57	500.00
73	Gareth PADDISON*	NZ	EX	77	73	70	74	75	77	446	14	716.57	500.00
74	Nicolas COLSAERTS*	Bel	EX	71	70	79	77	74	76	447	15	716.57	500.00
75	Jeppe HULDAHL*	Den	278	74	72	74	75	82	71	448	16	716.57	500.00
76	Per G NYMAN	Swe	281	76	75	75	71	79	72	448	16	716.57	500.00
77	Tomas Jesus MUÑOZ	Sp	277*	74	73	76	75	75	75	448	16	716.57	500.00
78	Jeff HALL	Eng	282	71	73	72	77	78	77	448	16	716.57	500.00
79	Manuel QUIROS	Sp	281*	74	75	75	74	75	76	449	17	716.57	500.00
80	Oyvind ROJAHN	Nor	267*	80	69	73	74	77	76	449	17	716.57	500.00
81	Iain STEEL	Mal	281*	71	77	73	77	74	77	449	17	716.57	500.00
82	Raphaël PELLICIOLI	Fr	272	69	77	77	75	80	74	452	20	716.57	500.00
83	Carlos QUEVEDO	Sp	278	71	74	79	74	76	79	453	21	716.57	500.00

The first 39 players became eligible for Category 11 Membership on The 2005 European Tour International Schedule

In 2005, for the second year in succession, The European Tour Qualifying School Finals were staged on the New and Old Courses at the San Roque Club

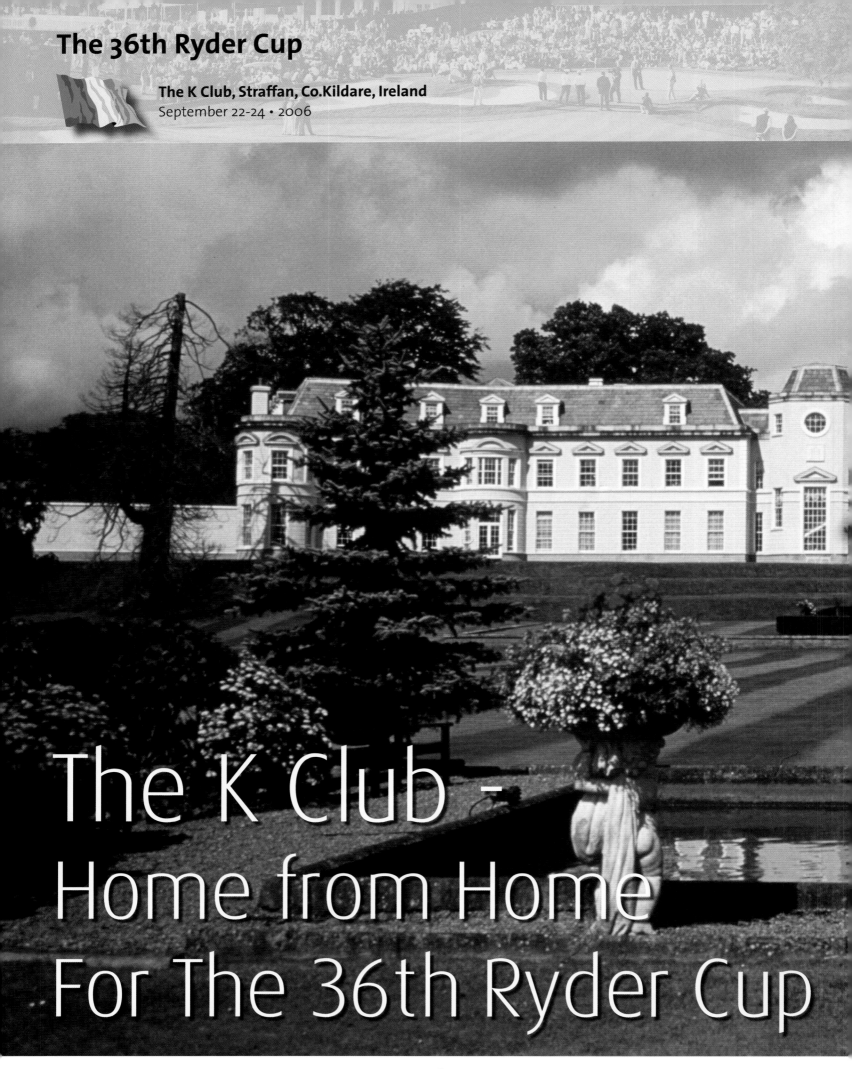

The K Club -
Home from Home
For The 36th Ryder Cup

Over eighteen holes, anything is possible.

Every two years, the greatest European and American golfers do battle for the world's most coveted golf trophy – The Ryder Cup.

It's a competition that rouses a rare passion. And when there is passion on a golf course – anything is possible. In 2006 The Ryder Cup will be played at The K Club. At AIB, we're delighted to play our part in making it possible.

AIB, proud partner to The 2006 Ryder Cup in Ireland.

Be with AIB.

RYDER CUP 2006
IRELAND
AIB
PROUD PARTNER

On a table behind the 18th green at The K Club, The Ryder Cup was proudly displayed. It was September 1995, the final day of the Smurfit European Open, and Tom Lehman had just completed a creditable performance as the lone representative of the defeated United States Team from Oak Hill a week previously.

The Winning 2004 European Ryder Cup Team Captained by Bernhard Langer

After signing his card, Lehman crept mischievously over to the table, picked up the trophy and pretended to sneak away with it under his arm. Little could he have imagined that, 11 years later, he would be pursuing that treasured prize in earnest, as Captain of the United States Team for The 2006 Ryder Cup at the Co. Kildare venue.

Back in April 1990, Arnold Palmer, whose design company had the target of completing The K Club's courses in time for an official opening 15 months later, also had The Ryder Cup on his mind. He was at Augusta National, reflecting on how the casting vote of the PGA Chairman, Lord Derby, had made The Belfry a compromise choice for the 1993

contest. "I realise that some people felt we were being over-ambitious in putting The K Club forward for 1993, but it was an entirely realistic application," he said.

This is what Palmer added at that time: "In fact I made it clear to The Ryder Cup organisers that we could have the course in play that fall, if we so wished. I believe it is a perfect setting for a Championship venue, offering a top-quality test in delightful surroundings. I would like to think that if The Ryder Cup passes it by, it would be considered for other prominent events such as the Irish Open."

The Ryder Cup, of course, will not pass The

K Club by. On September 22-24, 2006, The 36th edition of the biennial match between Europe and the United States will unfold on the Palmer Course at The K Club in Straffan some 18 miles from the city centre of Dublin.

We are informed that the history of the estate at Straffan, Co. Kildare, dates back nearly 1,500 years to 550AD, about a century after St Patrick had spread christianity to the Emerald Isle. Apparently a house or church then stood where the village is currently located.

Nothing further of note seems to have happened until the Norman invasion in

To enjoy the best golf coverage

including the 36th Ryder Cup, US Open, USPGA,

over 70 events from the European & PGA Tour and every

World Golf Championship event – join Sky digital.

Call 08702 424242

the latter half of the 12th century, when Richard FitzGilbert de Clare, better known as Strongbow, gave the lands at Straffan to compatriot Maurice FitzGerald, ancestor of the Dukes of Leinster. This grant was subsequently confirmed by King John of England, who signed the Magna Carta in 1215.

The land changed hands several times during the ensuing centuries until being bought in 1831 by Hugh Barton, who had founded a successful wine firm in Bordeaux. In fact he was reared there and was fortunate to escape the worst excesses of the French Revolution, including a planned encounter with the guillotine as a member of the wealthy, merchant classes.

As things turned out, a year after moving to Straffan, he commenced the construction of a grand new house for his family. It was this house which would ultimately form the basic structure of what is the east wing of the present-day hotel. The design was based on a great chateau in Louvesciennes, to the west of Paris. Indeed the outlines of the mansard roof, chimneys and windows can still be seen in the Kildare Hotel.

For Barton and his wife Anne, who was the daughter of a naturalised French subject of Scottish origin, Straffan became a haven of peace and serenity after the turmoil in France. Later on, as a finishing touch to the house, he added the Italian style companile tower, which is still there today and is similar to the tower built on Queen Victoria's estate at Osborne in the Isle of Wight.

Other refinements added by subsequent generations of Bartons were two suspension bridges to the island in the Liffey which is now home to the 16th green on the Palmer Course. At the beginning of the 20th century, the four-storey house had 30 bedrooms and

in 1963, the garden was given a parterre, linking the house with the river.

More recent owners included Stephen O'Flaherty, a legendary figure in the Irish motor industry and the first concessionaire for Volkswagen cars for these islands. He sold Straffan in the 1960s to Irish-American Kevin McClory, who will always be associated with James Bond as producer of "Thunderball" in 1965 and executive producer of "Never Say Never Again" in 1983.

Locals still recall the charity party he played host to in 1968, which went on for days and had Sean Connery, Shirley McLaine and Peter Sellers among the guests. Incidentally, when Connery returned to Straffan eight years later as an 11-handicap competitor in the Chris de Burgh Golf Classic, he made the admirable contribution of five net birdies to the fourth-placed team, which was led by none other than Christy O'Connor Snr, a long-time friend.

The estate consisted of 330 acres when Dr Michael Smurfit bought it in 1988 for €4.4 million. Four years later, he took an option on an additional 220 acres, at a cost of between €2,500 and €10,000 per acre, and subsequently went on to purchase a further 50 acres.

Dr Smurfit takes up the story: "When I was in my thirties (1970s) and I saw the way golf was being played in America and in parts of Europe, I got the idea of building a country club here, something of a truly international standard. In hindsight, it was probably fortunate that it didn't happen for some years, because such a venture would have been ahead of its time and probably wouldn't have taken off back then."

At first, David Adamson, who had been Dr Smurfit's personal assistant since 1972,

became the sole resident of the house. He recalled: "I was told it was haunted, which would explain why people looked at me a little strangely while enquiring if I had had any interesting experiences there. I regret to say that in the course of six months, I didn't. It was a lovely old estate, still with some horses, though not many."

Then, as part of Dr Smurfit's contract with the Jefferson Smurfit Group, whereby they had first option on any venture he embarked upon, the estate became part of the multi-national packaging company.

Ryder Cup Results 1985-2004

1985	The Belfry, Sutton Coldfield, West Midlands, England Europe 16½ - USA 11½
1987	Muirfield Village, Columbus, Ohio, USA Europe 15 - USA 13
1989	The Belfry, Sutton Coldfield, West Midlands, England Europe 14 - USA 14 (Europe retained Cup)
1991	The Ocean Course, Kiawah Island Resort, Kiawah Island, USA Europe 13½ - USA 14½
1993	The Belfry, Sutton Coldfield, West Midlands, England Europe 13 - USA 15
1995	Oak Hill Country Club, Rochester, New York, USA Europe 14½ - USA 13½
1997	Club de Golf Valderrama, Sotogrande, Spain Europe 14½ - USA 13½
1999	The Country Club, Brookline, Massachusetts, USA Europe 13½ - USA 14½
2002	The Belfry, Sutton Coldfield, West Midlands, England Europe 15½ - USA 12½
2004	Oakland Hills Country Club, Bloomfield Township, Michigan, USA Europe 18½ - USA 9½

IRELAND

A Natural Home for the
RYDER CUP 2006

Ireland, a golfer's paradise, with every shape, size and shade of green and the friendliest 19th watering hole on the circuit. Ireland has produced more than her share of Ryder Cup players and welcomed many of the world's top golfers. The 2006 Ryder Cup. Ireland, a perfect venue, an ideal host.

www.ireland.ie

Fáilte Ireland

For the last decade, the world's most prestigious golf
event has chosen to partner with Club Car. Now that's reliability.

Club Car®

Drive it once and you'll know.

With a view to developing it as a golf resort, the next step was to employ a designer and the original candidates were Seve Ballesteros, Peter Alliss and Clive Clark; Dave Thomas and John O'Leary and the American, Pete Dye. As the designer of Harbour Town and the fiendishly difficult Stadium Course at Sawgrass, Dye had many admirers internationally, but he declined the invitation to get involved at Straffan because he did not work outside of the United States.

Still anxious to have an American on board nevertheless, Dr Smurfit came up with the idea of approaching Palmer, who, with his partner Ed Seay, had become active in the design business by that time. In the end, it came down to a choice between him and Thomas and though more expensive, Palmer was deemed to have the edge in the context of global marketing.

Little more than a year after the official opening in July 1991, The K Club played host to the biennial PGA Cup in which the Americans retained the trophy with a 15-11 win. The Irish Professional Championship was also staged there in 1992 when Eamonn Darcy captured the title.

By then, Straffan House had been transformed into Ireland's only five red-star hotel. Despite Palmer's earlier view on the golf course, the hotel would have been too small had the 1993 Ryder Cup bid been successful so the first new wing was built, bringing the accommodation up to 36 rooms. The next expansion, which was planned in 1999 after the venue was officially awarded The Ryder Cup, was completed in 2001. It involved the addition of a further 33 rooms.

Meanwhile, in May 1998, The K Club had embarked on a further €12.5 million development, extending its facilities to 36 holes through the construction of the Smurfit Course, again by the Palmer company. It played host to the Smurfit European Open in 2004 when Retief Goosen triumphed and the tournament is scheduled to be played on that course in 2006 with the Palmer Course being prepared for The Ryder Cup.

The final piece of the resort jigsaw was completed in November 2004 with the official opening of a luxurious Spa, at a cost of €10 million. With this, The K Club now comprised a 78 bedroom hotel, two championship standard golf courses, significant housing costing up to €2.5 million per unit and two clubhouses, the newer of which measured a formidable 50,000 square feet.

All of which was bought back by the partnership of Dr Smurfit and wealthy club member, Gerry Gannon, in June 2005 in a deal valued at €115 million. "Though the entire development was a bit of a gamble, getting The Ryder Cup has confirmed that we made the right decision," said Dr Smurfit.

On a return visit for the Smurfit European Open in the summer of 2005, Lehman pointed to the new West Wing of the hotel. "That's where the American Team will be based," he said. "Europe with be at the other end." Somehow one sensed he was well pleased with the prospect of calling it home for a week in September, 2006.

Dermot Gilleece
Sunday Independent (Ireland)

Card of the Course

Hole	Yards	Metres	Par
1	418	382	4
2	413	378	4
3	170	155	3
4	568	519	5
5	440	402	4
6	478	437	4
7	430	393	4
8	173	158	3
9	461	422	4
Out	**3551**	**3246**	**35**
10	584	534	5
11	415	379	4
12	182	166	3
13	428	391	4
14	213	195	3
15	446	408	4
16	555	507	5
17	424	388	4
18	537	491	5
In	**3784**	**3459**	**37**

| Total | 7335 | 6705 | 72 |

The 36th Ryder Cup

The K Club, Straffan, Co.Kildare, Ireland
September 22-24 • 2006

The Palmer Course -
A Challenge with Personality and Atmosphere

Tom Lehman and Ian Woosnam, the respective Captains of the United States and European Teams for The 36th Ryder Cup, provide a unique in-depth survey of the 18 holes of the Palmer Course at The K Club where the match will take place from September 22-24, 2006.

Tom Lehman - 2006 United States Team Captain - *Reviews The Outward Half*

'My initial reaction is that it is a good driving course. With the rough up, you need to put the ball in the fairway. The greens are somewhat unique; there is a lot of personality to them. There are a lot of greens which are up higher and a lot of greens which go away from you and a lot of greens which slope to the right on the front and to the left on the back. It is a very good golf course and I enjoy playing it very much. The challenge is there and the firmer it gets the harder it will become.'

Hole 1

HOLE 1 (BOHEREEN ROAD) PAR 4 418 YARDS   382 METRES
The first hole is a great tee shot, a great way to get The Ryder Cup underway. It requires you to do something with the ball. You could hit a three wood up the left side short of the bunker, or you could take a driver and take a more aggressive route, although you can't hit it too far because the creek is waiting there for the longer hitters. The rough and the trees on the right mean that you are pretty much dead if you go in there. A decent drive gives you a shortish iron into the green and a good chance for an opening birdie.

Hole 2

HOLE 2 (THE TUNNEL) PAR 4 413 YARDS 378 METRES

This hole is quite similar in style to the opening hole. It has the one bunker you have to think about and right is no good at all. A decent drive in the fairway would give you a short iron to a green which I think is very receptive and it should be a chance for a birdie there too. If you are playing well and confident early on, it should give you a chance of a good start. If you are driving the ball well, you can be really aggressive.

HOLE 3 (THE ISLAND BEACH)
PAR 3 170 YARDS 155 METRES

This is a hole with a very shallow green and in a way there are really two greens. There is a ridge in the middle that separates the right side from the left side. The right side all breaks off to the right and the left side all breaks off to the left. Because it is so shallow it is a one club green. If the wind is blowing, the hole becomes way more difficult and tough to make the right club selection.

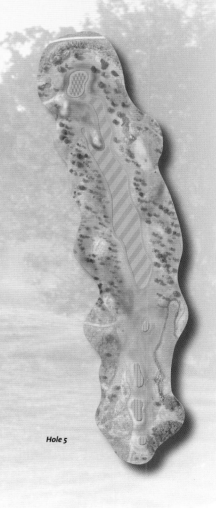

Hole 3

HOLE 4 (ARNOLD'S PICK)
PAR 5 568 YARDS 519 METRES

The first par five on the golf course and one where the long hitter definitely has a big advantage. You can take it way left and let it rip and hit it way down there leaving only an iron to the green for the longer guys. The green is kind of tucked back in behind the trees so you have to shape your second shot or take it up high and over. To me this is a definite birdie chance. As with most good holes, you need to pay attention to where the pin is which dictates where you need to put the ball if you miss it. If you are going to go for the green you can't just blast it up there and expect to chip and putt, you have to put it in the right spot.

HOLE 5 (SQUARE MEADOW)
PAR 4 440 YARDS 402 METRES

This is a very tough hole and usually plays into a left to right and hurting wind. It is a diagonal tee shot, right to left, so the guy who can draw the ball up the left side would get a bit of an advantage. The green is the real test with this hole because it is perched up on top of the hill and slopes away from you. The front left goes off the left side and the right side dumps into a hollow and the back goes away from you. Again the pin position dictates how you play the hole. In general being long is never a bad place to be apart from when the pin is front left.

Hole 4

Hole 5

Hole 6

Hole 8

HOLE 6 (THE LIFFEY STREAM)
PAR 4 478 YARDS 437 METRES

The tee shot is the key on this hole, simply because of the water which fronts the green. If you hit it in the rough you probably can't reach the green. You can actually aim it a bit further right than you think and take it aggressively over the rough and if you hit a good enough drive you can find the fairway and shorten up the hole. The second shot can be deceptively long but it depends again on the wind. The green has some nice possibilities for pin positions but it is all about the drive on this hole.

HOLE 7 (MICHAEL'S FAVOURITE)
PAR 4 430 YARDS 393 METRES

This is a very tough hole indeed. It is into the wind normally and all the new trees on the left have grown up so there is no way to miss left. There is also no way to miss right either because of the creek so again you have to find the fairway. If you don't, you are laying up or dropping. The green has water on two and a half sides which makes it a very tough golf hole. You have to hit a good drive, a good second, and the green is no piece of cake either with the slope in the middle. I would say that in a lot of the matches, if you make a par four, you have a good chance of walking off with the hole.

HOLE 8 (MAYFLY CORNER) PAR 3 173 YARDS 158 METRES

Again this hole all depends on the wind. If the wind turns and comes from the east and is in your face it can be a five iron or a four iron to the back, which is a very tough shot with the water to the right. If the wind blows the normal way and helps from the right then it is a short iron hole. The wind is also pushing you away from the water so that makes it an easier shot. You will see some birdies on the eighth hole.

HOLE 9 (THE EYE OF THE NEEDLE)
PAR 4 461 YARDS 422 METRES

This has been redesigned and has been lengthened with a new tee. The drive is crucial here because there is a big tree in the middle of the fairway and if you push it just a little bit you either get under the tree or behind it and it becomes a very tough hole from there. The green is a blind green and another one which goes away from you and you don't see much of the putting surface. It slopes hard to the left on the front and goes away from you at the back and when the greens get firm, if you don't hit the drive in the fairway, there is probably no way to hold the putting surface. As with a lot of the holes, it is judging how the ball is going to bounce on the green. There are not a lot of straight bounces on the greens, they are all kicking one way or the other so you really have to know the golf course. To me it is always a crucial hole either finishing a nine or starting a nine and it is a psychological boost if you can win the final hole of the front nine to turn into the back nine on a high. It will provide some excitement, that's for sure.

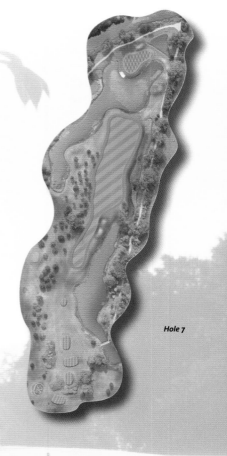

Hole 7

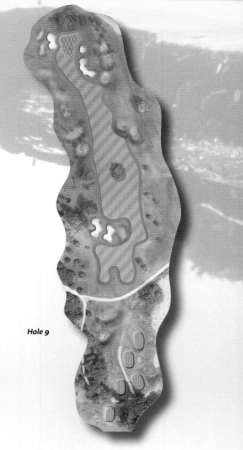

Hole 9

Ian Woosnam - 2006 European Team Captain - *Reviews The Inward Half*

‘This is just about as good as it gets for match play golf and it is going to be a brilliant setting for The Ryder Cup. Mind you, with the shots required for some of the possible pin positions, I'm pleased to be the Captain! Seriously, the combination of The Ryder Cup and this Arnold Palmer-designed course will create a very special atmosphere; the spectators are in for a fabulous festival of great golf. Subtle changes have been made to the course especially around the greens, where mown humps and hollows will allow for more creative chipping and putting as Arnold originally intended. The addition of trees in strategic areas has left nothing to chance in assuring that this will be a supreme test. ’

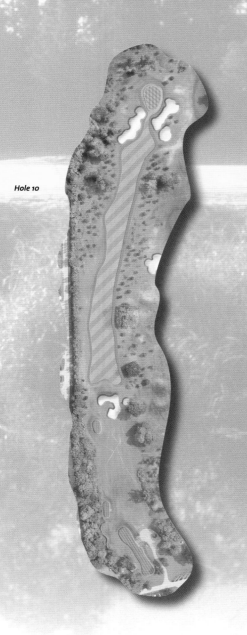

Hole 10

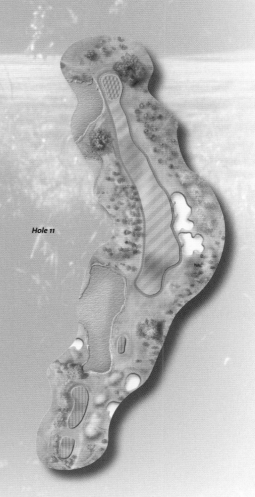

Hole 11

HOLE 10 (MICK HOLLY)
PAR 5 584 YARDS 534 METRES

Slight dogleg left to right off the tee. If you can get a big drive down there, maybe in the region of 310 yards/320 yards, you've got a good chance of getting onto this well protected green which is heavily bunkered left and right with a narrow entrance in. If you don't quite catch your drive you then have a decision to make. You either lay up to about 120 yards back or take the risk of trying to thread your ball through the bottleneck for about an 80-yard pitch. The green slopes right to left and the ball can run off into the little hollows leaving a variation of chip and runs. It's a very good hole; a good opportunity, especially in a match play situation, to go for the green in two.

HOLE 11 (LILY POND)
PAR 4 415 YARDS 379 METRES

Not the longest hole but a sharp dogleg right to left. A new tree down the left can restrict the long hitters from carrying the corner and forces them out to the right. The second shot therefore has to be played across the green, which slopes right to left towards the water. If your shot is left of the pin there is a good chance of your ball running into the water. The approach shot is as difficult as they come especially if it is windy.

The K Club, Straffan, Co.Kildare, Ireland
September 22-24 • 2006

HOLE 12 (THE DOMAIN)
PAR 3 182 YARDS 166 METRES

The water has been brought in closer and more in front of this new two tier green which slopes from right to left. There is also a new bunker back left of the green. If the pin is on the left any shot going long will end up in the back bunker. Anything left of the bunker will end up in the water. The green has also been extended on the back right hand side which gives another very good pin position on this top tier area.

HOLE 13 (LAUREL HEAVEN)
PAR 4 428 YARDS 391 METRES

Dogleg right to left. You need to hit it 275 yards to get a clear view to the green. There is water right of the green with a bunker on the left. If you miss the green to the right the ball will run down off the shaved bank into the water. The green slopes to the right with a little basin area back right. The further your drive the easier the shot because you play more into the slope of the green. The easiest pin position is back right and the hardest is front right.

HOLE 14 (CHURCHFIELDS)
PAR 3 213 YARDS 195 METRES

Usually the wind plays into you off the left. The green slopes left to right. There is a water hazard on the left - a lovely waterfall backdrop – but there is a nasty slope in the green from front to back with a spine running through it. If you are too far left your ball will kick towards the water. Plays in the region of a two iron to a four iron. It's a very strong par 3.

HOLE 15 (PHEASANT RUN)
PAR 4 446 YARDS 408 METRES

Very strong hole. From the tee shot there is a water hazard all the way down the right. The fairway slopes a little left to right towards the water as well and usually the wind plays off the left towards the water. The key is a good drive especially as the second shot is uphill to a green partially hidden by grassy mounds. The bunker about 30 yards short of the green on the left really protects the green that slopes from front to back. You can pitch the ball on the front and it will run to the middle of the green. Green slopes right to left.

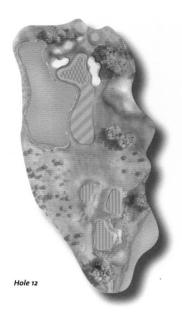

Hole 12

Hole 14

Hole 13

Hole 15

Hole 16

HOLE 16 (INISMOR)
PAR 5 555 YARDS 507 METRES

There is a double dogleg, left to right and then right to left. They call it the "greatest Par 5 in Ireland." I believe the back left tee will not be used so there is an opportunity to go for the green in two off the front tee. New trees down the right hand side, one at 280 yards and one at 300 yards, force the longer hitters to go down the left. The River Liffey runs in front of the green that has been extended so increasing the choice of pin positions. The green has also been redesigned. An exciting hole for The Ryder Cup as a lot of matches will be on the cusp of being won or lost coming to this hole. If you go for the green you're taking a risk; if you lay up you still have a good chance of making four.

HOLE 17 (HALF MOON)
PAR 4 424 YARDS 388 METRES

It has become a very demanding tee shot right to left since a new tee was put in 40 yards back The wind sometimes plays off the left. If the wind blows from the right it's an easier hole. If you bail out right hand side where there are three new trees you can face a very tricky second shot. The perfect place is to go down the left side of the fairway but it needs courage. The easier shot is to hit three wood or two iron off the tee but then that will leave a five iron into the green, and the longer the club the harder the shot. The more aggressive you get on this hole the easier it can be, although danger lurks. The green slopes severely from right to left towards the Liffey with a little mound just short of the green.

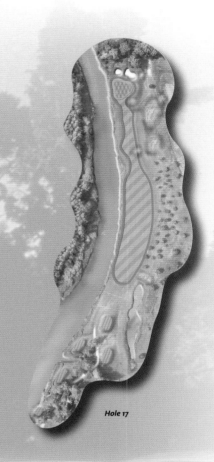

Hole 17

HOLE 18 (THE HOOKER'S GRAVEYARD)
PAR 5 537 YARDS 491 METRES

This often plays into the wind, it is uphill and it never ceases to deliver excitement – one way or another! Go down the right hand side and you need to carry the three new bunkers the first of which is 300 yards out. Go down the left and, although further from the green, the shot is a touch easier. Then for the approach there is water to the left and in front of the green and a cluster of bunkers to the right. If the pin is front left on this right to left sloping green then that only adds to the tension. If you've bailed out into those bunkers right then the recovery towards the water is fraught with danger.

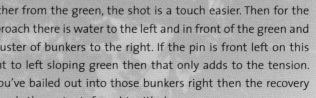

Hole 18

Images supplied by The Golf Business Ltd

WALES CYMRU
Golf as it should be

There's Stuffy Golf...

and there's Golf in Wales.

There's Overcrowded Golf...

and there's Golf in Wales.

Ian Woosnam MBE - 2006 European Team Captain

Vice Captains: Des Smyth, Peter Baker

Assistant Captains: Sandy Lyle, David J Russell

One of Ian Woosnam's many biographies claims that before fame and fortune settled on his broad shoulders the wee man used to travel Europe and eat tins of beans. Not true. He used to open the tins first and then eat the beans.

Mind you, if he had actually consumed the tin as well, few of us who know him would have been hugely surprised. Dynamite can arrive in a small package and Woosie, 5ft 4 1/2ins ("And don't forget the half," as he once told me sternly) tall, always has been an explosively impressive character.

Hard and muscular when he first hit The European Tour in 1977, he never has been a man to argue with. Debate, yes, but not argue. Woosnam wins most arguments. Even if his facts are occasionally dodgy his sheer force of personality can overwhelm an opponent so that eventually we have all conceded ground to the man born in Oswestry, England, but who always has claimed Welshness via his parents and the border that threads its path nearby.

Despite his lack of inches he was one of the longest hitters, a simple, unaffected swing on top of arms that could have been borrowed from Popeye, propelling the ball prodigious distances. After he would hit one of these zingers he would bend to pick up his tee-peg, grin and say to no-one in particular: "Not bad that."

Not bad at all. Excellent in fact. His problem as a player always has been his putting which has blown hot and cold over four decades now, but when the heat is up and the chicken bones are falling the right way and Woosnam is in the frame then he often is an unstoppable force. Forty-four titles worldwide, including, of course, the 1991 Masters Tournament at Augusta National, bear eloquent, statistical testimony to this thought.

His arm strength he has always put down to

the long hours he used to work on his dad's farm. Driving a tractor as a kid, hauling bales of hay around as a teenager did more than merely fine-tune this man. It turned him into a powerhouse. In Europe to begin with and then the world.

He is a member of the European Fab Five - the other four are Seve Ballesteros, Nick Faldo, Bernhard Langer and Sandy Lyle - but he had to work harder than the others when it came to winning events. While he was opening those tins, the others were already uncorking the champagne. But Woosnam never thought of giving up despite three nervous visits to The European Tour Qualifying School. Instead, the experience, if anything, made him even tougher mentally.

It also made him appreciate the good times when eventually they rolled in for him. Fact is that when he won his first European Tour title in 1982 he caught a great habit. Victories flowed after that breakthrough, his confidence at last in tandem with his talent and though he has all the trappings and toys of the seriously rich now - including residency in the rather choosy Channel Island of Jersey - he never has lost his common touch. Here, like his great pal Sam Torrance who made him a Ryder Cup Vice Captain at The Belfry in 2002, is a rich golfer who identifies with, and who is identified by, the average Joe.

With Woosie it always was a pint and a smoke. This casual, down to earth approach to life, the universe and pro golf has helped make him many friends over the years. It is this attractive quality on top of a natural ability to communicate with the great, the good and the others that will be his greatest

strength during his captaincy leading up to and at The K Club in Ireland.

He has respect because he has earned it, but he has affection because he deserves it. These are rich advantages to take into a match where the desire of his team members to purchase success for him may well be the difference between victory and defeat.

That remains to be seen. What is known now is that in Ian Harold Woosnam MBE, those with the power to choose have chosen well for he is a man for a battle, the right sort to have beside you when the wall is close and the opposition is closing in. He will also bring his own unique style to the event. What is this? Well, I suppose it is a directness and an openness as well as a keen golfing brain. Oh, and there is a champion's spirit in there as well. Those beans certainly worked.

Bill Elliott
The Observer / Golf Monthly

GREEN FEES   28€

NEW GOLF CLUBS   269€

PRIVATE LESSONS   35€

NOT LOSING THE BET
THIS TIME: PRICELESS

MasterCard

There are some things money can't buy.
For everything else there's MasterCard.
www.mastercard.com

EUROPEAN TOUR
OFFICIAL CREDIT CARD

Fan of the PGA European Tour
and Golfers Everywhere

Tom Lehman - 2006 United States Team Captain

Vice Captains: Corey Pavin, Loren Roberts

In the flesh Tom Lehman is a big guy, bigger certainly than he looks on television. At 6ft 2ins and 13st 8lbs he radiates not just size but power, his arms the sort that could have been attached to a blacksmith's body as easily as that of a professional golfer.

With Lehman, however, this impressive scale does not end with these trivial, physical dimensions. The reassuring news for most of us is that it really is true that size does not matter much. Except with regard to one organ...a man's heart. Here, too, Lehman appears to pass muster with a bit to spare.

This is good news for everyone connected to, or concerned about, The Ryder Cup. With Lehman in charge of the United States Team bound for The K Club, Ireland, in autumn 2006, Europe will be assured of a hard match, a fair tussle and one that should also include some real wit and wisdom from a man who can look inside himself and like the view.

As he approaches 47 years of age, Lehman can reflect on a professional career studded with grand moments. None of these are grander, of course, than his thumping victory in The Open Championship at Royal Lytham & St Annes in 1996, a major breakthrough that removed the malevolent monkey from his back that had attached itself a month earlier that year when he finished runner-up in the US Open Championship.

This failure to close a big deal - his second in a US Open - on top of the drive he whacked into a bunker at the last hole of the 1994 Masters Tournament when he was poised to win, had the idiot section of the chattering classes, as usual, digging out all those horny clichés about nerve and the lack of it.

Often this sort of thing from a bunch of people who can lose their own bottle over a changed deadline is rather silly. In Lehman's case it was inane to the point of ludicrously stupid. If ever I have seen a man with nerve and conviction then it is this bloke.

And, yes, he is driven. This drive to succeed, to overcome big odds, goes all the way back to his high school days in Alexandria, Minnesota, a town so small it would fit into the corner of a Steven Spielberg film set, a town so apple-pie American that Spielberg would like it there.

Anyway, when Lehman was 15 his high school patched together probably its greatest ever grid-iron team, a side that got all the way to the State Championship. And won, the 7,000 occupants of Alexandria decamping to the game. Lehman was part of this team. So why the long face? Because he was third choice quarter-back and never moved off the bench all year.

He recalls: "When we got back to town, we had a big parade then went back to the school gym to have a pep rally. Everyone was so excited. They had a big band playing and everybody was hugging and 'high-fiving'. But I remember just sitting there and feeling completely isolated, because I didn't really help the team win the championship. I felt like I was a failure. I just wasn't good enough. You get that a lot in sports. That sense of 'You're only as good as your last performance'.

"Shortly after I lost the two US Opens, I won the British Open and the Tour Championship on the PGA Tour. I was even ranked the best player in the world. But after all the celebrations, I was the same person with the same problems. You think victory will change your life, that life's going to be better because you won a golf tournament. But when things are all over, you still get mad and kick the dog and you even have new problems from all the sudden notoriety."

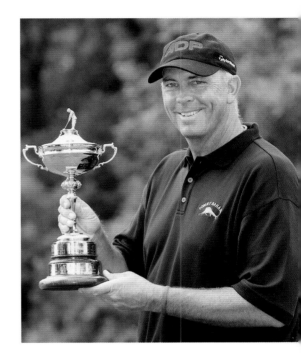

And, of course, your wife still might get mad at you. But what Lehman discovered all those years ago was religion and it is a comforting faith that has never left him. Those of us who struggle to believe that the alarm clock really will peep on time to catch the flight can only envy him the sort of strength this brings.

Watching the big man take on the little one - Ian Woosnam - in Ireland should be a thrill and, more than that, it will mean that two guys who strove to reach the top as players will enjoy the special challenge of being rival captains in a country which they both adore.

Bill Elliott
The Observer / Golf Monthly

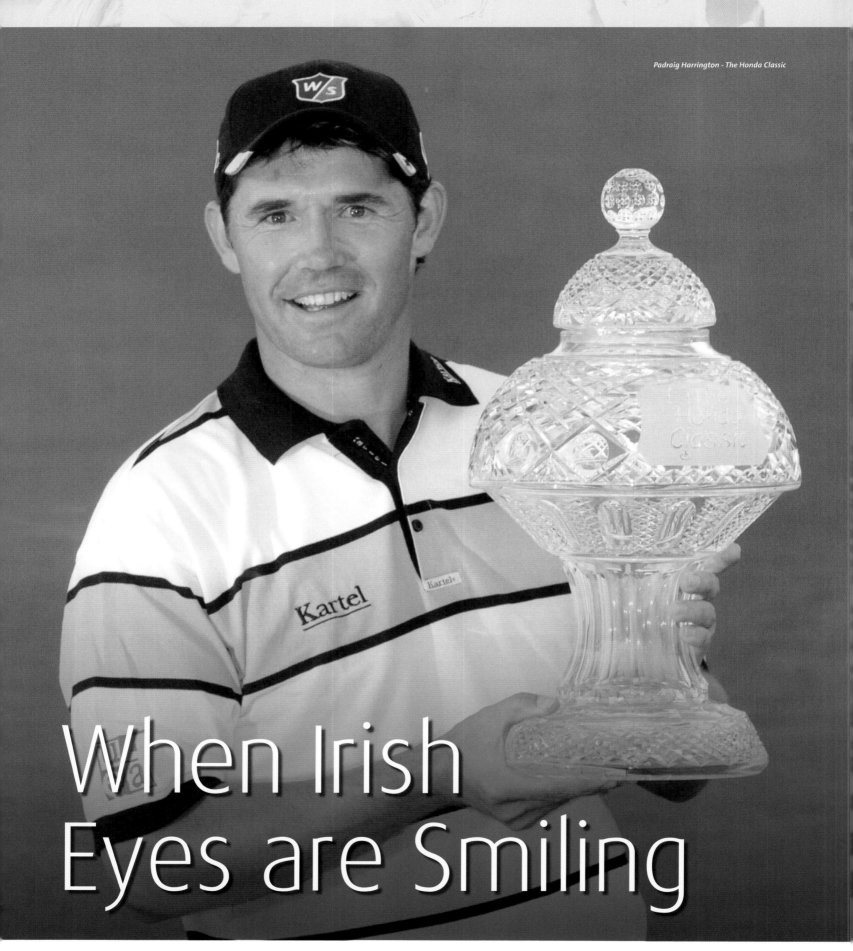

Padraig Harrington - The Honda Classic

When Irish Eyes are Smiling

Given the large Irish population in the United States, St Patrick's Day is celebrated with almost as much enthusiasm across the other side of the Atlantic as it is in the Emerald Isle itself. In 2005, however, the festivities took on an ever greater resonance thanks to the performance of two of Ireland's finest golfers.

On March 13 – four days before St Patrick's Day itself - both Padraig Harrington and Des Smyth triumphed for the first time in America: Harrington in The Honda Classic (pictured left) on the US PGA Tour and Smyth in the SBC Classic on the US Champions Tour. It was a truly memorable achievement and one of the highlights of yet another season where European Tour Members excelled around the globe.

In the final round of The Honda Classic at The Country Club at Mirasol in Florida, Harrington was pursued all the way by Joe Ogilvie and Vijay Singh. It came as no surprise when the trio ended their respective 72 holes tied at 14 under par 274. Ogilvie was eliminated from the play-off at the opening hole, and when Singh missed a two and a half foot par putt at the second extra hole the title belonged to Harrington.

"I'm sure I kept a few pubs open back home tonight," said the Dubliner, whose own place in the play-off was assured thanks to a superb final round 63. "It is great to be the first Irishman to win a US PGA Tour event – no-one can ever take that away from me."

With the Guinness already flowing, a few hours later in Drogheda there were additional calls for champagne when Smyth, the town's favourite son, came from behind with a closing four under par round of 68 to win the SBC Classic at the Valencia Country Club in California.

Matters were close between Smyth and eventual runners-up Mark McNulty and D.A. Weibring before the 52 year old Irishman broke clear on the back nine with birdies at the 12th, 13th and 15th to win by a shot on five under par 211. "I thought I might need

one more birdie, but as things turned out, I didn't," said Smyth. "We are all very happy about Padraig's win too – it is a truly great day for Ireland."

Not content with one success Stateside, both Harrington and Smyth went on to win again in 2005. Smyth's second US Champions Tour victory came five weeks later at the Savannah Harbor Golf Resort in Georgia where an opening round of 66 laid the foundations for an eight under par total of 208 and a two shot victory in the Liberty Mutual Legends of Golf tournament.

Harrington had to bide his time a little longer, until the end of June, for his second US PGA Tour win, but it was well worth the wait when a spectacular eagle putt from all of 65 feet on the final green of the Westchester Country Club in New York, saw him pip Jim Furyk by a shot to win the Barclays Classic.

Harrington closed with a 70 for a ten under par total of 274 and admitted: "To hole a putt like that on the final green is very special indeed. Normally you have a short putt or two putts to win a title and to be honest I was just trying to get it close."

Once more, over the course of the year, the United States proved a happy hunting ground for silverware for European Tour Members with Honorary Member Vijay Singh taking centre stage. Although he could not quite match his extraordinary haul of eight US PGA Tour titles in addition to the US PGA Championship in 2004, the 42 year old nevertheless won four times.

His first success came in January in the second event of the season, the Sony Open in Hawaii at the Waialae Country Club in

Des Smyth
- Liberty Mutual
Legends of Golf

Vijay Singh - Buick Open

Richard Green - Mastercard Masters

Wins Around The World

Simon Wakefield - Dimension Data Pro-Am

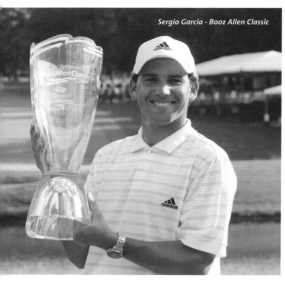

Sergio Garcia - Booz Allen Classic

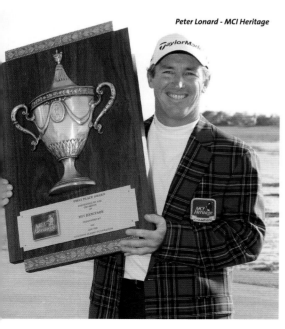

Peter Lonard - MCI Heritage

Honolulu, where a birdie four on the 72nd hole was enough for a 65 and an 11 under par total of 269, one shot better than the fast finishing Ernie Els, who closed with a 62.

Then at the end of April he won twice in the space of three weeks.

The first success did not come as a great surprise, being that it was Singh's second consecutive victory in the Shell Houston Open at the Redstone Golf Club in Texas and his third win in the event in four years. This time he ended level with John Daly on 13 under par 275 but took the title when the American found the water at the first play-off hole.

Two weeks later in the Wachovia Championship at the Quail Hollow Country Club in North Carolina, again via a play-off, the Fijian saw off Jim Furyk and Sergio Garcia after the trio had finished on 12 under par 276.

Singh also proved adept as a front runner, winning the Buick Open at Warwick Hills Golf & Country Club in Michigan at the end of July at a canter. A third round 63 put daylight between Singh and the rest of the field and although Tiger Woods mounted a final round charge to finish tied second with Zach Johnson, Singh's closing 70 for a 24 under par total of 264 was sufficient for a four shot victory. Singh eventually finished second in the 2005 US PGA Tour Money List behind Woods.

While Garcia had been disappointed to lose to Singh in the Wachovia Championship, having surrendered a six shot lead in the final round, the Spaniard put the chagrin behind him in admirable fashion four weeks later when he won the Booz Allen Classic at the Congressional Country Club in Maryland at the beginning of June.

Twelve months earlier, the title had gone to fellow European Tour Member Adam Scott and Garcia had good reason to thank the Australian, for it was a putting tip during the week that provided the catalyst for Garcia's

success, the 25 year old returning a 14 under par total of 270 to win by two shots from Ben Crane, Davis Love III and Scott himself.

"Maybe I should charge him," joked Scott, before adding: "Sergio's a good friend and I didn't like to see him struggling. I'd rather both of us playing our best and battling it out to see who's better."

Scott had enjoyed his own US PGA Tour victory in February when he won the rain-shortened Nissan Open at the Riviera Country Club in California. Torrential downpours meant competitors were only able to complete two rounds before Scott beat Chad Campbell at the first play-off hole after both had finished their respective 36 holes on nine under par 133.

Peter Lonard, another Australian, mounted the winner's rostrum at the MCI Heritage tournament at Hilton Head Island in South Carolina in April, a seven under par total of 277 good enough to finish two shots clear of Billy Andrade, Darren Clarke and Jim Furyk. This was Lonard's first US PGA Tour win, but when Retief Goosen claimed The International tournament at the Castle Pines Golf Club in Colorado in August he was winning for the sixth time on American soil.

The final day of the modified stableford event saw the competitors have to complete 36 holes on the hilly 7,619 yard course in one day, leaving Goosen's narrow victory – by 32 points to Brandt Jobe's 31 – a victory for stamina as well as skill.

There was a good deal of skill, too, in Mark James's second US Champions Tour victory in February when he birdied the final two holes at the Twin Eagles Golf Club in Florida for a 66 and a 13 under par total of 203 to finally see off the dogged challenge of Hale Irwin and win The ACE Group Classic.

"With Hale breathing down your neck, it is not a nice feeling," said the Englishman. "He

seemed like he only had to look at the ball today and it dived into the cup, it was quite incredible. So it was great to make those two putts myself at the end – it felt good."

Another man who found the bottom of the cup at the crucial time was Mark McNulty, who holed from 14 feet at the second play-off hole to end the hopes of Americans Don Pooley and Tom Purtzer in the Bank of America Championship at the Nashawtuc Country Club in Maryland. It was a fourth win for the former Zimbabwean, now a citizen of Ireland, on the US Champions Tour and came after the trio had ended on 12 under par 204.

It was not just in the United States, though, that European Tour Members flourished, with South Africa and the Sunshine Tour proving a happy hunting ground. In January, England's Simon Wakefield celebrated gaining his card at The European Tour Qualifying School Finals two months earlier by capturing the Dimension Data Pro-Am in Sun City. The 31 year old carded a final round 69 for a nine under par total of 279 and a five shot winning margin over South African Nic Henning.

Seven days later, host nation favourite Richard Sterne followed Wakefield into the winner's enclosure when a final round 70 for an 11 under par total of 269 saw him win the Nashua Masters at the Wild Coast Sun Country Club, before Zimbabwe's Marc Cayeux won the season-ending Vodacom Tour Championship at the Country Club in Johannesburg.

Cayeux was in scintillating form in the final round, carding nine birdies and an eagle three at the 18th in a superb closing 61 for a 20 under par total of 268 and victory by six shots. While Cayeux celebrated, there was also joy for South Africa's Charl Schwartzel, who confirmed his position as winner of the Sunshine Tour Order of Merit for 2004/2005. The main season might have ended in South Africa, but the onset of the Winter Tour did

nothing to dampen the title aspirations of the Members in action. First to succeed was Challenge Tour Member Desvonde Botes, who won both the Vodacom Origins of Golf Tour event at Pretoria Country Club with a 14 under par total of 202, and the Vodacom Origins of Golf Tour event at Pezula with an 18 under par total of 198, before Hennie Otto won the Vodacom Origins of Golf Tour event at Erinvale, matching Botes's winning 14 under par total of 202 at Pretoria.

While Schwartzel won the Sunshine Tour Order of Merit crown in South Africa, fellow European Tour Member Richard Green did the same in his native Australia, his win in the 2004 MasterCard Masters laying the foundations for him to claim the 2004/2005 PGA Tour of Australasia Order of Merit.

Green might not have won in 2005, but there were successes Down Under for Affiliate Member Steven Bowditch and European Tour Member Peter O'Malley. Bowditch's 11 under par total of 277 gave him a five shot winning margin in the Jacob's Creek Open at Royal Adelaide Golf Club, and the 22 year old nearly made it two wins in a row a week later in the ING New Zealand PGA Championship.

Having stormed home in a final round 63 on the Clearwater Resort course in Christchurch for a 14 under par total of 274, Bowditch found himself in a play-off with O'Malley, who closed with a 69. The duo halved the first three extra holes before O'Malley rolled in a 20 foot birdie putt on the fourth extra hole.

The scenery might have changed from Australasia to Asia four months later but the sweet smell of success remained in the air for Retief Goosen, Terry Pilkadaris, Adam Scott, and Thaworn Wiratchant as they each picked up titles on the Asian Tour.

Challenge Tour Member Pilkadaris started the ball rolling with an emphatic five shot victory in the Brunei Open at the Empire Hotel and Country Club, a final round 67 for

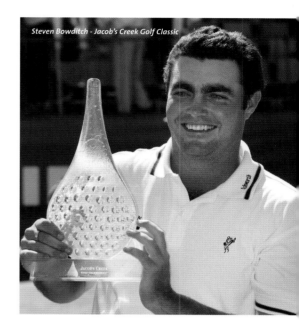
Steven Bowditch - Jacob's Creek Golf Classic

Retief Goosen - The International at Castle Pines Golf Club

Thaworn Wiratchant

a 19 under par total of 265 being the perfect start to his honeymoon the following week. Goosen won his 23rd title worldwide, a final round 64 for a 22 under par total of 266 giving him a six shot winning margin in the Volkswagen Masters – China at the Jinghua Golf Club. "It is great to win all around the world," said Goosen. "I've won in a lot of countries so it is good to win in China."

A man who had already sampled the delights of winning in Asia was Scott, following his success in the Johnnie Walker Classic on The European Tour at Pine Valley Golf Resort & Country Club in Beijing in April, and he thrilled his large Asian fan base once again in September with victory in the Singapore Open. He went one better than Goosen and won by seven shots at the Sentosa Golf Club's Serapong course, his final round 65 giving him a comfortable winning margin over fellow European Tour Member Lee Westwood.

Continuing the Asian Roll of Honour in 2005 was Wiratchant, the Thai golfer coming from behind with a spectacular closing 64 for an 18 under par total of 270 and a one shot winning margin over his fellow countryman Chapchai Nirat in the Taiwan Open at the Chang Gung Golf Club. Wiratchant followed this up by capturing the Hero Honda Indian Open at Delhi Golf Club with a 16 under par aggregate of 272, two ahead of India's Gaurav Ghei. It was Wiratchant's seventh win in Asia.

Then Northern Ireland's Darren Clarke successfully defended the Mitsui Sumitomo Visa Taiheiyo Masters title with a closing 68 on the Gotenba course at the Taiheiyo Club for an 18 under par 270.

While European Tour Members delighted in exhibiting their skills around the world, they were not averse to performing on home soil either, a point conclusively proven by Argentina's Angel Cabrera and Andres Romero and both Paul Lawrie and Padraig Harrington, who won their respective PGA

Championships. Cabrera followed wins in the 74th Abierto de Centro in Cordoba and the 39th Abierto de Norte in Tucuman by successfully defending the 18th Torneo de Maestros Copa Personal at Olivos Golf Club in Buenos Aires, and Romero won the inaugural Roberto de Vicenzo Classic the following week in the Argentine capital.

Lawrie's success in the Gleneagles Scottish PGA Championship came in August, the 1999 Open Champion claiming the flagship event on the Tartan Tour with a 13 under par total of 275, winning by four shots in the end from fellow Tour professional David Drysdale.

Harrington's victory at the Palmerstown House course proved to be a slightly harder fought affair, the 34 year old having to go to the first play-off hole to see off the dogged challenge of fellow European Tour professional Damien McGrane and Lisburn club professional Stephen Hamill, after the trio had ended their respective 72 holes on three under par 285.

Back in March, Harrington had remarked how his victory in The Honda Classic had no doubt kept a few pubs open in Dublin that night. It is a fair bet that his victory at home in September had a similar result especially with The 2006 Ryder Cup being so eagerly anticipated by all of Ireland.

Scott Crockett

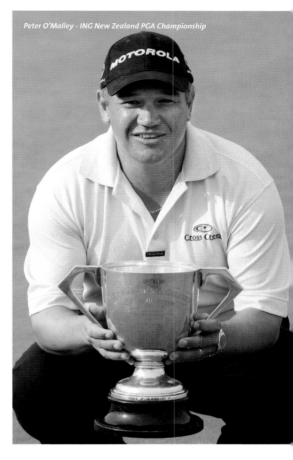

Peter O'Malley - ING New Zealand PGA Championship

Richard Sterne - Nashua Masters

The European Seniors Tour

On Top of the World

Sam Torrance OBE

From the majesty of the Alps to the mystery of the Pyramids, the 2005 European Seniors Tour Schedule offered the perfect blend of great golf and stunning scenery. In fact, there were times during the year when it seemed a little piece of history was being created at every turn, right down to the final putt when Sam Torrance claimed first place in the Order of Merit ahead of England's Carl Mason and Ireland's Des Smyth.

For Torrance not only achieved a lifetime ambition in finishing Number One in an Order of Merit, but he also completed a unique treble as Scottish compatriots Colin Montgomerie and Marc Warren had finished Number One on The European Tour Order of Merit and the European Challenge Tour Rankings respectively in 2005. It was the first time one nation had provided the Number One player on each of the three Tours.

Torrance received The John Jacobs Trophy awarded annually to the winner of the European Seniors Tour Order of Merit then said: "It feels awesome to be Number One. It is something I have wanted all my life. I'm very proud. I gave up playing in America last year to commit to the European Seniors Tour and it has proved fruitful."

In 2005 there were visits to new countries in the shape of Bahrain, Denmark and Egypt; an annual prize fund record of €6.75 million; six first-time winners in Bob Boyd, Giuseppe Cali, Mark James, Eduardo Romero, Smyth and Gery Watine; Terry Gale extending the longest current winning streak on Tour to four consecutive years; and Bob Lendzion equalling the lowest 54 hole winning total to par with an 18 under par mark of 198.

The Order of Merit contest developed into a head-to-head race between Mason, who was attempting to win The John Jacobs Trophy for the third year in a row, and Torrance, who, somewhat surprisingly given his long and illustrious career, had been denied a first place finish in The European Tour Order of Merit.

Mason initialy forged ahead but Torrance, following three wins in all of which he led from start to finish, edged in front in the penultimate event, the Algarve Seniors Open of Portugal, and at the season-ending Arcapita Seniors Tour Championship at Riffa Golf Club, Bahrain, he took his winnings to €277,420 (£187,397). Mason (€257,113; £173,679), who won twice, has now amassed €962,129 (£664,249) in three years and Smyth earned €229,514 (£155,036) for third place.

Denis O'Sullivan launched the 2005 campaign in March with victory in the DGM Barbados Open at Royal Westmoreland. Set against the backdrop of Caribbean white sands and palms trees that must have seemed a million miles from his native Ireland, he finished with a ten under par, three round aggregate of 206 to win by three shots from American John Grace.

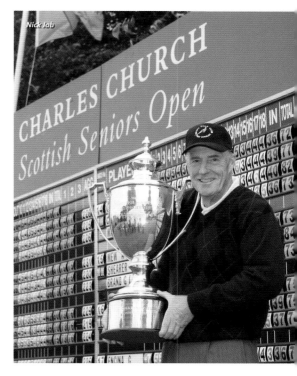

Nick Job

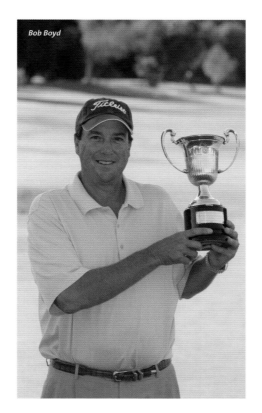

Bob Boyd

Jerry Bruner

273

The Tour then hopped across to Tobago where two Argentine brothers ensured the Tobago Plantations Seniors Classic was a truly family affair. Luis Carbonetti claimed victory at the Tobago Plantations Beach & Golf Resort by two shots with an eight under par score of 208 from his elder sibling Horacio and Scotland's Bill Longmuir who shared second.

While the one-two was a first for the Carbonetti clan in Seniors golf, history of a wider scale was made in April as the Tour embarked on its first visit to Egypt for the Jolie Ville Sharm El Sheikh Seniors Open at the Jolie Ville Golf Hotel.

With the desert conditions making the going hot, it was perhaps no surprise that Las Vegas resident Bob Lendzion should play the winning hand with a final round 66 to hold off South Africa's John Mashego and England's David J Russell. Lendzion finished on 18 under par 198 to equal the lowest 54 hole total to par, set by Australian David Good at the Tunisian Seniors Open in 2003, in the history of the European Seniors Tour.

Frenchman Gery Watine then became the fourth different nationality in the winner's enclosure when he beat Ireland's Eamonn Darcy in a play-off at the Nokia 9300 Italian Seniors Open at Circolo Golf Venezia, after both players had finished on 11 under par 205.

Bob Lendzion

Luis Carbonetti

After American Mike Reid claimed the US Senior PGA Championship at Laurel Valley Golf Club in Pennsylvania the Tour moved on to The Heritage at Killenard, Ireland, for the AIB Irish Seniors Open in association with Greenstar and Fáilte Ireland.

Luis Carbonetti again challenged but this time finished runner-up behind Australia's Noel Ratcliffe, who became only the second man after Seiji Ebihara to claim two AIB Irish Seniors Open titles when he closed with a 71 for a three round aggregate of six under par 210 to win by two strokes. Ratcliffe would go on to claim the Hardys Super Seniors Prize for the season, finishing ahead of American David Oakley in the competition for golfers aged 60 and over.

Then Torrance, who had gained one of his 21 European Tour victories in Jersey, again found the Channel Island a home from home as he captured the Irvine Whitlock Seniors Classic at La Moye Golf Club. Torrance led from the start and with rounds of 65, 68 and 72 for an 11 under par 205, he won by four from Russell.

Italian Giuseppe Cali scooped The Mobile Cup with an eight under par 208 at Collingtree Park Golf Club, England, but, sparked by Torrance's success, Mason then clicked into gear with back-to-back victories in the De Vere Northumberland Seniors Classic with a 16 under par score of 200 at De Vere Slaley Hall, England, and the Ryder Cup Wales Seniors Open at Royal St David's Golf Club with a five under par total of 202. This took to 11 the number of wins Mason had gained on the European Seniors Tour since his 50th birthday on June 25, 2003.

England's Jim Rhodes won the Nigel Mansell Sunseeker International Classic at Woodbury Park Hotel Golf & Country Club, England, with an eight under par 208 – three ahead of compatriot Tony Charnley – prior to the European Seniors Tour's flagship event, The Senior British Open

HARDYS SUPER SENIORS ORDER OF MERIT

Australia's Noel Ratcliffe won the Hardys Super Seniors Prize, presented by Andy Stubbs, Managing Director of the European Seniors Tour

Pos	Name	Country	Points
1	Noel Ratcliffe	(Aus)	11,450
2	David Oakley	(USA)	10,600
3	John Morgan	(Eng)	9,050
4	Tommy Horton	(Eng)	7,725
5	Malcolm Gregson	(Eng)	5,925
6	Bob Charles	(NZ)	3,675
7	Maurice Bembridge	(Eng)	3,525
8	Antonio Garrido	(Sp)	2,575
9	John Bland	(SA)	1,750
10	Bill Hardwick	(Can)	1,200

Giuseppe Cali

Championship, presented by Aberdeen Asset Management, unfolding. Buffeted by strong winds for the first two days, the tight Balgownie Links at Royal Aberdeen Golf Club proved to be a worthy challenge. Tom Watson of America tied with Smyth on four under par 280 – one ahead of Greg Norman and three ahead of Craig Stadler – and, after halving the 18th twice, Watson got down in two from just off the back at the 17th to regain the trophy he won in 2003 at The Westin Turnberry Resort, the venue where he will defend the title in 2006.

Torrance captured his second title of the season at the De Vere PGA Seniors Championship at the beginning of August – one week after American Allen Doyle won the US Senior Open at the NCR Country Club in Ohio – when he carded a three under par final round 69 for a 17 under par 271 to finish four shots clear of Russell at De Vere Carden Park.

Next to the Swiss Alps where Gale extended his record of consecutive winning years on the European Seniors Tour to four and gained his seventh win in all. "It's nice to know that when I have a chance I can still do it," admitted the 59 year old Australian, who finished on 11 under par 199 to claim the Bad Ragaz PGA Seniors Open at Golf Club Bad Ragaz by two strokes from Luis Carbonetti and Watine.

Another man who could not hide his delight was affable Argentine Eduardo Romero, who cruised to an eight stroke success with an 11 under par total of 205 in the Travis Perkins Senior Masters over the Edinburgh Course at Wentworth Club, England.

England's Nick Job took a share of second place behind Romero and he went one better the following week in the Charles Church

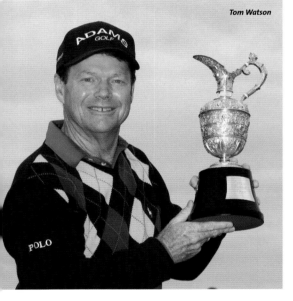

Tom Watson

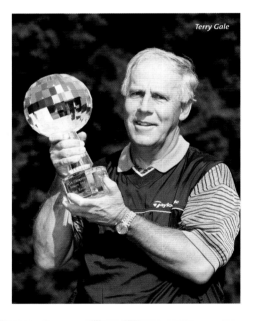

Terry Gale

Carl Mason

Gery Watine

Bill Longmuir

Des Smyth

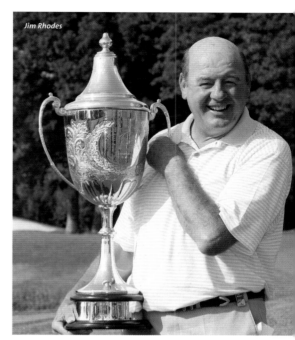

Jim Rhodes

Scottish Seniors Open, held at a windswept Roxburghe Hotel & Golf Course near Kelso, Scotland. It was Job's first win since 2001 and his third in all on the European Seniors Tour. Job carded a one under par 71 to hold off former professional footballer Jean-Pierre Sallat of France with a ten under par 206. It culminated in a glorious 210 yard four iron to the heart of the final green. "That was one of the finest shots I have ever hit in my life," he said.

Huge crowds watched the Bovis Lend Lease European Senior Masters in the regal setting of Woburn Golf Club and England's Mark James – the man who led The European Ryder Cup Team at Brookline in 1999 – had one hand on the trophy but could only smile wryly as his old friend and adversary, Torrance, the winning Captain from The De Vere Belfry in 2002, sank a birdie putt at the last to force a play-off with the pair locked on nine under par 207.

On their return to the 18th at the Duke's Course, Torrance appeared to have the advantage when, having been stuck in the trees to the left of the fairway, he conjured a miraculous low hook shot to within four feet of the pin. However, James holed from seven

feet for birdie and Torrance saw his putt drift fractionally right of the hole.

Leading Rookie Kevin Spurgeon of England, the overnight leader by three shots, finished in third place and while there was no fairytale ending for Spurgeon, the land of Hans Christian Andersen nevertheless produced a magical tale the following week when Longmuir won the Scandinavian Senior Open at the historic Royal Copenhagen Golf Club.

He fired a brilliant seven under par final round 64 and finished four strokes clear of Cali with a 17 under par 196 total.

The following week Longmuir received the warmest of welcomes on his arrival for the Bendinat London Seniors Masters at The London Golf Club where he is the touring professional, but Torrance was in no mood to let sentiment get in the way of his Order of Merit ambitions.

Torrance led from the front, carding a course record eight under par 64, and followed that with rounds of 67 and 70 for a 15 under par total of 201 and in so doing he denied Russell victory for a third time in

John Spanswick, Chairman and CEO of Bovis Lend Lease EMEA (left) and The Duke of Bedford (right) pose with England's Mark James

Denis O'Sullivan

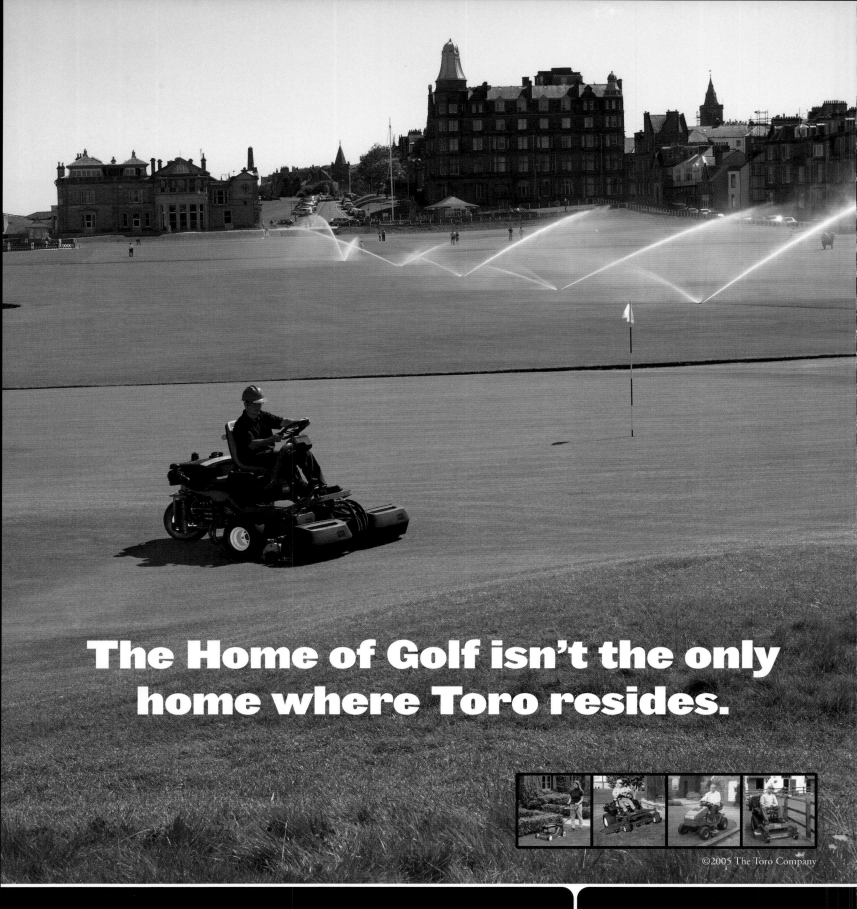

The Home of Golf isn't the only home where Toro resides.

©2005 The Toro Company

Eduardo Romero

David J Russell

John Chillas

2005. In fact Russell finished runner-up no fewer than four times in 2005.

American Bob Boyd produced a birdie-eagle-par finish to overtake Spain's José Rivero and Rhodes in the Castellón Costa Azahar Open de España Senior at Club de Campo del Mediterraneo the following week. He collected the title with an 11 under par total of 205.

The 'American Dream' continued when Los Angeles resident Jerry Bruner holed a 30 foot birdie putt at the 54th hole to capture the Algarve Seniors Open of Portugal at Quinta de Cima Golf by a stroke from Northern Ireland's Eddie Polland, Rivero and Torrance with an 11 under par 205. Mason finished tied sixth which meant that Torrance had earned enough to be €249 (£168) ahead entering the season-ending Arcapita Seniors Tour Championship at the Riffa Golf Club in Bahrain.

A decade after narrowly missing out on The European Tour Order of Merit when he was pipped by Colin Montgomerie in the final event on the 1995 season, Torrance secured the Number One spot with a superb closing 66 for a share of third place behind Smyth, who finished birdie-birdie for a two stroke win ahead of Scotland's John Chillas on ten under par 206. "It's a massive win for me," said Smyth. "My first on the European Seniors Tour and I'm very, very happy."

It was another piece of history at the end of a vintage year on the European Seniors Tour.

Steven Franklin

THE FINAL EUROPEAN SENIORS TOUR ORDER OF MERIT 2005

Pos	Name	Country	Played	€	£
1	Sam TORRANCE	(Scot)	(14)	277,420.76	187,397.08
2	Carl MASON	(Eng)	(18)	257,113.63	173,679.66
3	Des SMYTH	(Ire)	(5)	229,514.73	155,036.67
4	Luis CARBONETTI	(Arg)	(19)	199,412.07	134,702.39
5	Nick JOB	(Eng)	(20)	192,690.07	130,161.69
6	Giuseppe CALI	(It)	(21)	184,094.96	124,355.72
7	John CHILLAS	(Scot)	(21)	171,127.74	115,596.39
8	David J RUSSELL	(Eng)	(18)	167,982.46	113,471.76
9	Denis O'SULLIVAN	(Ire)	(22)	149,866.71	101,234.62
10	Bill LONGMUIR	(Scot)	(21)	146,161.90	98,732.03
11	Noel RATCLIFFE	(Aus)	(17)	143,172.43	96,712.65
12	Terry GALE	(Aus)	(19)	139,705.40	94,370.67
13	Martin GRAY	(Scot)	(19)	126,960.52	85,761.53
14	Bob CAMERON	(Eng)	(22)	124,284.82	83,954.11
15	Gery WATINE	(Fr)	(19)	122,227.72	82,564.54
16	Jim RHODES	(Eng)	(21)	113,646.05	76,767.64
17	Horacio CARBONETTI	(Arg)	(18)	113,378.36	76,586.82
18	Eamonn DARCY	(Ire)	(13)	111,907.98	75,593.58
19	Bruce HEUCHAN	(Can)	(19)	105,471.07	71,245.46
20	Delroy CAMBRIDGE	(Jam)	(20)	104,792.15	70,786.85
21	Kevin SPURGEON	(Eng)	(19)	97,586.98	65,919.77
22	Jerry BRUNER	(USA)	(20)	95,192.67	64,302.43
23	Gavan LEVENSON	(SA)	(21)	90,336.99	61,022.42
24	Ian MOSEY	(Eng)	(19)	85,032.18	57,439.04
25	Emilio RODRIGUEZ	(Sp)	(17)	84,520.61	57,093.48
26	Gordon J BRAND	(Eng)	(8)	81,804.43	55,258.70
27	Guillermo ENCINA	(Chl)	(18)	80,526.23	54,395.28
28	Bob CHARLES	(NZ)	(6)	77,388.13	52,275.50
29	Bob BOYD	(USA)	(10)	77,167.37	52,126.38
30	Tony CHARNLEY	(Eng)	(21)	76,343.90	51,570.13
31	Alan TAPIE	(USA)	(16)	75,023.48	50,678.19
32	David OAKLEY	(USA)	(20)	72,471.32	48,954.21
33	José RIVERO	(Sp)	(4)	70,516.25	47,633.56
34	Martin POXON	(Eng)	(17)	68,752.33	46,442.04
35	Tommy HORTON	(Eng)	(19)	63,186.39	42,682.26
36	John MASHEGO	(SA)	(17)	58,509.45	39,523.00
37	Jean Pierre SALLAT	(Fr)	(17)	58,317.58	39,393.39
38	David GOOD	(Aus)	(20)	57,485.57	38,831.37
39	Seiji EBIHARA	(Jpn)	(7)	54,514.35	36,824.32
40	Bob LENDZION	(USA)	(15)	54,184.09	36,601.23
41	Manuel PIÑERO	(Sp)	(15)	52,317.70	35,340.49
42	John MORGAN	(Eng)	(15)	51,681.07	34,910.44
43	Mike FERGUSON	(Aus)	(17)	51,376.79	34,704.90
44	Craig MALTMAN	(Scot)	(17)	51,246.44	34,616.85
45	Rex CALDWELL	(USA)	(17)	48,843.91	32,993.95
46	Eddie POLLAND	(N.Ire)	(19)	47,728.81	32,240.70
47	Gordon TOWNHILL	(Eng)	(19)	44,702.24	30,196.26
48	John BLAND	(SA)	(5)	43,942.99	29,683.39
49	John GRACE	(USA)	(8)	43,830.23	29,607.22
50	Martin FOSTER	(Eng)	(20)	41,594.47	28,096.97
51	Maurice BEMBRIDGE	(Eng)	(21)	40,651.96	27,460.30
52	Tony ALLEN	(Eng)	(16)	38,193.15	25,799.39
53	John BENDA	(USA)	(15)	37,708.36	25,471.91
54	Malcolm GREGSON	(Eng)	(18)	35,356.10	23,882.96
55	Denis DURNIAN	(Eng)	(17)	34,686.04	23,430.34
56	Hank WOODROME	(USA)	(18)	34,631.85	23,393.74
57	Mike MILLER	(Scot)	(21)	31,741.16	21,441.08
58	Adan SOWA	(Arg)	(18)	30,963.02	20,915.45
59	Bob SHEARER	(Aus)	(15)	30,723.89	20,753.91
60	Alan MEW	(T&T)	(16)	27,428.03	18,527.57
61	Simon OWEN	(NZ)	(17)	23,658.42	15,981.21
62	Armando SAAVEDRA	(Arg)	(19)	22,475.34	15,182.04
63	Antonio GARRIDO	(Sp)	(17)	22,328.27	15,082.69
64	Brian JONES	(Aus)	(16)	21,292.56	14,383.07
65	Pete OAKLEY	(USA)	(6)	21,049.24	14,218.71
66	David CREAMER	(Eng)	(19)	20,846.68	14,081.88
67	Bill HARDWICK	(Can)	(19)	20,760.33	14,023.55
68	Chuck MILNE	(USA)	(8)	18,007.29	12,163.89
69	Bob LARRATT	(Eng)	(12)	17,039.82	11,510.36
70	Neil COLES	(Eng)	(6)	16,864.29	11,391.79
71	Ray CARRASCO	(USA)	(14)	16,652.91	11,249.00
72	Donald STIRLING	(Aut)	(9)	14,496.34	9,792.24
73	Russell WEIR	(Scot)	(10)	13,640.60	9,214.20
74	Paul LEONARD	(N.Ire)	(10)	13,131.79	8,870.49
75	Lee CARTER	(USA)	(10)	12,624.93	8,528.11
76	John CURTIS	(Ire)	(14)	9,982.88	6,743.41
77	Gary WINTZ	(USA)	(10)	9,589.35	6,477.58
78	Jeff HAWKES	(SA)	(6)	9,559.65	6,457.52
79	Victor GARCIA	(Sp)	(14)	9,428.27	6,368.77
80	Bob BYMAN	(USA)	(7)	8,946.85	6,043.58
81	Neville CLARKE	(SA)	(11)	8,344.09	5,636.42
82	Liam HIGGINS	(Ire)	(12)	8,227.75	5,557.82
83	Keith WILLIAMS	(Wal)	(6)	7,695.01	5,197.96
84	Tony PRICE	(Wal)	(7)	7,117.55	4,807.89
85	Steve STULL	(USA)	(7)	6,873.40	4,642.97
86	Steve WILD	(Eng)	(11)	6,273.86	4,237.98
87	Ian STANLEY	(Aus)	(9)	6,250.18	4,221.98
88	Paul REED	(USA)	(4)	5,815.22	3,928.17
89	Mike GALLAGHER	(Eng)	(17)	5,710.40	3,857.36
90	Alberto CROCE	(It)	(7)	4,869.42	3,289.28
91	Jeff VAN WAGENEN	(USA)	(5)	4,738.91	3,201.12
92	Peter TOWNSEND	(Eng)	(7)	3,966.86	2,679.60
93	Philippe DUGENY	(Fr)	(7)	3,232.49	2,183.54
94	Manuel VELASCO	(Sp)	(7)	2,841.24	1,919.25
95	John IRWIN	(Can)	(4)	2,672.61	1,805.34
96	TR JONES	(USA)	(5)	2,538.15	1,714.52
97	Stephen CHADWICK	(Eng)	(5)	2,197.72	1,484.55
98	Scott DAVIDSON	(Eng)	(3)	1,214.94	820.69
99	Jay DOLAN III	(USA)	(6)	1,214.62	820.47
100	David CHILLAS	(Scot)	(6)	1,050.25	709.44
101	Peter DAWSON	(Eng)	(1)	927.06	626.22
102	Joe MCDERMOTT	(Ire)	(1)	800.00	540.40
103	Kurt COX	(USA)	(2)	555.58	375.29
104	Keith ASHDOWN	(Eng)	(1)	525.00	354.64
105	Bill BRASK	(USA)	(1)	495.51	334.71
106	Gerry MOCHE	(Arg)	(2)	464.29	313.62
107	Kenny STEVENSON	(N.Ire)	(1)	255.96	172.90
108	Vincent TSHABALALA	(SA)	(1)	246.56	166.55
109	Rene-Pierre BROUCHOUD	(Swi)	(1)	231.00	156.04

Ground-Breaking Adventure

The Final European Challenge Tour Rankings 2005

1 **Marc WARREN**

2 Carl SUNESON

3 Fredrik WIDMARK

4 Andrew BUTTERFIELD

5 Michael KIRK

6 Steven JEPPESEN

7 Benn BARHAM

8 Michael HOEY

9 Daniel VANCSIK

10 Richard McEVOY

11 Rafael GOMEZ

12 David HIGGINS

13 Paul DWYER

14 Andres ROMERO

15 Marco RUIZ

16 Ariel CANETE

17 Tom WHITEHOUSE

18 Ross FISHER

19 Stephen BROWNE

20 Toni KARJALAINEN

Marc Warren

The 2005 European Challenge Tour season was another year of first class golf fuelled by a ground-breaking sense of adventure as the Tour once again pushed the game's boundaries while continuing to unearth the stars of the future. With 30 events played in 22 countries in its 17th year, the Challenge Tour Members were afforded the opportunity to play the game in diverse locations all over the world, from Central America to Africa and from Europe to Central Asia, as they chased a place among the elite top 20 on the Rankings that would secure a passport to The 2006 European Tour International Schedule.

Marc Warren, who emerged as the Number One, is the embodiment of the kind of golfer the Challenge Tour aims to produce. The young Scotsman looks capable of becoming a European Tour champion of the future boasting, as he does, an impressive pedigree that is supplemented by an exceptional golf swing and a strength of mind that could take him all the way to the top of this most demanding of sports.

It was this mental toughness which helped him overcome a slow start to the season and emerge as the outstanding player of the year. Lying 88th on the Rankings halfway through the season, Warren began to make things happen in mid-July with a second place finish behind Sweden's Fredrik Widmark at the Texbond Open at Garda Golf, Garda, Italy, before he hit top gear two weeks later to collect his maiden professional victory in the Ireland Ryder Cup Challenge at the Killarney Golf and Fishing Club. He quickly followed this with his second win of the season in the Rolex Trophy at Golf Club de Genève, Switzerland.

Those two victories, allied to a further four top five finishes, accounted for the bulk of Warren's winning prize money total of €103,576 and ensured he would join former Challenge Tour players such as the 2005 US Open Champion Michael Campbell and Ryder Cup duo Thomas Björn and Ian Poulter on The 2006 European Tour.

"I want to get to the level guys like Campbell, Björn and Poulter have reached," Warren explained. "I want to be competing in Majors and believe I can get to that level. One thing the Challenge Tour teaches you is how hard you have to work and how hungry you have to be to get to and succeed at the top level. I think it's been the best way for me to learn and it felt awesome to come out as Number One at the end of the season.

"The next thing for me to do now is take what I have learned on the Challenge Tour and move up another level. Because of the Challenge Tour, I now know that I have the ability to win tournaments so I feel ready to move up to The European Tour."

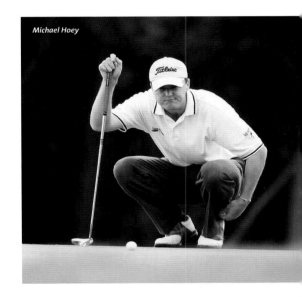
Michael Hoey

Andres Romero

Ireland – A golfer's paradise and so much more.

Ariel Canete

Steven Jeppesen

Carl Suneson

As it has done for the past three years the Challenge Tour season, in partnership with the Tour de las Americas (TLA), began in Central America with a record six events in the region, the increase indicative of the growing strength of the Challenge Tour's relationship with the TLA.

In 2005, five of the Challenge Tour's successful top 20 hailed from Latin America, namely the Argentine quartet of Ariel Canete (placed 16th on the Rankings), Rafael Gomez (11th), Andres Romero (14th) and Daniel Vancsik (ninth), as well as Paraguay's Marco Ruiz (15th).

Of those five, Gomez, Romero and Vancsik all won in 2005. Gomez, twice a winner of the TLA Order of Merit, took the first event of 2005 – the 47th Abierto Mexicano de Golf at the Club de Golf la Hacienda, Mexico City, Mexico – and added the XX Tessali-Metaponto Open di Puglia e Basilicata at Riva dei Tessali and Metaponto, Italy, midway through the season.

Romero secured his maiden Challenge Tour victory in the Morson International Pro-Am Challenge at the Marriott Worsley Park Hotel & Country Club, Greater Manchester, England, while Vancsik notched the third

Challenge Tour win of his career in the Tusker Kenya Open at the Karen Country Club, Nairobi, Kenya.

Before that visit to Africa, Richard McEvoy, of England, who took tenth place on the final Rankings, won the Panasonic Panama Open at the Coronado Golf & Beach Resort, Coronado Beach, Panama. McEvoy, winner of the 2003 European Tour Qualifying School, was then joined on the winner's rostrum by the American trio of Brad Sutterfield (TIM Peru Open 2004 at the Los Incas Country Club, Lima, Peru), Kyle Dobbs (Costa Rica Open 2005 American Express presented by BETonSPORTS.com at the Cariari Country Club, San Jose, Costa Rica) and Kevin Haefner (Summit Panama Masters at the Summit Golf and Resort, Panama City, Panama) while Argentina's Cesar Monasterio finished the Tour's Latin American Swing by securing the Abierto Telefonica Moviles de Guatemala title at the Hacienda Nueva Country Club in Guatemala City.

The first Challenge Tour event of 2005 to be played on European soil was the dual ranking Madeira Island Open Caixa Geral de Depositos in which former Challenge Tour Member Robert-Jan Derksen of The Netherlands triumphed on the stunning Santo da Serra course, Madeira, Portugal.

Andrew Butterfield

The European Challenge Tour

Stephen Browne

Tomas Jesus Muñoz of Spain was the next man to join the 2005 winners' circle with his victory in the Peugeot Challenge R.C.G. El Prat at the Real Club de Golf El Prat, Barcelona, Spain, followed by Frenchman Olivier David, who won the FIRSTPLUS Wales Challenge at the Vale Hotel Golf and Spa Resort, Wales.

Widmark's first victory of 2005 arrived at the Riu Tikida Hotels Moroccan Classic at Golf du Soleil, Agadir, Morocco. This victory was quickly followed by another Scandinavian success, this time for Finland in the shape of Toni Karjalainen who chose the inaugural Thomas Björn Open, presented by Multidata, at the testing Esbjerg Golfklub, Denmark, for his maiden victory on his way to twentieth place on the Rankings.

In mid-June the Challenge Tour moved from Denmark to the first of three visits to France, beginning with the ninth Aa St Omer Open – the second dual ranking event of 2005 - which was won by Sweden's Joakim

Bäckström at the Aa Saint Omer Golf Club. Bäckström took the title after a play-off with England's Paul Dwyer.

Seven days later, Englishman Gareth Davies won the second Challenge Tour title of his career at the Galeria Kaufhof Pokal Challenge at the Rittergut Birkhof Golf Club, Germany, before his compatriot, Benn Barham, took the Open Mahou de Madrid at the Club de Golf La Herreria, Madrid, Spain. Home favourite Ilya Goroneskoul then secured the Open des Volcans - Challenge de France at Golf des Volcans, Clermont Ferrand, France.

The Cadillac Russian Open - the third dual ranking event of the season – was won following a dramatic four hole play-off by Sweden's Mikael Lundberg. Andrew Butterfield of England may have lost out over extra holes at Le Meridien Moscow Country Club, Moscow, Russia, but his second place went a long way to seeing him claim the fourth Tour card on offer

Toni Karjalainen

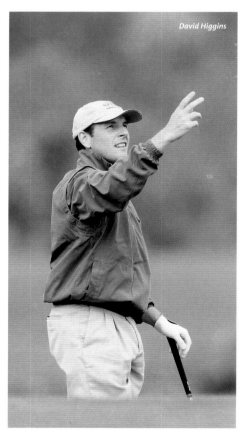

David Higgins

Ross Fisher

Fredrik Widmark

professional golf tournament in the country's history – the Kazakhstan Open – which was won by Ireland's Stephen Browne.

For trained baritone Browne there was good reason for him to launch into song for, as he sung Danny Boy, he knew that he could progress and earn a place on The European Tour which he eventually achieved. For all in golf, however, the Kazakhstan Open was truly ground-breaking.

Kazakhstan, once part of Russia where, since 1996, The Cadillac Russian Open has been played and which is now part of The European Tour International Schedule, is the first of the Central States – the country has borders with China, Kyrgystan, Russia and Uzbekistan – to embrace golf. The President of Kazakhstan, Nursultan Nazarbayev, and his chief minister, Nurtay Abykaev, are both passionate golfers. Indeed, Mr Abykaev teed-up in the event on a course which the players found to be in excellent condition

Rafael Gomez

through the final Rankings behind Warren, Carl Suneson and Widmark.

While Warren was winning the Rolex Trophy his fellow Scot, David Patrick, put the finishing touches to his maiden professional victory the same week at the Skandia PGA Open at the Arlandastad Golf Club, Sweden.

Northern Ireland's Michael Hoey triumphed at the stunning Fontana Golf Club, Vienna, Austria, in the BA-CA Golf Open presented by Telekom Austria, before Norway's Morten Hagen won the Telia Challenge Waxholm at the Waxholm Golf Club, Sweden. Seven days later Sweden toasted another Challenge Tour winner when Per G Nyman won the inaugural Rotterdam International Open at Golfclub Broekpolder, Vlaardingen, The Netherlands.

Then the golfing pioneers of the Challenge Tour travelled to Kazakhstan for the first

Tom Whitehouse

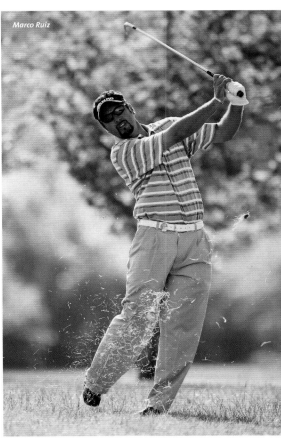
Marco Ruiz

San Domenico Golf

HOUSE OF THE APULIA GRAND FINAL

EUROPEAN CHALLENGE TOUR

Masseria Cimino
Guest House San Domenico Golf

72010 Savelletri di Fasano (Brindisi) - ITALY
Tel. +39 (0)80 4829200 - Fax +39 (0)80 4827944
e-mail: info@sandomenicogolf.com
www.sandomenicogolf.com

MEMBER OF

 ITALIA FIG

 IAGTO
INTERNATIONAL ASSOCIATION OF GOLF TOUR OPERATORS

The Class of 2005: Left to right: Richard McEvoy (Eng), Benn Barham (Eng), Stephen Browne (Ire), Toni Karjalainen (Fin), David Higgins (Ire), Michael Kirk (SA), Michael Hoey (N.Ire), Ross Fisher (Eng), Carl Suneson (Sp), Paul Dwyer (Eng), Marc Warren (Scot), Rafael Gomez (Arg), Daniel Vancsik (Arg), Andres Romero (Arg), Fredrik Widmark (Swe), Steven Jeppesen (Swe), Andrew Butterfield (Eng) and Tom Whitehouse (Eng). Ariel Canete (Arg) and Marco Ruiz (Par) not present

and which demanded accuracy off the tee. The tournament was an unequivocal success and tribute was paid to Martin O'Rawe, the agronomist, and the team of greenkeepers.

The Challenge Tour then returned to France and Sutterfield claimed his second title of the year in the Open de Toulouse at the Golf de Palmola, Toulouse, France. That was followed by the fourth and final dual ranking tournament of the year - the Abama Open de Canarias - where England's John Bickerton negotiated the Abama Golf Club, Tenerife, Spain, better than anyone although by finishing joint runner-up South African Michael Kirk catapulted himself towards a place on The 2006 European Tour International Schedule which he achieved by finishing fifth on the Rankings.

The class of graduates from 2005 also included Steven Jeppesen of Sweden (sixth), Ireland's David Higgins (12th) and the English duo of Tom Whitehouse (17th) and Ross Fisher (18th).

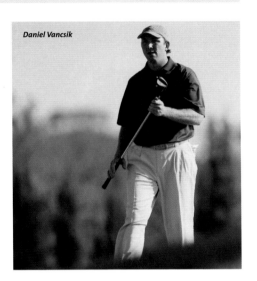

Daniel Vancsik

After 29 events, the Challenge Tour season came to its nerve-wracking dramatic annual finale in the Apulia San Domenico Grand Final at San Domenico Golf Club, Puglia, Italy, where the Challenge Tour's top 45 players did battle for those priceless 20 places on The 2006 European Tour. After a gripping final round, Carl Suneson of Spain took the title and the €42,800 first prize to propel himself to second place on the final Rankings and secure a return to golf's highest level.

Suneson said: "I can't describe what this feels like or means to me. It's awesome to be going back to The European Tour and hopefully I can stay there for years to come."

As the top 20 celebrated in the clubhouse at San Domenico after yet another momentous year on the Challenge Tour, their thoughts turned to The 2006 European Tour where their golfing education will continue alongside the best players in the world.

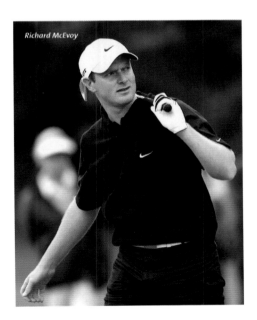

Richard McEvoy

Michael Gibbons

THE FINAL EUROPEAN CHALLENGE TOUR RANKINGS 2005

Pos	Name	Country	Played	€
1	Marc WARREN	(Scot)	(25)	103,576.62
2	Carl SUNESON	(Sp)	(23)	103,128.86
3	Fredrik WIDMARK	(Swe)	(16)	99,750.06
4	Andrew BUTTERFIELD	(Eng)	(21)	94,334.66
5	Michael KIRK	(SA)	(21)	90,619.98
6	Steven JEPPESEN	(Swe)	(21)	88,516.83
7	Benn BARHAM	(Eng)	(23)	86,258.66
8	Michael HOEY	(N.Ire)	(24)	86,123.74
9	Daniel VANCSIK	(Arg)	(24)	81,053.22
10	Richard MCEVOY	(Eng)	(24)	80,046.92
11	Rafael GOMEZ	(Arg)	(14)	79,880.46
12	David HIGGINS	(Ire)	(20)	77,258.69
13	Paul DWYER	(Eng)	(26)	73,479.41
14	Andres ROMERO	(Arg)	(21)	71,221.06
15	Marco RUIZ	(Par)	(25)	69,845.17
16	Ariel CANETE	(Arg)	(22)	66,087.02
17	Tom WHITEHOUSE	(Eng)	(21)	63,343.74
18	Ross FISHER	(Eng)	(25)	61,028.67
19	Stephen BROWNE	(Ire)	(8)	59,916.45
20	Toni KARJALAINEN	(Fin)	(18)	58,384.16
21	Brad SUTTERFIELD	(USA)	(20)	57,336.51
22	Kyron SULLIVAN	(Wal)	(23)	56,156.80
23	James HEATH	(Eng)	(18)	54,402.48
24	Denny LUCAS	(Eng)	(24)	54,281.32
25	Lee S JAMES	(Eng)	(26)	51,328.61
26	Miguel CARBALLO	(Arg)	(24)	49,705.95
27	David DIXON	(Eng)	(27)	43,555.94
28	Olivier DAVID	(Fr)	(20)	43,363.67
29	Shaun P WEBSTER	(Eng)	(26)	42,839.45
30	Cesar MONASTERIO	(Arg)	(18)	42,047.55
31	Sebastian FERNANDEZ	(Arg)	(20)	41,901.00
32	Sam WALKER	(Eng)	(23)	41,517.72
33	James HEPWORTH	(Eng)	(20)	41,141.01
34	Sion E BEBB	(Wal)	(22)	38,610.75
35	Gareth DAVIES	(Eng)	(25)	37,917.96
36	Stuart DAVIS	(Eng)	(27)	37,247.17
37	Michael JONZON	(Swe)	(9)	35,726.60
38	Peter WHITEFORD	(Scot)	(16)	35,602.77
39	Colm MORIARTY	(Ire)	(24)	35,402.09
40	David PATRICK	(Scot)	(21)	35,193.19
41	Tomas Jesus MUÑOZ	(Sp)	(12)	35,160.50
42	Anders S HANSEN	(Den)	(19)	35,028.04
43	Iain PYMAN	(Eng)	(22)	34,859.39
44	Marcus HIGLEY	(Eng)	(27)	33,718.87
45	Johan EDFORS	(Swe)	(17)	33,707.24
46	Michele REALE	(It)	(20)	31,494.71
47	Kariem BARAKA	(Ger)	(25)	31,213.83
48	Oliver WHITELEY	(Eng)	(21)	28,278.06
49	Gary CLARK	(Eng)	(24)	27,575.67
50	Roope KAKKO	(Fin)	(21)	27,113.77
51	Marco SOFFIETTI	(It)	(19)	25,915.84
52	Van PHILLIPS	(Eng)	(18)	25,375.69
53	Ivo GINER	(Sp)	(14)	24,969.31
54	Jesus Maria ARRUTI	(Sp)	(13)	24,348.93
55	Matthew MORRIS	(Eng)	(17)	24,063.57
56	Chris GANE	(Eng)	(24)	23,979.78
57	David ORR	(Scot)	(18)	23,900.70
58	Martin WIEGELE	(Aut)	(22)	23,668.65
59	Christian REIMBOLD	(Ger)	(15)	23,147.54
60	Oskar BERGMAN	(Swe)	(14)	22,501.35
61	Ilya GORONESKOUL	(Fr)	(7)	22,314.00
62	Jan-Are LARSEN	(Nor)	(9)	22,010.64
63	Per G NYMAN	(Swe)	(13)	21,981.43
64	Craig WILLIAMS	(Wal)	(16)	21,626.93
65	Iain STEEL	(Mal)	(12)	20,811.80
66	Thomas NIELSEN	(Den)	(26)	20,576.68
67	Magnus P. ATLEVI	(Swe)	(14)	18,353.58
68	Julien VAN HAUWE	(Fr)	(23)	17,909.95
69	Julien CLÉMENT	(Swi)	(19)	17,455.55
70	Mark PILKINGTON	(Wal)	(27)	17,270.21
71	Gareth PADDISON	(NZ)	(14)	17,151.73
72	Jean-Baptiste GONNET	(Fr)	(20)	17,094.12
73	Rodolfo GONZALEZ	(Arg)	(13)	16,833.12
74	Erol SIMSEK	(Ger)	(17)	16,815.15
75	Miguel RODRIGUEZ	(Arg)	(13)	16,559.88
76	Rafael ECHENIQUE	(Arg)	(14)	16,067.07
77	Alvaro SALTO	(Sp)	(13)	15,877.57
78	Edward RUSH	(Eng)	(17)	15,759.94
79	Sebastien DELAGRANGE	(Fr)	(10)	15,343.82
80	Mark MOULAND	(Wal)	(15)	14,831.06
81	José Manuel CARRILES	(Sp)	(9)	14,797.61
82	Jamie LITTLE	(Eng)	(25)	14,674.66
83	Knud STORGAARD	(Den)	(14)	14,585.50
84	Tuomas TUOVINEN	(Fin)	(8)	14,015.49
85	Birgir HAFTHORSSON	(Ice)	(9)	13,905.50
86	Jamie ELSON	(Eng)	(22)	13,884.77
87	Gustavo ROJAS	(Arg)	(14)	13,455.34
88	Raphael PELLICIOLI	(Fr)	(20)	13,388.33
89	Peter JESPERSEN	(Den)	(18)	13,197.96
90	Massimo SCARPA	(It)	(14)	13,197.07
91	Simon LILLY	(Eng)	(20)	13,167.89
92	Stuart MANLEY	(Wal)	(5)	12,453.97
93	Raphael EYRAUD	(Fr)	(15)	11,834.00
94	Kalle BRINK	(Swe)	(17)	11,756.55
95	Benoit TEILLERIA	(Fr)	(7)	11,435.50
96	Johan KOK	(SA)	(17)	11,397.60
97	Julien QUESNE	(Fr)	(18)	10,719.36
98	Hernan REY	(Arg)	(12)	10,713.78
99	Sam OSBORNE	(Eng)	(20)	10,683.61
100	Oskar HENNINGSSON	(Swe)	(13)	10,665.85

Exempt Status for 2006 European Tour International Schedule
10a - The top 10 from the 2005 Challenge Tour Rankings
11 - 11 - 15 from the 2005 Challenge Tour Rankings
11b - The top 30 and ties from The 2005 European Tour Qualifying School
11c - 16 - 20 from the 2005 Challenge Tour Rankings

The European Tour Golfer of the Month Awards 2005

The European Tour Golfer of the Month Awards are presented throughout the year followed by an Annual Award

ANNUAL WINNERS

2004	Vijay Singh	
2003	Ernie Els	
2002	Ernie Els	
2001	Retief Goosen	
2000	Lee Westwood	
1999	Colin Montgomerie	
1998	Lee Westwood	
1997	Colin Montgomerie	
1996	Colin Montgomerie	
1995	Colin Montgomerie	
1994	Ernie Els	
1993	Bernhard Langer	
1992	Nick Faldo	
1991	Severiano Ballesteros	
1990	Nick Faldo	
1989	Nick Faldo	
1988	Severiano Ballesteros	
1987	Ian Woosnam	
1986	Severiano Ballesteros	
1985	Bernhard Langer	

MICHAEL CAMPBELL - June

NICK DOUGHERTY - January

THONGCHAI JAIDEE - February

PADRAIG HARRINGTON - March

LUKE DONALD - April

ANGEL CABRERA - May

COLIN MONTGOMERIE - July

DAVID HOWELL - August

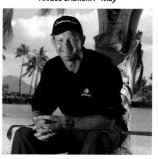

RETIEF GOOSEN - September

PAUL McGINLEY - October

The RBS Shot of the Month Awards 2005

The RBS Shot of the Month Awards are presented throughout the year followed by an Annual Award

ANNUAL WINNERS

2004   David Howell

2003   Fredrik Jacobson

COLIN MONTGOMERIE - September

NICK DOUGHERTY - January

MILES TUNNICLIFF - February

ERNIE ELS - March and April

DAVID HOWELL - May

MICHAEL CAMPBELL - June

NICLAS FASTH - July

EMANUELE CANONICA - August

Stroke Average

Rank	Player		Avg
1	Sergio GARCIA (Sp)	(38)	69.68
2	Ernie ELS (SA)	(44)	69.75
3	Colin MONTGOMERIE (Scot)	(86)	69.83
4	David HOWELL (Eng)	(63)	69.94
5	Henrik STENSON (Swe)	(90)	69.97
6	Luke DONALD (Eng)	(52)	70.02
7	José Maria OLAZÁBAL (Sp)	(56)	70.04
8	Vijay SINGH (Fiji)	(24)	70.08
9	Thaworn WIRATCHANT (Thai)	(38)	70.13
10	Thomas BJÖRN (Den)	(77)	70.27
11	Adam SCOTT (Aus)	(40)	70.43
	Miguel Angel JIMÉNEZ (Sp)	(86)	70.43
13	Retief GOOSEN (SA)	(42)	70.48
	Bradley DREDGE (Wal)	(94)	70.48
15	Lian-Wei ZHANG (PRC)	(46)	70.52
16	Gary ORR (Scot)	(50)	70.56
17	Paul MCGINLEY (Ire)	(84)	70.57
18	Angel CABRERA (Arg)	(56)	70.61
19	Paul BROADHURST (Eng)	(94)	70.64
	Steve WEBSTER (Eng)	(89)	70.64
21	Darren CLARKE (N.Ire)	(46)	70.65
22	Niclas FASTH (Swe)	(86)	70.67
23	Bernhard LANGER (Ger)	(28)	70.75
24	John DALY (USA)	(30)	70.77
25	Pierre FULKE (Swe)	(58)	70.79
26	David LYNN (Eng)	(81)	70.80
27	Johan EDFORS (Swe)	(30)	70.83
28	Mark HENSBY (Aus)	(32)	70.84
29	David BRANSDON (Aus)	(33)	70.85
30	Raphaël JACQUELIN (Fr)	(83)	70.86
	Simon KHAN (Eng)	(79)	70.86
32	Nick DOUGHERTY (Eng)	(108)	70.87
33	Trevor IMMELMAN (SA)	(50)	70.92
34	Maarten LAFEBER (NL)	(98)	70.94
35	Barry LANE (Eng)	(79)	70.96
36	Ivo GINER (Sp)	(46)	71.02
	Anders HANSEN (Den)	(88)	71.02
	Stuart LITTLE (Eng)	(86)	71.02
39	Michael CAMPBELL (NZ)	(72)	71.08
40	Martin ERLANDSSON (Swe)	(63)	71.13
41	Robert KARLSSON (Swe)	(88)	71.15
42	Robert-Jan DERKSEN (NL)	(93)	71.16
43	Thongchai JAIDEE (Thai)	(62)	71.19
44	Lee WESTWOOD (Eng)	(56)	71.21
45	Padraig HARRINGTON (Ire)	(50)	71.22
46	Anthony WALL (Eng)	(80)	71.24
47	Wade ORMSBY (Aus)	(81)	71.25
	Nick FALDO (Eng)	(24)	71.25
49	Peter SENIOR (Aus)	(47)	71.26
	José Manuel LARA (Sp)	(100)	71.26
51	Richard STERNE (SA)	(70)	71.29
52	Miguel Angel MARTIN (Sp)	(83)	71.33
	Peter HEDBLOM (Swe)	(86)	71.33
	Damien MCGRANE (Ire)	(101)	71.33
	Ian POULTER (Eng)	(60)	71.33
56	Søren HANSEN (Den)	(95)	71.34
57	Stephen DODD (Wal)	(75)	71.36
58	Steven O'HARA (Scot)	(83)	71.42
59	Søren KJELDSEN (Den)	(90)	71.44
60	Gonzalo FERNANDEZ-CASTANO (Sp)	(76)	71.45
	Ian GARBUTT (Eng)	(89)	71.45
62	Jeev Milkha SINGH (Ind)	(24)	71.46
63	Andrew MCLARDY (SA)	(67)	71.49
64	Peter LAWRIE (Ire)	(100)	71.51
	Amandeep JOHL (Ind)	(35)	71.51
66	Joakim HAEGGMAN (Swe)	(64)	71.52
67	Jamie SPENCE (Eng)	(60)	71.53
68	Ian WOOSNAM (Wal)	(59)	71.56
	Peter O'MALLEY (Aus)	(59)	71.56
70	Hennie OTTO (SA)	(30)	71.57
	Gregory HAVRET (Fr)	(87)	71.57
72	Nick O'HERN (Aus)	(52)	71.58
	Thomas LEVET (Fr)	(38)	71.58
	James KINGSTON (SA)	(74)	71.58
75	Christopher HANELL (Swe)	(63)	71.59
76	Jose-Filipe LIMA (Port)	(88)	71.60
77	Peter HANSON (Swe)	(96)	71.61
78	Graeme STORM (Eng)	(115)	71.64
79	Jonathan LOMAS (Eng)	(86)	71.65
	Nicolas COLSAERTS (Bel)	(52)	71.65
	Alastair FORSYTH (Scot)	(84)	71.65
82	Francesco MOLINARI (It)	(89)	71.66
83	Ricardo GONZALEZ (Arg)	(64)	71.67
84	Marcus FRASER (Aus)	(79)	71.68
85	François DELAMONTAGNE (Fr)	(77)	71.69
	Jyoti RANDHAWA (Ind)	(39)	71.69
	Edward MICHAELS (USA)	(26)	71.69
88	Richard GREEN (Aus)	(66)	71.70
	Simon WAKEFIELD (Eng)	(93)	71.70
90	Peter FOWLER (Aus)	(79)	71.72
91	Markus BRIER (Aut)	(80)	71.73
	Charl SCHWARTZEL (SA)	(73)	71.73
93	Christian CÉVAËR (Fr)	(80)	71.74
	Richard FINCH (Eng)	(77)	71.74
95	Graeme MCDOWELL (N.Ire)	(55)	71.75
	Brett RUMFORD (Aus)	(69)	71.75
97	Johan SKÖLD (Swe)	(86)	71.78
98	Jamie DONALDSON (Wal)	(79)	71.80
	Paul LAWRIE (Scot)	(91)	71.80
100	Scott DRUMMOND (Scot)	(84)	71.81
101	Peter LONARD (Aus)	(28)	71.82
102	Marcel SIEM (Ger)	(67)	71.84
103	John BICKERTON (Eng)	(85)	71.86
	Mattias ELIASSON (Swe)	(71)	71.86
105	Philip GOLDING (Eng)	(97)	71.87
106	Kyron SULLIVAN (Wal)	(24)	71.88
107	Paul CASEY (Eng)	(55)	71.89
108	Garry HOUSTON (Wal)	(93)	71.91
109	Simon DYSON (Eng)	(102)	71.92
110	Edward LOAR (USA)	(27)	71.93
	Kenneth FERRIE (Eng)	(87)	71.93
	Adam GROOM (Aus)	(58)	71.93
	Terry PRICE (Aus)	(73)	71.93
	Steven JEPPESEN (Swe)	(30)	71.93
115	Jean VAN DE VELDE (Fr)	(52)	71.94
116	Peter GUSTAFSSON (Swe)	(75)	71.95
	Miles TUNNICLIFF (Eng)	(76)	71.95
118	Gregory BOURDY (Fr)	(79)	71.96
	David PARK (Wal)	(81)	71.96
120	Phillip ARCHER (Eng)	(90)	71.97
121	Mårten OLANDER (Swe)	(73)	72.00
	Stephen SCAHILL (NZ)	(83)	72.00
	Michael JONZON (Swe)	(44)	72.00
124	Cesar MONASTERIO (Arg)	(32)	72.03
125	Emanuele CANONICA (It)	(93)	72.06
126	Mark ROE (Eng)	(73)	72.07
127	José Manuel CARRILES (Sp)	(36)	72.08
128	Roger CHAPMAN (Eng)	(64)	72.09
129	Mark FOSTER (Eng)	(102)	72.10
	Richard BLAND (Eng)	(79)	72.10
131	Harmeet KAHLON (Ind)	(28)	72.11
132	Gareth PADDISON (NZ)	(33)	72.12
133	Santiago LUNA (Sp)	(73)	72.14
	Ben MASON (Eng)	(79)	72.14
	Oliver WILSON (Eng)	(84)	72.14
136	Gary MURPHY (Ire)	(89)	72.15
137	Michael KIRK (SA)	(32)	72.16
138	Brian DAVIS (Eng)	(30)	72.17
	Jean-François REMESY (Fr)	(65)	72.17
140	Joakim BÄCKSTRÖM (Swe)	(70)	72.19
141	Alessandro TADINI (It)	(82)	72.21
	Gary EMERSON (Eng)	(85)	72.21
	Ignacio GARRIDO (Sp)	(66)	72.21
144	David DRYSDALE (Scot)	(73)	72.22
145	David GRIFFITHS (Eng)	(71)	72.23
	David CARTER (Eng)	(78)	72.23
147	Jean-François LUCQUIN (Fr)	(76)	72.24
148	Richard MOIR (Aus)	(24)	72.25
149	Jarrod MOSELEY (Aus)	(54)	72.28
	Robert COLES (Eng)	(82)	72.28

REUTERS — OFFICIAL STATISTICS

Driving Accuracy (%)

1	Andrew MARSHALL (Eng)	(86)	71.4
	Peter O'MALLEY (Aus)	(55)	71.4
3	Paul EALES (Eng)	(25)	69.4
4	Henrik STENSON (Swe)	(70)	69.2
5	Maarten LAFEBER (NL)	(88)	68.8
	Nick O'HERN (Aus)	(26)	68.8
7	Gary ORR (Scot)	(45)	68.5
8	Peter SENIOR (Aus)	(41)	68.1
9	Ben MASON (Eng)	(76)	67.9
10	Stuart MANLEY (Wal)	(85)	67.8
11	Andrew OLDCORN (Scot)	(53)	67.7
	Terry PRICE (Aus)	(71)	67.7
13	Miguel Angel MARTIN (Sp)	(81)	67.6
14	Philip GOLDING (Eng)	(94)	67.0
15	Søren KJELDSEN (Den)	(82)	66.8
16	Francesco MOLINARI (It)	(86)	66.4
	Wade ORMSBY (Aus)	(78)	66.4
18	Simon KHAN (Eng)	(71)	66.3
19	Jonathan LOMAS (Eng)	(79)	66.1
	Henrik NYSTROM (Swe)	(58)	66.1
21	Miguel Angel JIMÉNEZ (Sp)	(64)	66.0
22	Anders HANSEN (Den)	(84)	65.8
23	Costantino ROCCA (It)	(54)	65.5
24	Garry HOUSTON (Wal)	(90)	65.4
25	Luke DONALD (Eng)	(27)	65.2
	John BICKERTON (Eng)	(77)	65.2
27	Alastair FORSYTH (Scot)	(78)	64.9
	David GILFORD (Eng)	(25)	64.9
29	Colin MONTGOMERIE (Scot)	(64)	64.6
30	Simon WAKEFIELD (Eng)	(90)	64.5
31	Paul MCGINLEY (Ire)	(60)	64.4
32	Scott DRUMMOND (Scot)	(76)	64.3
33	Steven O'HARA (Scot)	(80)	64.2
34	Steve WEBSTER (Eng)	(78)	63.8
	Raymond RUSSELL (Scot)	(82)	63.8
	David PARK (Wal)	(77)	63.8
37	Hernan REY (Arg)	(44)	63.7
38	Jamie DONALDSON (Wal)	(77)	63.0
39	Peter HANSON (Swe)	(82)	62.7
	Phillip ARCHER (Eng)	(86)	62.7

Driving Distance (yds)

1	Angel CABRERA (Arg)	(40)	306.0
2	Robert ROCK (Eng)	(51)	305.6
	Joakim BÄCKSTRÖM (Swe)	(66)	305.6
4	Marcel SIEM (Ger)	(64)	305.0
5	Titch MOORE (SA)	(57)	304.3
6	Louis OOSTHUIZEN (SA)	(61)	303.8
7	François DELAMONTAGNE (Fr)	(74)	303.0
8	Ernie ELS (SA)	(32)	302.8
9	Nicolas COLSAERTS (Bel)	(50)	301.7
10	Pelle EDBERG (Swe)	(68)	301.3
11	Emanuele CANONICA (It)	(90)	300.6
12	Paul CASEY (Eng)	(38)	300.1
13	Hennie OTTO (SA)	(29)	299.7
14	Ricardo GONZALEZ (Arg)	(59)	299.1
15	Andrea MAESTRONI (It)	(43)	297.8
16	Robert KARLSSON (Swe)	(82)	297.6
17	Henrik STENSON (Swe)	(70)	297.3
18	Jose-Filipe LIMA (Port)	(83)	296.9
	Sebastian FERNANDEZ (Arg)	(28)	296.9
20	Mattias ELIASSON (Swe)	(67)	296.1
21	Stephen GALLACHER (Scot)	(71)	296.0
22	Hernan REY (Arg)	(44)	295.8
23	Peter GUSTAFSSON (Swe)	(71)	295.6
24	Charl SCHWARTZEL (SA)	(64)	294.7
25	Steve WEBSTER (Eng)	(78)	293.5
26	Ivo GINER (Sp)	(44)	293.2
27	Padraig HARRINGTON (Ire)	(32)	293.1
	Darren CLARKE (N.Ire)	(28)	293.1
29	Richard STERNE (SA)	(66)	292.9
	Fredrik ANDERSSON HED (Swe)	(77)	292.9
31	Stuart LITTLE (Eng)	(83)	292.8
32	Paul LAWRIE (Scot)	(83)	292.5
	Neil CHEETHAM (Eng)	(58)	292.5
34	Matthew KING (Eng)	(51)	292.4
35	Lee WESTWOOD (Eng)	(32)	292.3
36	Stuart MANLEY (Wal)	(85)	292.1
37	Gonzalo FERNANDEZ-CASTANO (Sp)	(73)	291.9
38	Cesar MONASTERIO (Arg)	(32)	291.7
39	Eduardo ROMERO (Arg)	(30)	291.6
40	Martin MARITZ (SA)	(77)	291.5

Sand Saves (%)

1	Philip WALTON (Ire)	(26)	75.0
2	Mark ROE (Eng)	(69)	69.0
3	Christopher HANELL (Swe)	(62)	68.3
4	Andrea MAESTRONI (It)	(43)	67.5
5	Gordon BRAND JNR (Scot)	(61)	67.3
6	Miguel Angel JIMÉNEZ (Sp)	(64)	67.2
7	Richard BLAND (Eng)	(76)	67.0
8	José Maria OLAZÁBAL (Sp)	(34)	65.7
9	Paul EALES (Eng)	(25)	64.9
10	Martin ERLANDSSON (Swe)	(60)	64.4
11	Trevor IMMELMAN (SA)	(34)	63.2
12	Robert-Jan DERKSEN (NL)	(90)	62.8
13	Richard GREEN (Aus)	(44)	62.7
14	Benoit TEILLERIA (Fr)	(58)	62.3
15	Paul CASEY (Eng)	(38)	61.8
16	Anders HANSEN (Den)	(84)	61.7
17	Joakim BÄCKSTRÖM (Swe)	(66)	61.6
18	Hernan REY (Arg)	(44)	61.0
19	Steven JEPPESEN (Swe)	(30)	60.9
	Paul BROADHURST (Eng)	(90)	60.9
21	Peter GUSTAFSSON (Swe)	(71)	60.8
22	Eddie LEE (NZ)	(24)	60.0
	Peter FOWLER (Aus)	(73)	60.0
	Christian CÉVAËR (Fr)	(76)	60.0
25	Richard STERNE (SA)	(66)	59.2
26	Alessandro TADINI (It)	(78)	59.1
27	Steve WEBSTER (Eng)	(78)	58.9
28	Jonathan LOMAS (Eng)	(79)	58.8
29	Andrew COLTART (Scot)	(77)	58.7
30	Nicolas COLSAERTS (Bel)	(50)	58.6
31	Paul MCGINLEY (Ire)	(60)	58.5
32	Bradley DREDGE (Wal)	(86)	58.3
	Jamie DONALDSON (Wal)	(77)	58.3
	Sam LITTLE (Eng)	(74)	58.3
35	Peter HANSON (Swe)	(82)	58.1
	Gonzalo FERNANDEZ-CASTANO (Sp)	(73)	58.1
37	Eduardo ROMERO (Arg)	(30)	57.5
38	Charl SCHWARTZEL (SA)	(64)	57.4
39	Padraig HARRINGTON (Ire)	(32)	57.1
40	Jamie SPENCE (Eng)	(62)	56.6

Greens In Regulation (%)

1	Ernie ELS (SA)	(32)	76.4
2	Henrik STENSON (Swe)	(70)	74.8
3	Peter O'MALLEY (Aus)	(55)	74.7
4	Terry PRICE (Aus)	(71)	73.9
	Miguel Angel MARTIN (Sp)	(81)	73.9
6	Miguel Angel JIMÉNEZ (Sp)	(64)	73.2
7	Colin MONTGOMERIE (Scot)	(64)	72.8
	Maarten LAFEBER (NL)	(88)	72.8
9	Ivo GINER (Sp)	(44)	72.5
10	Peter HANSON (Swe)	(82)	72.4
11	Gary ORR (Scot)	(45)	72.3
12	Angel CABRERA (Arg)	(40)	72.2
13	Steve WEBSTER (Eng)	(78)	71.6
14	Peter HEDBLOM (Swe)	(78)	71.1
15	Graeme STORM (Eng)	(108)	70.8
	Niclas FASTH (Swe)	(72)	70.8
17	Søren HANSEN (Den)	(88)	70.7
18	José Maria OLAZÁBAL (Sp)	(34)	70.4
	Luke DONALD (Eng)	(27)	70.4
20	Francesco MOLINARI (It)	(86)	70.1
	Ian WOOSNAM (Wal)	(52)	70.1
22	Paul MCGINLEY (Ire)	(60)	70.0
23	Thomas BJÖRN (Den)	(56)	69.4
	Costantino ROCCA (It)	(54)	69.4
25	José Manuel CARRILES (Sp)	(36)	69.0
26	Steven O'HARA (Scot)	(80)	68.8
27	Carlos RODILES (Sp)	(65)	68.7
28	Ignacio GARRIDO (Sp)	(59)	68.6
	Stuart LITTLE (Eng)	(83)	68.6
30	Hernan REY (Arg)	(44)	68.3
31	Paul EALES (Eng)	(25)	68.2
32	François DELAMONTAGNE (Fr)	(74)	68.1
	Cesar MONASTERIO (Arg)	(32)	68.1
34	Mikko ILONEN (Fin)	(78)	68.0
35	Richard FINCH (Eng)	(74)	67.9
36	Titch MOORE (SA)	(57)	67.8
	Gary EVANS (Eng)	(24)	67.8
38	John BICKERTON (Eng)	(77)	67.7
	Nick DOUGHERTY (Eng)	(90)	67.7
	Michael JONZON (Swe)	(43)	67.7

Average Putts Per Round

1	Christian CÉVAËR (Fr)	(76)	27.6
2	Luke DONALD (Eng)	(27)	28.0
3	Paul BROADHURST (Eng)	(90)	28.2
4	David HOWELL (Eng)	(44)	28.3
5	Jamie SPENCE (Eng)	(62)	28.4
	Padraig HARRINGTON (Ire)	(32)	28.4
	Pierre FULKE (Swe)	(54)	28.4
8	Lee WESTWOOD (Eng)	(32)	28.5
9	Thongchai JAIDEE (Thai)	(48)	28.6
	Bradley DREDGE (Wal)	(86)	28.6
	Darren FICHARDT (SA)	(66)	28.6
12	Stuart MANLEY (Wal)	(85)	28.7
	Brett RUMFORD (Aus)	(65)	28.7
	Jarmo SANDELIN (Swe)	(72)	28.7
	Eduardo ROMERO (Arg)	(30)	28.7
16	Simon DYSON (Eng)	(91)	28.8
	Darren CLARKE (N.Ire)	(28)	28.8
	Stephen DODD (Wal)	(59)	28.8
	Damien MCGRANE (Ire)	(98)	28.8
	Ian POULTER (Eng)	(32)	28.8
21	José Maria OLAZÁBAL (Sp)	(34)	28.9
	Thomas BJÖRN (Den)	(56)	28.9
	Marcus FRASER (Aus)	(74)	28.9
	Richard STERNE (SA)	(66)	28.9
	Peter GUSTAFSSON (Swe)	(71)	28.9
	Nick DOUGHERTY (Eng)	(90)	28.9
27	Andrew MCLARDY (SA)	(64)	29.0
	Paul MCGINLEY (Ire)	(60)	29.0
	Nick O'HERN (Aus)	(26)	29.0
	Richard GREEN (Aus)	(44)	29.0
31	Michael CAMPBELL (NZ)	(50)	29.1
	Andrew COLTART (Scot)	(77)	29.1
	Joakim HAEGGMAN (Swe)	(57)	29.1
34	Alessandro TADINI (It)	(78)	29.2
	Jose-Filipe LIMA (Port)	(83)	29.2
	David LYNN (Eng)	(78)	29.2
	Peter FOWLER (Aus)	(73)	29.2
	Steven JEPPESEN (Swe)	(30)	29.2
	Robert COLES (Eng)	(76)	29.2
	Gregory HAVRET (Fr)	(84)	29.2

Putts Per Green In Regulation

1	Luke DONALD (Eng)	(27)	1.684
2	Thongchai JAIDEE (Thai)	(48)	1.716
	Lee WESTWOOD (Eng)	(32)	1.716
4	Ernie ELS (SA)	(32)	1.730
	Brett RUMFORD (Aus)	(65)	1.730
6	Darren CLARKE (N.Ire)	(28)	1.732
7	Christian CÉVAËR (Fr)	(76)	1.737
	Andrew MCLARDY (SA)	(64)	1.737
9	Jamie SPENCE (Eng)	(62)	1.740
10	Bradley DREDGE (Wal)	(86)	1.741
11	Paul MCGINLEY (Ire)	(60)	1.742
	Padraig HARRINGTON (Ire)	(32)	1.742
13	David HOWELL (Eng)	(44)	1.743
	Ian POULTER (Eng)	(32)	1.743
15	Colin MONTGOMERIE (Scot)	(64)	1.747
16	Nick DOUGHERTY (Eng)	(90)	1.748
17	Thomas BJÖRN (Den)	(56)	1.749
18	Nick O'HERN (Aus)	(26)	1.750
19	Paul BROADHURST (Eng)	(90)	1.751
	Niclas FASTH (Swe)	(72)	1.751
21	Pierre FULKE (Swe)	(54)	1.752
	José Maria OLAZÁBAL (Sp)	(34)	1.752
	Martin ERLANDSSON (Swe)	(60)	1.752
24	Stephen DODD (Wal)	(59)	1.753
25	Eduardo ROMERO (Arg)	(30)	1.755
26	Darren FICHARDT (SA)	(66)	1.759
27	Peter GUSTAFSSON (Swe)	(71)	1.763
28	Peter FOWLER (Aus)	(73)	1.764
29	Simon DYSON (Eng)	(91)	1.765
30	James KINGSTON (SA)	(70)	1.766
31	Jose-Filipe LIMA (Port)	(83)	1.769
32	Miguel Angel JIMÉNEZ (Sp)	(64)	1.770
	Joakim HAEGGMAN (Swe)	(57)	1.770
34	Gary EMERSON (Eng)	(81)	1.771
35	Jarrod MOSELEY (Aus)	(53)	1.772
	Anthony WALL (Eng)	(76)	1.772
	Jarmo SANDELIN (Swe)	(72)	1.772
	Barry LANE (Eng)	(75)	1.772
	Richard GREEN (Aus)	(44)	1.772
	Raphaël JACQUELIN (Fr)	(80)	1.772

The European Tour Order of Merit 2005

Pos	Name	Country	Played	€	£	Pos	Name	Country	Played	€	£
1	Colin MONTGOMERIE	(Scot)	(25)	2,794,222.84	1,888,613.69	51	Stephen GALLACHER	(Scot)	(26)	462,550.80	312,637.83
2	Michael CAMPBELL	(NZ)	(22)	2,496,269.44	1,687,227.15	52	Charl SCHWARTZEL	(SA)	(22)	459,539.51	310,602.51
3	Paul MCGINLEY	(Ire)	(23)	2,296,422.77	1,552,150.89	53	Peter LAWRIE	(Ire)	(29)	445,405.71	301,049.48
4	Retief GOOSEN	(SA)	(13)	2,261,211.06	1,528,351.32	54	Thongchai JAIDEE	(Thai)	(18)	431,400.71	291,583.50
5	Angel CABRERA	(Arg)	(17)	1,866,277.30	1,261,415.80	55	Søren KJELDSEN	(Den)	(27)	429,944.87	290,599.50
6	Sergio GARCIA	(Sp)	(11)	1,828,544.74	1,235,912.39	56	Robert-Jan DERKSEN	(NL)	(27)	427,871.03	289,197.80
7	David HOWELL	(Eng)	(19)	1,798,307.50	1,215,475.06	57	Gonzalo FERNANDEZ-CASTANO	(Sp)	(26)	423,945.03	286,544.22
8	Henrik STENSON	(Swe)	(26)	1,585,749.73	1,071,807.38	58	Simon DYSON	(Eng)	(31)	417,179.74	281,971.56
9	Thomas BJÖRN	(Den)	(23)	1,561,189.62	1,055,207.21	59	Damien MCGRANE	(Ire)	(31)	408,581.53	276,160.03
10	José Maria OLAZÁBAL	(Sp)	(17)	1,489,016.29	1,006,425.30	60	Richard FINCH	(Eng)	(26)	406,245.02	274,580.79
11	Kenneth FERRIE	(Eng)	(28)	1,410,636.86	953,448.68	61	Brett RUMFORD	(Aus)	(24)	384,280.16	259,734.75
12	Luke DONALD	(Eng)	(15)	1,397,385.03	944,491.77	62	Brian DAVIS	(Eng)	(11)	381,247.26	257,684.81
13	Niclas FASTH	(Swe)	(26)	1,316,594.84	889,885.73	63	Anthony WALL	(Eng)	(27)	364,995.18	246,700.04
14	Miguel Angel JIMÉNEZ	(Sp)	(24)	1,115,455.83	753,935.99	64	Jonathan LOMAS	(Eng)	(27)	355,553.69	240,318.54
15	Nick DOUGHERTY	(Eng)	(31)	1,056,416.44	714,031.30	65	Stuart LITTLE	(Eng)	(26)	352,353.28	238,155.39
16	Bradley DREDGE	(Wal)	(25)	1,037,417.62	701,190.00	66	Thomas LEVET	(Fr)	(11)	341,230.45	230,637.48
17	Stephen DODD	(Wal)	(22)	1,033,942.11	698,840.91	67	Martin ERLANDSSON	(Swe)	(19)	329,431.61	222,662.65
18	Ernie ELS	(SA)	(11)	1,012,682.63	684,471.63	68	François DELAMONTAGNE	(Fr)	(24)	329,015.65	222,381.50
19	Ian POULTER	(Eng)	(17)	979,597.66	662,109.52	69	Gary ORR	(Scot)	(15)	324,990.45	219,660.87
20	Darren CLARKE	(N.Ire)	(14)	971,130.79	656,386.77	70	Steven O'HARA	(Scot)	(29)	320,515.77	216,636.43
21	Nick O'HERN	(Aus)	(15)	965,146.00	652,341.65	71	Wade ORMSBY	(Aus)	(28)	316,539.93	213,949.16
22	Paul BROADHURST	(Eng)	(27)	924,505.45	624,872.73	72	Gary EMERSON	(Eng)	(31)	311,068.91	210,251.31
23	Peter HANSON	(Swe)	(27)	837,223.52	565,878.92	73	Jose-Filipe LIMA	(Port)	(29)	310,464.18	209,842.57
24	Adam SCOTT	(Aus)	(11)	822,685.76	556,052.86	74	Scott DRUMMOND	(Scot)	(27)	308,240.67	208,339.70
25	Maarten LAFEBER	(NL)	(28)	820,227.02	554,391.00	75	Simon WAKEFIELD	(Eng)	(32)	307,313.99	207,713.36
26	Jean-François REMESY	(Fr)	(22)	732,837.16	495,324.23	76	Miles TUNNICLIFF	(Eng)	(24)	306,461.32	207,137.04
27	Lee WESTWOOD	(Eng)	(16)	724,864.88	489,935.78	77	Philip GOLDING	(Eng)	(29)	300,350.11	203,006.47
28	David LYNN	(Eng)	(23)	723,232.33	488,832.34	78	Ricardo GONZALEZ	(Arg)	(21)	283,033.01	191,301.86
29	Steve WEBSTER	(Eng)	(24)	716,906.11	484,556.45	79	Jamie DONALDSON	(Wal)	(27)	280,854.71	189,829.55
30	Trevor IMMELMAN	(SA)	(16)	712,205.05	481,379.00	80	Alastair FORSYTH	(Scot)	(26)	279,028.98	188,595.54
31	Graeme STORM	(Eng)	(32)	691,267.17	467,227.10	81	Gary MURPHY	(Ire)	(29)	274,178.26	185,316.94
32	Padraig HARRINGTON	(Ire)	(16)	671,615.93	453,944.84	82	Marc CAYEUX	(Zim)	(28)	266,547.13	180,159.06
33	José Manuel LARA	(Sp)	(30)	651,777.23	440,535.87	83	Andrew COLTART	(Scot)	(29)	265,448.42	179,416.44
34	Graeme MCDOWELL	(N.Ire)	(18)	588,674.84	397,885.00	84	John BICKERTON	(Eng)	(28)	264,528.19	178,794.46
35	Anders HANSEN	(Den)	(26)	583,221.54	394,199.12	85	Mårten OLANDER	(Swe)	(25)	262,926.31	177,711.75
36	Søren HANSEN	(Den)	(29)	580,910.89	392,637.35	86	Francesco MOLINARI	(It)	(30)	261,127.54	176,495.96
37	Raphaël JACQUELIN	(Fr)	(26)	579,687.88	391,810.72	87	Peter O'MALLEY	(Aus)	(19)	260,234.40	175,892.29
38	Robert KARLSSON	(Swe)	(28)	573,067.50	387,336.01	88	Ian WOOSNAM	(Wal)	(20)	259,728.58	175,550.41
39	Paul CASEY	(Eng)	(19)	564,647.65	381,645.04	89	Robert COLES	(Eng)	(28)	257,398.12	173,975.25
40	Simon KHAN	(Eng)	(23)	562,346.54	380,089.72	90	Andrew MCLARDY	(SA)	(22)	252,946.47	170,966.38
41	Emanuele CANONICA	(It)	(31)	556,844.27	376,370.74	91	Jamie SPENCE	(Eng)	(21)	245,881.14	166,190.93
42	Peter HEDBLOM	(Swe)	(26)	541,624.96	366,084.01	92	Joakim HAEGGMAN	(Swe)	(22)	245,872.96	166,185.40
43	Jean VAN DE VELDE	(Fr)	(16)	525,046.20	354,878.44	93	Jean-François LUCQUIN	(Fr)	(28)	240,171.01	162,331.45
44	Richard STERNE	(SA)	(22)	504,306.69	340,860.61	94	James KINGSTON	(SA)	(26)	234,929.53	158,788.74
45	Gregory HAVRET	(Fr)	(29)	491,778.19	332,392.61	95	Jyoti RANDHAWA	(Ind)	(13)	232,239.68	156,970.67
46	Peter GUSTAFSSON	(Swe)	(27)	491,637.86	332,297.76	96	Ian GARBUTT	(Eng)	(25)	229,901.91	155,390.57
47	Barry LANE	(Eng)	(25)	473,265.87	319,880.14	97	Oliver WILSON	(Eng)	(28)	229,537.26	155,144.11
48	Paul LAWRIE	(Scot)	(27)	468,680.50	316,780.89	98	Alessandro TADINI	(It)	(29)	223,845.38	151,296.97
49	Pierre FULKE	(Swe)	(19)	468,668.64	316,772.88	99	Marcel SIEM	(Ger)	(22)	221,443.58	149,673.59
50	Richard GREEN	(Aus)	(18)	467,172.39	315,761.56	100	Garry HOUSTON	(Wal)	(31)	220,622.75	149,118.80

Pos	Name	Country	Played	€	£
101	David PARK	(Wal)	(27)	219,450.46	148,326.44
102	Markus BRIER	(Aut)	(27)	209,985.28	141,928.94
103	Mark ROE	(Eng)	(24)	209,510.16	141,607.80
104	Nicolas COLSAERTS	(Bel)	(17)	203,115.13	137,285.41
105	Andrew MARSHALL	(Eng)	(30)	201,946.16	136,495.30
106	Christian CÉVAËR	(Fr)	(27)	201,074.95	135,906.45
107	Mark FOSTER	(Eng)	(31)	200,807.61	135,725.75
108	Marcus FRASER	(Aus)	(26)	198,952.03	134,471.57
109	David CARTER	(Eng)	(24)	197,361.39	133,396.45
110	Peter FOWLER	(Aus)	(26)	193,726.58	130,939.69
111	Richard BLAND	(Eng)	(27)	190,036.81	128,445.78
112	Miguel Angel MARTIN	(Sp)	(26)	185,522.14	125,394.31
113	Joakim BÄCKSTRÖM	(Swe)	(24)	182,442.98	123,313.11
114	Phillip ARCHER	(Eng)	(27)	179,587.66	121,383.20
115	Terry PRICE	(Aus)	(25)	176,066.14	119,003.01
116	Sam LITTLE	(Eng)	(28)	174,519.49	117,957.63
117	David DRYSDALE	(Scot)	(25)	173,933.28	117,561.41
118	Gregory BOURDY	(Fr)	(27)	173,299.94	117,133.33
119	Raymond RUSSELL	(Scot)	(29)	160,455.87	108,452.03
120	Johan SKÖLD	(Swe)	(28)	157,574.39	106,504.44
121	Titch MOORE	(SA)	(24)	155,173.99	104,882.01
122	Carlos RODILES	(Sp)	(28)	152,984.75	103,402.31
123	Neil CHEETHAM	(Eng)	(25)	150,037.46	101,410.24
124	Ignacio GARRIDO	(Sp)	(22)	149,815.11	101,259.95
125	Santiago LUNA	(Sp)	(25)	146,674.18	99,137.00
126	Johan AXGREN	(Swe)	(27)	142,970.69	96,633.81
127	Mattias ELIASSON	(Swe)	(24)	136,285.03	92,114.98
128	Stephen SCAHILL	(NZ)	(30)	134,946.46	91,210.24
129	Roger CHAPMAN	(Eng)	(19)	134,025.83	90,587.98
130	Fredrik HENGE	(Swe)	(27)	130,161.72	87,976.24
131	Peter SENIOR	(Aus)	(16)	129,648.99	87,629.68
132	Fredrik ANDERSSON HED	(Swe)	(29)	129,591.23	87,590.64
133	Thaworn WIRATCHANT	(Thai)	(11)	128,361.77	86,759.65
134	Ben MASON	(Eng)	(26)	126,173.74	85,280.76
135	Lian-Wei ZHANG	(PRC)	(12)	121,268.49	81,965.31
136	Hennie OTTO	(SA)	(11)	120,841.52	81,676.72
137	Leif WESTERBERG	(Swe)	(31)	118,662.71	80,204.06
138	Christopher HANELL	(Swe)	(25)	118,169.96	79,871.01
139	Louis OOSTHUIZEN	(SA)	(23)	117,060.15	79,120.89
140	Jarmo SANDELIN	(Swe)	(30)	115,893.34	78,332.25
141	Eduardo ROMERO	(Arg)	(14)	107,723.83	72,810.48
142	Rolf MUNTZ	(NL)	(27)	107,511.30	72,666.83
143	Klas ERIKSSON	(Swe)	(24)	107,195.11	72,453.11
144	Lee SLATTERY	(Eng)	(30)	105,461.14	71,281.12
145	Darren FICHARDT	(SA)	(24)	105,198.06	71,103.31
146	David FROST	(SA)	(11)	102,459.31	69,252.19
147	Stuart MANLEY	(Wal)	(31)	102,440.34	69,239.37
148	Sandy LYLE	(Scot)	(17)	92,317.05	62,397.04
149	Patrik SJÖLAND	(Swe)	(25)	90,784.14	61,360.95
150	Terry PILKADARIS	(Aus)	(14)	90,722.12	61,319.03
151	Martin MARITZ	(SA)	(30)	86,873.25	58,717.58
152	Jarrod MOSELEY	(Aus)	(21)	85,397.26	57,719.96
153	David GRIFFITHS	(Eng)	(25)	82,557.39	55,800.49
154	Mikko ILONEN	(Fin)	(32)	80,941.29	54,708.17
155	Mikael LUNDBERG	(Swe)	(7)	80,799.75	54,612.51
156	Henrik NYSTROM	(Swe)	(24)	80,586.75	54,468.54
157	Adam GROOM	(Aus)	(19)	79,534.70	53,757.46
158	David GILFORD	(Eng)	(11)	72,692.92	49,133.10
159	Brad KENNEDY	(Aus)	(31)	70,702.40	47,787.71
160	Peter BAKER	(Eng)	(18)	69,481.81	46,962.72
161	Ivo GINER	(Sp)	(14)	68,225.83	46,113.80
162	Mads VIBE-HASTRUP	(Den)	(28)	67,695.18	45,755.13
163	Michael KIRK	(SA)	(12)	65,844.44	44,504.22
164	Martin DOYLE	(Aus)	(5)	64,752.29	43,766.03
165	Andrew OLDCORN	(Scot)	(23)	63,622.39	43,002.34
166	Sven STRÜVER	(Ger)	(26)	61,373.66	41,482.42
167	Jan-Are LARSEN	(Nor)	(22)	60,439.21	40,850.83
168	Simon HURD	(Eng)	(24)	60,013.01	40,562.76
169	Adam FRASER	(Aus)	(10)	59,307.49	40,085.90
170	Gordon BRAND JNR	(Scot)	(23)	56,482.30	38,176.35
171	Johan EDFORS	(Swe)	(9)	53,699.07	36,295.17
172	Eddie LEE	(NZ)	(12)	53,030.37	35,843.20
173	Andrew BUTTERFIELD	(Eng)	(6)	51,467.94	34,787.15
174	David BRANSDON	(Aus)	(9)	51,256.28	34,644.09
175	Paul DWYER	(Eng)	(5)	51,033.19	34,493.31
176	Pelle EDBERG	(Swe)	(25)	50,701.09	34,268.84
177	Robert ROCK	(Eng)	(18)	49,406.66	33,393.94
178	Benoit TEILLERIA	(Fr)	(19)	48,440.69	32,741.03
179	Michael JONZON	(Swe)	(17)	48,259.72	32,618.72
180	Gareth PADDISON	(NZ)	(12)	47,331.66	31,991.44
181	Niki ZITNY	(Aut)	(23)	46,930.13	31,720.05
182	Oliver WHITELEY	(Eng)	(7)	45,620.78	30,835.06
183	Sebastian FERNANDEZ	(Arg)	(11)	45,543.32	30,782.71
184	David HIGGINS	(Ire)	(8)	45,164.64	30,526.76
185	Jason DAWES	(Aus)	(11)	44,150.35	29,841.20
186	José Manuel CARRILES	(Sp)	(10)	44,035.30	29,763.44
187	Amandeep JOHL	(Ind)	(12)	43,961.19	29,713.35
188	Jeev Milkha SINGH	(Ind)	(7)	42,844.79	28,958.77
189	Fredrik WIDMARK	(Swe)	(6)	42,253.06	28,558.82
190	Marcus BOTH	(Aus)	(10)	39,508.00	26,703.44
191	Paul EALES	(Eng)	(11)	37,663.45	25,456.70
192	Stephen BROWNE	(Ire)	(21)	37,604.48	25,416.84
193	Edward LOAR	(USA)	(8)	36,992.59	25,003.27
194	Tino SCHUSTER	(Ger)	(5)	35,511.70	24,002.34
195	Richard MOIR	(Aus)	(9)	33,555.41	22,680.08
196	James HEATH	(Eng)	(9)	33,038.27	22,330.55
197	Tom WHITEHOUSE	(Eng)	(7)	32,723.60	22,117.86
198	Ariel CANETE	(Arg)	(7)	32,581.04	22,021.51
199	Steven JEPPESEN	(Swe)	(12)	31,841.83	21,521.87
200	Edward MICHAELS	(USA)	(9)	31,235.73	21,112.21

Flags (M-Z)

 Malaysia
 Mexico
 New Zealand
 N. Ireland
 Paraguay
 Phillipines
 Portugal
 Qatar
 Russia
 Scotland
 Singapore
 South Africa
 Spain
 Sweden
 Switzerland
 Taiwan
 Thailand
 The Netherlands
 Trinidad & Tobago
 USA
 Wales
Zimbabwe

The European Tour International Schedule 2005

First Time Winners

STEPHEN DODD

CHARL SCHWARTZEL

NICK DOUGHERTY

THAWORN WIRATCHANT

PETER HANSON

STEVE WEBSTER

GONZALO FERNANDEZ-CASTANO

Date		Tournament	Venue
Nov	25-28	Volvo China Open	Shanghai Silport GC, China
Dec	2-5	Omega Hong Kong Open	Hong Kong GC, Fanling, Hong Kong
	9-12	dunhill championship	Leopard Creek, Mpumalanga, South Africa
Jan	20-23	South African Airways Open	Durban CC, Durban, South Africa
	27-30	Caltex Masters, presented by Carlsberg, Singapore 2005	Laguna National G & CC, Singapore
Feb	3-6	Heineken Classic	Royal Melbourne GC, Victoria, Australia
	10-13	Holden New Zealand Open	Gulf Harbour CC, Auckland, New Zealand
	17-20	Carlsberg Malaysian Open	Saujana G & CC, Kuala Lumpur, Malaysia
	23-27	**WGC - Accenture Match Play**	**La Costa Resort & Spa, Carlsbad, California, USA**
Mar	3-6	Dubai Desert Classic	Emirates GC, Dubai
	10-13	Qatar Masters	Doha GC, Qatar
	17-20	TCL Classic	Yalong Bay GC, Sanya, Hainan Island, China
	24-27	Enjoy Jakarta Standard Chartered Indonesia Open	Cengkareng Golf Club, Jakarta, Indonesia
	31-3	Estoril Open de Portugal Caixa Geral de Depositos	Oitavos Golfe, Quinta da Marinha, Portugal
Apr	**7-10**	**MASTERS TOURNAMENT**	**Augusta National, Georgia, USA**
	7-10	Madeira Island Open Caixa Geral de Depositos	Santo da Serra, Madeira, Portugal
	14-17	Jazztel Open de España en Andalucia	San Roque Club, Cadiz, Spain
	21-24	Johnnie Walker Classic	Pine Valley Golf Resort & CC, Beijing, China
	28-1	BMW Asian Open	Tomson Shanghai Pudong GC, Shanghai, China
May	5-8	Telecom Italia Open	Castello di Tolcinasco G & CC, Milan, Italy
	12-15	The Daily Telegraph Dunlop Masters	Marriott Forest of Arden, Warwickshire, England
	19-22	Nissan Irish Open	Carton House GC, Maynooth, Co. Kildare, Ireland
	26-29	**BMW CHAMPIONSHIP**	**Wentworth Club, Surrey, England**
June	2-5	The Celtic Manor Wales Open	The Celtic Manor Resort, Newport, South Wales
	9-12	The KLM Open	Hilversumsche GC, Hilversum, The Netherlands
	16-19	**US OPEN CHAMPIONSHIP**	**Pinehurst No.2, North Carolina, USA**
	16-19	Aa St Omer Open	Aa Saint Omer GC, Lumbres, France
	23-26	Open de France	Le Golf National, Paris, France
	30-3	Smurfit European Open	The K Club, Straffan, Co.Kildare, Ireland
July	7-10	The Barclays Scottish Open	Loch Lomond, Glasgow, Scotland
	14-17	**134TH OPEN CHAMPIONSHIP**	**Old Course, St. Andrews, Scotland**
	21-24	The Deutsche Bank Players' Championship of Europe	Gut Kaden, Hamburg, Germany
	28-31	Scandinavian Masters by Carlsberg	Kungsängen GC, Sweden
Aug	4-7	Johnnie Walker Championship at Gleneagles	The Gleneagles Hotel, Perthshire, Scotland
	11-14	**US PGA CHAMPIONSHIP**	**Baltusrol GC, Springfield, New Jersey, USA**
	11-14	The Cadillac Russian Open	Le Meridien Moscow Country Club, Moscow, Russia
	18-21	**WGC - NEC Invitational**	**Firestone CC, Akron, Ohio, USA**
	25-28	BMW International Open	Golfclub München Nord-Eichenried, Munich, Germany
Sept	1- 4	Omega European Masters	Crans-Sur-Sierre, Crans Montana, Switzerland
	8-11	Linde German Masters	Gut Lärchenhof, Cologne, Germany
	15-18	HSBC World Match Play Championship+	Wentworth Club, Surrey, England
	22-25	Seve Trophy*	The Wynyard Golf Club, Billingham, Tees Valley, England
	29-2	dunhill links championship	Old Course, St Andrews, Carnoustie and Kingsbarns, Scotland
Oct	**6-9**	**WGC - American Express Championship**	**Harding Park, San Francisco, California, USA**
	6-9	Abama Open de Canarias	Abama GC, Tenerife, Spain
	13-16	Open de Madrid	Club de Campo, Madrid, Spain
	20-23	Mallorca Classic	Pula GC, Majorca, Spain
	27-30	**Volvo Masters**	**Club de Golf Valderrama, Sotogrande, Spain**

\# Individual prize funds between the Tour and promoters/sponsors are contracted in different currencies.

* Denotes Approved Special Event   ** Denotes play-off victory

\+ Total Prize Fund and First Prize capped to €2,386,798 and €601,828 respectively.

Winner	Score	First Prize €	Total Prize Fund €
Stephen Dodd, Wal	68-70-70-68=276 (-12)	127,621	766,910
Miguel Angel Jiménez, Sp	65-64-71-66=266 (-14)	100,338	611,820
Charl Schwartzel, SA**	71-69-70-71=281 (-7)	120,576	732,090
Tim Clark, SA	68-71-68-66=273 (-15)	112,689	719,600
Nick Dougherty, Eng	68-67-68-67=270 (-18)	127,718	788,770
Craig Parry, Aus**	69-66-65-70=270 (-14)	225,367	1,207,000
Niclas Fasth, Swe**	65-63-75-63=266 (-22)	156,671	836,250
Thongchai Jaidee, Thai	64-66-67-70=267 (-21)	156,763	947,630
David Toms, USA	def Chris DiMarco 6&5	994,260	5,736,120
Ernie Els, SA	66-68-67-68=269 (-19)	277,877	1,692,170
Ernie Els, SA	73-69-69-65=276 (-12)	188,764	1,141,050
Paul Casey, Eng**	64-68-68-66=266 (-22)	123,772	744,890
Thaworn Wiratchant, Thai	63-63-66-63=255 (-25)	125,205	761,290
Paul Broadhurst, Eng	68-66-70-67=271 (-13)	208,330	1,259,350
Tiger Woods, USA**	74-66-65-71=276 (-12)	977,044	5,320,690
Robert-Jan Derksen, NL	67-70-71-67=275 (-13)	100,000	608,870
Peter Hanson, Swe**	70-68-71-71=280 (-8)	275,000	1,652,480
Adam Scott, Aus	63-66-69-72=270 (-18)	305,049	1,846,750
Ernie Els, SA	67-62-68-65=262 (-26)	191,307	1,156,400
Steve Webster, Eng	68-68-66-68=270 (-18)	216,660	1,301,950
Thomas Björn, Den**	73-68-73-68=282 (-6)	417,753	2,532,800
Stephen Dodd, Wal**	69-70-72-68=279 (-9)	333,330	1,011,980
Angel Cabrera, Arg	70-70-66-67=273 (-15)	666,660	4,006,000
Miguel Angel Jiménez, Sp	63-67-70-62=262 (-14)	362,567	2,207,900
Gonzalo Fernandez-Castano, Sp	66-70-66-67=269 (-11)	250,000	1,526,800
Michael Campbell, NZ	71-69-71-69=280 (L)	964,791	5,304,700
Joakim Bäckström, Swe **	72-70-68-70=280 (-4)	66,660	404,140
Jean-Francois Remesy, Fr**	68-69-67-69=273 (-11)	583,330	3,578,430
Kenneth Ferrie, Eng	75-70-70-70=285 (-3)	577,816	3,482,520
Tim Clark, SA	67-66-65-67=265 (-19)	592,316	3,564,990
Tiger Woods, USA	66-67-71-70=274 (-14)	1,047,362	5,607,610
Niclas Fasth, Swe**	68-66-72-68=274(-14)	550,000	3,319,780
Mark Hensby, Aus **	65-68-64-65=262 (-22)	266,660	1,611,970
Emanuele Canonica, It	70-71-69-71=281 (-7)	338,442	2,076,060
Phil Mickelson, USA	67-65-72-72=276 (-4)	949,138	5,299,720
Mikael Lundberg, Swe**	67-68-69-69=273 (-15)	67,599	405,610
Tiger Woods, USA	66-70-67-71=274 (-6)	1,046,024	5,986,080
David Howell, Eng	66-68-66-65=265 (-23)	333,330	2,000,000
Sergio Garcia, Sp	66-65-71-68=270 (-14)	283,330	1,717,790
Retief Goosen, SA	67-68-66-67=268 (-20)	500,000	3,009,000
Michael Campbell, NZ	def Paul McGinley 2 and 1	1,479,930	3,611,030
Great Britaln & Ireland beat Continental Europe 16 ½ - 11 ½			2,000,000
Colin Montgomerie, Scot	70-65-73-71=279 (-9)	662,415	3,986,410
Tiger Woods, USA	67-68-68-67=270 (-10)	1,078,120	6,144,040
John Bickerton, Eng	69-68-69-68=274 (-10)	75,000	450,680
Raphaël Jacquelin, Fr	64-64-64-69=261 (-23)	166,660	1,005,980
José Maria Olazábal, Sp	69-65-70-66=270 (-10)	250,000	1,522,370
Paul McGinley, Ire	74-68-65-67=274 (-10)	666,660	3,928,500

First Time Winners

JOAKIM BÄCKSTRÖM

MARK HENSBY

EMANUELE CANONICA

MIKAEL LUNDBERG

JOHN BICKERTON

RAPHAËL JACQUELIN

The European Tour supports The Golf Foundation
GOLF FOUNDATION
Developing Junior Golf

The European Tour

DIRECTORS

N. C. Coles, MBE, *Chairman*
A. Gallardo, *Vice Chairman*
R. Chapman
P. Eales
T. A. Horton, MBE
D. Jones
R. Lee
J. E. O'Leary
D. J. Russell
O. Sellberg
J. Spence
J. Van de Velde

Sir M. F. Bonallack, OBE
(Non Executive Tour Group Director)
P. A. T. Davidson
(Non Executive Tour Group Director, Finance)
B. Nordberg
(Non Executive Tour Group Director)
K. S. Owen
(Non Executive Tour Group Director, Broadcasting)

TOURNAMENT COMMITTEE

J. Spence, *Chairman* (Eng)
J. Van de Velde, *Vice Chairman* (Fr)
T. Björn (Den)
R. Chapman (Eng)
D. Clarke (N. Ire)
A. Coltart (Scot)
J. Haeggman (Swe)
M. A. Jiménez (Sp)
B. Langer (Ger)
R. Lee (Eng)
P. McGinley (Ire)
C. Montgomerie, OBE (Scot)
M. Roe (Eng)
H. Stenson (Swe)

EXECUTIVE DIRECTOR	G. C. O'Grady
DIRECTOR OF INTERNATIONAL POLICY	K. Waters
RYDER CUP DIRECTOR AND HEAD OF PLAYER RELATIONS	R. G. Hills
FINANCIAL DIRECTOR	J. Orr
GROUP MARKETING DIRECTOR	S. F. Kelly
DIRECTOR OF CORPORATE AFFAIRS AND PUBLIC RELATIONS	M. S. Platts
DIRECTOR OF TOUR OPERATIONS	D. W. Garland
MANAGING DIRECTOR, EUROPEAN SENIORS TOUR	K. A. Stubbs
DIRECTOR OF CHALLENGE TOUR	A. de Soultrait
CHIEF REFEREE	J. N. Paramor
ASSISTANT DIRECTOR OF TOUR OPERATIONS	D. A. Probyn
SENIOR REFEREE	A. N. McFee
SENIOR TOURNAMENT DIRECTOR AND QUALIFYING SCHOOL DIRECTOR	M. R. Stewart
CHAMPIONSHIP DIRECTOR, WORLD GOLF CHAMPIONSHIPS	P. Adams
DIRECTOR OF TOURNAMENT DEVELOPMENT	J. Birkmyre
GROUP COMPANY SECRETARY	M. Bray
DIRECTOR OF TOURNAMENT SERVICES	E. Kitson
DIRECTOR OF IT & NEW MEDIA	M. Lichtenhein
DIRECTOR, SPECIAL PROJECTS	M. MacDiarmid
SALES DIRECTOR	T. Shaw
DIRECTOR OF COMMUNICATIONS	G. Simpson

Photographers

Photography by gettyimages®

Main Contributors:
Andrew Redington, David Cannon, Ross Kinnaird, Warren Little, Stuart Franklin, Richard Heathcote, Ian Walton, Scott Halleran, Harry How

Additional Contributors:
Phil Inglis
Photosport
The Golf Business Ltd